CAPACITY FOR DEVELOPMENT
NEW SOLUTIONS TO OLD PROBLEMS

Edited by: Sakiko Fukuda-Parr • Carlos Lopes • Khalid Malik

Earthscan Publications Ltd
London and Sterling, Virginia

United Nations
Development Programme

First published in the UK and USA in 2002
by Earthscan Publications Ltd

ISBN: 1 85383 919 1 paperback
          1 85383 924 8 hardback

DISCLAIMER
The responsibility for opinions in this book rests solely with its authors. Publication does not consti-
tute an endorsement by the United Nations Development Programme or the institutions of the
United Nations system.

Design and layout by Karin Hug
Printed in the UK by The Bath Press

A catalogue record for this book is available from the British Library

Library of Congress Cataloging-in-Publication Data

Capacity for development : new solutions to old problems / edited by Sakiko Fukuda-Parr, Carlos
Lopes, and Khalid Malik.
        p. cm.
   Includes bibliographical references and index.
    ISBN 1-85383-924-8 (cloth) -- ISBN 1-85383-919-1 (pbk.)
     1. Industrial capacity--Developing countries. 2. Infrastructure (Economics)--Developing coun-
tries. 3. Economic development projects--Developing countries. 4. Technical
assistance--Developing countries. 5. Information technology--Economic aspects--Developing
countries. 6. Economic development. I. Fukuda-Parr, Sakiko, 1950- II. Lopes, Carlos. III. Malik,
Khalid, 1952-

HC59.72.C3 C36 2002
338.9'009172'4--dc21
                                                                        2002001691

Earthscan Publications Ltd
120 Pentonville Road, London, N1 9JN, UK
Tel: +44 (0)20 7278 0433. Fax: +44 (0)20 7278 1142
Email: earthinfo@earthscan.co.uk. Web: www.earthscan.co.uk

22883 Quicksilver Drive, Sterling, VA 20166-2012, USA

Earthscan is an editorially independent subsidiary of Kogan Page Ltd and publishes in association
with WWF-UK and the International Institute for Environment and Development

This book is printed on elemental chlorine-free paper

CONTENTS

PART 3: knowledge

"Scan globally, reinvent locally" (Joseph E. Stiglitz)

foreword

Developing capacity has been a fundamental component of international development assistance since the Marshall Plan. The huge success of that far-sighted programme, however, inadvertently generated an overly simplistic and optimistic view of what worked: Simply transfer capital and know-how to other countries, the thinking went, and swift economic growth will follow.

As we have learned over the past few decades, however, this view ignored—or at least underestimated—the importance of local knowledge, institutions, and social capital in the process of economic and social development. And for most of the Cold War, the problem was exacerbated by the phenomenon of aid driven by politics rather than results. Despite some significant achievements, successful and sustainable capacity development has remained an elusive goal.

Over the past decade, there have been several attempts to tackle these problems directly, most notably in the Conference on Technical Cooperation co-sponsored by the Organisation for Economic Co-operation and Development/Development Assistance Committee (OECD/DAC), the United Nations Development Programme (UNDP) and the World Bank in June 1994. That has in turn helped generate a welcome new emphasis on the need for development to be "locally owned": to ensure that development cooperation does not seek to do things for developing countries and their people, but with them.

There have been some notable successes in trying to make these principles work in practice but overall progress has so far been uneven.

If capacity development initiatives are to have a pivotal role in helping developing countries meet the challenge of the 21st century, in particular the Millennium

Development Goals, we now need to take this process a step further, looking more closely at the underlying assumptions about:

- the nature of development as a process of societal transformation, and the fundamental importance of indigenous capacity for this transformation;

- the nature of capacity and capacity development, including individual skills, institutions and societal capacities;

- the nature of knowledge, where it is located and how it can or cannot be transferred and shared; and

- the nature of the aid-donor-recipient relationship, which has profound consequences for success and failure in developing lasting capacities.

The United Nations system was a pioneer in the field of technical cooperation, and capacity development is its central mandate. UNDP has long played an important leadership role, both as a source of technical cooperation funds and advisory services, and as the home of innovative intellectual research and analysis on these questions. This book, which is part of a broader research effort that UNDP is carrying out with the support of the Government of the Netherlands, is aimed squarely at helping stimulate discussion around this important issue. As such it should be seen as the beginning of a process of debate and dialogue around the broader issue of improving effective capacity development.

The book contains a range of views from practitioners, academics and policy-makers about what has gone right with technical cooperation in recent years, what has gone wrong, and how to do it better and perhaps very differently. In so doing, it focuses on the questions of indigenous capacity, ownership, civic engagement and new possibilities for knowledge-sharing, for which the revolution in information and communications technologies offers ample opportunities. The book draws from the operational experience, policy analysis and intellectual work of UNDP, brought to bear through the three lead authors from the Evaluation Office, the Bureau for Development Policy and the Human Development Report Office.

Not everything in the book is new. Taken together, however, its conclusions may help point the way to a genuinely new vision of capacity development that is firmly founded on genuine ownership by the ultimate beneficiaries of development efforts: the governments and citizens of developing countries.

Mark Malloch Brown

MARK MALLOCH BROWN
Administrator
United Nations Development Programme

editors'
acknowledgements

This volume has a long history. As practitioners of technical cooperation for many years, each of the three coeditors has been confronted almost daily with the successes, the obstacles and the failures of technical cooperation. But in the mid-1980s, working in the policy unit of the Regional Bureau for Africa at the United Nations Development Programme (UNDP), we went on to reflect more systematically on why it sometimes succeeds and sometimes—or too often—does not. And we went further, to developing programmes that systematically improved the policy environment for more effective technical cooperation. The policy analysis and initiatives that were taken at this time are documented in an earlier publication, Rethinking Technical Cooperation: Reforms for Capacity-Building in Africa, coauthored by a UNDP team and Elliot Berg in 1993.

Ten years on, has the situation changed? Do we know more about making technical cooperation work better for capacity development? Our own thinking on the subject has evolved as we proceeded to other responsibilities—at UNDP country offices in Uzbekistan and Zimbabwe, to the Evaluation Office, the Human Development Report Directorate and the Development Policy Bureau at UNDP Headquarters. In these different capacities, the fundamental question of how to promote capacity development was never far from our minds.

In these ten years of momentous change in the world, with the end of the Cold War and the onset of globalization, development challenges have assumed a new topography. Yet the challenge of capacity development persists, as do constraints on the effectiveness of technical cooperation. It is time for looking at "old problems" in search of "new solutions." And new solutions are achieved only by challenging basic assumptions that underlie the practice of technical cooperation. This is why this volume is organized in three parts. Part 1 focuses on defining development as a transformative process, and the importance of capacity in this transformation. Part 2 examines the owner-ship that is critical to real progress in capacity development. Part 3 looks at dramatic changes in the way in which knowledge is being developed, accessed, used and rewarded.

We are grateful to all those who contributed to the report, starting with the con-tributing authors. Many thanks go to our Peer Reviewers: Marc Destanne de Bernis, Stephen Browne, Ryokichi Hirono, Bruce Jenks and Michael Sarris. This volume would not have been possible without the dedicated work of Marixie Mercado, who managed all aspects of production; Arleen Verendia, who provided logistical support; and the skillful editing and copyediting of Peter Stalker and Gretchen Sidhu.

This volume is part of the larger initiative on Reforming Technical Cooperation for Capacity Development at UNDP, and benefited from the results of its research, elec-tronic discussions, roundtables and country-level discussions. We are grateful for these opportunities to glean data, analyses and insights. The process has involved many individuals, including colleagues in the initiative's Advisory and Facilitation Group, the World Bank, UNDP, the European Center for Development Policy Management, Harvard University and the African Capacity Building Foundation. Many thanks in particular are due to: Pierre Baris, Heather Baser, Pim de Keizer, Gus Edgren, John Ennis, Sevil Etili, Ava-Gail Gardiner, Lina Hamadeh-Banerjee, Moira Hart-Poliquin, Volker Hauck, John Hendra, Mary Hilderbrand, Leonard Joy, Tony Land, Mahmood Mamdani, Nick Manning, Jyoti Mathur-Filipp, Paul Matthews, Peter Morgan, Huub Mudde, Christopher Ronald, Soumana Sako, Helen Sutch, Mark Suzman, Reynout van Dijk and Jean Zaslavsky. We're also thankful for the research support provided by Dalita Balassanian, Ghada Jiha, Daniela Mitrovich, Nadia Rasheed, Elizabeth Satow, Maki Suzuki and Teem-Wing Yip; and the administrative assistance offered by Lara Abrajano, Bibi Amina Khan and Zaida Omar.

Last but not least, particular thanks and recognition are due to Thomas Theisohn, Coordinator of the Reforming Technical Cooperation initiative at UNDP, who ensured the success of this collaborative effort.

Finally, the editors are especially grateful to the Government of the Netherlands for providing the financing for this publication; and to UNDP Administrator Mark Malloch Brown, UNDP Associate Administrator Zéphirin Diabrè and former UNDP Bureau for Development Policy Director Eimi Watanabe for lending the project sub-stantive support and much intellectual leeway.

With much gratitude for all the support they received, the editors and contributing authors assume full responsibility for the opinions expressed in this study.

SAKIKO FUKUDA-PARR
Director, Human Development Report Office

CARLOS LOPES
Director, a.i. Bureau for Development Policy

KHALID MALIK
Director, Evaluation Office

overview

INSTITUTIONAL INNOVATIONS FOR CAPACITY DEVELOPMENT

SAKIKO FUKUDA-PARR, CARLOS LOPES, KHALID MALIK[1]

The world at the beginning of the 21st century offers sights, sounds and experiences that continue to astonish anyone born even a few decades ago. Space and time have been shrunk by a multitude of communications devices. Geneticists decode and tinker with the alphabet of life. And millions of people each year casually soar across continents in search of work, pleasure and new experiences. Billions of people have the capacity to know and do things of which their parents or grandparents could scarcely dream.

Even more surprising—and disturbing—are the enduring scenes of poverty. Billions more people have far narrower horizons. They may see jetliners arcing across the sky, but they themselves scratch a living with simple tools from hard and unyielding land, or scavenge in city streets for the empty bottles or plastic bags that might be sold to buy the next meal. Certainly they have many of the universal human joys and excitements, and they often enjoy a rich cultural inheritance that many modern communities have allowed to slip away, but their capacities to know, explore and enjoy fully their own potential, let alone the wider world, are severely constrained.

Most shocking of all perhaps, these scenes, both of possessing every opportunity and confronting absolute exclusion, are frequently juxtaposed and intermingled. Even the world's richest cities have dark corners of deprivation, while enclaves in the

---

[1] This chapter is written by the authors in their personal capacities. It does not reflect the views of the United Nations Development Programme, of which they are staff members.

poorest countries house some of the world's wealthiest people. And running through all these scenes are threads of resentment and violence that can ignite at any time—around the next corner, or across the country, or across the world.

The world as a whole has made considerable progress over the past 50 years. Average life expectancy, for example, has increased by 10 to 20 years except where HIV/AIDS has made inroads. And the proportion of the world's people living in income poverty has fallen. But progress is not inevitable or universal. While some regions, countries and continents have propelled themselves in new directions, others languish at low-level equilibriums not far above the margins of survival. Since 1990, the number of income-poor people has increased every year in sub-Saharan Africa, South Asia, and Latin America and the Caribbean.

The complexities and frustrations of development have generated a voluminous literature, along with numerous institutions and organizations suggesting change and new directions. Many of these insights were embodied from the beginning of the 1990s in the concept of human development, which looked beyond a simple fixation on economic growth. Instead, it presented a broader and more inclusive view of people's capacities—not merely to gain a higher income, but to enlarge their choices, to know more and do more, and to have the health, the skills and the vigour to lead full and satisfying lives.

Though the objectives of development have been articulated more clearly than in the past, the mechanisms for achieving them have become more elusive. When the idea of "development" took hold in the middle of the last century, it seemed possible that all the poor countries had to do was to emulate the rich—following roughly the same development path towards a similar destination. Indeed, it was thought that the poorer countries should be able to do this even more rapidly. First, they could take advantage of the experience of their predecessors—by adopting the same proven measures and technologies. Second, they could also benefit from aid flowing from rich to poor countries—not just in the form of grants and loans to help build infrastructure (the roads, the factories, the schools and the hospitals) but also in the form of expertise, acquiring the information, skills and knowledge needed to run a modern industrial society.

As a result, thousands of experts and consultants fanned out around the world, taking up residence in ministries and project offices, partly to supervise aid projects, but also to plant their skills and expertise in this fertile new environment by working alongside local counterparts. Some of these expatriates arrived as part of "free-standing" programmes—aiming to develop capacities in communities and societies, in health, say, or education. Others arrived as parts of larger programmes—travelling along with capital investments to ensure that new installations ran as smoothly as possible and trying to transfer the skills needed to operate and maintain them.

The underlying assumption was that developing countries lacked important skills and abilities—and that outsiders could fill these gaps with quick injections of know-how. The vocabulary for this activity changed over the years. For the first few decades, aid as a whole was termed "development assistance," and that part of it concerned with the transfer of skills and systems was called "technical assistance." But development practitioners worried that "assistance" implied—and indeed reflected—inequality and dependency rather than a positive spirit of partnership. After a couple of decades, therefore, they started to refer to international aid as "development cooperation," and many correspondingly referred to knowledge transfer as "technical cooperation," although others, including the World Bank, still refer to this as "technical assistance" when it accompanies capital investment. It would also have been useful to find a substitute for the word "technical," which suggests an emphasis on science and technology—wrongly, for most cooperation has been, and is increasingly, in non-technological areas such as education, governance and judicial reform.

Much of this development cooperation and technical cooperation seemed likely to succeed. First, there had been the spectacular success of the Marshall Plan, without which European countries would have had much greater difficulty in revitalizing their economies and rebuilding their nations after the devastation of World War II. Second, a number of poorer countries, particularly the East Asian Tigers, made selective use of development cooperation to help launch themselves on decades of export-led growth. But elsewhere, and especially in recent years, the uneven record of countries in achieving economic and social transformation has left many questioning how effective development cooperation has been and can be.

Of all the elements of the development cooperation package, developing national capacity has emerged as the one particularly elusive goal. Thousands of people have been trained and thousands of "experts" fielded. Educational attainments have increased dramatically, to the point where unemployed graduates resort to driving taxis while others join the "brain drain." Yet development undertakings have constantly faced a lack of necessary skills and weak institutions. Donors can ship out four-wheel-drive vehicles, or textbooks, or computers; they can dispatch expatriate experts, whether on long-term secondment or on short-term consultancies. But they have not really appeared to transfer knowledge—or at least not in the catalytic way that might ignite a positive chain reaction throughout developing societies. Foreign experts certainly have proved that they can get the job done—helping to build dams or install irrigation systems. And they can run multiple seminars and courses that improve the individual skills of thousands of people. However, the capacity of local institutions and of countries as a whole has still not appeared adequate to meet the challenges of development. There have been positive micro-improvements, but not the kind of macro-impacts that build and sustain national capacity for development.

Donors have tried to address this issue, but mainly through drawing up cooperation programmes emphasizing the need for more technical cooperation, and new rounds of experts and training (Berg and UNDP, 1993; OECD, 1987). Technical cooperation expenditures totalled US $14.3 billion in 1999, according to the Development Assistance Committee (DAC) of the Organisation for Economic Co-operation and Development (OECD). This is a large amount, almost double the sum in 1969. If personnel and training in investment and other projects are included, the figure would be even larger, $24.6 billion (Baris et al., 2002).

Yet behind the rising figures lies the fact that over the past three decades, priorities have changed. Technical cooperation resources have actually declined for low-income countries, for the Least-Developed Countries (LDCs) and for sub-Saharan Africa—as reflected in total disbursements, per capita disbursements and as a proportion of overall official development assistance (see Figures 0.1-0.4)—even as these resources increased for the high-income countries, and for Asia and Eastern Europe. This is a disturbing trend. Countries most in need of capacity development are receiving less and less help. Even worse, as the world becomes increasingly dominated by a "knowledge economy," and globally integrated into a single market, developing countries need even more capacity to compete. Poor countries need more, not less technical cooperation, and they need forms of cooperation that are most effective in developing capacity. These technological, economic and social changes in the world offer new opportunities for capacity development that warrant a new look at technical cooperation—its past problems and future solutions.

Over the last two decades, concerns over the effectiveness of technical cooperation have provoked an almost constant process of reassessment. A number of donor evaluations in the 1980s led to debates in the donor community, most notably in the DAC, which held a series of seminars on this subject. In 1991, the committee issued a document entitled *Principles for New Orientations in Technical Co-operation,* which called for changes in existing practices. A high-level seminar was organized in 1996.

At the same time, the United Nations Development Programme (UNDP) launched a programme with over 30 governments in Africa to review the effectiveness of technical cooperation, and establish national policies and priorities. The originality of this process was that it was a national programme of reflection leading to adoption of a coherent national policy and priorities. Called the National Technical Cooperation Assessment and Programmes (NaTCAP), the process also provided unique insights, analyses and data on the successes and failures of technical cooperation, as seen from the recipients' points of view. The results of these experiences were published in the 1993 book *Rethinking Technical Cooperation: Reforms for Capacity-Building in Africa* (Berg and UNDP, 1993). Most of the country reviews reached similar conclusions: that technical cooperation had proven effective in getting the job done, but less effective at developing local institutions or strengthening local capacities; and that it was expensive, donor-driven, often served to heighten dependence on foreign experts, and distorted national priorities. As a result of these and other criticisms, donors worked with recipients to redesign many of the aid programmes—shifting away from the massive presence of expatriate teachers, engineers and other personnel, for example, and relying more on nurturing national professionals.

Through the 1990s, there was another stream of dialogue on developing better relationships between donors and recipients, and a growing concern with lack of "ownership" as an important element that undermined the effectiveness, not only of technical cooperation, but also of other forms of aid, especially structural adjustment lending (World Bank, 1998a). The donor community tried to build more balanced relationships with recipients—putting the emphasis on "partnership" and "policy dialogue." Through the 1990s, donors also gave a higher priority to "participation"—working not just with government agencies but also with nongovernmental organizations (NGOs) and other parts of civil society, as well as helping to create the conditions under which the private sector might flourish.

In 1994, for example, the OECD/DAC agreed on "new orientations for development assistance," emphasizing the need for local control and long-term capacity development, followed by a call for a new partnership to reshape the 21st century. More recently, the World Bank and the International Monetary Fund (IMF) have moved from top-down structural adjustment programmes to a more participative process that brings local stakeholders together to help define national social and economic policies for poverty reduction. The resulting Poverty Reduction Strategy Papers (PRSPs) are then used as the basis for decisions on aid and debt relief.

During the 1990s, many aid agencies also introduced results-based management (RBM). Recent comparative evaluation studies suggest that aid agencies have been successful in achieving better results over time. UNDP's *2001 Development Effectiveness Report* shows that the percentage of projects considered effective increased from 35 per cent in 1992-1998 to 60 per cent in 1999-2000. Similarly, the Department of International Development (DFID) of the United Kingdom also showed an upward trend from 66 per cent in the 1980s to 75 per cent in the 1990s of projects rated as satisfactory or better in terms of achieving their immediate objectives. At the World Bank, the percentage rated satisfactory or better with respect to outcomes increased from 72 per cent in the early 1990s to 81 per cent by the end of the decade (UNDP, 2001a).

Even so, the overall macro-impact of technical cooperation on developing national capacities remains worrisome. Research and country studies carried out for the project Reforming Technical Cooperation for Capacity Development confirm that many of the recommendations in the 1991 DAC Principles and *Rethinking Technical Cooperation* have not been implemented, and that many of the problems remain (UNDP/Reforming Technical Cooperation papers). Technical cooperation is still frequently criticized for:

- *Undermining local capacity:* Rather than helping to build sustainable institutions and other capabilities, technical cooperation tends to displace or inhibit local alternatives.

- *Distorting priorities:* The funding for technical cooperation generally bypasses normal budgetary processes, escaping the priority-setting disciplines of formal reviews.

- *Choosing high-profile activities:* Donors frequently cherry-pick the more visible activities that appeal to their home constituencies, leaving recipient governments to finance the other routine but necessary functions as best they can.

FIGURE O.1: TOTAL TECHNICAL COOPERATION BY REGION (1998 US $ MILLIONS)

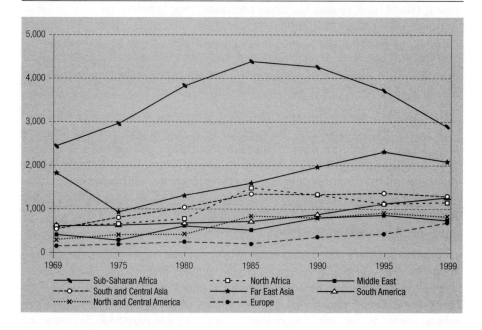

FIGURE O.2: TECHNICAL COOPERATION AS A PER CENT OF OFFICIAL DEVELOPMENT ASSISTANCE BY INCOME CATEGORY

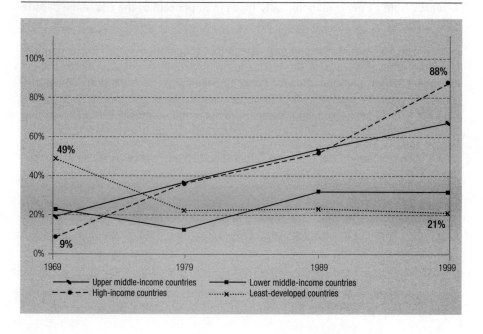

FIGURE 0.3: PER CAPITA TECHNICAL COOPERATION BY INCOME CATEGORY (1998 US $)

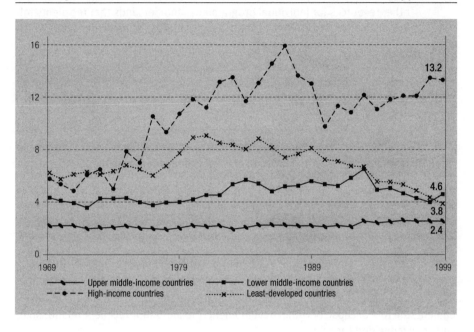

FIGURE 0.4: PER CAPITA TECHNICAL COOPERATION BY REGION (1998 US $)

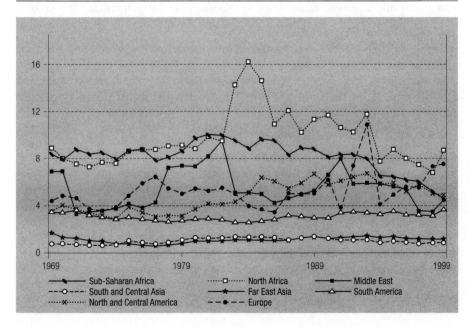

- *Fragmenting management:* Each donor sends its own package of funds and other resources for individual programmes, and demands that recipients follow distinctive procedures, formats and standards for reporting, all of which absorb scarce time and resources.

- *Using expensive methods:* Donors often require that projects purchase goods and hire experts from the donor country, although it would be far cheaper to source them elsewhere.

- *Ignoring local wishes:* The donors pay too little attention either to the communities who are supposed to benefit from development activities, to the local authorities, or to NGOs, all of whom should comprise the foundation on which to develop stronger local capacity.

- *Fixating on targets:* Donors prefer activities that display clear profiles and tangible outputs. Successful capacity development, on the other hand, is only intrinsically included.

Why do these old problems persist? We need to examine further the basic assumptions that underlie the old model of technical cooperation, which has remained unchanged to this day—including assumptions about the nature of development, the role of capacity within development, the aid-donor-recipient relationship, and knowledge and capacity.

The old model has been based on two mistaken assumptions in particular. The first is that it is possible simply to ignore existing capacities in developing countries and replace them with knowledge and systems produced elsewhere—a form of development as displacement, rather than development as transformation. The second assumption concerns the asymmetric donor-recipient relationship—the belief that it is possible for donors ultimately to control the process and yet consider the recipients to be equal partners.

Development As Transformation: The Central Role of Local Capacity

For all the universal theories about development, and the upheavals caused by wars and revolutions, most countries and societies have evolved organically, following their own logic and building on their own resources and strengths. So the assumption that developing countries with weak capacities should simply be able to start again from someone else's blueprint flies in the face of history. For these countries too, the most natural process is development as transformation. This means fostering home-grown processes, building on the wealth of local knowledge and capacities, and expanding these to achieve whatever goals and aspirations the country sets itself (see Part 3, Chapters 2 and 5).

What is capacity? In this book, it is defined simply as the ability to perform functions, solve problems, and set and achieve objectives. Each society has the capacities that correspond to its own functions and objectives. Non-industrial societies, for example, have few formal institutions, but they do have highly developed skills and complex webs of social and cultural relationships that are often difficult for outsiders to comprehend. Most important of all, by a process of cooperative and cumulative learning, typically passed on orally, they have worked out how to survive in often difficult and harsh conditions. Modern post-industrial societies have their own set of capacities, although they seem very different. They too have complex social structures, but tend to have more diverse and specialist activities, and rely on extensively codified knowledge bases, myriad organizations and a plethora of specialist skills, many of which can only be acquired over years of education and training.

As countries transform themselves, they have to develop different capacities. But it is important to recognize that they do not do so merely as an aggregate of individuals. National capacity is not just the sum total of individual capacities. It is a much richer and more complex concept that weaves individual strengths into a stronger and more resilient fabric. If countries and societies want to develop capacities, they must do more than expand individual human skills. They also have to create the opportunities and the incentives for people to use and extend those skills. Capacity development thus takes place not just in individuals, but also between them, in the institutions and the networks they create—through what has been termed the "social capital" that holds societies together and sets the terms of these relationships (see Part 1, Chapters 1 and 5). Most technical cooperation projects, however, stop at individual skills and institution-building; they do not consider the societal level.

Three Levels of Capacity Development

Capacity development needs to be addressed at three levels: individual, institutional and societal.

- *Individual:* This involves enabling individuals to embark on a continuous process of learning—building on existing knowledge and skills, and extending these in new directions as fresh opportunities appear.

- *Institutional:* This too involves building on existing capacities. Rather than trying to construct new institutions, such as agricultural research centres or legal aid centres, on the basis of foreign blueprints, governments and donors instead need to seek out existing initiatives, however nascent, and encourage these to grow.

- *Societal:* This involves capacities in the society as a whole, or a transformation for development. An example is creating the kinds of opportunities, whether in the public or private sector, that enable people to use and expand their capacities to the fullest. Without such opportunities, people will find that their skills rapidly erode, or become obsolete. And if they find no opportunities locally, trained people will join the brain drain and take their skills overseas.

All of these layers of capacity are mutually interdependent. If one or the other is pursued on its own, development becomes skewed and inefficient.

One source of confusion here is that capacity development is typically also understood as human resource development. This is unfortunate. Capacity development is a larger concept. It refers not merely to the acquisition of skills, but also to the capability to use them. This in turn is not only about employment structures, but also about social capital and the different reasons why people start engaging in civic action.

This more rounded view of capacity development contrasts with previous convictions that all that was required for the poorest countries to move forward was to slim down their public administrations and to reduce market distortions—to "get the prices right." This may have balanced national budgets, but it also tended to erode local capacity. There is an advantage to getting prices right, but it is even more important to get the capacities right (see Part 1, Chapter 1).

Capacity and Productive Processes

Capacity—including knowledge and technology—in getting things done also needs to be integrated into the knowledge systems and productive activities and structures that exist in any society. In developing countries, there are often two systems of knowledge and production operating in parallel: indigenous and modern. When new knowledge is not integrated into indigenous knowledge or production systems, it fails to be useful, despite its potential (see Part 1, Chapter 5; and Part 3, Chapters 2 and 5).

Of course, not all capacity development takes place through the public sector or technical cooperation. All countries are constantly engaged in multiple processes of capacity development, in the public sector, civil society and the private sector. Private enterprises, for example, are constantly transferring and modifying systems and technologies, and developing the capacities of different departments and subsidiaries. This often involves exchanging people and resources between affiliates in industrial and developing countries. But the private sector develops capacity according to the dictates of need and performance. The dynamics of this are complex and often a matter of trial and error, but the ultimate rewards and disciplines are clear. If capacity development works at both the individual and the corporate levels, this creates the prospect of higher productivity and higher profit. If it fails, there is the risk of takeover or bankruptcy.

The Asymmetric Relationship

The dynamics of capacity development through technical cooperation are very different. And this leads to the second mistaken assumption that has underlined technical cooperation in the past—that it is based on an equal partnership between donor and recipient. Instead, the relationships have tended to be more asymmetric, discontinuous and distorted. In reality, development institutions operate as bureaucracies of different size and complexity that exert power and domination (see Part 2, Chapter 3). The development industry creates *objects* out of development initiatives rather than *partners*. This is exemplified by the language of development, which is filled with terms of hierarchy and inequality: aid, developed and developing, donors and recipients, etc. (ibid.). The shift of control and power from the intended beneficiaries of development interventions to the providers of aid has naturally resulted from the fact that the financing of development interventions comes inevitably from the supplier and not the receiver. All parties are, of course, fully aware of the necessarily asymmetric relationship, but the old model of technical cooperation conveniently wishes this away and ignores the fact that this can be an obstacle to building partnerships. Although at the highest level, those involved may feel they are driven by shared development objectives, for most practical purposes the incentives and interests of the stakeholders—donors, consultants, governments and local communities—often diverge widely (see Part 2, Chapter 2).

Donor Priorities

Donors will have a long-term vision of what they want to contribute to—a better health system, perhaps, or an efficient judiciary, or a more skilled civil service. At the same time, however, they remain accountable to their constituencies at home. They feel more comfortable, therefore, if they can point to visible activities—courses, training manuals, computer systems—which encourages a bias towards self-contained and pre-ordained packages. This may make the process more "manageable," but it also closes off options for creative learning or incremental discovery.

Donors also want to retain as much control as possible and avoid accusations that hard-earned taxpayer funds are being squandered through inefficiency, incompetence or corruption. One way of achieving this kind of assurance has been to send expatriates as gatekeepers. In the past, donors have ensured that almost every development cooperation programme or project was escorted by a technical cooperation component. This seemed reasonable. There was little point in attempting to create a new infrastructure for a national vaccination programme, say, without ensuring that the necessary skills were in place to manage both the equipment and staff. But a strong technical cooperation component also offers crucial levers for control. When donors have consultants in place, even for a short term, they also have eyes and ears in situ — keeping them abreast of developments, and generating numerous reports and statistics. Donors have thus used technical cooperation to lubricate the cogs of a self-perpetuating engine that pumps large volumes of money to developing countries.

Donors have certainly addressed some of these problems. Nevertheless, many of the fundamental issues remain, and technical cooperation is driven more by donor supply than recipient demand (see Part 3, Chapter 3).

Nor are consultants likely to rock the boat. They have a strong interest in the status quo. Although they may vociferously lament the inadequacies of both donor and government paymasters, they are usually content to accept highly paid assignments in congenial locations. Consultants can justify their fees by doing their job well within its own limited terms, but they have little incentive to criticize the basic system. If they do, they will soon be replaced by more compliant staff (ibid.).

The Recipient Governments

The recipient governments too find themselves locked into a cycle of dependency and conformity. Ministries of finance, for example, will be reluctant to reject billions of dollars worth of support and foreign exchange, even as their budgets are under attack from every direction—including from international financial agencies convinced that the best form of government is small government. In 1989, for example, for the countries of sub-Saharan Africa, excluding Nigeria, technical cooperation was equivalent to 14 per cent of government revenues. For ten countries, it was equivalent to at least 30 per cent.

Meanwhile, government departments that spend money on development are also enmeshed in ongoing relationships with donors. They may or may not agree with donors about priorities, but they will have a strong incentive to conform—or to promise to conform—to what donors propose. And the civil servants who work in these departments may also be wary of fully taking ownership if they believe this will create more work and possibly deprive them of some of the perks they use to supplement their often meagre salaries (see Part 2, Chapter 2).

These factors have two damaging impacts. The main one is that technical cooperation is ultimately not driven by demand, but by supply. This might succeed, but the odds are against it. The only people who will guarantee that resources are used well are those who are hungry for them. Thus, unless government officials really feel they need to know what is being said to them in one training course after another, they may do little more than transfer information from blackboards to notebooks.

But the donor-recipient relationship has a further and more insidious impact. Even when donors are offering something useful and the recipients have helped shape the decisions on how it might be delivered, the donor-recipient relationship too often leads to a lack of commitment by the recipient, and even to resentment, both of which are demotivating.

The healthiest relationship is where the country concerned has set its own priorities and has established its own momentum for societal transformation. At that point, it can seek external assistance and draw upon the resources it needs to meet those objectives, whether the resources come from the World Bank, Grameen Bank, UNDP, McKinseys, Transparency International or local NGOs.

Where such a relationship does not exist, donors will tend to fill the vacuum.

Turning the Process Inside Out: From Knowledge Transfer to Acquisition

The issue of effective demand is also closely linked with what generations of teachers know about the basic mechanisms of learning. Teachers and trainers can offer information and ideas and different forms of knowledge codified in textbooks or handbooks. Technical cooperation has long been predicated on this kind of transfer, with the adviser analysing the knowledge gap and prescribing solutions that might enable counterparts to improve their performance. The underlying premise is that poorer countries can simply adopt a template that has been refined over time in the richer countries. No need to reinvent the wheel.

To be sure, most people have acknowledged that this is at least partly wrong— that there have been inevitable misalignments and poor fits, and that there is a need for some local adaptations. What has not been appreciated, however, is just how catastrophically wrong the entire approach has been. The process really needs to be turned inside out, with the first priority being encouragement for recipients to initiate the process. This starts from a deep understanding of local knowledge and practice— assessing the capabilities and potential of individuals, institutions and the society as a whole, and working out ways to build on these incrementally. The process is also likely to be, in the broadest sense, a political one—appreciating the different interests involved and anticipating how conflicts might be resolved (see Part 1, Chapter 2; and Part 3, Chapters 2, 3 and 5).

This approach also resonates with a more realistic view of learning. Most teachers at any level will say that learning only takes place effectively when students have motivation and appetite. Indeed, some teachers would argue that they cannot transfer knowledge at all. The most they can do is create the conditions under which people can learn. They can certainly offer information. But knowledge is more than information; knowledge is something that learners have to acquire for themselves.

This may seem like a subtle distinction. And when it comes to some facts about the world this may be true. Take the information that malaria is transmitted by a mosquito, or that certain pesticides are appropriate for particular crops. In this case, a trainer or a book can state the fact, and the reader or the learner can immediately absorb it. But knowledge in its fullest sense involves more than the transmission of facts. Most useful knowledge is tacit—and at a deeper level (see Part 3, Chapter 3). This kind of knowledge, which enables people to size up new situations and take the appropriate action, cannot be delivered as a simple package. Rather, it has to be steadily absorbed, tested and modified. And this requires a constant process of willing acquisition. So unless the individual genuinely wants to learn, he or she will not be able to expand their capacities. Many education systems do still rely on teaching by rote and attempt to transfer knowledge by dint of forceful repetition. Some information thrown at pupils or trainees in this way will stick; many students will feel that what they are being offered is just what they need. But for most learners most of the time, such methods are irrelevant and wasteful.

This lesson has not been lost in the commercial world. Businesses that consider themselves to be information-based "learning organizations" now rely less on routine training courses and more on on-the-job learning, or mentoring, or having people with different levels of skills work in teams with a constant process of interaction and learning.

A more home-grown process also addresses the problem of a disconnect between technological development and production systems. If indigenous knowledge and production systems (organizations and other indigenous entities) cannot easily make use of foreign technology, then they are likely to reject it and continue much as before (see Part 3, Chapter 2).

Rather than starting from a mail-order catalogue of standard parts to be forced into likely looking slots, the challenge instead should be fully to understand the local situation and move forward from there—step by step. The major implication of this proposal is that it puts a high premium on local rather than international expertise.

From Partnership to Ownership and Beyond

These two core concerns—the need to appreciate development as transformation and to recognize the asymmetry of the donor-recipient relationship—have profound implications for technical cooperation. And to some degree, both are already being addressed. As ever, the first thing to change is the jargon. A few years back, attempts to equalize the relationship resulted in the promotion of the term "partnership," coupled with efforts to achieve local participation or empowerment. Now the clarion call is for "ownership."

Ownership is also about self-confidence, without which there can be no leadership, commitment and self-determination. An indispensable part of ownership, empowerment in the development context is about expansion of recipients' capabilities, involving enhancement of choices and freedoms, and as such is not only a means but also an end in itself. The problem of initiating and fostering local ownership in the context of the asymmetry of power relationships, as discussed above, requires the consideration of three key issues: What exactly are national and indigenous approaches? What is the role of the development "industry"? What is the time-span for development interventions? (See Part 2, Chapter 1.)

As a result of political, financial and planning imperatives, there has been an urge for achieving results quickly. Transformation, however, is a slow and ongoing process, and development aid practices should adjust to reflect that tendency by using a long-term time-frame. Furthermore, local ownership necessitates a clear accountability structure and processes embedded in the local value system. In order to enhance access to external support while preserving local ownership, national agents need not only actively participate, but must also have full control over the initial idea as well as the execution of the project and its integration in national processes (ibid.).

The role of the state in this context needs further consideration. While the state is no longer the only interlocutor for development initiatives, the lack of recognition of its role has produced tension, confusion and a leadership crisis (see Part 2, Chapters 1 and 2). Unless developing country governments fully "own" technical cooperation programmes, having already agreed on their objectives and shaped their content, they will never have the commitment needed to make such programmes work. There is evidence to support this claim. Research and evaluation findings reveal that programmes commanding a sense of ownership by target beneficiaries and stakeholders have clearly performed better than those than did not (UNDP, 2001a; World Bank, 1998a).

Among the most successful technical cooperation programmes in recent years have been those in several of the former communist countries of Eastern Europe. But in many respects, these were special circumstances, not unlike those of the Marshall Plan 50 years earlier. Here much of the social capital, including a highly literate population and a highly developed public sector, was already in place. So, although the flows of assistance were one-way, and to some extent donor-driven and conditional on policy reform and the promotion of market economies, the policies and interests of donors and recipient governments were already reasonably well aligned.

The situation for the poorest countries is very different; there is a much greater gulf between donor and recipient. And this creates something of a catch-22 scenario. The LDCs are said to require technical cooperation precisely because their social and institutional infrastructures are weak. But this weakness also inhibits their ability and confidence to get into the driving seat, choose the direction in which to travel, and acquire and absorb appropriate resources that will be needed on the journey.

Worse still, technical cooperation can undermine local capacity. First, there are opportunity costs. Even "free" outside assistance takes up local resources, demanding counterpart budgets and mechanisms as well as the time to meet donor needs. Second, technical cooperation can open channels through which existing capacity can drain out as the best officials are tempted away to work on donor projects or for NGOs—leaving their remaining colleagues demoralized, overworked and susceptible to corruption.

Addressing Asymmetry

The asymmetry issue is inevitable. Donors will always ultimately control the funds and where they are disbursed. The recipient's final recourse is the exit option—simply to reject any assistance with which it is dissatisfied. Nevertheless, it is possible to level the playing field, or at least reduce the gradient. But the first step is to recognize that this is a fundamental issue—not merely that donor control and the lack of local autonomy are unfortunate defects or brakes on otherwise worthwhile activities, but that for some countries they can throw development into reverse.

Exactly how this asymmetry can be tackled will depend on local circumstances. Many countries have been able to pursue autonomous development strategies by making some or little use of aid funds and going their own way—Brazil, Botswana, Cape Verde, China, Costa Rica, Malaysia, Mauritius and Singapore, for example. Eastern and Central European countries too have been pretty successful in utilizing technical cooperation funds. But what about the poorest and politically weakest countries, who now find themselves in a dependent position? Alarmingly, countries with the least capacity have been the ones whose technical cooperation flows have decreased—by one quarter since 1994 (see Figure 0.3).

One of the most deliberate attempts to address this issue has been a pioneering effort in Tanzania (Helleiner, forthcoming 2002). In 1997, the Government of Tanzania, following an earlier initiative from the Nordic countries, agreed with the donors as a group on a radical change of rules and roles between the partners in development, which included what subsequently became 18 specific steps on which progress in the aid relationship could be monitored by an independent assessor. While the assessor's 1999 report did note considerable progress on both the donor and recipient side in many aspects of development cooperation, the least progress seemed to have been in technical cooperation, which continued to serve donor interests and which the Government regarded as wasteful.

Another way to help level the playing field is to strengthen the voice of recipient countries in debates about aid policy. On the international level, the donors already have the OECD/DAC. No such forum exists for developing countries to share their experiences, find common positions and develop aid guidelines with a southern perspective. Southern forums on development cooperation could be an important platform for balancing the donor-recipient relationship. A good entry point for such cooperation might be existing regional or subregional mechanisms.

Innovative Funding Channels

The most direct solution to the asymmetry problem in technical cooperation would be for the donors simply to support the national budgets of the recipients. This would mean an integration of external support into national planning processes and accountability systems. It would allow governments to exercise ownership over those funds and determine what inputs, advice, training, etc. is suitable to national capacity-development needs. It would contribute to aligning incentives and allow an improvement of overall civil service conditions. One may thus argue that budget support should be the starting proposition—the rule to which exceptions need to be negotiated.

A more targeted version of this would allow donors to retain a degree of control by channelling resources through specific technical cooperation funds with a clear general purpose. As long as the recipients deployed the funds to achieve agreed overall objectives, they could use them as they saw fit. As an extension of this, a group of donors could come together and pool funds that could be used in a similar way. A part of the Tanzanian experiment, for example, has been for donors to contribute to "baskets" of funds. There are variants of this type of mechanism, such as establishing autonomous development funds—public but politically independent institutions that can cater to both government and civil society. A technical cooperation window accessible to civil society may in any case be a useful complement to pure budget transfers.

The precise mechanism can be chosen according to local circumstances, but the central principle would be that of modifying the link between donors and programmes so as to achieve real national ownership. Most importantly perhaps, the pooling of resources, ideally as budget transfers, would dramatically simplify the aid relationship and would help resolve many other issues, including the obstacles created by vested interests.

If the development partners were prepared to explore other funding mechanisms, then many of the problems of ownership would start to recede and recipient governments would have much stronger incentives to get value for money. Some donors have indeed moved in this direction. The Netherlands has sharply reduced its use of long-term expatriate experts. And Norway and Sweden have done away with technical cooperation altogether to concentrate on local capacity development. The United Kingdom is actively exploring the implications of budget support.

The Accountability Challenge

Without strong accountability systems, support for pooled funds would not be feasible. What sanctions are available to enforce accountability? The two common responses are conditionality and selectivity. The weaker national accountability systems are, the more donors are tempted to subject disbursements to prior conditions, and tighten requirements and control mechanisms, which are difficult to comply with precisely because of weak institutions. The logical consequence is that donors disengage from countries where conditions are deemed insufficient. Both parties actually aggravate the situation for the poorest people.

Accountability should also be viewed in a wider context. Donors are accountable to their home constituencies, and they in turn set certain performance criteria for recipient governments. Missing from this perspective is accountability—on performance, on impact, and on finance—to the intended beneficiaries, the people of the developing countries.

Civil society, in the form of NGOs and the media, is stepping in to monitor what is happening. Why is the health service using an expensive western information technology consultant when similar expertise is available for a fraction of the price locally or from another developing country in the region? Wasting someone else's resources is one thing; wasting one's own is quite another. This kind of transformation would of course also be a huge breakthrough for the donors, who could demonstrate far more convincingly to their constituencies that their funds are being used wisely.

As a way of strengthening local accountability, recipient countries could also establish a national forum for all the stakeholders—including government, civil society, the private sector, the development industry and donors—to set priorities and monitor progress in a transparent way. Such a forum could help bridge a leadership gap and get reforms underway, particularly in countries where governance structures are weak.

Capacity Development in the Network Age

Regardless of whether donors or recipients are prepared to take such steps, the old-style linear forms of technical cooperation will to some extent be overtaken by events. Globalization—and the counter-reactions to it—is creating multiple new links, networks and alliances that change the topography of knowledge. In this globalized environment, the idea of being propelled along a linear development path by knowledge emanating from a single distant country will increasingly be seen as antiquated and irrelevant. New institutional forms of global support to capacity development are becoming possible. This will bypass the constraints of asymmetry and knowledge transfer (see Part 3, Chapter 1).

New technology is creating myriad alternative tools for capacity development. Information on agricultural technology, for example, that might previously have remained lodged in the minds of overseas experts or expensive foreign manuals or textbooks can be summoned from wherever it is, through an Internet connection and the click of a mouse. Information and communication technologies can also create networks and communities of practice. People in governmental and nongovernmental institutions across the world can now engage with each other horizontally and directly without passing through formal channels. Many NGOs have already discovered the potential for exchanging information internationally and for planning joint activities and campaigns. Governments or other institutions are now in a better position to locate expertise independently and assess its worth, just as the private sector does in garnering the best skills and abilities from wherever they are worldwide (see Part 3, Chapter 4).

These changes in technology are also taking place at a time when development expertise itself has become more widely dispersed. At the beginning of the 21st century, some of the most relevant and useful knowledge on how to achieve rapid human development now resides in the countries that have the most recent records of success. The notion that the only ideas for development that are worth trying are those that derive from the North looks less and less plausible (see Part 3, Chapter 3).

It can still be argued that circumstances in Bangladesh, China, Costa Rica or Mali are unique and distinct, and that the experience in one country will not necessarily translate to another. But once it is accepted that there is very little generic development knowledge—that all knowledge has to be gathered and then analysed, modified, disassembled and recombined to fit local needs—the source is immaterial. The new motto is: "Scan globally, reinvent locally."

This philosophy can turn networks into an empowering tool of capacity development. An extraordinary sociological transformation over the last decade has been the rise of networks—formal and informal, in almost all areas of life. Information networks are proliferating, as corporations, governments, research institutions, NGOs and millions of individuals collaborate to share ideas, information and knowledge. They can share information nationally, as with the South Africa Health Network, for example, which enables health practitioners to swap experience on topics ranging from malaria to traditional medicine. Or they can share regionally, as with Electronic Networking for Rural Asia Pacific, supported by the International Development Research Centre (IDRC) and the International Fund for Agricultural Development (IFAD). Or they can share internationally, as with the OneWorld global network for NGOs. These networks and many others offer a striking alternative to the old model of one-way North-South information flows. Now, the flows can be in every direction—within and between countries of both South and North.

The network approach to capacity development can truly be demand-driven. For example, the International Budget Project, supported by the Ford Foundation, is a network of NGOs across the world involved in social audits of budgets. The project develops the capacity of network members by providing a forum for exchanging information and ideas, tools and methodologies, training, and moral support. The success of a project with such a design will depend on effective demand, and therefore cannot be simply supply-driven.

UNDP and the World Bank are actively promoting the development of networks, starting within their own organizations. But as some of these experiences show, networks can also fall into the same problems experienced with donor-driven agendas, particularly the trap of asymmetry. If they are hierarchically organized and tightly controlled, they can once again be constrained by a supply-driven agenda. To avoid this outcome, networks have to be managed so as to be truly open, participatory and demand-driven. When they are, they open up exciting new possibilities for empowering people to scan globally and reinvent locally (see Part 3, Chapter 1).

At the same time, however, while there are now greater rewards for exploiting these opportunities in a knowledge-based market environment, there are also greater penalties for being left behind (see Part 3, Chapter 1). As knowledge becomes the foundation for more and more economic activity, it also becomes the basis for a competitive edge. India's rapid emergence as a world leader in information and communication technology skills is but one example. Brazil's success in building on local and international knowledge for its pharmaceuticals industry is another. However, many other countries and industries have not been able to develop their capacities in this fashion, and risk being marginalized from the global economy.

Conclusions: A New Paradigm for Capacity Development and Institutional Innovations to Solve Old Problems

If technical cooperation is to work for capacity development, only institutional innovations—new models—most appropriate to today's social and economic environment will overcome the well-known constraints. This means:

-   starting with the motto "scan globally, reinvent locally";

-   trying out new methods—such as networks that make the best use of new types of learning; and

-   trying out innovations that address asymmetry in donor-recipient relationships, such as pooling technical cooperation funds and developing forums for discussion among southern nations.

Perhaps the biggest obstacle in developing such innovations lies in the human mind itself, which can remain imprisoned in old assumptions and practices. Institutional innovations will have to be built on new assumptions about the nature of development, effective development cooperation, the aid relationship, capacity development and knowledge. These assumptions have to shift to new assumptions in order to build a new paradigm. The key elements are listed in Table 0.1.

TABLE 0.1: A NEW PARADIGM FOR CAPACITY DEVELOPMENT

	Current paradigm	New paradigm
Nature of development	Improvements in economic and social conditions	Societal transformation, including building of "right capacities"
Conditions for effective development cooperation	Good policies that can be externally prescribed	Good policies that have to be home-grown
The asymmetric donor-recipient relationship	Should be countered generally through a spirit of partnership and mutual respect	Should be specifically addressed as a problem by taking countervailing measures
Capacity development	Human resource development, combined with stronger institutions	Three cross-linked layers of capacity: individual, institutional and societal
Acquisition of knowledge	Knowledge can be transferred	Knowledge has to be acquired
Most important forms of knowledge	Knowledge developed in the North for export to the South	Local knowledge combined with knowledge acquired from other countries—in the South or the North

Capacity development is arguably one of the central development challenges of the day, as much of the rest of social and economic progress will depend on it. To begin with, it is an imperative for economic survival in today's knowledge-based market environment. But if the purpose of human development is to extend human capabilities, then capacity development is not merely a stepping stone towards higher levels of human development; it is an end in itself. For individuals, for institutions and for societies, this demands a continuous process of learning and relearning—from each other and from the world around them.

If all the stakeholders are to make fundamental progress, they will need to experiment with new approaches and seize fresh opportunities presented in the network age. Jointly, through this new paradigm, they will need to design institutional innovations to support capacity development.

References

Baris, Pierre, Nadia Rasheed and Jean Zaslavsky. 2002. "Repenser la coopération technique: revue des données statistiques (1969-1999)." Paper prepared for Reforming Technical Cooperation for Capacity Development. United Nations Development Programme.

Berg, Elliot, and the United Nations Development Programme (UNDP). 1993. Rethinking Technical Cooperation: Reforms for Capacity-Building in Africa. New York: United Nations Development Programme.

Edgren, Gus and Paul Matthews. 2001. "Preliminary Synthesis of Emerging Research Findings: Post-Turin Researcher Workshop." Paper prepared for Reforming Technical Cooperation for Capacity Development. United Nations Development Programme.

Fukuda-Parr, Sakiko. 1996. "Beyond Rethinking Technical Cooperation." Journal of Technical Cooperation, 2(2), 145-157.

Helleiner, Gerry. 2002 (forthcoming). "Local Ownership and Donor Performance Monitoring: New Aid Relations in Tanzania?" In *Journal of Human Development* 2002, 3(2). New York: United Nations Development Programme.

Organisation for Economic Co-operation and Development/Development Assistance Committee (OECD/DAC). 1987. Development Assistance Committee Preparatory Meeting on Technical Co-operation. Note on background issues. Paris.

———. 1991. *Principles for New Orientations in Technical Co-operation.* Paris.

———. 1992. *Principles for Effective Aid: Development Assistance Manual.* Paris.

United Nations Development Programme (UNDP). 2001a. *Development Effectiveness: Review of Evaluative Evidence.* New York.

———. 2001b. Human Development Report 2001. New York: Oxford University Press.

World Bank. 1998a. Assessing Aid: What Works, What Doesn't, and Why? Washington, DC: World Bank and Oxford University Press.

———. 1998b. "What is Knowledge Management?" Background paper for World Development Report 1998-1999: Knowledge for Development. Washington, DC.

1 *capacity and development*

1.1 TOWARDS A NORMATIVE FRAMEWORK: TECHNICAL COOPERATION, CAPACITIES AND DEVELOPMENT

KHALID MALIK

Successful development transformation affects not only what we do, but also how we do it...in the end, successful development must come from within the country itself, and to accomplish this, it must have institutions and leadership to catalyse, absorb, and manage the process of change, and the changed society.

   Joseph E. Stiglitz (Prebisch Lecture, 1998)

Introduction

In understanding technical cooperation[1] (TC) and capacity development[2] and their contribution to development, it is necessary to examine the notion of development itself

---

[1] Technical cooperation comprises the provision on concessionary terms of resources aimed at the transfer of skills and know-how and at capacity-building within national institutions to undertake development activities. It includes resources in the form of personnel (international, national, and long- and short-term). TC is broadly divided into two categories: i) investment related, and ii) "free-standing" general institutional support (UNDP, 1989).
[2] Capacity development is defined in this paper as the ability of actors (individuals, groups, organizations, institutions, countries) to perform specified functions or specified objectives effectively, efficiently and sustainably.

and consider how different capacities contribute to development. An exclusive focus on either TC or capacity-building is unlikely to draw out the essential synergy they bring (or could bring) to accelerating progress in developing countries.

Development is fundamentally about transformation of the production system and of society. It is rarely a linear process, and in that sense, it differs substantially from the current process of growth in developed countries. Development strategies, of which TC is a part, must aim to facilitate the transformation of society by identifying barriers and catalysts for change. If technical cooperation is to serve as a useful catalyst for national and international development strategies, a better understanding of its relationship to efforts to overcome these barriers is at least as necessary as analysing the forms in which TC is delivered.

This chapter addresses these relationships in three parts. First, there is a review of the issues connected to the concept of development as transformation and what this implies for development policies and practices. This emphasis on development as transformation produces in turn a related paradigm shift based on the proposition that "getting capacities right" may be at least as important as "getting prices right" for the sustainable progress of developing countries. Second, there is an attempt to identify the critical capacities required in development transformation and what these imply for the role of government and civil society in such development change. Finally, the chapter analyses current TC and aid practices in relation to their development effectiveness and assesses how the framework outlined in the following pages may influence the way TC and aid are provided in the future.

From Growth to Transformation

Traditional explanations of growth and development draw upon the neoclassical production function, which highlights the roles played by capital, labour and land. The failure of these approaches to explain differences in growth across countries and in the process of development has meant a search for explanations that lie behind the production function.

An important addition to this search was the concept of human capital, an idea put forward in the 1960s by economists such as T. W. Schultz and Gary Becker. Trained, skilled labour clearly influences the prospects of a nation; much of the success of the East Asian model has been attributed to this factor of production.[3] Radelet and Sachs (1998a), for example, posit that quality institutions, schooling and an overall stock of human capital, together with outward-oriented trade policies, placed the region very favorably to kick-start a trend of high growth rates that were sustained for over a generation. Literacy rates in East and South East Asia were 73 per cent in 1970, compared with 30 per cent in sub-Saharan Africa, and had reached 87 per cent by 1990.[4]

---

[3] Growth rates in a select group of East Asian countries between 1965 and 1990 stood on average at 5.5 per cent per annum, implying that national incomes were doubling every 13 years or so. A comparable rate in South Asia was 1.7 per cent (Radelet and Sachs, 1998b).

[4] Econometric results, however, show that the relationship between growth and education is weaker than other variables, which is attributable to measurement problems and differences in the *quality* of education (Radelet and Sachs, 1998b).

There exist other explanations. Some economists have picked up on a theme identified by Alfred Marshall—the importance of external economies of scale. While external economies concepts, together with the general process of growing division of labour and specialization as markets widen, have been helpful in explaining how growth and innovation get started and how they might be maintained, they still do not provide a complete understanding of development as such. Similarly, studies linking growth with differences in knowledge cite asymmetries in access to knowledge that draw on differences in initial income conditions and even geographic specificity. Hausmann (2001) argues, for instance, that development outcomes may be shaped by geography, as most poor countries happen to be either landlocked, or located in the tropics, or both, a conclusion that does not fully explain historic shifts in the development ranking of countries.

While strides have been made in attempts to identify sources of growth beyond asset accumulation, such as a recent focus on institutions and economic geography, the overarching message in all these avenues of inquiry is that we still do not know too much about the variables that trigger and sustain development.

Despite their well-documented limitations, the neoclassical approaches have had a strong influence on development policies. Further, they have contributed to a premise that development is intrinsically a technical problem requiring technical solutions—such as increasing the capital stock, better resource allocation and preventing market failures (Stiglitz, 1998). One particular challenge is to take a broader view of development, by beginning to understand better how societies work, how societal forces interact with each other, and how they help or hinder development progress.

Adding Social Capital

The term "social capital" can be of some value in the analysis of development. It seeks to respond to the challenge of integrating the social and historical context in which the different factors of production are brought together. Though it is widely accepted that the relationships between society and development are important, there has been, until recently, surprisingly little interest by mainstream economists in societal forces.

Classical economists, notably Karl Marx, were of course deeply concerned with understanding the relationships between society and production systems. But it was the sociologists and political scientists who coined terms like social capital, defined broadly as "the norms and networks facilitating collective action for mutual benefit" (Woolcock, 2000).

Communities with high levels of trust and strong networks are seen to be better off than those without. Social capital is reflected in better jobs, in fewer disputes and in a more prompt response to citizen concerns (Putnam, 1993b and 1995). The policy conclusion becomes an obvious one: Nurture and strengthen social capital, which requires understanding how social relations are structured and how they can be leveraged for the purposes of development. Woolcock (1998) refers to a four-hour journey from Madras to Singapore in bringing out the sharp differences in social capital as expressed in levels of organization related to matters such as forming queues, the order in boarding, procedures for deplaning, etc. Like the Italy Putnam (1993a) studied, some societies may be better endowed with a package of civic virtues that not only help them function better, but also cope with crises and manage transformations well. There can, of course, be "bad" social capital, such as criminal gangs who meet the criteria of trust and collective action, and there can be "dysfunctional" social capital, when different social groups are unable to function in harmony.

Putnam (1993b) argues that in the same way that money is more efficient than barter, "a society that relies on generalized reciprocity is more efficient than a distrustful society," implying that avoidable transaction costs impede economic progress. When networks of civic engagement are dense, reciprocity and trust are fostered, "lubricating social life." Further, coordination and communication among agents "amplify information about the trustworthiness, or the general reputation of other individuals, reducing incentives for opportunism and malfeasance."

The association between social networks and growth has also been extensively explored. Fukuyama (1995) elaborates on the virtue of trust in spurring economic growth by drawing a distinction between "low trust" and "high trust" societies, with particular reference to the East Asian model of "network capitalism." Coleman (1990) points out that social capital facilitates access to high-quality, relevant and timely information at lower cost. Adler and Kwon (1999) point out that, like trust, solidarity is also a product of social capital, which, they argue, "encourages compliance with local rules and customs, and reduces the need for formal controls."

The concept of social capital has its detractors. The term is considered too broad. There is a view that it lends itself to being interpreted in contradictory ways when being used to justify specific public policy prescriptions (Woolcock, 2000). Solow (1997) goes further and questions both whether social capital can even be compared to capital (as a product of past investments), and the feasibility or usefulness of measuring such "capital." In some ways, social capital (and more broadly the notion of capacities) may be usefully viewed as influencing the nature of the production function itself, rather than being treated on par with other factors of production such as capital or labour. Dasgupta (2000) refers to it as a shift in the production function, affecting (positively or negatively) the outcome of the mixing of different factors of production. Further, it could be argued that a positive, durable form of social capital may even determine the sustainability of the production function. If trust breaks down, groups may find it difficult to interact efficiently in the production process, an extreme example of which is civil strife.

Without adding to the controversy—the debate has often been both strident and confusing—the interest here is to use terms like social capital to understand better how society organizes itself, how development takes place, and what critical capacities are required to make transformation work.

The term social capital may help in understanding more fully the interplay between markets, social groups and networks, and the development process. Markets can empower individuals, but groups may not be strengthened, which may carry a specific downside for development change. In certain situations where market relations are not well developed, networks may complement markets, but equally they may compete with them if they substitute for or hinder market development (Dasgupta 2000). Public policy can have a large influence on the form and content of social capital. Equally, a robust engagement of civic society may have profound consequences on development outcomes, as argued by Sen (1984) in his seminal work on poverty and famine in India.

Social capital complements traditional economic theory, which starts with the individual and aggregates up to the economy. Traditional public policy prescriptions are based on how individuals behave, how they save or invest. When the individual's behaviour is a function of change, i.e., when it becomes an endogenous variable, the analysis forces us to look at broader societal issues. In particular, this requires us to examine the notion of social norms and how change influences behaviour—such as how people save and invest, for instance. Individual behaviour is the product of social interaction and the point in history at which different societies find themselves. Without this broader approach, analysis can be limited and may produce insufficient understanding.

Critical Capacities, Production Processes and Development Change

The literature on capacity development (CD) is vast. Much of it is focused on the needs and purposes of organizations—the ability of institutions to identify and solve development problems over time (UNDP, 1995). It is task-driven and mission-oriented, referring to the capacity to perform certain functions. For some, CD serves both as an objective and an approach, with an accent on participatory processes that are particularly valuable for their attention to the capacity of individuals to play more active and productive roles in development. Others take a broad view, a "systems" perspective, and by extension examine societal and organizational contexts. In this broader view, CD incorporates social-capital concerns. CD becomes "an effort to change a society's rules, situations and standards of behaviour. Capacity in this sense is about the self-organization of a society and the will, the vision, cohesion and values to make progress over time" (Morgan and Qualman, 1996). Whatever the definition, the concept of capacity development has clearly emerged as an organizing principle for development efforts and by extension TC.

Finding the Right Balance

Yet the value of capacities can be most usefully assessed in relation to their development purpose. In understanding the contribution of capacity-building, a development effectiveness filter therefore has to be applied, although even this approach is not entirely straightforward. A key question is to look at a capacity's contribution to development outcomes. This perspective forces attention on the different options available to meet the intended outcomes, and assesses whether the capacities at hand are necessarily the right ones to focus on. This broader approach encourages going beyond technical factors alone, so that options and alternatives are kept in mind. Health care services, for instance, are part of a web of social services, some modern, some traditional. By adopting a systems approach, each system can find its right place, and overall health care delivery may improve more than under a narrowly focused development effort. The same applies to institutions. Setting up institutions may require more than the knowledge of their purpose.

Linking capacities to development impact in turn begs a normative question: What capacities are key to development, especially when development is defined as transformation? What capacities are required to meet the challenge of designing policies, institutions and programmes based on an understanding of social conditions and with a view to the transformational requirements of development? There is a dynamic aspect to this issue. Some capacities may be more critical than others at a given time. Following independence, planning commissions were established in virtually every developing country as a way to plan and direct development. They performed useful roles. Yet it can be argued that these institutions also lagged behind development challenges. India represents a classic example. Following the principles of Fabian Socialism from 1947 through the mid-1980s, India's growth rates were disappointing, at around 3 per cent, especially when contrasted with those of East Asia. Apart from "inappropriate policies,"[5] Bhagwati (1993) faults the heavy hand of the state with its distrust of markets in favour of bureaucratic plans. Planning commissions were charged with the tasks of allocating and managing development resources, rather than rethinking their role (and the capacities needed) in more market-driven environments.

The issue of capacities can be looked at in three interlocking categories (see Figure 1.1.1). While policies and markets do matter, their sustainability is intimately connected with having the capacities to direct and manage the policies within a broader vision of societal transformation. The challenge becomes one of finding the right balance through:

1. Setting priorities ("vision") and identifying the right mix of policies and market approaches. This especially includes taking a view of the preferred nature of development and the process adopted. Emerging from World War II, Europe pursued very different development paths than the United States, partly because it faced different challenges. While both stressed the importance of markets, the role of the state in protecting society and in its relationship to the individual and social groups varied significantly. Broad-ranging debates are necessary in developing countries so that development visions can be consciously constructed in line with national culture and social conditions.

2. Developing the appropriate capacities to direct and support these policies ("institutions"). While this can be understood to mean the administrative capacity of government, it can also imply a debate on the role of government and how it can complement markets. Keeping society together and functioning with essential social capital facilitates and supports development change. Development requires an understanding of both current and preferred

---

[5] As the three fundamental obstacles, Bhagwati blames i) the paradigm of state-led industrialization (with a substantial public sector involvement beyond the confines of public utilities and infrastructure), ii) inward-looking trade and investment policies, namely import substitution, and iii) the "License Raj" with its extensive bureaucratic controls over production, trade and investment.

FIGURE 1.1.1

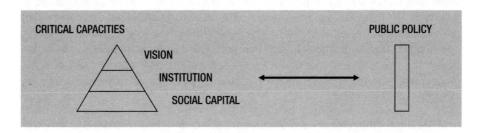

social norms and attitudes. Modernization demands an adjustment in institutions and in these norms.[6]

3. Establishing a conscious policy to balance and link social norms and cultural
   values with development ("social capital"). Whether social capital is defined
   as social cohesion or social capabilities, transformation produces pressures
   that are large and need to be understood—including the relentless forces of
   globalization, which are leading to growing competition and specialization.
   There is a complex interplay of external and internal forces that are not only
   the backdrop for the application of economic and social policies, but also
   intimately influence their content.

The critical capacities identified and categorized here as vision, institution and
social capital are integral components of capacity development, and hence of the formulation and implementation of public policies designed for sustainable
development. The nature of and the interplay between these categories have a direct
influence on how and what public policies are encouraged or instituted by governments and other prominent players participating in the development process.
However, the relationship between the categories identified above and public policy,
rather than being unidirectional, is synergistically interlocked. Public policy is shaped
by but also shapes the visionary scope, institutional robustness and the social-capital
content of a society. Well-established capacity strengths provide the necessary
groundwork for sound and effective public policies, which in turn promote further
development of critical capacities.

This close interrelationship invites a discussion of the necessary role of the state
in influencing societal transformation, and inevitably the appropriate role of institutions
in that process. Increasingly, pragmatic approaches are being taken to the role of
governments. A new "third way" has been proposed, even by economists reared on
neoclassical thinking (De Long, 1999). They view governments and markets as necessary
complements, with the government having a critical role in ensuring "equality of

---

[6] The term "institutions" deserves a more rigourous elaboration. While it is broadly understood in the
political science literature as "stable, valued, recurrent patterns of behaviour," North (1990) specifically describes institutions as "any form of constraint that human beings devise to shape human
interaction." North also offers a useful distinction between organizations and institutions, with the former associated more with actors (political parties, churches, universities, etc.) and the latter with *rules*,
or the way games are played in national life. North argues that both organizations and institutions are
there to provide "structure to human interaction."

opportunity," while accepting and occasionally responding to the inequality of outcomes depending on the political imperatives. Too little government can be as destructive as too much. The Asian crisis of the 1990s and the US savings and loan crisis of the 1980s have been attributed to the failure of government to perform key regulatory tasks. Aid and TC have taken strong positions on the content of development policies and in particular the role of government. The issue ultimately is one of smart and effective government, and the need for ongoing assessments of the effectiveness of the key functions of government.

The three categories are profoundly connected, and their relationships vary with country and over time as development takes place. Personal relationships and social habits are part of institutions and influence their performance. Woolcock's reference (2000) to the "social embeddedness of institutions" implies, inter alia, that transformation requires a more sensitive appreciation of the factors involved in change than passing decrees and new laws. The combination of the three capacity categories requires a country- and region-specific understanding of what is possible and what should be done. Fundamental questions on direction and development purpose are best answered by the people themselves and their representatives. The relationship between the three is likely to vary with country conditions, so the fundamental challenge is to find a balance.

The discussion of TC and related capacity-building has tended to be about the first and second categories, with less consideration of the third; rarely has there been much examination of the factors that promote a balance of the three.

Managing the Alignment

Traditional societies may have high levels of organizational and social capital, though this may not be in the form that facilitates change (Stiglitz, 1998). What stock of social capital exists might be destroyed during development transformations, or, as in Russia, transitions may happen without the emergence of a new social order and capital. This perspective leads to the proposition that public policy needs to go beyond narrowly defined capacities to consider approaches that promote social capabilities—institutions, incentives and social structures that encourage productivity, thrift and entrepreneurship.

In a traditional society, there may well be alignment between the three categories: a coherent vision of society with established priorities; institutions that manage them; and social capital that fits in with the priorities. Development change and the imperatives of new production systems in turn demand new social systems and capacities. Understanding that development is fundamentally about transformation, the real challenge then is in properly managing the transformation from a traditional to a modern society (see Figure 1.1.2). Transformation should focus not on the dismantling of entrenched institutions and capacities, but on the judicious management of the development process to create a social environment that sustains and enriches new social structures and alignments conducive to a modern society. In periods of rapid change, there is bound to be profound misalignment among the three components, making transformation management a daunting task. Development policy has to be concerned

FIGURE 1.1.2

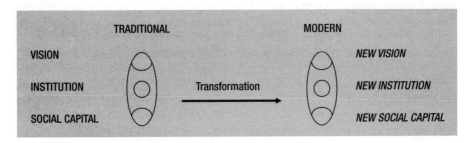

with all three, not only to ensure their proper transformation but to align them together to realize effective development.

Development aid can have surprisingly large influence. The experience of Russia is instructive. The disastrous results are well known—the collapse of incomes, a huge rise in inequality, shortened life spans—some were unprecedented since World War II. Dramatic new policies were introduced (with support from the international community) without thinking through their implications for the new institutional capacities needed, and even more fundamentally, without understanding the implications of the new social norms and networks needed to make the policies work. One of the reasons fostering this situation has been that "experts" and agencies charged with assisting the transition saw it as a conventional problem of weak markets and democratic institutions requiring standard solutions in the form of more financial and human resources, i.e., more loans and technical cooperation (Putnam, 1993a).[7]

An obvious arena where the state can step in to influence social norms and practices, hence social capital, is in instances of discriminatory and exclusionary practices linked with race, gender, ethnicity and religion. The *World Development Report 2000/2001* argues that these anomalies can be redressed by understanding the nature of the problem. Some forms of exclusion can be eased by improving the outreach of public services to areas of neglect—for example, by setting up primary schools and hospitals in rural outposts. Stronger manifestations of discrimination ought to be dealt with legally through institutions of the state or special policies such as affirmative action.

Moving from one system to the other raises issues of absorption and sequencing. Much of the debate on "absorptive" capacities has been linked to the role of public policy in influencing the ability of developing countries to absorb "new ideas, norms and techniques" (Koo and Perkins, 1995). In South Korea, this led to investing in education first so that the transfer of skills and knowledge through TC could be better absorbed.

The East Asian crisis is a different example. Here the role of governments was well established, with generally strong, well-managed institutions and a mix of policies mostly regarded as growth-friendly. And, perhaps even more important, these countries

---

[7]Jeffrey D. Sachs, himself an adviser to the Russian President from 1991 to 1994, has observed, "(W)e were witnessing a profound transition of a social, political, and economic system of a scale unprecedented in history, and we sent a handful of fiscal accountants to manage that transformation" (noted during a presentation at a Kennedy School of Government seminar, 2000).

had succeeded to a considerable extent in transforming their societies. So what went wrong? While critical observers have faulted the volatility of short-term capital flows and inadequate external advice (Radelet and Sachs, 1998a), there has also been serious questioning of key aspects of the Washington Consensus,[8] such as premature capital account convertibility. The East Asian crisis represented a combination of risky lending and inadequate financial sector supervision in developed countries, hence calling for more, not less, governmental action, and for more and better international financial supervision.

Rethinking the Role of Governments (and Civil Society)

The incorporation of social-capital issues in the analysis of development, and defining development as transformation, raises the bar for social policy. In some ways, the role of social policy itself has to change. It has to go beyond policies concerned with how society treats the poor and other vulnerable groups. The transition that is occurring today in the newly independent countries of the former Soviet Union is much more than a transition from central planning to a market-oriented economy. It is an attempt to transform society, and in that process to develop a new relationship between social norms and development. Part of this has to do with how people interface with their government, and whether a new political culture emerges with preferred attributes such as greater transparency and accountability (Griffin, 1995).

This broader, society-driven approach affects how we look at traditional policy instruments. Macroeconomic policies, for instance, are rarely "poor neutral." National budgets and their composition have to be seen in their political and social context. Partly because of the perception that these are technically complex areas best left to the experts, macroeconomic policies have avoided public scrutiny, despite a growing realization that the consequences of these technical decisions can have substantial implications for the development of nations and societies (Cagatay et al., 2000). The policy conclusions, for instance, are likely to be very different if education or health budgets are viewed as expenditures or investments. Mahbub ul Haq, the founder of the United Nations Development Programme's (UNDP) series of Human Development Reports, was fond of cautioning finance officials that it is unwise to "balance budgets on the backs of the poor."

A larger, transformative role for governments is not without precedent. In the early stages of development, governments of the more advanced economies did play key roles in laying the conditions for later economic and social progress, be it in Japan after the Meiji Restoration of 1868, or in postwar Germany. The role of the Government in coordinating decisions about investments in heavy industry in Germany, for example, stands in contrast to the more spontaneous growth of industry in the United Kingdom. It can be argued that it is only when fundamental policies were flawed or institutions ill-equipped that even a proactive role of the state produced little results, as in the communist bloc (Kornai 1992). The content and sequencing of transformative development policies becomes important in determining the speed and efficacy of the transformation path.

---

[8] Broadly understood to cover packages of policy prescriptions endorsing privatization, stabilization and liberalization.

How do states and civil society connect? Narayan and Woolcock (2000) argue that states must invest in the organizational capacities of the poor and help them build bridges with other social groups, suggesting the use of participatory processes. Their argument is that social networks of the poor are one of the primary resources they have for managing risk and vulnerability. Narayan and Woolcock add that states can identify virtuous cycles that link "structural" social capital (institutions) with "cognitive" social capital (norms and values). They can assist the growth of new linkages between the state, markets and citizens, e.g., among enterprises that pursue profits but distribute them for social ends, or through social policies that deliver effective child care without burdening women. States can also be aggressive and crowd out civil society organizations. The links are both obvious and subtle and need careful consideration.

A Necessary Digression on Crisis Situations

Civil wars are a major source of poverty. The worst-deprived societies, regardless of whether they are measured by human development indicators or GDP per capita, tend to have had major civil conflicts or wars. A staggering half of all low-income countries have experienced major political violence (Stewart, 2000). Preventing conflict requires an understanding of the economic and social causes of conflict, and the design of polices that strengthen social capital. In looking at conflict among organized groups, factors such as economic and social differentiation (group identity, etc.) and the political ambition of opportunistic leaders stand out. A basic reason, however, behind group conflict is relative inequity and perceived denial of "rights." Prevention of conflicts requires countervailing pressures such as a strong state and/or communities. Dysfunctional social capital can easily overwhelm institutions created when society was more stable. Repairing institutions alone without a concomitant rebuilding of social capabilities is unlikely to be lasting. "Good" policies become insufficient if the government is not broadly based and groups do not feel appropriately represented.

In war-torn societies, the systematic destruction of social capital requires in equal measure a systematic approach to the creation of such capital, with emphasis on trust and confidence-building. Many African analysts have argued that past social capital in traditional societies in Africa is fast eroding as a result of pressures emanating from recent conflicts, with little attempt to restore such a social-capital base.

Stewart also identifies some trigger events that have implications for TC. Changes may be brought about by development policies that sharply affect relative access to jobs and incomes. Several development thinkers have argued that the structural adjustment policies promoted by the World Bank not only negatively affected the first two capacity categories but in the end reduced social capital by changing some of the basic social dynamics. In cases such as Rwanda and Guinea Bissau, this led to open conflict. Sharp reduction in aid has in cases like Liberia and Sierra Leone also been identified as among the causes of conflict. More than ever, country conditions need to be better understood so that international aid efforts are not only better targeted but also contribute to polices that that more likely to have some useful impact.

Technical Cooperation, Social Capital and Development Effectiveness

The rethinking of the development paradigm requires the rethinking of TC. TC has played and continues to play a large role in setting global agendas and in the design of both international and national development policies. Its substantive content has generally been shaped by the Washington Consensus (see Part 2, Chapter 1). There is remarkable lack of attention to empirical evidence (of what works and why) or to learning from those countries that have been successful in developing their economies and societies. In short, there is both promise and concern in aid and TC as transfer mechanisms and catalysts for development.

Aid has two basic functions: as a capital transfer and as a knowledge provider. Investing in infrastructure with support from international agencies like the World Bank (through low-cost lending) has been seen as a key factor in the conditions promoting accelerated growth in East Asian economies. The UN's original development mandate (principally through UNDP) was directed towards developing skills and establishing institutions required for the running of newly established countries. By the 1990s, the overlapping of the mandates of the World Bank and UNDP testified to the growing complexity of the development process in a rapidly globalizing and connected world.

It can be argued that aid and TC function in an imperfect market. Driven in large part by governmental and intergovernmental concerns, this market is regulated by its own institutional frameworks and motivations. The growing emphasis on results and the waves of new aid priorities has meant that aid flows are no longer an exclusive function of need. In 1999, Africa received 29 per cent of total aid flows, compared to 40 per cent in 1989, in a period of stagnant or negative growth in development (Baris et al., 2002).

Since the early 1990s, the development aid market has been characterized by a sharp shift away from "aid as entitlement" concepts towards an emphasis on results and performance. It is possible to identify supply-and-demand factors: On the supply side are the specific policy interests of donors, bilateral and multilateral, who, in pursuit of their respective political mandates, supply financing, grants and performance incentives to achieve their objectives. They promote their own projects largely in the thematic areas of their choice and are willing to develop partnerships with other aid providers in that context. On the demand side are the requests of governments to finance or co-finance their programmes and projects within a specific policy framework. While governments may be concerned with the proliferation of "third-party" financing, they are understandably interested in not missing funds that could help them to pursue their development agenda. In this context, the World Bank and UNDP could be viewed as brokers who try to reconcile the demands of countries with the funding supply provided by donors.

In principle, the monitoring of results, assessments of impact and the growing interest in comparative performance assessments can be seen as attempts to construct a resource allocation substitute for price signals in an imperfect market environment. It is, however, important to underscore that aid and TC transfers are not unique mechanisms. The aid-dependent TC market does in some ways compete with private sector markets, especially involving multinational corporations, which transfer skills and support capacity-building as part of the process of investment in the productive sector. South Korea in the 1970s and 1980s provides a good illustration of skills transfer and institutional upgrading provided through the private sector. There is also considerable synergy between the TC and private sector markets. As was the case in South Korea, the sequencing of investing first in education and skills development, before receiving aid or TC transfers, facilitates the transfer of ideas and knowledge taking place in the private sector (and the production process).

To be helpful, TC has to be transformed into national policies, strategies and programmes. And to be effective, the proposed policies and programmes have to have positive development impact. This requires an assessment of the value of the knowledge transfer mechanisms used in the aid and TC markets.

That the traditional donor-recipient and TC-counterpart models have not worked well is amply documented. In 1993, these issues were the subject of an important book by Elliot Berg and UNDP. Yet, as is argued in this chapter and as the World Bank (2000) also acknowledges, it is difficult to impose change from the outside. Ownership is a critical ingredient for sustainable development. Without it requisite capacities cannot be developed, and without capacities transformation cannot take place. This position questions the value of conditionality: whether imposed at the policy level by the Bank and the International Monetary Fund (IMF) or at the implementation level by the UN or bilateral aid agencies. While it is difficult to question the demand for performance, a concern in principle equally shared by the recipient, the question must be raised as to how effective existing conditionality regimes have been and whether they have influenced capacity creation.[9]

Development effectiveness also requires a closer examination of the forms of technical cooperation. A principal vehicle for the transfer of development aid has been through projects. Study after study has pointed to the inadequacy of this microperspective (UNDP, 2000). Projects may be termed a success, but may not lead to an improvement in development conditions, let alone creating anything sustainable.[10] The new performance-driven approaches are producing sharp changes in development practice. Emphasizing the essential value of partnerships puts the accent on cooperation, not just between a donor and a recipient but between all key actors and

---

[9] Despite the practical deficiencies of conditionality, Collier (1999) presents a theoretical justification for conditionality as an instrument to acquire credibility. His premise is that lack of private investment in Africa is a result of risks associated with non-credible governments, and the two ways to cure problems of credibility are signaling or lock-in. Both these mechanisms could be achieved by creating what he calls an agency of restraint. Such agencies can be external in nature, e.g., through membership of regional trading blocs, or internal, say in the form of central bank independence, sustainable fiscal deficits, etc. By extension, donor conditionalities that require governments to commit to a set of irreversible policies are also considered to constitute an agency of restraint. Conditionalities, if credible, are potential instruments for future punishment of governments that renege on pledges, and because private investors know this ex-ante, they spend money assured of little risks over damaging policy reversibility.
[10] The failure of piecemeal, project-based development assistance has led to reforms in devlopment agencies. Examples include the introduction of results-based management in UNDP, with a greater focus on outcomes (the development changes being promoted) and on demonstrating impact. It has highlighted the importance of partnerships, since no single agency despite large resources can exclusively influence development change.

institutions involved in change. This heightens the potential value of evaluation, which becomes not only an exercise to judge the effectiveness of specific interventions, but also serves as a pointer to institutions and incentive regimes that promise more effective strategies for sustainable development.

The record of TC in delivering on its capacity-development mission is problematic at best. It has been argued that the dominant roles of donors (and some forms of TC) have actually led to the destruction of emergent national capacities. Often, the transfer of developed country expectations onto a developing country environment has meant that tasks or conditions were disproportionately placed on poorer, less capable governments. Examples range from the 100-plus IMF conditions placed on Burkina Faso for the release of funds from the Structural Adjustment Facility, to the demands placed on small developing countries to produce data of internationally comparable quality for expenditure surveys. There appears an almost inverse relationship between the number of conditions imposed and the level of national capacities.

At the same time, it is probably misleading to leave an impression that TC and aid are synonymous with external factors. TC is no longer exclusively of external origin. Over the last decades, TC in many countries has developed national roots, a phenomenon that has to be factored in when talking about national ownership. The strong nongovernmental organization (NGO) community in Bangladesh, for example, has equally strong links with the international NGO world. It could be argued that facets of social capital (norms, networks) are now increasingly international, a consequence of globalization and perhaps the forms in which development cooperation has evolved. The UN global conferences of the 1990s have produced a "global compact" with values and norms that are now accepted as global standards. These conferences and international agreements have had large consequences at country level. Witness the women's movement galvanized by the Beijing Conference, whose platform of action serves as a global charter for women's movements everywhere. In turn, these global agreements and the more recent endorsement of global targets presented as the Millennium Summit goals are emerging as the framework for bringing together bilateral and multilateral donors.

Social Capital and Implications for Development Policy

Traditional societies may have high levels of organizational and societal capital, although this may not be in the form that facilitates change (Stiglitz, 1998). Whatever stock of social capital that exists might be destroyed during development transformations; or, as in Russia, transitions may happen without the emergence of a new social order and capital. It has been argued that individuals and agencies charged with assisting the process of transition in Eastern Europe saw the challenge as a conventional problem of weak markets and democratic institutions requiring standard solutions in the form of more financial and human resources, i.e., more loans and technical cooperation. But building on Putnam (1993b), it could be further argued that deficiencies in the new social capital in these countries is alarming, and that attempts should have focused on rebuilding "shards of indigenous civic associations that have survived decades of totalitarian rule," ranging from philanthropic agencies to chess clubs.

New approaches to development will need to find and articulate a clearer link between social capital and development. Development may have mostly failed because of misguided polices and flawed institutions. But even in the rare instances when policies and institutions were right, ignoring the social issues led to a development path that produced "incomplete transformation," with the social construct not tallying with institutional and policy innovation. When all three don't exist synergistically, the process is distorted and none of the sectors perform optimally.

Are there specific roles that state institutions can assume, or policies that support or hinder advancement of social capital? If public policy is an instrument and productive social capital a target, can a workable link between the two be established? If not, why? If yes, how? Can national public policies and international aid administrations (through TC) help social-capital formation, or at least stop the destruction of existing social capital?[11] What kind of capacities do we require to create new development processes that engender productive social capital, which can then be leveraged for "good development"? Certainly, social capital as a concept is difficult to quantify, and so it is hard to make it an integral part of hard public policies.

Social capital does, however, point us towards a direction that is immensely useful in development—it helps us focus on how and under what terms we associate with each other. Woolcock (2000) highlights the following points. First, if a low stock of bridging capital makes it difficult for information and resources to flow among groups, larger socio-economic-political forces that divide societies—such as discriminatory practices along gender, caste and ethnic lines—make the situation even less conducive to growth. Second, if social capital offers an effective risk management strategy in crises, its absence implies a difficult time for countries at times of volatility. Third, institutions affect how communities draw on social capital to manage risks and opportunities. In countries where states are weak and the norm includes rampant corruption, bureaucratic obstruction, suppressed civic liberties, and a lack of the rule of law, it will be very difficult to showcase schools, hospitals and roads that are well maintained, for example. Vehicles, in the form of effective institutions, are needed to leverage social capital for "good development."

The bigger agenda of social capital, however, has the risk of being belittled by development practitioners, because as Edwards (2000) points out, attributes such as trust, tolerance and nondiscrimination are hard to engineer, and the tendency for development organizations is to focus on things that are measurable in the immediate run, such as the number of NGOs and civic organizations. This can be useful, but it is assisting "forms" not "norms" of social capital. Edwards suggests the following in relation to TC and social capital: First, the Western understanding of non-Western contexts of civil society and social capital is shallow, and dominated by Western preconceptions. TC should thus incorporate indigenous viewpoints about how civil society and social relations are structured. Narayan and Woolcock (2000) also advocate

---

[11] Putnam (1995) cites examples of policy-induced social-capital formation and destruction: community colleges, tax deductions for charitable contributions and slum clearance through urban renewal projects.

for a social institutional analysis to identify the range of stakeholders and their inter-relations. Second, rather than picking winners, TC should focus on creating an enabling environment for social-capital formation by strengthening the legal, regulatory and fiscal frameworks. All these considerations have large consequences for both the content and the forms of TC.

Some Concluding Observations

In understanding TC and capacity development, and their role in development, it becomes necessary to ask difficult questions about the aim of development itself: What are the objectives? What promise does development hold for all segments of the population? How does the development process take place? Understanding develop-ment better requires digging deeper into societal forces, and examining how norms and attitudes are formed and how in turn they connect to production processes. This process leads to some interesting and potentially far-reaching conclusions: not only do good policies and institutions matter, but so do good norms and attitudes. And careful attention has to be placed on the role social policy can play in transforming society so that development progress can not only be initiated but also sustained. This requires that considered thought be given to the sequencing of measures. For TC to be effective in creating capacity, the ground has to be made ready in terms of literacy and education. Above all, there is a need for governments to play an active and effective role.

Historically, several rationales have driven the provision of aid, from altruistic rea-sons, such as helping those in need, to more practical justifications, which recognize that in a global, connected world, poverty and disease and civil conflict constrain the progress of all nations. Yet despite TC's potential value, the record has been less than stellar. Partly, this is a consequence of less than adequate levels of aid. But perhaps even more importantly, the aid industry has been unable to meet adequately the chal-lenges of development. If the aid industry is seen as operating in a market context, even if it is imperfect, then certain factors may be necessary for the market to perform better. Since aid donors, bilateral and multilateral, drive this market, issues of market regulation and oversight have to be thought through. The aid market cannot be left to regulate itself.

Aid constituencies have to be revitalized. When aid works, it represents a high return on investment. Yet despite the global commitment to 0.7 per cent of GDP, aid levels have continued to decline and are today at the lowest level ever (0.22 per cent of GDP of the countries of the Organisation for Economic Co-operation and Development). This reflects a lack of strong constituencies in developed countries. To reverse this trend, aid performance has to be more convincingly demonstrated. This requires, inter alia, serious and regular assessment of what works and why, and an examination of how different agencies, both bilateral and multilateral, contribute to development as transformation.

There have been and continue to be calls for reforming the aid architecture. But what-ever the forms and specific roles assigned to institutions, there is a more fundamental need for aid partnerships to become exactly that—partnerships. Current approaches have to be rethought so that the overall strategic framework is a shared one, and so that not only is there broad-based ownership, but also shared accountability. The Millennium Summit agreement and related action plans have set clear targets adopted by all the countries of the United Nations. This agenda has been widely endorsed by civil society at a variety of forums. As such, these agreements and targets potentially provide a coherent, widely shared platform for change. They represent as such a global compact. Aid agencies can come together in a coordinated fashion to help countries and country institutions develop and implement policies and programmes to translate these goals into reality.

Development agendas must change if the basic premise outlined in this chapter—that development is about transformation—is to be taken seriously. This requires helping nationals and country institutions to come together to set their own visions and priorities. In the early 1990s, UNDP launched the national long-term perspective studies (NLTPS) programme. While many countries in Africa did produce national vision documents with broad national ownership, their limitation was that the vision was not linked to specific national policies and programmes, and in many ways the agenda was not sufficiently transformative in nature. Transformation requires a development dialogue based on specific country conditions, which in turn leads to specific policies and development actions. It requires a revamp of the current global aid regime based on built-in asymmetries between donors and recipients, and the imposition of conditions and fads. This approach must gradually be replaced by more home-grown development strategies that governments themselves are clearly accountable to.

Finally, transferring ideas and institutions requires the existence of local capacities to undertake this adaptation. As Stiglitz (1999) puts it, "(T)he chances of a successful transplant are much larger than if the tree is simply pulled up in one place and planted in another." Advisers from developed countries or international aid agencies may not always appreciate the value of this adaptive approach to the transfer of development knowledge, or its importance, especially given the need to show quick results. Adaptation may take longer, but this process ensures that the policies that arise are "better prepared for the local soil."

References

Adler, P., and S. Kwon. 1999. "Social Capital: The Good, the Bad and the Ugly." Paper presented at the 1999 Academy of Management meeting. Chicago.

Baris, Pierre, Nadia Rasheed and Jean Zaslavsky. 2002. "Repenser la coopération technique: revue des données statistiques (1969-1999)." Paper prepared for Reforming Technical Cooperation for Capacity Development. United Nations Development Programme.

Berg, Elliot, and the United Nations Development Programme (UNDP). 1993. *Rethinking Technical Cooperation: Reforms for Capacity Building in Africa.* New York: United Nations Development Programme.

Bhagwati, J. 1993. *India in Transition: Freeing the Economy.* Oxford: Clarendon Press.

Bourdieu, P. 1985. "The Forms of Capital." In the *Handbook of Theory and Research for Sociology of Education,* edited by J. G. Richardson, 241-58. New York: Greenwood.

Cagatay, N., et al. 2000. *Budgets As If People Mattered: Democratizing Macroeconomic Policies.* New York: United Nations Development Programme.

Civic Practices Network. (www.cpn.org/sections/tools/models/social_capital.html.)

Coleman, J. 1990. *Foundations of Social Theory.* Cambridge: Harvard University Press.

Collier, P. 1999. "Learning from Failure." In *The Self-Restraining State: Power and Accountability in New Democracies,* edited by Schedler, Diamond and Plattner. Boulder: Lynne Rienner Publishers.

Dasgupta, P. 2000. "Economic Progress and the Idea of Social Capital." *In Social Capital: A Multifaceted Perspective,* edited by P. Dasgupta and I. Serageldin. Washington, DC: World Bank.

De Long, B. 1999. "Review of Stiglitz Book Proposal: The Economic Role of the State." (www.j-bradford-delong.net/Econ_Articles/Reviews/stiglitz_role.html.)

Dreze, J., and A. K. Sen. 1995. *Economic Development and Social Opportunity.* Oxford: Clarendon Press.

Edwards, M. 2000. "Enthusiasts, Tacticians and Skeptics: The World Bank, Civil Society and Social Capital." A World Bank draft paper.

Esman, M., and N. Uphoff. 1984. *Local Organizations: Intermediaries in Rural Development.* Ithaca: Cornell University Press.

Falk, I., and S. Kilpatrick. 1999. "What is Social Capital? A Study of Interaction in a Rural Community." Discussion Paper Series. Centre for Research and Learning in Regional Australia, University of Tasmania.

Fukuyama, F. 1995. *Trust: The Social Virtues and the Creation of Prosperity.* New York: Free Press.

————. 2000. "Social Capital and Civil Society." An International Monetary Fund working paper, WP/oo/74. Washington, DC: International Monetary Fund.

Griffin, K. 1995. "Social Policy and Economic Transformation in Uzbekistan." An International Labour Organization paper.

Hanifan, L. J. 1916. "The Rural School Community Center." *Annals of the American Academy of Political and Social Science,* 67, 130-138.

Hausmann, R. 2001. "Prisoners of Geography." *Foreign Policy,* 122 (January and February).

Koo, B. H., and D. Perkins. 1995. *Social Capability and Longer Term Growth.* Cambridge: Center for International Development, Harvard University.

Kornai, J. 1992. *The Socialist System.* Princeton: Princeton University Press.

Morgan, P., and A. Qualman. 1996. "Institutional and Capacity Development: Results-Based Management and Organizational Performance." Paper prepared for the Canadian International Development Agency.

Narayan, D. and M. Woolcock. 2000. "Social Capital: Implications for Development Theory, Research and Policy." *The World Bank Research Observer,* August.

North, D. 1990. *Institutions, Institutional Change and Economic Performance.* Cambridge: Cambridge University Press.

Portes, A. 1998. "Social Capital: Its Origins and Application to Modern Sociology." *Annual Review of Sociology,* 98, 1320-50.

Putnam, R. 1993a. *Making Democracy Work: Civic Traditions in Modern Italy.* Princeton: Princeton University Press.

———. 1993b. "The Prosperous Community: Social Capital and Public Life." *The American Prospect,* 4 (13).

———. 1995. "Bowling Alone: America's Declining Social Capital." *Journal of Democracy,* 6(1) [January].

———. 2000. *Bowling Alone: The Collapse and Revival of American Community.* New York: Simon and Schuster.

Radelet, S., and J. Sachs. 1998a. "The East Asian Financial Crisis: Diagnosis, Remedies and Prospects." Brookings Papers on Economic Activity, p. 1-90.

———. 1998b. *Emerging Asia.* Manila: Asian Development Bank.

Sen, A. 1984. "Poverty and Famines: An Essay on Entitlement and Deprivation." Oxford: Oxford University Press.

Solow, Robert M. 1997. *Learning from "Learning by Doing": Lessons for Economic Growth.* Stanford: Stanford University Press.

Stewart, F. 2000. "Tackling Horizontal Inequalities." In *Evaluation and Poverty Reduction: Proceedings from a World Bank Conference,* edited by O. Feinstein and R. Piccirto. Washington, DC: World Bank (Operations Evaluation Department).

Stiglitz, J. E. 1998. "Towards a New Paradigm for Development: Strategies, Policies, and Processes." Prebisch Lecture. Geneva: United Nations Conference on Trade and Development.

———. 1999. "Scan Globally, Reinvent Locally: Knowledge Infrastructure and the Localization of Knowledge." Keynote address at the First Global Development Network Conference. Bonn.

United Nations Development Programme (UNDP). 1989. *NaTCAP Methodology.* Regional Bureau for Africa. New York.

———. 1995. *Capacity Development for Sustainable Human Development: Conceptual and Operational Signposts.* New York.

———. 2000. *Development Effectiveness Report.* New York.

————. 2002. *Revue des Donnees Statistiques 1969/1999.* Prepared for the Reforming Technical Cooperation for Capacity Development project. New York.

Woolcock, M. 1998. "Social Capital and Economic Development: Toward a Theoretical Synthesis and Policy Framework." *Theory and Society,* 27, 151-208.

————. 2000. "The Place of Social Capital in Understanding Social and Economic Outcomes." *Canadian Journal of Policy Research,* 2(1), 11-17.

————. 2001. "Microenterprise and Social Capital: A Framework for Theory, Research and Policy." The Journal of Socio-Economics, 30, 193-198.

World Bank. 1998. "Assessing Aid: What Works, What Doesn't, and Why?" Washington, DC.

————. 2000. *World Development Report 2000/2001.* Oxford: Oxford University Press.

1.2 AUTONOMY-RESPECTING ASSISTANCE: TOWARDS NEW STRATEGIES FOR CAPACITY-BUILDING AND DEVELOPMENT ASSISTANCE

DAVID ELLERMAN[1]

Introduction and Overview

Development Assistance As Helping People Help Themselves

The purpose of this chapter is to analyse the old strategies for technical cooperation, capacity-building and, in broader terms, development assistance in a way that will point to new strategies. It is a very old idea that the best form of assistance is to *help people help themselves*. We are all familiar with the ancient Chinese saying that if you give people fish, you feed them for a day, but if you teach them how to fish—or rather, if you help them learn how to fish—they can feed themselves for a lifetime.[2]

The Helper-Doer Relationship

To begin by establishing some concepts and terminology: Development assistance is analysed as a relationship between those offering assistance in some form, the helper or helpers, and those receiving the assistance, the doer or doers.[3] The helpers could be individuals, NGOs, or official bilateral or multilateral development agencies, and the doers could be individuals, organizations or various levels of government in the developing countries. The relationship is the helper-doer relationship.

The Fundamental Conundrum of Development Assistance

The assumed goal is transformation towards autonomous development on the part of the doers, with the doers helping themselves. The problem is how can the helpers supply help that actually furthers rather than overrides or undercuts the goal of the doers helping themselves? This is actually a paradox: If the helpers are supplying help that is important to the doers, then how can the doers really be helping themselves? Autonomy cannot be externally supplied. And if the doers are to become autonomous, then what is the role of the external helpers? This paradox of supplying help to self-help, "assisted self-reliance"[4] or assisted autonomy, is the *fundamental conundrum* of

---

[1] The findings, interpretations and conclusions expressed in this chapter are entirely those of the author and should not be attributed in any manner to the World Bank, to its affiliated organizations, or to the members of its Board of Directors or the countries they represent.

[2] In Pierre-Claver Damiba's "Foreword" to Berg and UNDP (1993): "Improved policy-making and better economic management—and *self-reliance* in these matters—are the central objectives of technical cooperation" (emphasis added).

[3] Doing includes thinking; "doer" is not juxtaposed to "thinker." Instead, the "doers of development" (Wolfensohn, 1999) actively undertaking tasks are juxtaposed to the passive recipients of aid, teaching or technical assistance.

[4] The phrase is from Uphoff, Esman and Krishna (1998). David Korten terms it the "central paradox of social development: the need to exert influence over people for the purpose of building their capacity to control their own lives" (1983, 220). See also Chapter 8 of Fisher (1993) on the "central paradox of social development."

development assistance. Over the years, the debates about aid, assistance and capacity-building keep circling around and around it.

My aim is not to provide a new blueprint for development assistance but to point the way for new strategies by trying to deepen the understanding of this basic conundrum and the kinds of "unhelpful help" that reduce the effectiveness of so much technical cooperation and other forms of development assistance.

Unhelpful Help

There are many strategies for development assistance that may supply help in some form but actually do not help people help themselves. The forms of help that override or undercut people's capacity to help themselves will be called "unhelpful help."[5]

There are essentially two ways that the helper's will can supplant the doer's will to thwart autonomy and self-help:

1) The helper, by social engineering, deliberately tries to impose his will on the doer; or
2) The helper, by benevolent aid, replaces the doer's will with her will, perhaps inadvertently.

"Override" or "undercut" are shorthand terms for these two conceptually distinct yin-and-yang forms of unhelpful help (which may be combined, as when benevolence hides the desire to control).

Unhelpful Help #1: Social Engineering

The overriding form of unhelpful help is a type of social engineering. The helpers supply a set of instructions or conditionalities about what the doers should be doing. They also offer motivation to follow this blueprint through various forms of aid to override the doers' own motivations. If we use the metaphor of the doers as trying to work their way through a maze, then the helpers as social engineers perceive themselves as helicoptering over the maze, seeing the path to the goal, and supplying instructions (knowledge) along with carrots and sticks (incentives) to override the doers' own motivation and push the doers in the right direction.

The alternative to providing motivation is to give some resources (perhaps with a strong matching requirement) to enable the doers to undertake development projects and programmes that they were already motivated to do on their own.[6]

Unhelpful Help #2: Benevolent Aid

The second form of unhelpful help occurs when the helper undercuts self-help by inadvertently supplying the motivation for the doer to be in or remain in a condition to receive help. One prominent example of this is long-term charitable relief. The world is awash with disaster situations that call for various forms of short-term charitable relief. The point is not to oppose these operations but to point out how charitable

---

[5]For related notions, see Gronemeyer (1992) on "help (that) does not help" and Ivan Illich's notion of "counterproductivity" (1978).
[6] The inability to engineer intrinsic motivation harks back to Socrates' point about the unteachability of virtue.

relief operates in the longer term to erode the doers' incentives to help themselves—and thus creates a dependency relationship. In this sense, charitable relief in the longer term is an undercutting form of unhelpful help.

All aid to adults based on the simple condition of needing aid risks displacing the causality. The working assumption is that the condition of needing aid was externally imposed (e.g., a natural disaster); the aid recipient shares no responsibility. But over the course of time, such aid tends to undermine this assumption as the aid becomes a reward for staying in the state of needing aid,[7] all of which creates dependency and learned helplessness. Thus relief becomes the unhelpful help that undermines self-help.

It would be hard to overstate the problem this poses for today's development industry. Official development assistance is shot through with practices that can charitably be seen as constituting charitable relief.[8] Relief to those who can help themselves needs to be time-bound and, above all, separated as if by a Chinese wall from the promotion of development.

The Scylla and Charybdis of Development Assistance

The benevolent impulse to give charitable relief and the enlightened impulse to do social engineering are the Scylla and Charybdis of development assistance. Several major difficulties lie in the path of adopting and implementing new strategies of assistance based on the idea of the transformation of capacities in the direction of self-help and autonomous development. The first difficulty to be overcome—the *pons asinorum* to be crossed—is the simple recognition of the pitfalls of social engineering on the one hand and of benevolent aid on the other hand.

Again and again, one finds social engineering blueprints to "do X" being defended on the grounds that the doers should indeed do X. But there seems to be little or no real recognition that if the doers do X only to satisfy conditionalities and thus receive aid, then the motive will falsify the action, the reforms will not be well implemented, and the policy changes will not be sustained. Hence all the arguments about the beneficial nature of doing X miss the point. Paraphrasing Kierkegaard, it is not so much the "what" of reform that counts but the "how" of reform, if the reform is to take root and be sustainable.[9]

And again and again, one finds benevolent aid being defended as doing good in the sense of delivering resources to the poor without any real recognition as to how this undercuts the incentives for developing self-reliance. All the arguments about the

---

[7] See Murray (1984) or Ellwood (1988) on the "helping conundrums."

[8] I said "charitably be seen" because many protests against the major development agencies see the agencies as pursuing political or even corporate goals. Without gainsaying the protests, my point is different. Even if the agencies are pursuing pure-hearted charitable relief, that itself cuts across and conflicts with the longer-term developmental goals of the agencies. And, unfortunately, many of the protests seem driven by the goal that the development agencies *should* pursue more pure-hearted charitable relief.

[9] "All ironic observing is a matter of continually paying attention to the 'how,' whereas the honorable gentleman with whom the ironist has the honor of dealing pays attention only to the 'what'" (Kierkegaard, 1992, 614). For a more recent critique of conditionality-based reforms, see Assessing Aid (World Bank, 1998).

relief being "help" miss the point. It is an unhelpful form of help that in the longer term undercuts capacity-building and autonomous development.

The other major difficulty to be overcome is the gap between rhetoric and reality. Development agencies are quite adept at adopting the language of being against charity and blueprint-driven social engineering, and being in favor of helping people help themselves. The challenge is that it is a rather subtle matter to overcome the basic conundrum and supply help in a way that does not override or undercut the development of the capacity for self-help. Yet reborn managers in restructured agencies regularly use recycled rhetoric to launch reconfigured programmes in social engineering or charitable relief or both.

The First Don't: Don't Override Self-Help Capacity with Conditional Aid

The Mental Imagery of the Expert Surgical Intervention

One major source of social engineering[10] programmes is the mental imagery or "development narrative" of the expert helper who performs the surgical operation that restores the patient to health, a health that is thereafter self-reinforcing. If the patient were able to cure himself, then the operation would not be necessary. But, realities being what they are, the helper must take control to ensure success and must supply the motivation for the doer to undergo the operation. Afterwards, with health restored, the doer can go his own way.

A variation on this narrative is where the expert helper makes a surgical intervention to install a new and improved way of doing things, accompanied by technical training for the counterpart doer. The doer will absorb the required know-how and, seeing the benefits, the reforms will be sustained on their own.

This question is complicated by the fact that there are some cases where such expert interventions might work well—and then the success in these cases prompts the development industry optimistically to extend the strategy to the vast majority of cases, where it is quite inappropriate. For instance, there are certain stroke-of-the-pen or *pro forma* reforms, such as striking down a tariff, tax or licensing requirement, which might be implemented to satisfy a conditionality and thereby to receive aid. Once a tax is surgically removed, the tax-payers will readily comply so, in that sense, the socially engineered intervention will be effective. But these cases are the exception, not the rule.

The Spectrum of Institutional Reforms

Auturo Israel (1987) envisaged a spectrum of institutional reforms where the reforms were ranked in terms of specificity. At one end of the spectrum are the highly specific stroke-of-the-pen reforms that can be socially engineered. At the other end are the highly non-specific institutional reforms such as the rule of law, the ethos of fulfilling

---

[10] In terms of professions, social engineering is now sponsored largely by economics, not classical engineering.

contracts and paying back loans, the fair adjudication of disputes and the general shift to the private sector market mentality.

Particularly vexing are those reforms that are like icebergs, with a specific stroke-of-the-pen reform showing above the water and a massive below-the-water change in behaviour (which involves attitudes, norms and culture) needed to implement the reform. Again and again, above-the-water reforms are engineered with strong conditionalities enforced by output-based aid geared to the passage of laws. Years later, the reforms are discovered to be ineffective due to the lack of below-the-water changes in behaviour. Instead of learning how the below-the-water changes actually take place and making a fundamental shift in development strategy away from social engineering, the economics-engineering frame of mind is constantly rededicating itself to better indicators of outputs upon which to base tougher conditionalities for new and improved output-based aid.

The Indirect Approach

The notion of autonomous development provides the clue to a new approach. (see box 1.2.1) Autonomous action is based on intrinsic motivation. Any action based on the externally supplied motivation of carrots and sticks is heteronomous. Any attempt to engineer autonomous action with external carrots or sticks would be self-defeating; the means are inconsistent with the motive and thus defeat the end. This problem is often illustrated using the horse-to-water metaphor; externally engineered pressures can lead a horse to water, but that sort of motivation cannot make him drink.

BOX 1.2.1: John Dewey on the Indirect Approach

The indirect approach was well-developed both in educational theory and in broader social affairs by John Dewey:

> We are even likely to take the influence of superior force for control, forgetting that while we may lead a horse to water we cannot make him drink; and that while we can shut a man up in a penitentiary we cannot make him penitent.... When we confuse a physical with an educative result, we always lose the chance of enlisting the person's own participating disposition in getting the result desired, and thereby of developing within him an intrinsic and persisting direction in the right way (Dewey, 1916, 26-7).

Dewey also saw the general case for the indirect approach as the best way to help people help themselves:

> The best kind of help to others, whenever possible, is indirect, and consists in such modifications of the conditions of life, of the general level of subsistence, as enables them independently to help themselves (Dewey and Tufts, 1908, 390).

The whole idea of imposing or engineering change with supplied motivation might be termed the "direct" approach. That formulation then points to the alternative as being an "indirect" approach to helping, which implies not supplying motivation to the doers but finding the existing intrinsic motivation of the doers and offering help on that basis.

If social engineering schemes don't work (outside a few special cases), then what is the blueprint and where is the motivation for the alternative? This question is ill-posed.

The alternative is not having a different blueprint, but having an active and adaptive learning approach instead of a blueprint approach.

BOX 1.2.2: Gilbert Ryle on the Helper-Doer Conundrum in Education

The fundamental conundrum of development assistance occurs in all the helper-doer relationships across the range of human interaction (Ellerman, 2001). The philosopher Gilbert Ryle gave a particularly clear statement of the same conundrum in education:

> (H)ow, in logic, can anyone be taught to do untaught things? ...How can one person teach another person to think things out for himself, since if he gives him, say, the new arithmetical thoughts, then they are not the pupil's own thoughts; or if they are his own thoughts, then he did not get them from his teacher? Having led the horse to the water, how can we make him drink? (Ryle, 1967, 105 and 112).

Ryle's answer was a motive inconsistency argument: There is no way to heteronomously impose autonomous action.

> How can the teacher be the initiator of the pupil's initiatives? The answer is obvious. He cannot. I cannot compel the horse to drink thirstily. I cannot coerce Tommy into doing spontaneous things. Either he is not coerced, or they are not spontaneous...(Ryle, 1967, 112).

> How in logic can the teacher dragoon his pupil into thinking for himself, impose initiative upon him, drive him into self-motion, conscript him into volunteering, enforce originality upon him, or make him operate spontaneously? The answer is that he cannot—and the reason why we half felt that we must do so was that we were unwittingly enslaved by the crude, semi-hydraulic idea that in essence to teach is to pump propositions, like "Waterloo, 1815," into the pupils' ears, until they regurgitate them automatically (Ryle, 1967, 118).

Ryle mentions that the "crude, semi-hydraulic idea" of the rote teaching of facts like "Waterloo, 1815" is mistaken as a general model of teaching. Similarly, we have seen that the simple example of engineered stroke-of-the-pen reforms is mistaken as a general model of institutional reforms.

In terms of motivation, the alternative does not involve a different set of carrots and sticks to motivate change, but instead comprises change that is based on intrinsic motivation. The key is for the doers to embark on projects or programmes motivated by themselves. Thus, money *cannot* be the leading edge of the helpers'assistance. The direct link between money and motivation must be broken.[11] Money can only play a role as a secondary or background enabler for what the doers *independently* want to do. Development transformation cannot be bought, but where it is afoot on its own there will be costs of change that could be partly covered by development assistance agencies. Where, however, aid money takes the lead, it will distort the dynamics and will end up essentially paying the costs of not changing.

Since intrinsic motivation cannot be based on external carrots and sticks, the helpers cannot *supply* this motivation ("virtue") to the doers; they can only *find* it. Yet aid-seeking doers will nonetheless try to fake or mimic intrinsic motivation for real reforms, so the helpers face a difficult task of judgment. But the difficulties of judgment

---

[11] For a consumer, a subsidy only on certain goods skews motivation, while a lump-sum subsidy may allow one to buy what one already wanted to buy. Similarly, aid conditional on certain actions skews motivation, whereas pooled aid and similar sector-wide approaches break the link with specific donor sponsored actions and may enable the doers to do what they were *already* motivated to do. The doers' activities, motivated by themselves, might be to launch raids on their neighbors or to launch real reforms. The helpers need to judge independently if these activities should be enabled.

are little in comparison with the pressures to "move the money" in the lender and donor agencies. One would expect large Type II errors (i.e., accepting faux-motive projects), particularly as the aid-seeking doers evolve better means of mimicry and the money-moving helpers supply more corroboration for the theory of cognitive dissonance (i.e., judgment bending to be more consonant with self-interest).[12] Thus there is grave doubt that any agency with an organizational business plan based on providing aid by moving money could implement an autonomy-respecting indirect approach to development assistance . To lessen Type II errors, the agency must be able to say, "No."

BOX 1.2.3: Socratic Helper and Active Doer

Instead of claiming that the "answers" should be disseminated from expert-helper to counterpart-doer, Socrates displayed the humility of knowing that he did not know. He did not put learners in a passive role, but helped them to try actively to answer questions or resolve problems.

> That real education aims at imparting knowledge rather than opinion, that knowledge cannot be handed over ready-made but has to be appropriated by the knower, that appropriation is possible only through one's own search, and that to make him aware of his ignorance is to start a man on the search for knowledge—these are the considerations that govern and determine the Socratic method of teaching (Versényi, 1963, 117).

Indeed, the key to the indirect approach is for the helper as midwife to facilitate the doer taking the active role. In a slogan: "Stop the teaching so that the learning can begin!" As George Bernard Shaw put it: "If you teach a man anything he will never learn it" (1961, 11). Or as management theorist Douglas McGregor said: "Fundamentally the staff man...must create a situation in which members of management can learn, rather than one in which they are taught..." (1966, 161). José Ortega y Gasset suggested: "He who wants to teach a truth should place us in the position to discover it ourselves" (1961, 67). Or as Myles Horton, founder of the Highlander Folk School, maintained: "You don't just tell people something; you find a way to use situations to educate them so that they can learn to figure things out themselves" (1998, 122).

The Second Don't: Don't Undercut Self-Help Capacity with Benevolent Aid

The Mental Imagery of Relief and Gap-Filling Aid

One major source of encouragement for disguising benevolent aid as development assistance is the mental imagery of aid that allows doers to get back on their feet after some externally caused calamity so that they can thereafter help themselves. A second scenario is that given a genuine self-help project with a resource-gap, the gap-filling aid enables the self-help project to go forward.

These marvelous images might actually come true in a few cases, but it would be inappropriate to take them as a general model for development assistance. In each case, there is the time-consistency problem that the continuing offer of aid tends to make the motivation aid-driven. In the case of disaster relief, the continuing offer of aid takes the sting out of staying in a needful condition. While the needful condition was initially exogenous or independent of aid, staying in that condition may become a means for getting more aid. In the second case of gap-filling aid, the continuing offer

---

[12] See "Problems Encountered in Buying Virtue through Aid" in Hirschman (1971, 205-7).

of aid leads to projects based partly on the incentive of the aid offer. Instead of self-help projects that were initially afoot on their own, doers may create aid-seeking projects camouflaged in a rhetoric of self-help.

In short, whenever money becomes the leading edge of assistance, then the supply of aid seems to create and perpetuate the demand for it—which might be labeled Say's Law of Development Aid.[13] Aid that might in a few cases be autonomy-respecting ends up chasing its own tail by funding needs or projects induced by the offer of aid—all to the detriment of building self-help capacity. What starts as a benevolent impulse thus becomes one of the major problems in the postwar effort towards capacity-building and development. Organizational reforms in the development agencies will need to separate development assistance from benevolent aid—as if by a Chinese wall.

The Example of Social Funds

This problem is illustrated by the debate about social funds (e.g., Tendler, 2000), which seems to recapitulate some forms of North-South unhelpful help at the community level. Social funds (SFs) are currently something of a policy fad; they are often described using the imagery of promoting self-help with gap-filling aid. The funds are typically set up by national governments to deliver quickly resources to poor people, bypassing the regional and local governments. They are funded by grants from donors or by hard currency loans with a payback beyond the political horizon of the central government. One of their main activities is to make grants (or near-grants with small matching requirements) to fund small infrastructure projects. Lenders and donors tend to like the social funds since they move the money with tangible outcomes (more schools, tube wells, health clinics, warehouses and so forth), which in turn rewards the benevolent impulse in the lender and donor agencies.

The problem is that social funds are more instruments of relief in the sense of "quickly delivering fish to poor and hungry people," rather than instruments of capacity-building and development in the sense of "helping poor people learn how to fish for themselves." There is disagreement less about the facts than about the choices between short-term aid and long-term capacity-building.

By using a new, separate and clean organization of the central government, supporters argue that SFs circumvent unresponsive, incompetent and perhaps corrupt regional and local governments to help quickly satisfy the needs of poor people. Critics see the same reality as central government largess buying or rewarding local support, as an elite special agency (often outside the civil service) attracting good talent out of the ministries, and as a bypass of sustainable reforms and capacity-building in the lower levels of government. Since no one argues that SFs should actually replace local and regional governments, the net result is a plus for short-term relief and a minus for long-term government reform.

Supporters see the process of local people choosing their preferred local infrastructure project from a menu funded by the social fund as being bottom-up, demand-driven community empowerment. Critics see the same reality and argue that

---

[13] The original Say's Law in economics is usually paraphrased as: "Supply creates its own demand."

local people soliciting and receiving largess from an agency funded by and solely accountable to the central government is more top-down paternalism than bottom-up community empowerment. Eliciting demand for grant-funded projects is hardly demand-driven in the sense of projects that are afoot on their own (i.e., with doers covering enough of the costs to ensure that they wanted to do the project anyway). Empowering people to buy outcomes with an external grant is rather different from building the community's own capacity to reach those outcomes in a fiscally sustainable manner. Thus the social fund debate provides an illuminating example of how Orwellian the rhetoric can become, and how phrases like "bottom-up," "demand-driven" and "community empowerment" can be used to describe almost the opposite reality.

Social funds, like all good policy fads, seem to have self-reinforcing loops that keep them rolling. To close these loops, the funds need to be evaluated. Supporters argue that they have done the research and have the impact evaluations to show that SFs have a good impact. Critics argue firstly that impact evaluations are independent of cost. A true *project* evaluation would have to look at whether the impact was obtained with US $10 or $10 million. Secondly, the impact evaluations compare communities that receive social fund grants with otherwise similar counterfactual communities that receive no grants. Not surprisingly, the studies tend to show that the communities that receive the funds have better facilities (more "impact") than the communities that don't receive funds. Sometimes the difference is not that significant, but the real point is that a well-specified counterfactual would be a community that had the *same* resources available for the best alternative approach to community development (e.g., see the 18 cases of assisted self-reliance in Krishna et al., 1997).

Relief Assistance As Generalized Moral Hazard

The First Don't deals with social engineering as a form of unhelpful help that overrides (hopefully temporarily) any self-help capacity in order to get the doers to do the right thing. The Second Don't concerns benevolent aid that, unless very temporary, will tend to undermine the capacity for self-help. Sometimes aid is sought by a country because of a self-perceived lack of efficacy. Aid granted out of benevolence, even without carrots and sticks, has the adverse effect of reinforcing the lack of self-confidence and doubts about one's own efficacy. Eleemosynary aid to relieve the symptoms of poverty may create a situation of moral hazard that weakens reform incentives and attenuates efforts for positive change to eliminate poverty (see Maren, 1997). Such aid *"tends to render others dependent,* and thus contradicts its own professed aim: the helping of others" (Dewey and Tufts, 1908, 387). The Two Don'ts are interrelated when dependency-creating aid leaves the doers vulnerable to more social engineering control as well as more charity in a vicious circle that drives them away from autonomous development.[14]

Moral hazard refers to the phenomenon where excessive insurance relieves the insured from taking normal precautions so risky behaviour might be increased. The phrase is applied generally to opportunistic actions undertaken because some arrangement has relieved the doers from bearing the full responsibility for their actions. Benevolent help softens the incentives for people to help themselves.

---

[14] See the "shifting the burden" to the helper as the "generic dynamics of addiction" in Senge (1990, 104-113).

BOX 1.2.4: John Dewey's Critique of Benevolence

We saw previously that John Dewey criticized the controlling engineering approach to help as not promoting people's capacity to help themselves. Dewey also criticized "oppressive benevolence" as undercutting that capacity development. He was inspired in this by Chicago reformer Jane Addams' critique of industrialist George Pullman's paternalism towards "his" workers in her essay "A Modern Lear" (Addams, 1965), an essay that Dewey called "one of the greatest things I ever read both as to its form and its ethical philosophy" (quoted by Lasch in Addams, 1965, 176). Christopher Lasch developed some of the same ideas in his contrast of the "ethic of respect" with the "ethic of compassion" (Lasch, 1995).

According to Robert Westbrook, Dewey held that:

> (S)elf-realization was a do-it-yourself project; it was not an end that one individual could give to or force on another. The truly moral man was, to be sure, interested in the welfare of others—such an interest was essential to his own self-realization—but a true interest in others lay in a desire to expand their autonomous activity, not in the desire to render them the dependent objects of charitable benevolence (Westbrook, 1991, 46-7).

An incapacity for beneficial self-activity was assumed to be part of the condition of the poor, so reformers would treat them accordingly.

> The conception of conferring the good upon others, or at least attaining it for them, which is our inheritance from the aristocratic civilization of the past, is so deeply embodied in religious, political, and charitable institutions and in moral teachings, that it dies hard. Many a man, feeling himself justified by the social character of his ultimate aim (it may be economic, or educational, or political), is genuinely confused or exasperated by the increasing antagonism and resentment which he evokes, because he has not enlisted in his pursuit of the "common" end the freely cooperative activities of others (Dewey and Tufts, 1908, 303-4).

Thus development assistance as benevolent aid does not help people help themselves and it may even lead to antagonism and resentment—all of which is baffling to those who derive moral satisfaction from doing good and making others happy.

> To "make others happy" except through liberating their powers and engaging them in activities that enlarge the meaning of life is to harm them and to indulge ourselves under cover of exercising a special virtue.... To foster conditions that widen the horizon of others and give them command of their own powers, so that they can find their own happiness in their own fashion, is the way of "social" action. Otherwise the prayer of a freeman would be to be left alone, and to be delivered, above all, from "reformers" and "kind" people (Dewey, 1957, 270).

David Thoreau noted, "If I knew for a certainty that a man was coming to my house with the conscious design of doing me good, I should run for fear that I should have some of his good done to me" (quoted in Carmen 1996, 47; and in Gronemeyer, 1992, 53).

In the insurance example, the limit case of no insurance (which means complete self-insurance) certainly solves the problem of moral hazard since the individual then has a full incentive to take precautions to prevent accidents. Yet the no-insurance option forgoes the benefits of insurance. There is no first-best solution of complete insurance without moral hazard, but there are partial solutions in the form of co-payments and deductibles so that the insured party retains some risk and thus some incentive to take normal precautions.

In a similar manner, the conservative approach of no assistance could be seen as the "tough love" limit case. It certainly solves the problem of softened incentives for self-help, but it foregoes forms of positive assistance that might be compatible with autonomy. The idea of co-payments carries over to the idea of non-trivial matching funds from the doers as a commitment mechanism to show that they are dedicated on their own account to the programmes.[15] The idea of deductibles carries over to the concept of second-stage funding, where the doers show commitment by funding the first stage of a programme on their own.

This problem suggests the possibility that the post-World War II development assistance effort from the developed countries to the developing world has created a massive generalized moral hazard problem. Among development economists, Peter Bauer (1976 and 1981) has developed these arguments about aid with particular force. William Easterly (2001) has summarized the empirical results that, on the whole, document the lack of success in the last half century of development assistance based on various combinations of social engineering and benevolent aid.

Surely one bright spot was the Marshall Plan, which, in many ways, provided a model for later development efforts. Yet it also contained the seeds of moral hazard. Robert Marjolin, the French architect of the Marshall Plan, noted in a 1952 memo that American aid continuing over a longer term could have precisely that effect:

> Although American aid has been a necessary remedy over a period, and will continue to be for a time, one is bound to acknowledge that in the long run it has had dangerous psychological and political effects.... It is making more difficult the task of the governments of Western Europe trying to bring about a thorough economic and financial rehabilitation. The idea that it is always possible to call on American aid, that here is the ever-present cure for external payments deficits, is a factor destructive of willpower. It is difficult to hope that, while this recourse continues to exist, the nations of Western Europe will apply, for a sufficient length of time, the courageous economic and financial policy that will enable them to meet their needs from their own resources without the contribution of external aid (quoted in Marjolin, 1989, 241).

However, the demands of the Korean War and the lack of a permanent aid bureaucracy resulted in the winding down of American aid. If the industrial countries of Western Europe faced moral hazard problems in the short-lived Marshall Plan, one can only begin to fathom the extent of the moral hazard problem in developing countries that face well-established professional aid-providers in the developed countries who constantly reinvent ways to move the money.

Money is a mixed blessing—to the extent that it is a blessing at all in development assistance. As long as money continues to be the leading edge of development assistance,[16] then the problems of moral hazard will only be compounded.

---

[15] A programme like the African Management Services Company (AMSCO) that provides help only by topping off doer-supplied funds would be enabling without engendering faux-motive projects. AMSCO is a joint initiative between the United Nations Development Programme, the African Development Bank and the International Finance Corporation (see www.amsco.org).

[16] One sees the evidence every day in calls by leaders of the development industry to address this or that development problem with US $X billions more in funding—rather than undertaking the difficult and subtle reforms for a more effective approach where money has a background role.

The Two Dos

The First Do: Start from Where the Doers Are

The *via negativa* of the Two Don'ts needs to be supplemented by Two Dos that can help guide a more autonomy-respecting approach to development assistance. To be transformative, a process of change must start·from and engage with the present endowment of institutions. Otherwise, the process will only create an overlay of new behaviours that is not sustainable (without continual bribes or coercion).

Yet this is a common error. Reformers oriented towards utopian social engineering (see Popper, 1962) aim to wipe the slate clean in order to install a set of ideal institutions. Any attempt to transform the current flawed, retrograde or even evil institutions is viewed as only staining or polluting the change process. For instance, in the transitional economies such as Russia, the "leap over the chasm" imposed by institutional shock therapy fell far short of the other side, since people "need a bridge to cross from their own experience to a new way" (Alinsky, 1971, xxi). It will take the country much longer to climb out of the chasm than it would have taken if a bridge over the chasm had been built step by step.

Similar considerations support the argument for an evolutionary and incremental strategy in poor countries rather than trying to jump to new institutions.

> The primary causes of extreme poverty are immaterial, they lie in certain deficiencies in education, organization and discipline.... Here lies the reason why development cannot be an act of creation, why it cannot be ordered, bought, comprehensively planned: why it requires a process of evolution. Education does not "jump"; it is a gradual process of great subtlety. Organization does not "jump"; it must gradually evolve to fit changing circumstances. And much the same goes for discipline. All three must evolve step by step, and the foremost task of development policy must be to speed this evolution (Schumacher, 1973, 168-9).

Given a choice between helpers using the momentum of bottom-up involvement in "flawed" reforms and the top-down social engineering of "model" institutions, the start-from-where-the-doers-are principle (the First Do) argues for the former.[17]

The Second Do: See the World Through the Doers' Eyes

If a social engineer could perform an "institutional lobotomy" to erase present institutional habits, then development advice would not need to be tailored to present circumstances. Generic advice would suffice; one message would fit all blank slates. But failing that, it is necessary to acquire a deeper knowledge of the present institutions. This is done by, in effect, learning to see the world through the eyes of the policy-makers and people in the country. "The change agent must psychologically zip him or herself into the clients' skins, and see their situation through their eyes" (Rogers, Everett; 1983; 316).

---

[17] Applied to technical cooperation, it would be better for the helpers to train local doers to do the job—even if locals do it poorly at first, so long as there is a learning mechanism—than for the helpers to do the job well but with little or no local capacity-building. Sometimes the best form of training is for the helper to broker horizontal learning between the doers and those who have already successfully done a job under similar circumstances.

An interaction between teacher and learner that is compatible with autonomy requires that the teacher have an empathetic understanding with the student. If the teacher can understand the learning experience of the student, then the teacher can use his or her superior knowledge to help the student. This help does not take the form of telling the student the answer or solution, but of offering advice or guidance, perhaps away from a dead-end path, to assist the student in the active appropriation of knowledge. The teacher, according to Dewey's learner-centered pedagogy, must be able to see the world through the eyes of the students and within the limits of their experience, and at the same time apply the adult's viewpoint to offer guideposts. Similarly, in Carl Rogers' notion of client-centered therapy (1951), the counselor needs to enter the "internal frame of reference of the client" in order to give assistance that respects and relies upon the actual capacity of the person.[18]

In describing the process of an aid agency trying to help a developing country, Albert Hirschman recommends a process of familiarization—of walking in their shoes and looking through their eyes at the array of problems facing the country.

> Little by little, after getting committed and "seeing," that is, learning about the country's problems, some hypotheses should emerge about the sequence in which a country is likely to attack successfully the multifarious obstacles. In the search for the best hypothesis, those who administer aid programmes should use what Dr. Carl Rogers, the psychotherapist, calls "client-centered therapy" (Hirschman, 1971, 185).

In the context of adult transformation, how does the educator/investigator find out about the client-student's world? One way is through Paulo Freire's notion of dialogue. In the non-dialogical approach to education, the teacher determines the appropriate messages to be delivered or "deposited" in the students, as money is deposited in a bank. Instead of ready-made best-practice recipes, Freire, like Dewey, saw the educational mission as based on posing problems, particularly those stemming from the learners' world:

> In contrast with the anti-dialogical and non-communicative "deposits" of the banking method of education, the programme content of the problem-posing method—dialogical par excellence—is constituted and organized by the students' view of the world, where their own generative themes are found (Freire, 1970, 101).

Yet often to development "professionals, it seems absurd to consider the necessity of respecting the 'view of the world' held by the people" (Freire, 1970, 153-4).

Albert Hirschman's Model of Unbalanced Growth

Within development theory, the best exposition of the alternative indirect approach (including the Two Dos and Two Don'ts) is the still-classic work of Albert Hirschman. I previously used the image of the social engineer helicoptering over a maze giving both instructions and motivation to the doers in the maze to do the right thing. In the context of Hirschman's work, the social engineer was the development planner designing an integrated development plan of balanced growth for a country to make the big push out of

---

[18] Maurice Friedman emphasizes the importance of seeing through the eyes of the other in Buber's notion of dialogue. "The essential element of genuine dialogue...is 'seeing the other' or 'experiencing the other side'" (Friedman, 1960, 87).

the low-level traps and to take-off on the path of self-sustained growth. But the planners have neither the knowledge nor the motivational powers for such plans to be implemented.

Instead of having a clear view of the path out of the maze, social engineers often have preconceived plans based on economic theory. Hirschman provides an example from his own experience as a development adviser in Colombia:

> But word soon came from World Bank headquarters that I was principally expected to take...the initiative in formu-lating some ambitious economic development plan that would spell out invest-ments, domestic savings, growth and foreign aid targets for the Colombian econ-omy over the next few years. All of this was alleged to be quite simple for experts mastering the new programming technique: Apparently there now existed adequate knowledge, even without close study of local surroundings, of the likely ranges of...all the key figures needed....
>
> My instinct was to try to understand better *their* patterns of action, rather than assume from the outset that they could only be "developed" by importing a set of tech-niques they knew nothing about (Hirschman, 1984, 90-1).

Instead of preconceived blueprints, a local learning process was necessary. Hirschman has often noted the problems created in developing countries by the tendency that Flaubert ridiculed as *la rage de vouloir conclure* or the rage to conclude (see Hirschman, 1973, 238-40). And the same attitude is common in development agencies. Indeed, there is a self-reinforcing lock-in between developing countries that *want* "The Answer" and development agencies that *have* "The Answer."

> (Policy-makers) will be supplied with a great many ideas, suggestions, plans, and ideolo-gies, frequently of foreign origin or based on foreign experience.... Genuine learning about the problem will sometimes be prevented not only by the local policy-makers' eagerness to jump to a ready-made solution, but also by the insistent offer of help and advice on the part of powerful outsiders.... (S)uch practices (will) tend to cut short that "long confrontation between man and a situation" (Camus) so fruitful for the achievement of genuine progress in problem-solving (Hirschman, 1973, 239-40).

In addition to replacing imported blueprints with a local learning process, an alternative indirect approach also has to find a substitute for the external carrots and sticks that drive programmes in the social engineering vision—a "picture of pro-gramme aid as a catalyst for virtuous policies (that) belongs to the realm of rhapsodic phantasy" (Hirschman, 1971, 205). Instead of supplying exogenous motivation for a faux-virtuous reform, the idea is to *find* in the small where "virtue appears of its own accord" (Hirschman, 1971, 204) and then to recognize and strengthen it.

Endogenous motivation for change is based on problem-solving. Not all problems can be attacked at once so attention and aid is first focused on the sectors or locali-ties where some of the preconditions are in place and where problem-solving initiative is afoot on its own. The initial small successes will then create pressures through the forward and backward linkages to foster learning and change that is nearby in sectoral or regional terms. The successes, when broadcast through horizontal learning to those facing similar problems, will start to break down the paralyzing beliefs that nothing can be done and will thus fuel broader initiatives that take the early wins as their benchmark. Unlike a model that assumes large-scale organized social action on the balanced-growth model, directed by the government under the pressure of external conditionalities, the parties in Hirschman's unbalanced growth model, like the pieces on Adam Smith's human chessboard,[19] are responding to local endogenous pressures and inducements from their economic partners or to opportunities revealed by others in a similar position.

One thing leads to, induces, elicits or entrains another thing through chains of "tensions, disproportions and disequilibria" (Hirschman, 1961, 66). Hirschman at one point refers to the principle of unbalanced growth as "the idea of maximizing induced decision-making" (1994, 278). The problem-solving pressures induced by unbalanced growth will call forth otherwise unused resources and enlist otherwise untapped energies. As a project or programme moves from one bottleneck and crisis to another (in comparison with the smooth, planned allocation of resources), then "resources and abilities that are hidden, scattered or badly utilized" (1961, 5) will be mobilized.

Conclusion: The Two Paths

After a half-century of official development assistance, we still find ourselves wandering in a dark wood. But starting from the fundamental conundrum of helping people to help themselves, it is becoming clear that there are two divergent paths. The well-worn path is the direct approach of conventional money-based and knowledge-based aid. If the goal is to help the doers of development to help themselves, then I have argued that the direct path tends to override (with conditional aid) or undercut (with benevolent aid) the doers' capacity for self-help.

Perhaps it is time to consider the less-trodden path of the indirect approach, which emphasizes forms of assistance based on respect for the autonomy of the doers. Initial steps on the indirect path were described with the Two Dos: Start from where the doers are and see the world through their eyes. Perhaps it would be useful to have a Third Do as an overall description of the indirect approach: Respect the autonomy of the doers.[20]

On the direct path, the helper helps the doers by supplying distorted motivation (conditional aid) and "managed" knowledge (*ex cathedra* answers buttressed by one-sided research and public relations campaigns) to get the doers to do what the helpers take as the right thing. On the indirect path, which respects autonomy, the helper helps the doers to help themselves by supplying not motivation but perhaps some resources to enable the doers to do what the doers were already motivated to do themselves. On the knowledge side, the helper who respects autonomy supplies not answers but helps in a Socratic manner to build learning capacity (e.g., by enabling doers' access to unbiased information and developing their ability to hear all sides of

---

[19] "The man of system...seems to imagine that he can arrange the different members of a great society with as much ease as the hand arranges the different pieces upon a chessboard; he does not consider that the pieces upon the chessboard have no other principle of motion besides that which the hand impresses upon them; but that, in the great chessboard of human society, every single piece has a principle of motion of its own, altogether different from that which the legislature might choose to impress upon it" (Smith, 1969 (1759), 342-3).
[20] See Ellerman (2001) for a treatment of the Two Don'ts and Three Dos in the works of Hirschman, Schumacher, McGregor, Dewey, Freire, Alinsky, Rogers and Kierkegaard.

an argument) that allows the doers to learn from whatever source in a self-directed learning process.

Direct methods can help others, but they cannot help others to help themselves. That requires autonomy-respecting indirect methods on the part of the helpers and autonomous self-activity on the part of the doers. Doers need not only to participate but also to be in the driver's seat in order to make their actions and learnings their own. It is the psychological version of the old principle that people have a natural ownership of the fruits of their own labor. The helpers can use indirect and enabling approaches to provide background assistance. But the doers have to take the initiative and then keep it from being overridden or undercut by external aid. And then they will be the doers of their own development.

References

Addams, Jane. 1965. "A Modern Lear." In *The Social Thought of Jane Addams,* edited by Christopher Lasch, 105-23. Indianapolis: Bobbs-Merrill.

Alinsky, Saul. 1971. *Rules for Radicals.* New York: Vintage.

Bauer, Peter. 1976. *Dissent on Development.* Cambridge: Harvard University Press.

———. 1981. *Equality, the Third World, and Economic Delusion.* Cambridge: Harvard University Press.

Berg, Elliot, and the United Nations Development Programme (UNDP). 1993. *Rethinking Technical Cooperation: Reforms for Capacity-Building in Africa.* New York: United Nations Development Programme.

Carmen, Raff. 1996. *Autonomous Development.* London: Zed Books.

Dewey, John. 1916. *Democracy and Education.* New York: Free Press.

———. 1957. *Human Nature and Conduct: An Introduction to Social Psychology.* New York: Modern Library.

Dewey, John, and James Tufts. 1908. *Ethics.* New York: Henry Holt.

Easterly, William. 2001. *The Elusive Quest for Growth: Economists' Adventures and Misadventures in the Tropics.* Cambridge: Massachusetts Institute of Technology Press.

Ellerman, David. 2001. *Helping People Help Themselves: Toward a Theory of Autonomy-Compatible Help.* World Bank Policy Research Working Paper 2693. (http://econ.worldbank.org/view.php?type=5&id=2513.)

Ellwood, David. 1988. *Poor Support: Poverty in the American Family.* New York: Basic Books.

Fisher, Julie. 1993. *The Road From Rio: Sustainable Development and the Nongovernmental Movement in the Third World.* Westport: Praeger.

Freire, Paulo. 1970. *Pedagogy of the Oppressed.* New York: Continuum.

Friedman, Maurice. 1960. *Martin Buber: The Life of Dialogue.* New York: Harper Torchbooks.

Gronemeyer, Marianne. 1992. "Helping." In *The Development Dictionary: A Guide to Knowledge as Power,* edited by Wolfgang Sachs, 51-69. London: Zed Books.

Hirschman, Albert O. 1958. *The Strategy of Economic Development.* New Haven: Yale University Press, 1961.

———. 1971. *A Bias for Hope: Essays on Development and Latin America.* New Haven: Yale University Press.

———. 1973. *Journeys Toward Progress.* New York: Norton.

———. 1984. "A Dissenter's Confession: The Strategy of Economic Development' Revisited." In *Pioneers in Development,* edited by G. Meier and D. Seers, 87-111. New York: Oxford University Press.

———. 1994. "A Propensity to Self-Subversion." In *Rethinking the Development Experience: Essays Provoked by the Work of Albert O. Hirschman,* edited by L. Rodwin and D. Schön, 227-83. Washington, DC: Brookings Institution.

Horton, Myles, with Judith and Herbert Kohl. 1998. *The Long Haul: An Autobiography.* New York: Teachers College Press.

Illich, Ivan. 1978. *Toward a History of Needs.* New York: Pantheon Books.

Israel, Arturo. 1987. *Institutional Development.* Washington, DC: World Bank.

Kierkegaard, Søren. 1992. *Concluding Unscientific Postscript to Philosophical Fragments.* Edited by Howard and Edna Hong. Princeton: Princeton University Press.

Korten, David C. 1983. "Social Development: Putting People First." In *Bureaucracy and the Poor: Closing the Gap,* edited by D. Korten and F. Alfonso, 201-21. West Hartford: Kumarian.

Krishna, Anirudh, Norman Uphoff and Milton Esman, eds. 1997. *Reasons for Hope: Instructive Experiences in Rural Development.* West Hartford: Kumarian Press.

Lasch, Christopher. 1995. *The Revolt of the Elites and the Betrayal of Democracy.* New York: Norton.

Maren, Michael. 1997. *The Road to Hell: The Ravaging Effects of Foreign Aid and International Charity.* New York: Free Press.

Marjolin, Robert. 1989. *Architect of European Unity: Memoirs 1911-1986.* Translated by William Hall. London: Weidenfeld and Nicolson.

McGregor, Douglas. 1966. *Leadership and Motivation.* Cambridge: Massachusetts Institute of Technology Press.

Murray, Charles. 1984. *Losing Ground: American Social Policy 1959-1980.* New York:Basic Books.

Ortega y Gasset, José. 1961. *Meditations on Quixote.* New York: Norton.

Popper, Karl. 1962. *The Open Society and Its Enemies: The High Tide of Prophecy: Hegel, Marx, and the Aftermath.* New York: Harper and Row.

Rogers, Carl R. 1951. *Client-Centered Therapy.* Boston: Houghton Mifflin.

Rogers, Everett. 1983. *Diffusion of Innovations,* third edition. New York: Free Press.

Ryle, Gilbert. 1967. "Teaching and Training." In *The Concept of Education,* edited by R. S. Peters, 105-19. London: Routledge & Kegan Paul.

Schumacher, E. F. 1973. *Small is Beautiful: Economics As If People Mattered.* New York: Harper and Row.

Senge, Peter. 1990. *The Fifth Discipline: The Art and Practice of the Learning Organization.* New York: Currency Doubleday.

Shaw, George Bernard. 1961. *Back to Methuselah.* Baltimore: Penguin.

Smith, Adam. 1969 (1759) *Theory of Moral Sentiments.* New Rochelle: Arlington House.

Tendler, Judith. 2000. "Why Are Social Funds So Popular?" In *Local Dynamics in the Era of Globalization,* edited by S. Yusuf and S. Evenett, 114-29. Oxford: Oxford University Press for the World Bank.

Uphoff, N., M. Esman, and Anirudh Krishna. 1998. *Reasons for Success: Learning from Instructive Experiences in Rural Development.* West Hartford: Kumarian Press.

Versényi, Laszlo. 1963. *Socratic Humanism.* New Haven: Yale University Press.

Westbrook, Robert. 1991. *John Dewey and American Democracy.* Ithaca: Cornell University Press.

Wolfensohn. James D. 1999. "Coalitions for Change." Annual meetings address (World Bank). Washington, DC; 28 September.

World Bank. 1998. *Assessing Aid: What Works, What Doesn't, and Why.* Washington, DC.

1.3 TECHNICAL COOPERATION AND INSTITUTIONAL CAPACITY-BUILDING FOR DEVELOPMENT: BACK TO THE BASICS

DEVENDRA RAJ PANDAY

Introduction

Development capacity has been on the forefront of development thinking and practices from the time the economic and social status of the former colonies and other emerging states became a matter of international concern in the postwar world. The origin and rise of technical cooperation has been part of the same process, specifically geared to fashioning institutions and practices to support the development objectives of these countries. The role of development aid was originally conceived fundamentally as a means of bridging the savings gap, and it emphasized the importance of capital more than any other factor of development. There was also an understanding of the need to establish or upgrade capabilities for planning and implementation in the recipient countries, at the macro as well as the sectoral and project levels.

In addition, most donor-funded projects, both from bilateral and multilateral sources, have usually had an institutional component to complement physical development work. This has been the case with nearly every World Bank financed scheme (Israel, 1987, 18). In projects financed by regional development banks in Asia and Africa, too, there has been a practice of introducing institutional development even as a condition for loan approval and disbursement. The emphasis on policies that later came to assume a dominant position in aid programmes shaped by the Washington Consensus was similarly supported by institutional initiatives, with and without the conditionality element. These institutional processes have ranged from deregulation, privatization and downsizing of the public sector to civil service and financial sector reforms. More recently, as donors have woken up to the malaise of corruption, accountability and transparency have also been of concern.

Academic institutions and scholars have similarly been engaged from the early years of international development efforts, assisting in building institutions and streamlining management systems for designing and executing development. They have laboured hard, particularly to reconceive and reconceptualize the principles and practices of public administration, as traditionally understood, and to transform them into the principles and practices of "development administration" that is capable of meeting the new challenges facing governments freshly initiated to development. This has been an interactive process, lending, perhaps, a substantive meaning to the term "cooperation." The literature in this field from the early years illustrates that academic work has been enriched to a considerable degree by the learning opportunities offered by technical cooperation schemes, as executed in the developing world, with its intellectually challenging diversity. Now we have the benefit of the more comprehensive and inclusive concept of "governance." This, too, is the product of similar engagements and experiences—that is, an outcome of the continuing search for development capacity.

What, then, is the special significance of the present interest in institutions, development capacity-building and the role of technical cooperation? Why revisit a subject that has been a part of development thinking for a long time, and about the significance of which there should be little controversy? There are several reasons, some of which will come up during the discussions that follow. In short, one may approach the exercise fundamentally as a part of the learning process that the international development community is going through. Our knowledge about development seems to grow more from a process of trial and error—and, as far as the poor countries are concerned, more error than trial—than any established theoretical wisdom. Everyone is, thus, constantly on a learning curve.

Lessons Learned

In the innocence of the early days of international development efforts, the government was seen as the "engine of development," with the five-year plans it produced and the foreign aid it attracted providing the energy to enable the engine to speed up. Community institutions at the local or national level—there were few in the latter category—were not noticed. The people were supposed to be the beneficiaries of the benevolent process the system promised, not rightful participants or recognized stakeholders. However, the potential capacity of the private sector was not altogether ignored. After all, the most important donors of the time, as now, carried with them the experience, wisdom and interests of the capitalistic mode of development. But the private sector was either overwhelmed by the emphasis on the value of an overactive state, or its entrepreneurial prowess was simply taken for granted. Even within the government, the emphasis was merely on building the capacity of public institutions as managers of public policy and programmes. That the policy environment, ownership and accountability constituted a part of institutions for development—especially as they affected the incentive structures for other possible development agents or actors—generally escaped the wisdom of the time. Development capacity was considered neutral to the character of the political regime of the country as long as, perhaps, it was not a communist state. Authoritarian states flourished all over the third world, though not in an enduring manner, with the support or benign neglect of their international development partners.

The problem arose when many governments floundered in their attempts to manage national political economies amidst competing interests, and tended to succumb to predatory allure or the proclivity to self-serving populism, rather than rational policy-making to match development goals. The result was widespread government failure that overshadowed the earlier convictions about market failure. Contradictions in the international political economy also played a role in bringing this about. Even as international cooperation in development became a novel characteristic of the era, the unequal relations inherent in trade and in the distribution of information and technology, among other factors, adversely affected the welfare of the developing countries.

At the same time, the influential centres of knowledge and development finance engineered a radical reorientation of development strategies, which entailed a shift in the principles of economic management and in development policies. This basically required a country pursuing development to put more faith in the impersonal forces of the market rather than in the undependable wisdom of the state.

The important donors also began to be more open to suggestions that, in many cases, their understanding of the issues in relation to aid and development left much to be desired. Some of them were also humbled by their own performance, which was found wanting. The poverty and deprivation submerging the peoples of many lands, variously called least-developed, low-income or poor, were an embarrassment not only to the donors, but also to the social science community, which supplied knowledge and practical wisdom on how to organize and accomplish development. The donors also saw loopholes in their approaches to liberalization and privatization, as the national and global rent-seekers made a mockery of their theoretical potential, even as the sufferings of the poor in sub-Saharan Africa and elsewhere became worse. In the case of some donors, including the international financial institutions (IFIs), their own internal evaluations showed gaping holes in their strategies and performance (French, 1994; Kapur, 1997; Berg and UNDP, 1993). In the policy domain, structural adjustment, by itself, was no longer sacrosanct; poverty reduction regained its place in the development discourse and policy designs.

The less-than-satisfactory experiences of structural adjustment and economic reform initiatives in several important cases have produced two results relevant to this discussion. First, as stated, the donor community and its think-tanks were required to approach the subject with some humility. Second, a recognition arose, even for those who had argued for a minimalist state, that the incentive system inherent in a market economy would not be triggered, or could even misfire, if the required set of institutions were not in place (World Bank, 1993, 1997 and 2001). It may also be the case that as the debate oscillated between two extremes, a middle ground emerged as a natural course (Stiglitz, 2001; also see Collier, 2001; Rodrik, 2001).

At the moment, this middle ground is not so much about ideology as about finding gaps in earlier approaches to development (market-led as well as state-led) and making amends for them. For the ideologically motivated, for example, the market system may be an institution by itself, but the markets, too, need an encompassing institutional foundation to work according to their "design capacity." The middle ground seems to recognize that this foundation has to be provided by the state, on the one hand, and traditional and new community institutions, on the other. If there is any ideology in this, it may be about the "back to the basics" of a mixed economy, though there is now less inclination to accept the government as an economic agent as in the period before 1970.

Premise and Scope

The purpose of this chapter is to explore or retrace, in the light of these experiences and emerging tendencies, some critical approaches to capacity-building for development that may complement and support related measures for the development of the poor countries. Given the fact that many countries have failed miserably in governance, the interest here is in examining how and under what conditions the governments, which have failed to bring development to their people on their own, can help the market to do the job for them. And since, as with the state in the past, the framework of institutions necessary for the market is now a priority area for donor consideration and support, the interest will be on the role of technical cooperation to that end. In line with our theme of "back to the basics," we see that, even today, the donors are apparently conceding that their technical cooperation has to concentrate more on public institutions than the private sector. If so, this effort should help create not only efficient markets, but also effective governments.

In what follows, we will try, very briefly, to cull the key messages on the promises of market-friendly institutions and on the associated debate. The next step will take us back to the struggle with the complexity of the task of establishing effective state institutions that can support the legitimate purposes of the market. The role of technical cooperation will be examined in that context and within the framework of development cooperation in general. The emphasis will be on the need to promote institutions that support democratic values, sustainability and self-reliance, and country ownership of the development mission and enterprise.

This chapter is inspired, in particular, by the conditions and needs of the poor, low-income or least-developed countries, which are also called here "nonperforming." There is no doubt that many developing countries have demonstrated their capacity for development, which has enabled them to radically transform their economies, especially in the last two decades. Some have used the political potential of the state as well as the invisible hand of the market to their advantage. In the process, some of them have even graduated from the third world community to the first world or the near-first world. However, many others who seem condemned to poverty and deprivation continue to suffer, though international attention and access to available capital, knowledge and technology have not been denied to them—at least, one should add, until the Uruguay Round and the emergence of the intellectual property rights regime. If it were not for these nonperforming countries, the discourse on development and capacity-building and the role of technical cooperation would not probably be as relevant or challenging to human intellect and sensitivities.

Reviewing the Debate

To begin with the market-centric argument, the developing countries have much to benefit from promoting markets that function as "incentive-compatible institutions," with internally inspired self-enforcement mechanisms that promote human ingenuity and enterprise. When the poor and the rich alike freely participate in income-earning activities commensurate with their potentials, the result is a boost for economic growth and reduction of poverty. To perform to their full capacities, markets need institutional support that helps to transmit information, protect property rights, enforce contracts, and manage—or, if necessary, regulate—competition in the interests of the society. In this sense, market institutions must comprise "rules, enforcement mechanisms and organizations" that serve such purposes. It is the responsibility of the government to create and ensure the proper functioning of these institutions, though the people also have a role to play in signaling the demand for them (World Bank, 2001).

Such institutional functions are also available in norms, networks and traditions in the form of the "unwritten" laws of a society. These informal mechanisms can be efficient in terms of low transaction costs, risk-sharing, and physical and political proximity to the poor. They need to be harnessed. Opportunities should also be seized for a higher level of efficiency where it can be achieved through formal institutional intervention. As markets develop and become integrated, the importance of formal institutions grows. Demand for new institutions arises in order to respond to new opportunities and new incentives, and to address new threats to competition. The developing countries need to build such institutions to make their market-oriented policies work better and produce the expected results (World Bank, 2000 and 2001).

The Catch-22 Situation

The role of the state is constrained by two major problems. One, the government in power usually cannot take firm measures to develop institutions and policies that might be unpopular among supporters who supply "political resources," including financing. Two, governments are prone to arbitrarily exercise state power and stifle private initiatives through overtaxation, corruption and so on. Nonetheless, the foundation of the arguments about markets and market institutions is related to the premise that governments will create institutions necessary for the markets. Among other requirements, governments have to make laws and establish organizations; enforce and adjudicate property rights and contractual obligations; and generally maintain the rule of law (Rodrik, 2001; also World Bank, 2001). Similarly, government intervention may be necessary because not all community norms may support efficient market operations. One example is the caste system and the social environment affecting the status of women and other excluded sections of the population in India, Nepal and elsewhere. This throws up high barriers to the entry of specific communities into the markets. One is forced to go back to the basic problem of dealing with states, which are, as argued, and often as experienced, inherently predatory. It is more than a catch-22 situation. We need markets, because governments cannot do what the society needs; but the markets need governments to produce the public goods that the markets require in order to perform for the society.

There are other issues in the debate that merit recalling before we consider what can be done. Some historical and social analyses and our own experience tell us that the poor countries are poor today because generally they lack some fundamental prerequisites that would otherwise allow them to benefit from the operations of the market. The institutions these countries lack are not only those related to the market. This is illustrated by the possibility that in these countries, the state also suffers from many of the same institutional and other social and global factors that inhibit markets from performing efficiently. In fact, narrowly conceived reform measures that may be initiated under such conditions can exacerbate the rent-seeking tendencies of a predatory state and other segments of the society. As Stiglitz (2001) puts it, "When predatory states seem to reform, shouldn't political economy arguments lead to worries that the seeming reform is not really a reform, but a change in the manner of acquiring rents—and not necessarily in ways that reduce the adverse effects?" State institutions might receive recognition from some unlikely quarters for the service they provide to the markets. But this does not change the historical and cultural environment within which a judge, a legislator or a police officer has to work (Rodrik, 2001)—or within which a nation has to develop, for that matter.

If development, indeed, means "social transformation," which some influential mainstream economists now acknowledge (e.g., Stiglitz, 1998), then reforms in state institutions are necessary *for their own sake* and for the sake of an integrated development of *all* societal institutions relevant to such transformation, including the market. A society cannot change in a manner that is way out of step with some of its own constituents. And a state is, after all, a constituent that, in addition, exercises "coercive power" over the rest of the society, albeit, in a democracy, with the latter's consent.

It is necessary to improve the state's capacity for other reasons, too. In Nepal, for example, the Asian Development Bank (ADB) claims that much of its technical assistance is geared towards capacity-building and institutional strengthening. The reason for this is not difficult to see. After more than 30 years of lending and advisory technical assistance, the ADB is still struggling with the problem of aid utilization and effectiveness. Of the 45 loans that have been evaluated, only 56 per cent were "generally successful" (ADB, 2001, 7). The principal reasons identified for a lack of success in project implementation were "weak project preparation and design, and inherent institutional weaknesses" of the executing agencies. One might think of auctioning off these executing agencies under the rules of the market! But the ADB also reports that the "poor quality of consultants and contractors [who are market-players] has also contributed to the poor performance of projects."

For all the clarity and purity of ideas that market economics tries to project, implementing these ideas in practice for the purpose of development may still come down to living with the "on the one hand, and on the other" syndrome that economists are often accused of displaying. There are many positive features of a market-oriented policy framework on which there can be universal agreement, just as there will be the same about the state, *when it works perfectly.* The key is to find policies and methods that work in the conditions present on the ground. It is hard to argue with the idea that the aim of any reform should be not "to define what should be done in an ideal world, but what can be done in today's world" (World Bank, 2001, 4). This message may be applicable as much to the actual potential of the markets as of the governments.

The key point, of course, may be striking a balance. But the balance needs to be pursued not only between the relative roles of the market and the state, but also in terms of how we view development. The existing literature on capacity-building recognizes this point. Some donors already see capacity-building as development itself. For others, "a vision of development and the kind of society to be nurtured" is a precondition for capacity-building (UNICEF, 1999, 19). We have to understand that capacity is a generic, neutral concept. Hence, it is naturally relevant to ask: The capacity to do what? The balance may differ from country to country and, within one country, from one time period to another. In every case, the responsibility for defining it falls on the country's leadership and the political process, which cannot be ignored.

Major Challenges for the Future

The essence of the debate on institutions, as briefly reviewed above, is that development institutions are not only about enabling, facilitating or even regulating the markets. They are about finding a mandate, based on the view of development as social transformation, for setting policies and deploying resources accordingly. A situation should be avoided where the institutional capacity-building effort may fail for the same reason that the periodic paradigm shifts have failed—because they were viewed too narrowly (Stiglitz, 1998, 2). If markets need "good" government institutions, including the policies they embrace, then the need for building the capacity of the government becomes paramount. Importantly, such institutions serve interests that go beyond the markets. A good governance structure that guarantees the rule of law, enforces contracts and protects the rights of citizens is necessary everywhere, regardless of the country's stage of development. The critical question is how to go about this task in light of our experience so far.

The *World Development Report 2002* claims that the report is about the "how," not just the "what," of necessary reforms (World Bank, 2001, 4). But it seems to contain few practical messages on "how the government can change ways of thinking and institutional arrangements" (Stiglitz, 2001). The underlying complexity of the task has been a challenge for the poor countries all along. In many cases, the governance structures are getting weaker by the day, with civil strife and violence further taxing their meagre institutional resources. The underlying problems of political economy embedded in the historical and cultural experiences of these countries cannot be oversimplified.

As we shall see shortly, the currently popular governance paradigm, too, falls short of providing practical messages and methods that touch at the core of the problem. Institutions, whether related to national governance or international development, that claim to look at the interests of the poor may need something different to guide them, something in addition to the universal principles of management and capacity-building. This may be about values (Edwards and Sen, 2000), where the change-agents may articulate and pursue their self-interests in broader terms than is the case when development is merely a career. In a technical cooperation context, it is difficult to come to grips with these issues, but we may have to face them sooner or later. There is a considered point of view that the technical practitioners might be better suited than theologians to promote a "global ethic" for human societies, because they can hopefully do so without moralizing too much or unduly emphasizing moralism as against the "functional value" of morality (Kung, 1999). The moral capacity of a nation and the institutional processes influencing it may soon emerge as an important agenda item in development discourse. An element of it can already be observed in the growing concerns with corruption.

Understanding Capacity-Building

There are many definitions of capacity-building, although in general there are basically two ways of looking at the concept. We can look at it from a management perspective, focusing on some specific, but possibly disjointed organizational areas needing reform, including the state organs or the legislative framework. Or we can look at it as something intimately close to the nation-building process, and as requiring a broader and more integrated perspective. The first approach makes it easier for a desperate donor to find entry points for project formulation and financing. To focus its capacity-building effort, each donor can look for a suitable niche in such areas as governance, policy advocacy, corporate governance, human resource development, decentralization or specific public organizations. This approach may, however, be insufficient for producing the expected results, and can be even counterproductive if some fundamental issues are not addressed simultaneously.

The point may be illustrated by recalling a particularly comprehensive definition of capacity-building, as articulated by the United Nations Development Programme (UNDP, 1997) on one occasion. UNDP defines capacity-building as "the process by which individuals, groups, organizations, institutions and societies increase their abilities to: 1) perform core functions, solve problems, and define and achieve objectives; and 2) understand and deal with their development needs in a broad context and in a sustainable manner." This definition suggests that capacity-building be not merely about devising management tools and instruments or some other technocratic frames and frameworks. It should be about the community's *ability to appreciate organizational goals,* and to build and use its resources to that end. If so, everything becomes important—from the nature of the polity and regime structure to the sense of self-respect and self-reliance among the leaders and members of the institution (in this case, the host nation).

Amidst frustrations, mixed with genuine concerns, the donor think-tanks have sometimes a tendency to seek comfort by experimenting with reforms in the vocabulary of development, amounting only to what one scholar has called, in a different context, an attempt at "explanation by redefinition."[1] The new concepts, frameworks or even the so-called development paradigms have their value, but only if they embody new ideas and practical methods in place of the old ones that did not work. These ideas and methods, in turn, have to be grounded on some *foundational values* that can ensure long-term consistency in institutional behaviour, and also inspire popular support. If, for example, the UN system wishes to promote its "development assistance framework" on the basis of a rights-based approach, it has to be recognized that the departure it seeks is about values, about how the partners in

---

[1] Writing about political disorder in some Indian states, Kohli worries about "the greatest danger" that "problems of political disorder will simply be redefined as problems of institutionalization, in the belief that something has thus been explained" (1991, 6).

development cooperation are to value human life and human dignity and solidarity. These values have to be reflected in how people see the roles of the government, the markets, the civil society (including the community organizations and households), and, obviously, the donors.

The premise that guides the rest of this chapter is that unless we try to come to grips with important foundational issues with critical implications for the outcomes of capacity-building efforts, the progress on any other front can be elusive or, if at all achieved, not enduring. To make the discussion manageable, we focus on three issues that are not new, but extremely challenging for technical cooperation in relation to capacity-building. They are democracy, sustainability, and ownership and partnership.

Democracy

There is a good deal of emphasis in the literature, as well as in capacity-building pro-grammes and projects, on the role of the rule of law, transparency and accountability, and, generally, corruption-free governance. The expectation that civil society and citizens in general demand institutions that support their interests indicates an assumption that democracy is, indeed, at the foundation of capacity-building efforts (World Bank, 2001). However, after the significant advancements of the last two decades, many countries are, again, demonstrating that there is a big gap between a country's ability to introduce democracy and the ultimate capacity to nurture it in the traditions of liberal democracy (Huntington, 1997). The democratic regimes that rode the tide of the "third wave" have generally failed to demonstrate a capacity to develop and demonstrate pluralistic culture that should go with its manifest structural form. Nor have many of them been able to come up with a dependable policy framework that takes into account the challenges of a "traditional" society, polarized by diverse conditions, interests and aspirations affecting the people. The interest of the important sections of the donor community in promoting and defending democracy may also be eroding precisely when the unsatisfactory outcomes of their efforts so far in the post-cold-war era may require greater commitment from them.

After aggressively trying to promote democracy in the third world for some years, there are signs of some reticence in the case of some donors. More importantly, there is a lack of consistency in views, or at least in emphasis. At one point, democracy may be considered responsible for a hostile or unreceptive institutional environment (e.g., World Bank, 1991, 132-3). At other times, the emphasis is more on presenting the system as a precondition for institutional change (e.g., World Bank, 2000, 113). For a realistic practitioner of development wanting reform through technocratic initiatives, democracy can indeed be a hindrance. It is certainly easier to implement economic liberalization and austerity measures when they are not subject to popular scrutiny, as they are in a democracy that is open to dissent and a competition of ideas and visions (Thomas, 1999; Panday, 2000). The increasing ambivalence about democracy among some donors, however, may also be explained by the mixed findings of empirical studies on the relationship between democracy and long-run economic growth rates. In addition, the instances of political instability in many "third wave" democracies may even support the view that, on the basis of the experience so far, democracy need not be valued much because it disturbs social stability and peace and, therefore, development.

If development, indeed, means social transformation, we have to look at the relation between democracy and development from a different, more broad-based perspective. Irrespective of the growth rates recorded, there are other social processes and values that only a democratic regime embedded in a pluralistic culture and legitimized by an inclusive policy outlook can guarantee and sustain (Bhagwati, 1995). The natural dissent and divisions in the society about public policy may give an impression that democracy is an inefficient or status-quo-oriented political system. But when democracy is functioning well, it demonstrates its capacity to manage such dissent, resolve conflict and also build consensus for policy changes. This is the essence of democratic policy-making and of the accountability of a democratic government to its domestic constituency (Panday, 2000). It is another matter that the consensus so reached may be different from what the "global community" has in mind for the country at a given time. The point is that an adherence to democratic norms should, in the end, provide for principled partnership that yields "fulfilling conclusions" from the process (Edwards and Sen, 2000)—for all concerned.

The interest of the donors in "democracy assistance" has not completely dissipated. But there is a possibility of further withdrawal as they find that there are no workable strategies they can implement in this complex area. It is difficult to imagine a more curious situation than one where the rule of law and public accountability are valued (for the sake of markets), but a democratic regime (for the people) cannot be nurtured. Some optimistic scholars have gone to the extent of identifying 57 specific initiatives that the United States can take to promote democracy (Allison Jr. and Beschel Jr., 1992). The difficulty is that it is uncertain how the donors can help a country to democratize in this manner if the country's leadership on its own fails to tackle the underlying social conflicts and tensions in a consensual manner, as is now the case in many struggling democracies. Certainly, one does not wish to see the powerful nations in the West install "democratic leadership" in the third world countries the way they enshrined the authoritarian ones in some countries in the past.

The new and very popular discourse and intervention on "governance" has also not been able to go beyond formal, organizational aspects. The concept has added little to the arsenal of analytical tools for enabling the leaders and citizens committed to institutionalizing democracy, as they struggle with multifarious conflicts and contradictions of a social and historical nature. One also gets an impression that the concept of governance has become handy to development practitioners and aid managers who may wish to divorce development from politics and the underlying issues of equity and justice. Even decentralization can be implemented in an apolitical manner, as when all that is accomplished is the delegation of authority to implement projects financed by aid, giving the donors a foothold in local governance.

The donors cannot be faulted for not being able to influence the political culture of a developing country, which, obviously, is the task of national institutions and actors. They may, instead, have to be mindful of the possibility that the technical cooperation programmes launched in the name of governance reform or capacity-building do not become counterproductive. The system of development cooperation has certain fault lines, where the harder the donors try for results under adverse conditions, the worse the situation may become. It may be necessary in some countries to take efforts to support legislatures, the judiciary and civil society, and to augment the legislative framework and support the rule of law. But these are matters that the host society institutions, including the government, should be interested in on their own. If they are not, the donors may succeed only in legitimizing a regime that is not interested in the principles of pluralism, justice or development. Similarly, introduction of anticorruption measures as an element of governance reform in an environment where the government has no intention or ability to do anything in that direction can further legitimize a corrupt regime. It is claimed that donors' practice of supporting electoral processes has driven up the "cost of democracy" without improving the content of the process (Ottaway and Chung, 1999; also Santiso, 2001).

The nascent civil society institutions, including the nongovernmental organizations (NGOs), provide some entry points for donors interested in the promotion of democratic governance under such circumstances. There are NGOs in many developing countries that play a very positive role in the field of human rights, including minority rights, the rights of women and children, environment, media development and so on. In Bangladesh (Sobhan, 1998), there is plenty of evidence that NGOs can make far-reaching contributions by mobilizing group action and promoting linkages and solidarity among the poor, especially by empowering women. Such approaches need to be supported. However, they need not be romanticized too much (Streeten, 1999).

First, the civil society in many developing countries is not a homogenous entity in terms of the genesis, agenda and interests of its constituent elements. It is also misleading to think that it invariably pursues "noble causes" with committed public-spirited actors (Carothers, 1999-2000; also Dahal, 2001). Supported almost exclusively by the donors, the nascent civil society movement in many countries is perceived as donor-driven, with an agenda addressed to the supporters outside the country, rather than the domestic constituency. The civil society institutions, in many cases, also project a mirror image of distortions brought by foreign aid to the state sector. When the spirit of volunteerism, so essential for a genuine civil society movement, is lacking, the unsustainably high cost of running an organization—including the high salaries of the promoters and other functionaries and staff—raises questions about the movement's propriety as well as its sustainability (Ottaway and Chung, 1999).

There is a more critical, substantive point on the subject of civil society and democracy. With the donors working directly with local government institutions and civil society, the domain of policy-making has extended beyond the state apparatus and the usual framework of dialogue and negotiations between the donors and the recipient governments. This is part of a deliberate policy, which has been adopted as a response to the general ineffectiveness of the policy frameworks and institutions inspired and supported by the donors in the past. In some cases, the process has helped to temper and improve upon the guidelines that local governments and civil society organizations use in shaping programmes and policies impacting on the environment, human rights and so on. Taking the agenda of development to the grassroots may also create some possibility of enriching its substantive content in favour of the poor, and ensuring compliance by all parties concerned.

This cultural shift in development cooperation can, however, have an adverse effect on the political process and the fragile state institutions of the host country. If an elected government does not represent the public interest in the eyes of the donors, the civil society cannot fill that political void. Besides, it may not be for the donors to decide who the real representatives of the people are, who the civil society is, and who the international partners should deal with. This is so especially if the donors' own judgement about the value of democracy in a recipient country lacks conviction.

Moreover, with important sections of civil society simultaneously engaged in partisan politics in many developing countries, the dialogue with civil society can degenerate into a "convocation of the opposition," as some public officials in Latin America complained to a visiting dignitary (Summers, 2001; also Santiso, 2001). The vibrant civil society cultivated by the Weimer Republic in Germany became handy for Hitler's later machinations (Berman, 1997; Encarnacion, 2000). To put it more ideologically, there can be a civil society that mediates between capital and labour or one that just represents capital. There can be another that mediates between the state and the citizens, and also yet another that may become the handmaiden of the more powerful, including, in the present context, the donor community. These all have their uses for different purposes, but our interest should be with those that help to promote democratic legitimacy in the society.

The problem with governance, in most cases of democratic decay or erosion (Santiso, 2001), is that the country's political leadership is unable to manage the special interest groups as they seek to advance their careers in a competitive political system. The answer to this problem does not lie in further surrendering political autonomy to yet another actor, civil society, but in enabling the leadership and other political forces to come to terms with their responsibilities. An enduring relationship between the state, civil society and the market cannot be developed in a situation where engagements between donors and civil society (Encarnacion, 2000) may look like a coalition for cutting the state to its size, and putting it in its place, as it were. Civil society needs to be promoted with these risks and opportunities in mind.

Capacity-Building

An important lesson that can be learned from history is that most of the successful economies have emphasized mobilization and use of national resources, not foreign aid, for capacity-building and development in general. Institutions for development, therefore, should be about building domestic capacity, including the cultivation of values and norms that determine a nation's appreciation of the concept of development and the role of foreign aid in it. It has become a fashion to talk about and pursue sustainable development in the developing countries. Capacity-building is directly related to this objective, because only domestic capacity can make the development process sustainable. However, this is not possible, *if the message of sustainability itself has to come from foreign aid.*

There is more to development than aid and its management, and more to aid than its financing role. Concessional aid is but a fraction of the total financial flows in the developing world. The share of the IFIs is only 5 per cent of the total, prompting the Meltzer Commission to recommend far-reaching structural changes in the International Monetary Fund (IMF) and the World Bank nearly three years ago (Meltzer, 2001). Even for the poor countries that concern us here, and for whom such aid is immensely important, aid effectiveness may be defined and determined *more by the character of the aid delivery system and the donor practices* than by the substantive policies and programmes being financed.

Until some time ago, the characterization of development cooperation as an industry used to be considered almost derogatory. Now, the US $50 billion strong global development industry, one quarter of which is attached to technical cooperation, is accepted with reverence and as a challenge to be coped with in the aid market. As argued, aid is not an entitlement. The logic may be that if the recipients are not entitled to it, the middle-people are not either, and that they have to compete in the market on the basis of their products and performance (see Part 2, Chapter 1; Berg and UNDP, 1993). This is a novel approach to building the capacity of technical assistance delivery institutions. And competition should be good for the process. However, the idea that the aid industry, which is driven by so many motives and conflicting interests, can mix with market principles may be somewhat incongruous.

Technical cooperation, the way it works, may be about finding ideas and experts that money can buy. One difficulty is that the ideas—not to mention the values, which may be missing the most in the nonperforming countries—are not offered in the market. One of the cruel ironies of development cooperation is that the support of external partners has a tendency to become less effective precisely in areas that are critical to development, such as building democratic institutions and traditions. With or without the aid market, the scope for a substantial contribution to sustainable governance institutions through technical cooperation may be limited in any case, except in countries where what might be called foundational capacity already exists.

The perceptions and arguments about aid as an industry arise basically from the declining trend of aid resources, on the one hand, and the growth in the number of intermediaries, on the other. As the most prominent, if not also the largest source of technical assistance, the position of UNDP in this respect may be educational. The changing financing framework within UNDP can be observed in the declining role of its core resources, and the more prominent role of non-core programmes. The core expenditures have declined sharply from US $1.1 billion in 1990 to below $700 million in 2000. The non-core expenditures had increased to $1.6 billion during the same period, representing 75 per cent of total UNDP spending (Ruffat, Andic and Weisner, 2001, 7-8).

The dependence of UNDP on non-core resources has pushed the institution into a situation of several contradictions. First, UNDP, like any other development financing institution, would claim that its programmes are demand-driven—that is, they are determined by the conditions observed, needs assessed and priorities identified in the field. But dependence on non-core resources means essentially responding to the priorities of donors who supply UNDP with the non-core funds. It could be claimed that there is a commonality in the interests and objectives of the institutions concerned. And this may be so. But there is no guarantee that the recipient country's interests and objectives coincide too. Instead, there is a danger that the country may be drawn into making commitments in areas that the government cannot sustain on its own.

The temptation to produce "replicable" ideas and programmes, with or without the technical cooperation framework being transformed into an industry, is a risk to be avoided in the future. As we know by now, even the structural adjustment programme was not replicable. Institutional capacity-building is a less generic proposition than macroeconomic policy-making (Stiglitz, 2001). The literature is full of warnings against the one-size-fits-all idea. On the ground, however, there is plenty of practical interest in it, as projects are designed and implemented in different countries and cultures, often by the same consultants using the same project parameters and organizational approaches. The push for locating the so-called "best practices"—and their articulation and presentation, at times, in relevant reports—might be responsible for one of the more common, yet harmful, sins of the profession. The only attraction here is the opportunity to market the product and promote replicability, regardless of the need and suitability in given conditions.

The replicability myth makes the life of aid administrators and development consultants more comfortable than it would be otherwise. But this is not how development works. And when the donors become disappointed with their methods, the blame is often put on the cultural deficiencies of the country that rejects them. It is not possible to pursue a universal paradigm of development and replicable institutions to support the markets everywhere, and also blame the "local policies, economies, polities and cultures" when you meet with failure (Mishra, 2000). Now, market economics seems to take notice of and also value social capital, including community norms and practices for their functional relations with the market. If so, it may also help to remember that there was culture before many of the other things, including, obviously, markets (Escobar, 1997). If market economics sees value in community norms and traditional practices as a part of a self-enforcing set of rules supporting the market, it may also be necessary to be careful of distortions and perversions that may be introduced when aid is delivered to these countries without adequate sensitivity to them.

Ownership and Partnership

From the beginnings of technical cooperation, or development aid for that matter, it has been recognized that economic and social development is the responsibility of the governments and the people of the developing countries. Of all the areas of development, this message is most relevant for capacity-building. External partners can provide support, but cannot do what a committed leadership and the dedicated people of the host country must do on their own. Experience has validated this principle, as we observe the better performers of East Asia, on the one hand, and many nonperformers in sub-Saharan Africa or even South Asia, on the other. Surprisingly, despite the agreement in principle and the demonstrated experience on the ground, country ownership of capacity development efforts remains a contested field in practice. Some clarity on this issue and honesty in application may be important preconditions for the success of other related efforts in the future.

For the source of the confusion, we have to go back, again, to the unsatisfactory outcomes of models and practices applied in the past. The more the states and leadership of the developing countries floundered in their mission, even with the adoption of recommended shifts in development policies and strategies, the greater the possibility became of giving a wider and more flexible meaning to such concepts. As the donors tried harder with new paradigms and new approaches, they became involved in policy designs, implementation and monitoring of the programmes with an intensity that could not be consistent with the proclaimed wisdom about and commitment to country ownership. The situation became more complex and contradictory with the emergence of conditionality in the IFI-financed structural adjustment programmes and other associated reforms.

There are lessons to be learned here. In the design, negotiation, approval and implementation of capacity-building programmes, there must be an effort to avoid the kind of mistakes committed in the era of structural adjustment (World Bank, 1997, 83-4). It must be remembered that the acquiescence of the government of an aid-dependent country to a reform programme or a project "recommended" by important donors does not constitute its ownership of that programme. The interest may be only in not missing the funds (see Part 1, Chapter 1). Buying ownership is one of the corrupt practices that some donors may indulge in by offering incentives that may vary from personal to societal. But the most they can have is the support of individual counterparts, and not of the recipient system as a whole. This applies to civil society institutions as well.

In the context of structural adjustment and economic reforms, the methodology followed in designing, implementing and monitoring the "aid for reform" packages was such that it could not but weaken the host country capacity (Collier, 2001) to develop its own policy packages. In many African countries, it has been found that their "natural capacity to manage the macroeconomy" could not develop "while international financial institutions continued to hold technical analysis and decision-making captive to their programmes and conditionalities" (UNDP, 1996, 52).

The problems become worse when insensitive donor representatives develop a patronizing attitude towards their counterparts and exploit the generally less favourable psychological and material condition of the latter for speedy project execution or, worse, in the interest of a personal career. One of the most serious capacity problems in many developing countries is the way the public officials have, in effect, abdicated the responsibility of the positions they hold. Individuals and institutions have lost their capacity to analyse (Collier, 2001) and understand their own reality. Across Africa and in most South Asian countries, the planning commissions, line ministries, and, now with decentralization, the local government bodies are becoming increasingly donor-dependent not only for financing but also for their routine functions.

Together with ownership, the idea of partnership is growing in popularity. The two approaches can be mutually supportive but also *internally inconsistent* if we are not careful about the details of how one goes about the process. Both concepts are multidimensional and might be interpreted more inclusively or exclusively in different times and different places. First, if ownership is to mean country ownership rather than mere government ownership, then the partnership idea requires a framework where all responsible national actors have a forum to debate and arrive at a consensus on the national vision and the mission. Ordinarily, in a well-functioning democracy, existing institutions and processes would ensure that this happens, to the extent realpolitik permits, nearly automatically. The government, representing the nation, would claim ownership of policies and be answerable to its partners, that is, the various sections of the society, under a defined accountability framework. In the absence of such a system, the donors can play the mediating role, which, however, contradicts the idea of country ownership.

Second, since partnership also means including the donors in the cooperative framework, country ownership should mean the government taking the lead in framing strategies and policies, following the process just mentioned. A representative, responsible government would produce a strategic plan that the donors would be constrained to argue against, though their constructive inputs could add value to the exercise. Because such an ideal situation rarely exists in a developing country, both the concepts are plagued by ambiguity and controversy in reality. There are plenty of examples of "tokenism" or donor-created "islands of participation" (Sobhan, 2000), and partnerships that run counter to the objectives pursued.

One does not have to go very far to look for ideas on what to do in the future. In 1993, the Operations Evaluation Department of the World Bank published a study that suggested four criteria for assessing country ownership. They are: "(a) the locus of the initiative for the policy or project must be in the government; (b) the key policy-makers responsible for implementation must be intellectually convinced that the goals to be pursued are the right ones; (c) there must be evidence of public support from the top political and civic leadership; and (d) there must be evidence that the government is building consensus among the affected stakeholders and can rely on their support and cooperation."[2] One could add one additional criterion: that ownership is not something to be offered by the donors. The government and other concerned institutions, that is, the designated "owners," must claim ownership and also be held accountable to other stakeholders.

The related tendency to claim the rights and the role of stakeholders has become prominent in recent years as the donors, frustrated by the nonperforming states, actually

---

[2] Cited in *Partnership for Development: Proposed Actions for the World Bank* (a discussion paper) by a team in Partnerships Group, Strategic and Resource Management, 1998.

look for surrogate partners. The old idea of the two parties in action—the donors and the recipients—became untenable amidst a record of pitiful results and nontransparent systems of aid management. The traditional norms of international diplomacy, including aid diplomacy, and the sovereignty of the recipient governments are sacrificed in the name of a purposeful dialogue and promotion of an accountability process in the society. Special care should be taken that broadening the partnership ensures national ownership without diluting the framework of accountability.

Conclusions

The concrete situations we face in the world are diverse and challenging. The ideologues will not be bothered by them; they have their preconceived notion about what is good and what is bad or what is desirable and what is not for this world. Development specialists or thinkers, on the other hand, have to approach the subject with less certainty and more humility, given the sufferings they have not been able to help heal. No ideology can hide the fact that, for all the economic and technological advancements the world community has made, the number of the least-developed countries has grown to 49 today from the original 25 in 1971. The 600 million people living in these countries in absolute poverty and at least as many living elsewhere are awaiting a life with dignity and security in the new century. This section of the world population suffers the worst capacity deprivation; ultimately, it is the capacity of these people we should be addressing with a view to enabling them to "signal," both to the government and the market, for the goods and services they need or could offer.

Limitations

The rules, mechanisms and organizations that are considered essential for markets are also needed for maintaining the rule of law, dispensing justice and generally protecting the public good. Institutions for promoting development capacity must, therefore, be built on the foundation of democracy and a development culture that values basic democratic principles. The challenge for development cooperation in general and technical cooperation in particular is compounded by the fact that the external partners may not really have much to contribute here, other than using gentle persuasion or some threat where possible, and providing moral support to the reform-oriented national actors.

There is also the danger that the "institutions for market" paradigm may meet the same fate, at least, in some countries, as the earlier initiatives for policy reforms. This is so especially if the incentive structure associated with development cooperation does not change and nonperforming recipients accept it as yet another mode of accessing fungible resources in the name of yet another paradigm.

Need for Donor Patience and Restraint

Capacity-building is a long-term and never-ending process. In many countries of our concern, the governments and the people seem to be a long way from covering even the few initial and enduring steps as far as the foundational and strategic direction is concerned. The domestic actors who should be doing something about this are often busy asking the ordinary people to be patient. Ironically, however, the donors, especially their technical representatives, tend to be more impatient and short-term oriented. It is widely believed that the incentive structures of the aid system—which mix the career prospects and earnings of aid officials and experts with immediate successes in programming and execution of projects, rather than their sustainable contribution—is partly responsible for this mindset. This needs to be looked into, because this system also has implications for the motivation and morale and, therefore, the capacity of the most important partner in the process: the national counterparts.

Among those who serve in all the areas of development cooperation, the "capacity-builders" should be more aware than others that there is just no alternative to trying patiently to work with governments and other national institutions in their reality. If governments and the people of the host countries do not show necessary commitment, the donors cannot fill that void by just trying harder. For example, many countries may need fresh programmes to build their critical institutions; but it is also the case that many countries are not utilizing their existing capacities. The legal framework is one example. In a number of third world countries, law abidance suffers because the citizens as well as the responsible functionaries in the legislature, judiciary and the executive are not sensitive to the value of justice, fairness and the rule of law. The donors competing to help draft and promulgate new legislation can contribute but little under such conditions.

The same may be the case with planning, budgeting, civil service reforms or decentralization. Even with brain drain, resulting from the development of individual as opposed to institutional capacities, much knowledge exists within most poor countries and in their governments for articulating appropriate development policies, designing management practices and executing them. The hindrance, as we are fond of repeating, is the absence of political will, which donors cannot generate even with their conditionalities. If this is the case, it may be more appropriate for technical cooperation not to get involved in such areas at all. The nonexistent partnership only dilutes responsibility and may provide an excuse for a nonperforming government to abdicate it altogether.

Coordination and Possible Specialization

Leaving the principal responsibility of building capacity to the recipients themselves, the donors can do the next best thing in this respect. They can concentrate on continuing the reforms in areas where they have greater control. We will refer to only one of them, the problem of donor coordination, because this issue has a direct impact on national capacities.

The old problem of aid coordination has now become more complicated, due to the new concerns, priorities and practices presently surrounding international cooperation. First, there are strategic frameworks at the global level, like the Comprehensive Development Framework (CDF) of the World Bank. Many other donors, too, have similar strategic guidelines. Then there are country strategies adopted by the same donors. For each donor, there may be little problem in matching global and local. But integrating and transforming them into a coherent national strategy and then implementing the strategy is a very difficult proposition for a poor country whose coordinating capacity is swamped from all directions. Not only the number of donors but also the number of recipients—the nonstate institutions the donors deal with directly—has proliferated in each country. The "coordinators" have to cope also with the consequences of the horizontal and vertical expansions of the policy-making domain, covering the market, civil society and the local bodies, apart from the state institutions.

In the last decade or so, donors have made special efforts for better coordination among themselves, by introducing various innovations to the traditional mechanisms of "consultative groups" and aid programming. There are now sectoral groups, thematic groups and like-minded groups of donors that meet to coordinate their approaches and activities in areas of mutual concern and priority. Such attempts need to be continued and built upon so that they can, in turn, help national agencies to integrate their efforts with those of the other set of partners in the country, the national actors.

There have been many good ideas floating around for some time as a response to the much-acknowledged problem of aid coordination. Some of them may be too idealistic for the real world, like the suggestion that all donors pool their resources into one pot and then allow the recipients to use them in accordance with priorities and conditions agreed under some kind of a compact. There are some other suggestions that may, however, be doable, in the light of the progress already made. The donors are now more inclined than before to work together and share their strategies for better harmonization of their programmes. This may be the right time to take that one additional step—towards a division of labour based on the specialized knowledge and demonstrated experience of each individual donor.

To give some provocative examples, governance programmes, or at least the parts dealing with state institutions, are best left to those bilateral donors who have decades and centuries of experience in their own countries in this respect. The United Kingdom and other similarly placed donors must have the best comparative advantage when it comes to democratization and democratic governance, for example. The World Bank and regional banks like the Asian Development Bank could withdraw from these fields and concentrate elsewhere, one possible area being the capacity-building of the private sector in conditions where a corporate culture is still alien to the mainstream business communities. The IFIs know governments mainly as borrowers or, maybe, as their corporate members. They have rarely had to deal directly with the complex bundle of history, economic interests, social demands, political conflict, and a large and diverse citizenry that the morally fragile and harassed politicians have to handle in many poor and polarized societies.

The World Bank is already a "knowledge bank" as well. It could concentrate more efforts in that direction and help build research capacities in institutions in the recipient countries, which can do more than provide consulting services for them. The capacities of national universities must be upgraded if development capacity in a developing country is ever to be supported by indigenous and sustainable means.

UNDP can feel satisfied that some of the critical ideas about human-centered development it floated with its *Human Development Reports* in the 1990s are now an integral part of global discourses and development policy-making. The important ideas already resonate, for example, in the CDF of the World Bank and in the Poverty Reduction Strategy Papers (PRSPs) many poor countries are formulating. But UNDP will be hard-pressed to compete with the World Bank in knowledge-building and dissemination. On the other hand, UNDP, the United Nations Children's Fund (UNICEF) and, in fact, the United Nations as a whole have established a splendid reputation in humanitarian programmes, including those addressed to the poor, women, children and other excluded groups. UN agencies also have a proven record in nation-building programmes in post-conflict situations, though they have not succeeded everywhere. This is a challenge that is likely to grow. The United Nations is also the most likely candidate for "genuine global secretariat" (Streeten, 1999), should this increasingly felt need materialize in the foreseeable future. The point is that if the idea is to assist the developing countries, and if they are to be patient with the reality there and not try to do too many things by themselves, there is plenty to do for all competent organizations in development cooperation. There should be no need for any one of them to overstretch or overlap with the others.

Advisory Support or a Turnkey Assignment?

Finally, some additional questions on the modalities. The reach and domain of technical cooperation today is very different from the past, when technical assistance schemes could be easily differentiated from physical development projects, although both were supported by external financial assistance. Technical cooperation is now a mainstream endeavour, not an adjunct to larger projects that may include small technical assistance components or some stand-alone advisory services. With increasing stress on policy reforms, institutional development and governance, a donor can now provide fungible resources to the recipient government as a grant or a loan with the attached technical assistance component for designated reforms taking care of the more substantive part of the cooperative effort. The activities under a typical governance reform programme today would also be a part of a technical assistance project as defined in the past. Their scale, sources of financing and management structures, however, including separate project offices and mandate, make them look like a regular present-day capital project. Yet, the nuts and bolts of technical assistance projects have not changed much.

The partnership structure is now broader, as discussed, and a civil society actor in the recipient country can also be the beneficiary of technical cooperation. But a national partner still expects to receive from an external collaborator in a technical cooperation scheme the same package of experts, training (including overseas visits) and commodities, which may now include computers and other useful and not-so-useful gadgets, in addition to the traditional four-wheel drives. One difference is that the humble advisers of yesteryear are now replaced by more "rational" consultants maximizing their personal utility function. The team of experts may include host country nationals who, too, may be driven by the same values.

Is it possible that the potential of technical cooperation to contribute to domestic capacity-building was higher in the old days, when technical assistance meant advisory services, where advisors attached to government offices, and when project experts worked together with national counterparts who were formally designated as their understudies? Have the notions of partnership and even ownership produced, to some extent, perverse results, where the national political, civic and bureaucratic leadership has forgotten to respect the notion of self-reliance and the sense of personal responsibility?

Earlier, it was an accepted principle that the understudy would eventually take over from the expert, who would then be redundant in that context. This method may look anachronistic at a time when the distinction between technical cooperation and a composite development project has blurred. But capacity-building is not a task that can be organized like a capital project, which may be completed on a turnkey basis. Building institutions is no less intricate a task than producing physical development in economic or social sectors. For greater effectiveness of technical cooperation in this area, the concerned actors and activities must be integrated fully with the national institutions to be supported, including imbuing them well with the values and norms we want to create or replace. This idea may deserve a fresh interrogation.

References

Allison Jr., Graham T., and Robert P. Beschel Jr. 1992. "Can the United States Promote Democracy." *Political Science Quarterly,* 107(1), 81-98.

Asian Development Bank. 2001. *Nepal: Background Paper for the 2001 Country Portfolio Review Mission.* Kathmandu: Nepal Resident Mission.

Berg, Elliot, and the United Nations Development Programme (UNDP). 1993. *Rethinking Technical Cooperation: Reforms for Capacity-Building in Africa.* New York: United Nations Development Programme.

Berman, Sheri. 1997. "Civil Society and the Collapse of the Weimar Republic." *World Politics,* 49 (April), 401-29.

Bhagwati, Jagdish. 1995. "Democracy and Development: New Thinking on Old Questions." *Indian Economic Review,* XXX(1), 1-18.

Carothers, Thomas. 1999-2000. "Civil Society." *Foreign Policy,* 117 (Winter).

Collier, Paul. 2001. "Consensus Building, Knowledge, and Conditionality." In *Annual World Bank Conference on Development Economics 2000,* 67-83. Washington, DC: World Bank.

Dahal, Dev Raj. 2001. *Civil Society in Nepal: Opening the Ground for Questions.* Kathmandu: Center for Development and Governance.

Edwards, Michael, and Gita Sen. 2000. "NGOs, Social Change and the Transformation of Human Relationships: A 21st Century Civic Agenda." *Third World Quarterly,* 21(4), 605-16.

Encarnacion, Omar G. 2000. "Tocqueville's Missionaries: Civil Society Advocacy and Promotion of Democracy." *World Policy Journal,* XVII(1) [Spring], 9-18.

Escobar, Arturo. 1997. "The Laughter of Culture." *Development* (journal of the Society for International Development), 40(4), 20-4.

French, Hillary F. 1994. "Rebuilding the World Bank." In *State of the World,* edited by Lester R. Brown et al. Washington, DC: World Watch Institute.

Huntington, Samuel P. 1997. "After Twenty-Five Years: The Future of the Third Wave." *Journal of Democracy,* 8(4) [October], 3-12.

Israel, Arturo. 1987. *Institutional Development: Incentives to Performance* (a World Bank publication). Baltimore: Johns Hopkins Press.

Kapur, Devesh. 1997. "The New Conditionalities of the International Financial Institutions." In *International Monetary and Financial Issues for the 1990s, Vol. VIII.* New York: United Nations.

Kohli, Atul. 1991 (first Indian edition, 1992). *Democracy and Discontent: India's Growing Crisis of Governability.* New Delhi: Foundation Books.

Kung, Hans. 1999. "Global Ethics in World Politics: The Middle Way Between 'Real Politics' and 'Ideal Politics'." *International Journal of Politics, Culture and Society,* 13(1).

Meltzer, Allan H. 2001. "IFI Reform: A Plan for Financial Stability and Economic Development." *Economic Perspectives* (electronic journal of the US Department of State), 6(1) [February], 9-12.

Mishra, Chaitanya. 2000. "Nepal: Five Years Following the Social Summit." *Contributions to Nepalese Studies,* 27(1) [January].

Ottaway, Marina, and Theresa Chung. 1999. "Debating Democracy Assistance: Towards a New Paradigm." *Journal of Democracy,* 10(4) [October].

Panday, Devendra Raj. 2000. "Matching Democray and Development Policymaking in an Aid-Dependent Country: An Illustration from Nepal." *Harvard Asia Quarterly,* IV(1) [Winter].

Rodrik, Dani. 2001. "Development Strategies for the 21st Century." In *Annual World Bank Conference on Development Economics 2000,* 85-108. Washington, DC: World Bank.

Ruffat, Jean, Fuat Andic and Eduardo Weisner. 2001. *Evaluation of UNDP Non-Core Resources Report.* New York: United Nations Development Programme.

Santiso, Carlos. 2001. "Development Cooperation and the Promotion of Democratic Governance: Promises and Dilemmas." *International Politics and Society,* 4, 386-97.

Sobhan, Rehman. 1998. *How Bad Governance Impedes Poverty Alleviation in Bangladesh.* OECD Technical Papers No. 143. Paris: Organisation for Economic Co-operation and Development.

———. 2000. "Aid Governance and the Policy Ownership: Agenda for the Paris Aid Club." An occasional paper. Dhaka: Centre for Policy Dialogue.

Stiglitz, J. E. 1998. "Towards a New Paradigm for Development: Strategies, Policies, and Processes." Prebisch Lecture. Geneva: United Nations Conference on Trade and Development.

———. 2001. "Development Thinking at the Millennium." In *Annual World Bank Conference on Development Economics 2000,* 13-38. Washington, DC: World Bank.

Streeten, Paul. 1999. "Globalization and Its Impact on Development Cooperation." *Development* (journal of the Society for International Development), 42(3) [September].

Summers, Larry. 2001. "Remarks at the (World Bank's) Country Directors' Retreat." 2 May.

Thomas, Chantal. 1999. "Does the 'Good Governance Policy' of the International Financial Institutions Privilege Markets at the Expense of Democracy." *Connecticut Journal of International Law,* 14(2) [Fall], 551-63.

United Nations Children's Fund (UNICEF). 1999. *Literature Review: Definitions of Capacity-building and Implications for Monitoring and Evaluation.* New York.

United Nations Development Programme (UNDP). 1996. Building Sustainability: Challenges for the Public Sector. Office of Evaluation and Strategic Planning. New York.

———. 1997. "Capacity Development." In *Capacity Development Resource Book,* Management Development and Governance Division. New York.

World Bank. 1991, 1993, 1997, 1999, 2000 and 2001. *World Development Report.* Washington, DC.

1.4 CIVIC ENGAGEMENT AND DEVELOPMENT: INTRODUCING THE ISSUES

KHALID MALIK AND SWARNIM WAGLÉ[1]

This chapter has a simple purpose. By pulling together a disparate set of arguments, we put forward the case that civic engagement, a critical part of social capital, has an essential role to play in successful development transformation (Stiglitz, 1998; see Part 2, Chapter 1). From this premise, some key conclusions are drawn: a) that civic engagement, often argued as an end in itself from a moral-philosophical perspective, is also an important means through which social capital and effective development efforts can be fostered; b) development efforts are likely to yield better long-term benefits if they build in components of civic engagement; and c) this focus on civic engagement has significant implications for strengthening country capacities to manage development processes for which international resources might be necessary. The chapter reviews civic engagement as a concept, looks at its critical attributes and examines some policy implications. The recent example of the Poverty Reduction Strategy Papers (PRSPs) is illustrated as one important attempt to influence development policy through civic engagement.

The Link Between Social Capital and Civic Engagement[2]

Despite growing appreciation of the concept of social capital, literature on the subject is diffuse. Though arguably different in character from human and physical capital, social capital can also be understood as a factor that influences productivity. As Putnam (2000) puts it, social networks have value, and, like physical capital (machines) and human capital (education), social contacts influence the productivity of groups and individuals. If human capital is embodied in individuals, social capital is embodied in relationships. Woolcock (2000) is more succinct when he limits the understanding of social capital to "norms and networks that facilitate collective action," cautioning that any definition of social capital should differentiate between its "sources" and "consequences." In this context, social capital would, for example, exclude "trust" from its definition, since it is an outcome, not a source, of social relations that foster repeated interactions. Social capital is linked to the idea of civic virtue, which is most powerful when embedded in a dense network of reciprocal social relations.

The concept of social capital came out of its character of civic engagement. Its first use is attributed to Lyda J. Hanifan, who, as a Superintendent of schools in West Virginia in 1916, highlighted the importance of community involvement in the success of state schools. The theme was independently picked up by social scientists in subsequent decades, including in the late 1980s by James Coleman. The notion's

[1] Khalid Malik is the Director of the Evaluation Office of the United Nations Development Programme in New York and Swarnim Waglé is a consultant at the World Bank in Washington, DC. The opinions expressed here are personal and should not be attributed to the institutions with which the authors are affiliated.
[2] Draws on Waglé (2001).

scholarly credibility reached new heights, however, only with the publication in 1993 of Putnam's 20-year experimental study, *Civic Traditions in Modern Italy,* which sought to establish linkages between successes in regional governance and stocks of social capital in different Italian provinces. In the early 1970s, 20 regional governments, identical in form, were implanted in provinces with very different characteristics. Some failed; some succeeded. Putnam attributed this difference in quality of performance not to party politics and ideology, not to affluence and population movements, but to traditions of civic engagement—voter turnout, newspaper readership, membership in choral societies and literary circles, soccer clubs, etc. Putnam places this finding in the context of an observation that Alexis de Tocqueville made in the 1830s about civic engagement and the successful working of democracy in the United States. He had noted, "Americans of all ages, all stations in life, and all types of disposition...are forever forming associations."

Putnam (1993a) argues that when networks of civic engagement are dense, reciprocity and trust are fostered, "lubricating social life." Coordination and communication among agents amplify information about the trustworthiness, or general reputation, of other individuals, reducing incentives for opportunism and malfeasance (Putnam 2000). The association between social networks and economic growth has been extensively explored in the economics literature. Fukuyama (1995) elaborates on the virtue of trust in spurring economic growth by drawing a distinction between "low-trust" and "high-trust" societies. He identifies their respective abilities to generate social capital as being key to mitigating the adverse consequences of the discipline that market economies impose. The success of some East Asian economies in making giant material advances within a generation has been partially attributed to the positive externalities of "network capitalism."

Social capital and civic engagement, of course, have downsides. Establishing and maintaining relations may require a level of investment that may not be cost-effective. Adler and Kwon (1999) cite a study that argues that while social capital may generate informational benefits, these may be costly to maintain. The same forces of solidarity that "help members bind can turn into ties that blind," as over-embedded relationships stop the flow of new information and ideas into the group, and create non-economic obligations that hinder entrepreneurship. Dreze and Sen (1995), for example, attribute high dropout rates for girls from schools in India to family obligations and pressures to fulfill community expectations. Indeed, it has to be recognized that religious cults, terrorist organizations, gangs and drug cartels are groups with strong internal ties among members that nonetheless impose severe damage to society.

Defining Civic Engagement

In the confusing yet obvious domain of social capital, civic engagement is a key subset. If the term civic engagement is understood as a process that organizes citizens or their entrusted representatives to influence, share and control public affairs, then we see this contributing to social capital through interactions between people and the processes they engage in for a positive public outcome. More generally, civic engagement contributes to social capital and to development efforts through the channels of voice, representation and accountability. This link between civic engagement and development can be organized in a variety of ways, both formal and informal. The latter refers to processes that may complement the formal processes of electing officials or making development plans in a consultative manner.

Discussions here use the terms "civic engagement" and "participation" interchangeably for convenience, with both terms concurring broadly with the definition that participation is a process through which stakeholders influence and share control over development initiatives, and the decisions and resources that affect them (World Bank, 1996). However, it is still worth noting that civic engagement is a more specific term than participation, with an emphasis on civic objectives and concerns. The United Nations Development Programme's (UNDP) *Human Development Report 1993* sees participation in similar terms, describing it "as a process, not an event, that closely involves people in the economic, social, cultural and political processes that affect their lives." The report places the issue within a wide developmental, and in some ways even philosophical, paradigm—seeing it as both a means and an end. Because the paradigm of human development stresses investment in human capabilities and the subsequent functional use of those capabilities to allow people to lead the kind of lives they choose, participation is viewed as facilitating the use of human capabilities, hence serving as a means for socio-economic development. In this context, by allowing people to realize their full potential and enhance their personal fulfillment, participation is also seen as an end in itself (Sen, 1981; UNDP, 1993).

Korten (1988) frames civic engagement as an issue of governance, stating, "If sovereignty resides ultimately in the citizenry, their engagement is about the right to define the public good, to determine the policies by which they will seek that good, and to reform or replace those institutions that no longer serve." This is a useful definitional reference for the purposes of this chapter, because our attempt here is also to talk about activities among entities at the macrolevel—the higher echelons and departments within the central government—whose work is usually difficult to access and influence by common citizens, both procedurally, because of centralization or bureaucratic restrictions, and substantially, because of technical content. This perspective on governance in a sense draws upon the notion that members of groups and society at large enter into social compacts that present mutual or reciprocal obligations, and that civic engagement is an active process of exercising these obligations. In this sense, exercise of this obligation implies the essential right of every citizen to voice their concerns and to enforce accountability.

At a more technical level, the scope of the term civic engagement is best understood on a continuum that spans information-sharing to empowerment. Following Edgerton et al. (2000), this continuum can begin with: a) a one-way *flow of information* to the public in the form of, say, media broadcasts or dissemination of decisions; and progress on to; b) bi- or multilateral *consultation* between and among coordinators of the process and the public in the form of participatory assessments, interviews and field visits; c) *collaboration* encompassing joint work and shared decision-making between the coordinators and the stakeholders; and d) *empowerment,* where decision-making powers and resources are transferred to civic organizations, in the form of say, forestry or irrigation user groups. It might also be useful to highlight the concept of "exit," which was originally highlighted by Hirschman (1972). He contrasts the issue of voice, or the capacity to influence policy and debate within an institution, with the capacity of a group to get what it wants by choosing a specific institution or switching to another, i.e., an exit. This concept is interesting insofar as it reminds us that people choose to express dissatisfaction with an institution or process by ignoring or moving away from it rather than necessarily working from within. More broadly, it might be useful to recognize the existence of a complex interplay between different forms of civic engagement, and the role and function of state institutions—rather than civic groups only being on the receiving end of the process, for instance as communities or groups who need to be involved in projects or programmes in order to make development more effective.

The Conundrum of Policy Implications

Are there specific roles and policies that state institutions can assume or introduce that support or hinder advancement of civic engagement? If public policy is an instrument, and productive civic engagement as a form of social capital is a target, can a workable link between the two be established? If not, why? If yes, how? What kind of capacities do we require to create productive social capital, which can then be leveraged for development transformation?

Social capital, including more specifically civic engagement, can be thought of as a missing block in many development parcels, but it is not a solution to all ills, and while its influence should be recognized, it ought not be exaggerated. It does, however, point us toward a direction that is useful in development—it helps us focus on how and under what terms we associate with each other. Woolcock (2000) highlights the following points. First, if the low stock of bridging capital makes it difficult for information and resources to flow among groups, larger socio-economic-political forces that divide societies, such as discriminatory practices along gender, caste and ethnic lines, will stand in the way of growth. Second, if social capital is part of an effective risk-management strategy in crises, its absence implies a difficult time for countries at times of volatility. Third, institutions affect how communities manage risks and opportunities. In countries where a corrupt bureaucracy and a lack of the rule of law are the norm, it will be difficult to showcase well-maintained schools and roads, for example. It is rare that one witnesses cases where a country is characterized by strong features of positive social capital and simultaneously weak systems of government responsiveness to citizen concerns.

Can we then find a role for public policy to nurture, or create, or at least stop the destruction of the positive aspects of social capital? Social relations are neither culturally determined in a permanent way, nor are they always shaped by the responses of rational agents. Institutions and history play a big role in shaping social relations. Public policy can shape institutions that support social relations that in turn sustain high levels of productive social capital. The *World Development Report 2000/2001* cites an example where the Brazilian state devised a health programme that increased vaccination and reduced infant mortality, and in the process created social capital in the form of building trust between government workers and poor people.

An arena where the state can step in to influence social norms is in instances of exclusionary practices linked with race, gender and ethnicity. Some forms of exclusion can simply be redressed by improving the outreach of public services to areas of neg-lect—such as rural primary schools and hospitals. Stronger manifestations of discrimination ought to be dealt with legally through institutions of the state or special policies such as affirmative action. The bigger agenda of social capital, however, risks being belittled by practitioners, because as Edwards (2000) points out, attributes such as trust and tolerance are hard to engineer, and the tendency for development organizations is to focus on things that are measurable in the short run. This focus can be useful, but it assists "'forms" not "norms" of social capital. Helping countries build social capital is complex, however, as assistance dedicated to "building other people's civil societies by investing in their social capital" encourages the idea of picking winners, which spreads mistrust among groups, and even backlash as indigenous groups become associated with foreign interests (Edwards, 2000).

In sum, as Narayan and Woolcock (2000) put it, a new consensus is emerging about the importance of social relations in development: a) they provide opportunities for mobilizing growth-enhancing resources; b) they don't exist in a vacuum; and c) the nature and extent of interactions between communities and institutions hold the key to understanding development prospects in a given society. Edwards (2000) para-phrases Ramon Daubon in likening social capital to the Indian Ocean: "Everyone knows where it is, no one cares where it begins or where it ends, but we know we have to cross it to get from India to Africa."

Going Beyond Civic Engagement as an Instrument

At a broader level, though, the virtues of social capital can only be exploited fully by internalizing civic interaction in mainstream political and development processes. Narayan and Woolcock (2000) call for social capital to be seen as a component of such orthodox development projects as dams, irrigation systems, local schools and health clinics. Quoting Esman and Uphoff (1984), they posit, "Where poor communities have direct input into the design, implementation, management and evaluation of projects, returns on investments and the sustainability of the project is enhanced."

The idea of civic engagement at the grassroots level has been tested, and has generally been seen to generate benefits that contribute to better planning, imple-mentation and sustainability of projects. Civic engagement has costs and constraints, of course, but it is to the credit of the successes at the microlevel that questions are now being asked about the desirability of scaling civic engagement up to the macrolevel. But equally, there is a growing question as to the development value of microinterventions, however successful or well meaning they might be, along with a corresponding search for improved understanding about the necessary factors and conditions that can more fundamentally ensure broader progress in the issues raised. A concrete example is microfinance, where however successful or well designed individual schemes might be, the larger development outcomes of increased access to credit by the poor can only be tested by examining the functioning of capital markets, and how they might be adjusted (institutions, approaches, etc.) to allow for such access.

Civic Engagement at the Microlevel

The term civic engagement has been in frequent use since the early 1960s in the narrower arena of people's engagement in small projects. It is, however, only in recent years that it has received much academic attention as an important development theme. Following the gradual replacement of the coercive socialist order by democratic regimes in many countries around the world, together with the heightened quest for new ways to achieve a sustained rise in standards of living for the world's poor, participation has been rediscovered as an instrument that can be used both to consolidate democratic systems of governance and to strengthen the global project of development. The fundamental premise is that the people have the urge as well the right to be part of events and processes that shape their lives.

Benefits, Costs and Constraints

A compelling body of empirical evidence exists that makes a strong case for people's participation at the microlevel (Uphoff et al., 1979; World Bank, 1996). Such has been the wave that most foreign-aid-financed programmes in the developing world today make participation an essential component of project design and implementation. Theoretically, the channels through which participation is seen to contribute usefully to the effectiveness and sustainability of development outcomes are: information-driven efficiency, ownership, transparency and accountability, and constructive partnerships. It is very hard to quantify success in these broad terms, and this is probably one of the reasons why it is difficult to make a strong case for civic engagement even when the gains seem obvious. While attempts at quantifying success can be made, the best indicators are likely to continue to be qualitative—whether people perceive the processes to be successful or not.

By involving the beneficiaries in a project's design, one can expect a more accurate perception of needs based on the direct exchange of information (Robb, 2000). When the people are not consulted, policy-makers work on assumptions that are subject to problems of information asymmetries, such as moral hazard and adverse selection, as discussed extensively in the economics literature. Participation can be expected to alleviate these problems to some extent by allowing a more accurate flow of information that translates into better decisions. Informed decisions are more efficient in terms of resources consumed and outcomes generated than those that are not. Often, there may not have been demand for the project, or it might not have been a priority. With people's participation, not only can the most important needs be identified, but by having people play a role in the entire project cycle—formulation, adoption, implementation and monitoring—ownership can be ensured, and with it the sustainability of the project (World Bank, 1996). In a study of 121 diverse rural water-supply projects in 49 countries in the developing world, the World Bank provided evidence of how there exists a strong correlation between project success and high levels of beneficiary participation. It claimed that of the 49 projects with low levels of participation, only 8 per cent were successful, while of the 42 projects with high levels of participation, 64 per cent were successes (World Bank, 1997). When coordinators of projects are subject to civic scrutiny of their decisions and actions, this forces them to be more accountable and responsive to the needs of beneficiaries. By getting rid of the vacuum in communication between the two groups, bureaucratic obstructions can be overcome, which can make government more answerable.

If public policy is about deciding the most efficient allocation of scarce public resources, policy decisions often take the form of analysing trade-offs between options. Participation of the people, especially differing groups with divergent interests, can allow an exchange of each other's positions and interests, which can kick-start a deliberative process of mutual understanding of the trade-offs involved in the collective decision. Not only can the groups then enter into constructive alliances, but they are also likely to be less combative and disruptive to the processes and programmes subsequently decided on.

Beyond its instrumental roles in ensuring better decisions and sounder implementation, participation is also seen as a good in itself that deepens democracy. By giving citizens an opportunity to access and shape governance and the exercise of power, participation complements the systems of electoral competition that may fail to meet citizen needs directly (Agrawal, 1999). Along these lines, participation has also been viewed as a process that politically educates citizens in the art of governance, and the pursuit of rights and civic roles (Freire, 1970).

The virtues of participation are, however, not unanimously appreciated. Concerns often raised about participatory processes are: costs in terms of money, time and management (high transaction costs); risks of elite capture; the possibility of instability; and legitimate representation. In addition, Brinkerhoff and Goldsmith (2000) suggest that participatory processes may also result in policy stalemates and unrealistic expectations on the part of those involved.

Civic engagement as a process needs to be managed and requires resources. In developing countries, where many equally deserving ends compete for scarce resources, opportunity costs in terms of money and bureaucratic capacities diverted to manage a participatory process may be significant. While all development and all politics is about, and for, the people, any argument to avoid their engagement in these processes on the pretext of "inconvenience" can confuse ends with means. While participatory processes impose real costs in terms of time, money and management, a balanced tally indicating clearly the benefits and costs of the process may justify a better case for civic engagement.

Scholars further talk about the danger of elite capture when development and political processes become more open and participatory. The fear is that as more opportunities become available for citizen participation, local elites may become more dominant and reap a disproportionate share of the possible benefits that emanate from benign processes aimed at bringing "governance closer to the governed" (Agrawal, 1999). When opportunities for grassroots participation in development and political processes are extended to the village level, the local elite, who are better off financially as well as in power relations, may be the first ones to capture control of the local administrative and political bodies. Roodt (1996) adds that local elites monopolize power and are hostile to the widespread participation of common people, which they attempt to prevent from occurring by using their power positions. For every optimist who sees participation as a genuine tool for transformation, it seems there is a less-optimistic person who views it as a mere legitimizing tool for top-down implementation.

A related fear expressed by scholars like Huntington (1968) — and even John Stuart Mill, in an earlier context of whether democracy is well suited for all countries — is that a society without strong institutions to set and enforce rules may easily create environments where greater participation, without the institutional safeguards, leads to anarchy. It is in this spirit that one hears arguments such as, "A high level of participation could be antithetical to democracy, for it may endanger freedom and rights, impede governability and destroy pluralism" (Agrawal, 1999). This has, of course, been countered by arguments that in the absence of broad-based citizen participation, electoral democracies may instead run into the risk of becoming hostage to the manipulations of the powerful minority.

On balance, however, there is a growing recognition in the global development movement today of the conditional virtues of civic engagement. As Oakley et al. (1991) note, "Whereas up to ten years ago a review of project-based literature would probably highlight technological effectiveness, good planning and management, and resource efficiency as the key ingredients of project success, today participation figures prominently; some would say that it is the single most important ingredient."

Scaling Up Participation: The Leap from the Microlevel to the Macrolevel

If we recognize that the experiment of civic engagement at the microlevel has been, on balance, a positive experience, it might be reasonable to expect similar outcomes at the macrolevel. Is it realistic to expect to reap there the microlevel benefits of enhanced efficiency through better information flow, improved programme effectiveness through solicitation of local knowledge, greater accountability, stronger ownership and partnerships, and empowerment of stakeholders? If yes, what are the channels? Is there a higher-order case for civic engagement as an essential part of democracy and development sustainability, and as a key channel for strengthening the "glue that binds and holds society" together, especially in circumstances of development transformation? (See Stiglitz, 1998.)

Expected Benefits

Brinkerhoff and Goldsmith (2000) suggest that the outcomes of civic engagement at the macrolevel can be expected to be very similar to those at the grassroots. They, among others, posit that inclusive participatory processes can create: a) better socio-macroeconomic policy content based on better information; b) social consensus on policy priorities because of civic involvement in the discourse; c) a positive signaling effect to international donors and investors because of national consensus; d) equitable policies and distribution of benefits to the vulnerable, such as the poor; e) accountable and responsive government; and f) better implementation of policy and programmes.

While these are a direct extension of anticipated benefits at the macrolevel, based on the microlevel evidence, there also exists a set of related reasons that can be presented to strengthen the case for civic engagement at higher levels.

- Participation and Economic Stability

Rodrik (2000) presents empirical evidence on the association between participatory political regimes and lower levels of aggregate economic instability, suggesting that this may be because participatory political regimes moderate social conflict and better induce compromises among citizen groups. While there does not exist convincing econometric evidence on the link between democracies and long-term economic growth, evidence on the positive link between democracies and volatility (annual standard deviations in GDP growth rates) is statistically significant. Because economic volatility triggers high welfare losses in a world with incomplete insurance markets and inadequate levels of intertemporal trade, Rodrik accords this finding much importance. It suggests that participatory processes induce cooperation and generate stability. First, as individuals meet and discuss, they "understand each other's viewpoints, develop empathy, recognize the value of moderation, internalize the common interest and de-emphasize self-interest." Participatory regimes induce cooperation not by "changing the constraints we face, but by changing the type of people we are," or by altering the preferences of agents. Second, democracies with constitutional provisions that prevent the majority from suppressing the minority, or the winners from marginalizing the losers, induce cooperation among groups ex ante who are aware of the costs of noncooperation. Third, cooperation among groups is ensured by the possibility of repeated interactions. As long as this probability is strong and past actions influence future behaviours, groups who have a sufficiently long-term time horizon have an incentive to cooperate rather than renege on negotiations for short-term gains (Rodrik 2000).

- Participation and Prevention of Famines and Extreme Destitution

Similarly, building on an observation by Sen (1993) that "there are no famines in democracies," T. Besley and R. Burgess (as cited in World Bank, 2000) highlight the importance of the free press in preventing famines in India—the world's largest democracy. In participatory political regimes, where informed citizens can exact accountability from politicians on the speed of relief programmes, responsiveness to disasters is swift, preventing major calamities. Besley and Burgess find that for a given shock, in the form of a drought or flood, higher newspaper circulation leads to greater public food distribution or relief spending. Their hypothesis is that an "informed population can link inefficiency to a particular politician and elicit a greater response to a crisis" (World Bank, 2000). Freedom of the press can be thought of as a reasonably good proxy for the freedom and the scope of the activities of civic organizations.

- Participation and Strength of State Capacities

It has also been argued that civic engagement strengthens state capacities in two additional ways. First, when citizens can express and press for demands legally, states acquire some of the credibility to govern well. This is partly because wide-ranging and open discussion of policy goals tends to avoid the risk of a small elite or minority influencing the course of government. Second, where public services are inefficient because of weak state capabilities and incentive problems, the user groups and citizen associations can inform public officials of their needs and press for improvements (World Bank, 1997). It has been argued in the Kenyan context, for example, that better information flows from the supposed beneficiaries lead to better decisions, resulting in the kind of efficiency that alleviates budgetary pressures on central governments — a crucial point in resource-starved nations (Smoke, 1993).

Costs and Constraints

The costs and constraints briefly discussed above for microactivities apply to the following section as well. It is important to note, however, that when an argument in favor of civic engagement is presented as being supportive to the legitimacy of the state, etc., there may exist inherent difficulties in attaining this goal. As Mathur (1997) describes, central governments and the bureaucrats usually are very reluctant to give up powers, as they consider their decision-making authority an exclusive preserve. Government institutions and their staff are quite suspicious and feel threatened by people who organize themselves for participation; hence the often lacklustre or even hostile reception of participatory initiatives by government officials. As Ghai (1988) adds, "Many participatory initiatives have to contend with hostility, harassment and attempts at suppression. Certainly few attract resources of the type and amount reserved for more conventional development projects." This, he contends, is because the dominant groups mistakenly tend to equate participatory movements with subversion or revolutionary doctrine. It is in this context that Agrawal (1999) views participation as a thoroughly political process. He argues that, among the many factors related to the success of participation, two key issues are: the management of political relationships at the central level in order to extract commitment from powerful actors, and the creation of institutional mechanisms at the local level.

The Distinctive Case of Macrolevel Policy-Making[3]

While cases may be made for both advocating and downplaying the roles of civic engagement in policy processes, and it is also recognized that civic engagement is

---

[3] Co-author S. Wagle was a member of a team that interviewed several economists at the World Bank and the International Monetary Fund about the option of incorporating elements of civic engagement

certainly not a solution to all things wrong with policy-making or programme implementation, there is a broad acceptance now that participation is a necessary if not solely sufficient ingredient for attaining successful policy outcomes.

Some areas of macroeconomic policy-making, however, are slightly different. Neoclassical economists point to the technical nature of macropolicies, for example, noting that monetary policies about interest rates or decisions on currency devaluation should not be issues subject to civic influence. Similarly, it may be unreasonable to expect informed public debates to take place on issues such as optimal credit targets or the sustainability of fiscal deficits. But where participation can play a role is in public education about the consequences of these technical decisions, and, perhaps even more importantly, about the role macropolicies can play in development transformation (see Part 1, Chapter 1). On issues such as the inevitability of short-term pains to reap medium-term benefits in inflation-reducing policies, for example, the public ought to be informed and convinced about the rationale for short-term austerity. (Although even on this there is disagreement, for instance, over how short-term austerity is to be achieved, whether expenditures on health or education are protected or not, and so on.) On questions of public sector reform, or privatization, there are economic and political choices to be made, and bringing groups with varying priorities to a common forum to hear and understand each other and deliberate on trade-offs can be helpful.

It has also been pointed out that since macropolicies are public goods, which, by definition, are characterized by people's understatement of their willingness to pay for them, there may be situations when outcomes of certain participatory mechanisms ought to be overruled, e.g., when externalities are involved. Along these lines, it has been argued that participation, when used as a management tool, as in a farmer's ownership of irrigation systems, may also give rise to problems of moral hazard through incentives for excessive risk-taking.

When macroeconomic decision-making on resource allocation is subject to popular influence, there is a fear that participatory processes might generate an outcome that is not only "populist," but also one that is laden with conflicting demands from different segments of the society (e.g., simultaneous calls for imposition and removal of import tariffs, specific subsidies, low taxes and greater expenditures).

Broad-based consultative exercises can result in lengthy lists of demands. It becomes a challenge then to square the wish list of people with the budgetary realities. After the agenda is defined, reality presented, and trade-offs regarding revenue and expenditure examined through a process of consultation, the elected government officials ultimately have to decide how to proceed. While scope for participation in macropolicies may well be limited, it is by no means a given. Citizen groups can be engaged in debates over trade-offs among priorities, e.g., between low inflation and growth-generating high public expenditures.

---

at the macrolevel in June 2000. Those consulted were H. Bradenkamp, S. Devarajan, M. Katz and D. Morrow, among others.

A recurring concern about participation pertains to an apparent contradiction. While participatory processes are usually credited as instruments that lend legitimacy and credibility to policies, valid questions may be asked about stakeholder identification and representation. Who exactly does a particular civic group represent, and who is it accountable to? Furthermore, by creating ad hoc participatory processes in addition to established political-legal processes, a question that can emerge is whether the former subverts the latter, and if it does, whether that is desirable. Since participation does not have a constitutional "feel" to it, practitioners suggest that governments should be drawing on established institutional resources, not bypassing them, in order to reap the kinds of benefits that civic engagement could be expected to generate.

One area where the participation of people, especially the poor, has been found to be valuable in formulating national-level strategies is the arena of poverty reduction, where policies have relied extensively on information fed through Participatory Poverty Assessments, which employ flexible visual and verbal techniques of inquiry, as opposed to predetermined statistical questions asked in household surveys. Robb (2000) argues that these participatory approaches have resulted in a broader definition of poverty and better-informed public policies that are more responsive to the needs of the poor. She draws on a range of African examples to conclude that broad policy dialogue on poverty typically widens the constituency for reform and strengthens a country's sense of ownership of policies.

Weighing the competing claims and arguments about the virtues and the vices of participatory processes, it is clear that, at a theoretical level, while participation can be expected to yield benefits, the channels through which this may happen are specific and conditional on an array of circumstances. The challenge for policy entrepreneurs is to identify the right channels and the circumstances for employing processes of civic engagement.

PRSPs: A Case of Macrolevel Civic Engagement

Between 1999 and 2001, around 50 countries prepared interim or full Poverty Reduction Strategy Papers (PRSPs). They are now the primary source of 1171 lending for most poor countries. Although triggered by the Group of Seven (G-7) initiative to relieve the debts of the Highly Indebted and Poor (HIPC) countries, and by the World Bank and International Monetary Fund (IMF) requirement that countries must articulate how they have sought to channel resources to fight poverty after debt relief, the PRSPs have now developed into an elaborate development policy vehicle of their own. According to the World Bank, there is a renewed emphasis on six basic approaches: a) a country-driven process, b) results-orientation, c) comprehensive coverage of issues, d) prioritizing of issues for improved implementation, e) a strong base in partnerships, and f) a long-term perspective. A feature most worth noting in the PRSPs is that they are supposed to be prepared in a participatory manner. While in the interim PRSPs participation is not mandated—the only requirement is a plan indicating how participation will be cultivated—at the full PRSP stage countries are required to follow a participatory process.

Over the past two years of PRSP preparations, there have been numerous assessments by leading nongovernmental organizations (NGOs) and agencies external to the World Bank and the IMF. Some of the recurring findings on civic engagement that emerge are as follows: a) there is considerable divergence in the conceptual understanding of civic engagement; b) the breadth and depth of civic engagement is insufficient, with the real poor, ethnic minorities and the poor outside urban areas not generally consulted; c) civic engagement has enriched and widened the description and analysis of poverty, but has not influenced much the technical areas of macroeconomic choices and public expenditures; d) the participatory processes have spun off many positive externalities, such as new legal developments and creation of civil society alliances; and e) correlates of an open regime, such as freedom to speak and to form socio-political organizations, seem conducive for the flourishing of civic engagement processes, although little direct link is observed between a political regime per se and the quality of a civic engagement process.[4]

Concluding Remarks

Following the publications of UNDP's flagship *Human Development Reports,* and the increased operational orientation of large institutions like the World Bank to more "human" arenas such as education and health over the past decade,[5] the development debate has refocused on the basics of the ends and means of development. What are we seeking to achieve? For whom? And how? People informed by both personal value judgments as well as empirical results make cases for specific policy measures. Our attempt in this chapter has been to introduce one such notion of social capital. If one recognizes this to be a desirable input, output and outcome of development, then the question that policy professionals need to ask is: Can it be created or nurtured? This chapter explores the theme of civic engagement as one possible policy response, and we discuss its many dimensions, appreciating its perceived successes at the microlevel and positing whether it could be up-scaled and out-scaled to the macrolevel. We also briefly talk about a practical example of the PRSPs in this context.

Increasingly, what we do in development is becoming as important as how we do it (Stigltiz, 1998). The thesis of development as transformation emphasizes the process as much as the product, and as various disciplines—from philosophy to sociology, and from urban planning to economics—converge to shape the multidimensional field of development, concepts and issues that were hitherto ignored as irrelevant to the basic pursuit of enhancing national incomes have emerged as important ingredients to meaningful and sustainable development. By presenting an array of issues and positing hypotheses in the area of social capital and civic engagement, we hope this chapter will modestly nudge the policy debates into appreciating more the multidimensional color of the developmental puzzle.

---

[4] Co-author S. Wagle led a team in December 2001 to review over 60 distinct documents on participation in PRSPs, including 33 interim PRSPs, 9 PRSPs and over 20 external assessments. A volume that synthesizes the findings is expected from the World Bank in early 2002. Please consult this for details.
[5] Over 25 per cent of World Bank lending has gone to the social sector in recent years, with the agency becoming the largest source of funds for education, health and HIV/AIDS programmes in the world.

References

Adler, P., and S. Kwon. 1999. "Social Capital: The Good, the Bad and the Ugly." A paper presented at the 1999 Academy of Management meeting. Chicago.

Agrawal, A. 1999. *Decentralization in Nepal: A Comparative Analysis.* Oakland: ICS Press.

Brinkerhoff, D., and A. Goldsmith. 2000. "Participation in Macroeconomic Policy: Experience and Implications for Poverty Reduction Strategies." A draft paper. World Bank.

Dreze, J., and A. K. Sen. 1995. *Economic Development and Social Opportunity.* Oxford: Oxford University Press.

Edgerton, J., et al. 2000. "Participatory Processes in Poverty Reduction Strategy." In *Poverty Reduction Strategy Sourcebook*, chapter two. Washington, DC: World Bank.

Edwards, M. 2000. "Enthusiasts, Tacticians and Skeptics: The World Bank, Civil Society and Social Capital." A World Bank draft paper.

Esman, M., and N. Uphoff. 1984. *Local Organizations: Intermediaries in Rural Development.* Ithaca: Cornell University Press.

Freire, P. 1970. *The Pedagogy of the Oppressed.* New York: Herder and Herder.

Fukuyama, F. 1995. *Trust: The Social Virtues and the Creation of Prosperity.* New York: Free Press.

Ghai, D. 1988. "Participatory Development: Some Experiences from Grassroots Experiences." Discussion Paper No. 5. Geneva: United Nations Research Institute for Social Development.

Hanifan, L. J. 1916. "The Rural School Community Center." *Annals of the American Academy of Political and Social Science,* 67, 130-8.

Hirschman, Albert O. 1972. *Exit Voice and Loyalty: Responses to Decline in Firms, Organizations, and States.* Cambridge: Harvard University Press.

Huntington, S. 1968. *Political Order in Changing Societies.* New Haven: Yale.

Korten, D. C. 1981. "Social Development: Putting People First." In *Bureaucracy and the Poor,* edited by David C. Korten and Felip Alfonso. Singapore: McGraw Hill International.

———. 1988. "Third Generation NGO Strategies: A Key to People-Centered Development." *World Development* (supplement), 15.

Mathur, H. M. 1997. "Participatory Development—Some Areas of Current Concern." *Sociological Bulletin,* March.

Narayan, D., and M. Woolcock. 2000. "Social Capital: Implications for Development Theory, Research and Policy." *The World Bank Research Observer,* August.

Oakley, P., et al. 1991. *Projects with People: The Practice of Participation in Rural Development.* Geneva: International Labour Organization.

Pritchett, L., and D. Narayan. 1997. "Cents and Solidarity: Household Income and Social Capital in Rural Tanzania." A World Bank working paper.

Putnam, R. 1993. *Making Democracy Work: Civic Traditions in Modern Italy.* Princeton: Princeton University Press.

———. 1993a. "The Prosperous Community: Social Capital and Public Life." *The American Prospect,* 4(13).

———. 2000. *Bowling Alone: The Collapse and Revival of American Community.* New York: Simon and Schuster.

Robb, C. 2000. "How Can the Poor Have a Voice in Government Policy?" *Finance and Development,* December.

Rodrik, D. 2000. "Participatory Politics, Social Cooperation, and Economic Stability." *American Economic Review,* May.

Roodt, M. J. 1996. "Participatory Development—A Jargon Concept?" In *Reconstruction, Development and People,* edited by J. K. Coetzee and J. Graaf. Johannesburg: International Thomson Publishing.

Sen, A. K. 1981. *Poverty and Famines: An Essay on Entitlement and Deprivation.* Oxford: Clarendon Press.

———. 1993. "The Economics of Life and Death." *Scientific American,* May.

Smoke, P. 1993. "Local Government Fiscal Reform in Developing Countries: Lessons from Kenya." *World Development,* 26(6).

Solow, R. 1997. "Tell Me Again What We Are Talking About." *Stern Business,* 4(1).

Stiglitz, J. E. 1998. "Toward a New Paradigm for Development: Strategies, Policies and Processes." Prebisch Lecture. Geneva: United Nations Conference on Trade and Development.

United Nations Development Programme (UNDP). 1993. *Human Development Report.* New York: Oxford University Press.

Uphoff, N. 1992. *Learning from Gal Oya: Possibilities for Participatory Development and Post-Newtonian Social Science.* Ithaca: Cornell University Press.

Uphoff, N., J. Cohen and A. Goldsmith. 1979. *Feasibility and Application of Rural Development Participation: A State of the Art Paper.* Ithaca: Cornell University Press.

Waglé, S. 2001. "Social Capital and Development: A Survey." A draft paper.

Woolcock, M. 2000. "The Place of Social Capital in Understanding Social and Economic Outcomes." *Canadian Journal of Policy Research,* 2(l), 11-17.

World Bank. 1996. *The World Bank Participation Sourcebook.* Washington, DC.

———. 1997. *World Development Report.* New York: Oxford University Press.

———. 2000. *World Development Report 2000/2001.* New York: Oxford University Press.

1.5 SOCIAL CAPITAL AND INDUSTRIAL TRANSFORMATION

SANJAYA LALL[1]

Introduction

This chapter is an exploration of the social-capital needs of industrial development. "Social capital" has attracted considerable recent attention in socio-political analysis, and we are now beginning to see its application to development economics. However, there has not to my knowledge been any application of the concept to industrialization. This essay is a preliminary attempt to remedy this gap, although it is more an exploration than a completed piece of research.

The analysis of social capital in industrialization may, to start with, need some justification since there now seems to be a presumption in development thinking that industrial development is best left to the market. The dominant Washington Consensus view, supported by leading development and aid agencies, is that the key to efficient industrialization is "market-friendly" policies. Drawing upon the success of the export-oriented East Asian newly industrializing economies, market friendliness is taken to mean rapid and full exposure to international trade, investment and technology flows, and the removal of all government interventions in the allocation of investment resources. This interpretation of the Asian experience remains controversial, as discussed below. More important for present purposes is the fact that the social factors that affect the process are rarely taken into account. There is an implicit assumption that such factors do not matter, or that if they do, market-friendly policies will by themselves ensure that social norms will automatically adapt to economic needs.

There is growing evidence that this view is oversimplified and possibly harmful. Economies are not equally equipped to cope with international competition and globalization: A few do very well, but a large number flounder. Take the well-known figures on growing disparities in incomes between countries: Per capita income in the richest 5 per cent of all countries was 30 times higher than that in the poorest 5 per cent in 1960. In 1997, the ratio was 74 times. Inequality in the manufacturing industry has risen even more sharply. The ratio of per capita manufacturing value added (MVA) in the 5 per cent most industrialized countries to that in the 5 per cent least industrialized rose from 95 to 566 during 1985-98 (UNIDO, 2002). This disparity also rose within the developing world. While the five industrial leaders in the developing world did quite well vis-à-vis highly industrialized countries (with the ratio of per capita MVA narrowing from 2.3 to 2.2), the ratio for the five developing leaders to the five laggards rose from 42 in 1985 to 261 in 1998.

[1] I am grateful to Khalid Malik for encouraging me to undertake this foray into a new—and very important—field, and for his comments and suggestions. I have drawn heavily on the survey of the social-capital literature by Waglé (2001) and would not have been able to produce even this exploratory draft without this.

All the relevant measures of industrial performance reinforce this impression of massive and rising disparity. Take a measure of competitive industrial performance, manufactured exports. The leading ten exporters in the developing world (a group of 58 developing countries with sizeable industrial sectors) accounted for 76 per cent of manufactured exports in 1985; by 1998 they accounted for 80 per cent. The share of the bottom 30 countries in this group fell from 2.2 to 1.3 per cent over this period (UNIDO, 2002). In skill- and technology-based exports, the levels of concentration were even higher. A large part of the developing world has been dropping out of the dynamics of global industrial activity.

A similar picture emerges from the data on the inputs into industrial growth. Inflows of foreign direct investment (FDI) into manufacturing were highly concentrated, with the leading 10 developing countries accounting for 80 per cent of the total. While data on FDI in export-oriented manufacturing are not separately available, this was probably even more concentrated (UNIDO, 2002). To the extent that FDI constitutes the engine of globalization and integration of countries into world production and trade systems, this is a worrying sign. Productive resources and knowledge are more mobile today than before, but where they "stick" depends very much on local economic and social capabilities. National capabilities are very unevenly distributed. Take an indicator of skills as an indicator of capabilities: The leading 10 countries accounted for nearly 70 per cent of the total number of developing country enrolments in tertiary education in 1997. These countries also accounted for over 97 per cent of enterprise-funded research and development (R&D).

These figures imply that there are major structural forces at work. Theory and evidence suggest that there are pervasive market and institutional failures holding back the supply response of many developing economies (Stiglitz, 1996 and 1998). Divergence in economic performance can therefore go on rising. While endogenous growth theory can explain divergence based on cumulativeness, increasing returns and externalities, it assumes that the solution for developing countries is simply to open up to investment and technology inflows. It neglects the fact that investment and technology need strong absorptive capacities (below). As such, it oversimplifies the nature of the development challenges facing modern industry in the developing world.

A branch of the development literature has dealt at length with these capabilities and their policy needs in economic terms (for a review, see Lall, 2001). It has not, however, considered the equally vital *social capacities* that allow economic capabilities to be developed and efficient policies to be designed and implemented. Without a consideration of the social capital that provides the basic precondition for structural change and policy, the analysis is clearly incomplete. There are also important and salutary lessons for development economists who give policy advice. We often feel that the prescriptions we dispense, based on best-practice policies and institutions in the developing world, have a rather low chance of success in many countries. Whatever the reason—poor design and implementation, rent-seeking, lack of commitment, low skill levels and so on—there is often a strong underlying social-capital element. If we ignore this, we are being partial or naïve.

Other chapters in this volume deal better with the problems in imposing solutions from outside when local commitment and ownership are lacking. We simply note that the issues are as important for industrialization as in other spheres. Within the industrial sphere also, "it is time that social groups and social capital be integrated in a broader, more complete framework of the understanding of development" (see Part 1, Chapter 1).

Concepts

The concept of social capital can be a powerful aid to development analysis. In simple terms, social capital comprises the ability of individuals in a group to form relationships of trust, cooperation and common purpose. For Putnam (1993), social capital is valuable because "a society that relies on generalized reciprocity is more efficient than a distrustful society," and its benefit lies in its ability to facilitate collective action. For Fukuyama (2000), the norms provided by social capital promote "cooperation between two or more individuals": in the economic sphere, this can reduce transaction costs, and in the political one it can promote the association necessary for the success of modern democracy. The World Bank's *World Development Report 2002* uses a concept very similar to that of social capital: "informal institutions."[2] Informal institutions comprise social norms or networks that supplement or supplant formal laws and institutions; where they work well, they can lower the costs and risks of economic transactions, improving information flows and spreading risks.

While the concept and uses of social capital originate in sociology, they can be complementary to economic analysis. The conventional economic approach to growth deals mainly with physical and human capital and technology. Even when it includes broader factors like economic capabilities, structures or policies, it neglects the *social* factors that allow these broader factors to be used effectively (see Part 1, Chapter 1). However, it is widely accepted that interactions between groups and social structures, on the one hand, and productive systems, groups and governments, on the other, are critical to economic performance. Countries with similar factor endowments and policies often perform very differently in economic terms because their modes of social and political interaction differ. Or, where policies differ, the transfer of best-practice policies from successful economies often fails because the social glue or commitment and ownership that makes them work in some cases is absent in others.

The presumption is that groups or countries with strong social capital are able to function better: Members interact more closely with each other, spend less effort on formal methods of enforcing contracts, reach greater consensus on common aims and are able to implement joint actions more efficiently. In economic terms, therefore, social capital can reduce transaction costs, facilitate information flows, lower risks, allow joint action (say, to realize externalities or offer insurance), and supplement formal contracts and property rights.

---

[2] On the distinction between formal and informal institutions, see Chapter 9 of the *World Development Report 2002* (World Bank, 2002). Formal institutions are "formal constructs of governments and modern organizations" (such as legal systems), while informal ones are "systems based on social norms or networks...[that] are a central means of facilitating market transactions" (p. 171). While there is a general trend from informal to formal institutions with economic development, informal institutions remain vital to the efficient functioning of formal institutions even in mature societies.

Social capital is valuable everywhere: Without it, the costs of many economic transactions would be prohibitive, even in countries with sophisticated institutions and legal systems (World Bank, 2002). However, its value is likely to be much greater in developing economies that lack such institutions and systems and are undergoing difficult economic, political and social transformations. Many of the mechanisms and structures needed to facilitate the transformation are absent. Since markets are not well developed, there is a need for policy measures to strengthen them—but the social capacity to mount such policies effectively is generally weak. Rapid technological changes, liberalization and globalization add to the stresses while reducing the shelter earlier offered by protection from world market forces. In these conditions, social capital can help countries or communities to cope better and facilitate more effective policy.

This need not imply that *all* forms of social capital are desirable. As analysts have noted, some forms of social capital can be discriminatory and harmful to those excluded from the group. Social capital may also be used to further antisocial objectives, as in fundamentalist religious organizations, or among terrorist and criminal groups. Traditional social values even in well-intentioned groups can hold back economic progress and modernization (World Bank, 2002, 174-6; Stiglitz, 1998). Social capital may be ineffective if groups grow beyond a certain size or try to pursue multiple objectives. The risk of negative effects of social capital in fact often leads analysts to regard it as less valuable than physical, human or technological capital (Fukuyama, 2000). Some economists also question the validity of social capital as an economic concept: It is almost impossible to measure and is generally not accumulated deliberately (by reducing consumption).

Many of these criticisms are valid. There *are* undesirable forms of social capital, and it *is* difficult to include it in the usual economic models. This does not, however, mean that the concept is not useful: The existence of "bad" social capital only strengthens the case for analysing how "good" social capital comes into being and how it can be created. Problems of measurement do not preclude qualitative analysis; many other important development issues share this problem. As Wagle (2001) notes, several writers have forcefully defended the economic validity of the social-capital concept.

Nevertheless, it is true that the concept of social capital remains vague and is used by authors in different ways. In its narrowest (and original) sense, it refers to the very microlevel. For instance, the Civic Practices Network defines it as the "stocks of social trust, norms and networks that people can draw upon to solve common problems...[at the level of] neighbourhood associations, sports clubs and cooperatives" (CPN, 2001). Putnam (1993) extended the scope of social capital to the role of individual connections that allowed more or less effective coordination and cooperation in regional governments. Woolcock (2000) extends it further, noting seven disparate fields where the concept is being applied, one of them being economic development. There is, however, a risk of stretching it to cover the entire institutional, cultural, political and social framework within which economies have to function.

It is not the purpose here to explore the semantics or theory of social capital. Accepting that the lines between social capital are strictly defined and the larger cultural or political settings are porous, we confine social capital to the norms that permit groups and networks (in civil society, enterprises, institutions and governments) to cooperate, share information, and formulate and act towards common objectives. We apply this concept of social capital to one important aspect of development—industrialization—and draw upon the experience of successful industrializing countries to illustrate the kinds of social capital that may be necessary.

Industrialization and Economic Transformation

Despite the recent hyperbole on the information age, structural and economic transformation in developing countries still depends vitally on industrialization. Historically, almost all societies that have developed have done so by moving from traditional low-productivity activities like agriculture or simple services to manufacturing and high-value services. Manufacturing has been the engine of the transformation process for several reasons: It allows greater scope for the continuous application of new technology; yields greater economies of scale, scope and learning; has more spillover effects; and is a major source of innovation and skill formation. It is also a powerful modernizing agent, changing work and entrepreneurial attitudes, creating new institutions and ownership forms, and raising the productivity of traditional activities. The information age is itself the outcome of technical progress in manufacturing. For poor societies, there seem to be few development alternatives to industrialization, at least for some time to come.

Before considering the social capital that industrial development requires, it would be useful to start with the changing setting for industrialization. Perhaps the most important feature is that, unlike a few decades ago, industry has to become internationally competitive if it is to survive and grow, and it must do so in the context of rapid, pervasive and continuous technological change. In the past, many governments—in the presently mature countries as well as in the dynamic newly industrializing economies—used such tools as protection, subsidies, procurement and the like to promote local industry. In the early days, high transport and communication costs (with large gaps in information and standards) also provided considerable "natural" protection.

The setting today is very different. Most governments are rapidly reducing interventions in trade, finance and investment. At the international level, this trend is strengthened by new rules of the game. Production is being integrated across national boundaries under common ownership or control—often at the hands of a relatively small number of large private companies—making it even more difficult to isolate economies from world market forces. Technological change is eroding natural protection. The end result of all this is that enterprises are exposed to global competition with an immediacy and intensity rarely seen before. Thus, competitiveness is essential.

Reaching best-practice competitive levels within firms involves much more than importing new technology in the form of equipment, designs or patents. Technical knowledge has large tacit elements that cannot be codified or embodied in these forms—the user of the new technology has to engage in a process of building new capabilities. This process is often long, costly, difficult and uncertain. It involves seeking new information, creating new skills, experimenting, devising new routines and making mistakes. Firms do not operate in the certain, clear world of neoclassical textbook economics, where there is perfect information (past, present and future), all markets are complete and efficient, and the job of the industrial enterprise is to maximize profits mechanistically. Instead, they struggle in a fuzzy world of incomplete information, deficient markets and constant uncertainty (Stiglitz, 1996). Their world is rife with externalities, and their learning processes are closely intertwined with those of other firms around them (and sometimes far away). A dense and rich information environment is increasingly the essence of industrial competitiveness.

Competitiveness also has stringent requirements at the national and regional level. Governments must provide the right framework conditions: security, good economic management, sound and enforceable legal and property rights, transparent and predictable policies, well-functioning institutions and an environment with low transaction costs. They must also mount trade, industrial and technological policies that lead firms to invest in building dynamic capabilities, and then support them in doing so. At the sectoral level, suppliers of inputs and infrastructure must meet international standards of cost, quality and delivery. Markets for labour, capital and information, along with their supporting institutions, must work reasonably efficiently. At the cluster level, there must emerge strong networks of enterprises willing to combine competition with appropriate collective action. This is the essence of what Michael Best (1990) calls the "new competition."

In the new competition, competitive industrial activity takes new forms. Low costs arising from the traditional advantages of developing countries (cheap, unskilled labour or natural resources) do matter, but are of diminishing importance. Inexorably, such things as innovation, flexibility, reliability, service and quality are becoming more critical. This is as true of developing as of industrial countries. The most successful developing countries are those that have been able to master and build upon new technologies, develop strong technological capabilities, and build efficient supply and information networks (Lall, 2001). The determinants of industrial success constitute a "national industrial learning system"[3] in that the main elements interact with each other in a systematic way. The system comprises the incentive framework (trade, industrial and technology policies, the macrosetting, legal system and so on), factor markets (including skills, finance and industrial linkages) and support institutions. A good learning system stimulates investments in competitive capabilities by firms, embedding them in a rich information environment and providing them the factors and institutional support they need. A weak learning system leads, by contrast, to poor capabilities that do not equip firms to face the competitive challenges of a globalizing economy.

---

[3] The concept is similar to that of "national innovation systems" used in developed countries (see Nelson, 1993). However, I prefer to use "national learning systems" to emphasize that developing countries are concerned with mastering and using existing technologies rather than with innovating on the frontier.

What does this mean for social capital? An industrial learning system able to cope with the new competition needs various forms of social capital not generally found in developing countries. Social capital, for instance, is needed for the ownership and effective implementation of new strategies and policies. It is also needed to create and operate new institutions, legal systems and property rights, and to facilitate closer interaction between major stakeholders (firms, employees, policy-makers and institutions). At the microlevel, it is needed to promote new modes of behaviour within firms and institutions (see below). The emergence of new forms of social capital must, in other words, match the development of new industrial capabilities.

Some of these new forms may well arise as a consequence of exposure to new economic incentives and information flows, but others may not. As with capabilities, policies and assistance may be necessary to create or foster new social norms and relationships. This may prove to be the most difficult part of effective development strategy: It is relatively easy to design or imitate good economic policies.[4] How well these policies work in practice is another matter entirely, and differences in social capital are certainly one major reason why the response to globalization has been so varied across the developing world.

Social-Capital Needs of Dynamic Industrial Learning Systems

An efficient and dynamic industrial learning system is one in which enterprises are able to access, absorb, master, adapt and deploy in production modern technologies, and, over time, develop innovative capabilities. Such a system is becoming the sine qua non of industrial success in all developing countries, and it needs social capital at every level. To illustrate, new forms of social norms and relationships are needed to:

- build the interactions that allow new, competitive industrial capabilities to be developed and deployed by firms;

- encourage new forms of entrepreneurship based on the use of new technologies and aimed at international competitiveness, particularly in small- and medium-sized enterprises (SMEs);

- strengthen networking, trust and information flows between firms in geographical clusters, value chains and global production systems, and to facilitate closer links between backward regions and activities in the mainstream;

- promote stronger supply and information linkages between large firms and SMEs, and in particular between local affiliates of multinational enterprises and local suppliers;

- strengthen institutions providing skills and financial, technological and marketing support to industrial enterprises, and intensify their linkages with

---

[4] The content of "good" development policies remains controversial, but this is not the main issue here: Practically all forms of sensible development policy—that is, apart from the extreme version of the *laissez-faire* doctrine—need new forms of social capital.

firms, again by building new capabilities (within institutions) and improving linkages and trust between them;

- strengthen international networks and links that allow developing country enterprises to link with global markets and technology suppliers, access foreign resources, and keep close tabs on the changing market and technical situation;

- improve corporate governance, competition systems and the legal systems within which modern industry functions;

- finance the costly and uncertain process of technology acquisition, mastery and development, and at higher levels to finance innovation;

- create government capabilities to manage industrial development; and

- link the government effectively to other stakeholders, create local ownership of policies and ensure flexible implementation.

FIGURE 1.5.1: FORMS OF SOCIAL CAPITAL NEEDED FOR INDUSTRIAL DEVELOPMENT

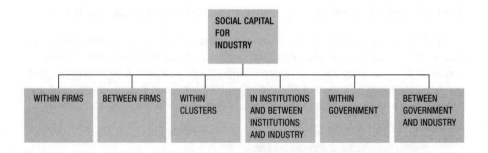

We can organize these new forms into the six categories shown in Figure 1.5.1.

Within firms: The new technological setting has significant effects on the way firms are managed and organized, and on how they create skills and work-systems. There are four main types of organizational change. The first change is work-teams. This approach "lies at the core of the new systems" (ILO, 1998, 42), and involves greater group responsibility, broader skills on the part of workers and frequent job rotation. The second change is involvement in off-line activities, such as problem-solving, quality improvement, health and safety. The third change is a flattening of organizational hierarchies, with greater responsibility by shop-floor workers and more intense information exchange. The fourth change is links to human resource policies. Work reorganization can only be successful if training and remuneration systems are changed to prepare and reward employees for the new responsibilities.

The use of new technologies, in particular information-based technologies, calls for more, better and newer kinds of skills (ILO, 1998, 39). The technological reasons for this are self-evident, but there are also organizational reasons. New skills and norms are entailed in setting up and working effectively with new work-production systems. For instance, skills have to be complemented with different attitudes to work, new occupational categories, new work relationships and new management systems.[5] All developed and successful developing countries are raising the skill profiles of their industrial workforces.

There are matching changes in management and organization. The need to facilitate information flows causes firms not just to introduce ICT, but also to cut management hierarchies and build new tools to handle information. On the shop floor, the use of new technologies requires not just new skills but also more continuous training, "multi-skilling," work-teams, close involvement of workers in quality and productivity improvement, and so on (ILO, 1998). Information technology is now pervasive in new work methods, plant layouts, process control, quality management, continuous improvement, lean production and "just-in-time" inventory systems. Other ICT applications include computer-aided design, manufacturing or engineering; manufacturing and enterprise resource planning; product data management; automation; robotics and flexible manufacturing systems. ICTs are being applied to the automation of design, manufacturing and coordination, and are changing the technology of the innovation process itself.

These new systems are not easy to set up and manage, particularly in developing countries. They need not only training and advanced infrastructure—which is demanding enough—but also new systems of contracting, greater trust and openness, and new forms of management-worker interaction (Mansell and Wehn, 1998). Information-sharing, networking and flexibility are the new weapons in the competitive armoury, with large potential benefits in terms of efficiency, innovation and flexibility. In many developing countries, inherited business cultures are not conducive to these practices. In those with a small base of modern industry and associated skills, new forms of management, organization and worker training are difficult to adopt, particularly in traditional small enterprises. In those with significant industrial sectors nurtured behind high protective barriers on Fordist methods of organization and family-dominated management, the change is also quite difficult. Confrontational union attitudes, traditional work divisions, and mistrust of new technologies and management can severely constrain the adoption of new organizational forms.

Between firms: Firms do not learn, innovate or build capabilities in isolation. They rely heavily on formal and informal interactions with each other. The new technological setting strengthens the role of networking and information flows between firms, within the same industry and vertically along the value chain. With greater concentration by firms on "core competencies," there is increased use of long-term supply

---

5 Thus, "the demand for professionals and technicians has increased in all countries, as their analytical, cognitive and behavioural skills equip them better to adapt to more sophisticated technology. However, even within these high-skilled jobs, the trend is increasingly towards multi-skilling—combining specialized professional expertise with business and management skills…. [Even for production workers,] the trend is towards up-skilling and multi-skilling. A study of 56,000 production workers over an eight-year period shows that skill requirements in production jobs have changed across the board. It is not only that each job has experienced up-skilling, but the overall distribution of production jobs has shifted away from the less skilled to the more skilled" (ILO, 1998, 47).

linkages with suppliers. With the accelerating pace of technological change and skill requirements, firms have to share information and resources to survive and compete. Even global corporations are contracting out what used to be internal functions, including R&D, to other firms.[6] Some are going the other way, specializing in R&D and marketing, leaving the entire manufacturing and logistics process to contractors. It is likely that industrial firms in developing countries will have to adopt similar organizational forms, both within their domestic sectors and within global value chains.

Vertical inter-industry relations have always involved dense networks of cooperation and trust, but the nature of networks has changed, and the intensity of interaction has increased, under new technological and competitive pressures. The growth of these organizational forms involves new (formal) contractual relationships, but such relationships can only work efficiently if there is a concomitant development of trust, information exchange, corporate governance and openness.

Within clusters: Another organizational change lies in the rising importance of geographical clustering, particularly of SMEs (Best, 1990; Humphrey and Schmitz, 1998). The benefits of clusters lie in external economies like access to information and personal interaction, or proximity to pools of skilled workers, specialized suppliers and customers. These economies tend to be cumulative and path-dependent, and can increase the competitive advantages of clusters over time if they are able to keep up with new technologies. Clusters can also attract new technological and skill resources from outside; thus, multinational companies now look for cluster economies in siting production and other activities abroad.

In recent years, the competitive success of industrial districts in "Third Italy," where groups of small firms became world leaders in products like clothing, footwear, leather products and engineering goods, has illustrated the strength of SME clusters. New high-tech clusters are spreading across the developed economies. Efficient clusters are also found in developing countries, and firms located within them have been found to be more competitive than those located outside. In the new competitive setting, however, effective clustering involves more than just being passively located in an agglomeration. It needs deliberate cooperation and joint action by cluster members to identify common problems and find and implement common solutions. This requires vision, trust, information-sharing and coherence, along with continuing competition: a very different form of social capital than what is found in traditional agglomerations in most developing countries.

---

[6] We can illustrate this with reference to innovation. The rising costs and risks of R&D and the pressures of competition are forcing even industry leaders to establish collaborative relations with other firms. "Large firms no longer 'make' all their innovations in-house, in large corporate laboratories, but increasingly 'buy' in order to keep abreast of the competition. There are several channels through which firms can gain access to the required knowledge.... [But] innovation surveys suggest that interfirm collaboration is generally the most important channel of knowledge-sharing and exchange" (OECD, 2000, 32). There are two main forms in which enterprises share in innovation. The first is with enterprises in the same value chain. The automobile industry is a good example: Major manufacturers involve first-tier suppliers in developing new models, expecting them to take on the full burden of designing and developing new components and sub-assemblies. The other important means of collaboration is between competitors, within and across countries. The rising costs and risks of innovation drive this trend (particularly in the basic, pre-commercial stages), with strategic alliances and consortia used with greater frequency. Thus, there were some 5,100 strategic alliances formed during 1990-98.

Clusters need not only comprise SMEs. They can be made up of large "lead" firms surrounded by key input and service providers of all sizes. Again, taking such linkages into the new realm of technological dynamism and competitive efficiency often needs closer relations and trust than what is found under old social and business norms. Where clusters are deliberately formed or strengthened by policy—say, in technology parks—there is a need for cooperation between governments, institutions like universities, or technology services and enterprises.

Without the base of norms, cooperation and trust that allow linkages and clusters to function effectively, the industrial economy loses greatly. Transaction costs between enterprises are higher, innovation lower and specialization constrained. Small size is a more severe constraint if SMEs cannot cooperate to realize external and scale economies jointly. Formal legal instruments and industrial infrastructure can provide the framework and setting for increased cooperation, but these are irrelevant if social capital does not evolve appropriately.

Institutions: Industrial development and capability-building needs interaction between enterprises, and between enterprises and support (or intermediary) institutions. These institutions fulfil a range of functions. They provide the public goods of industrial activity or innovation, like technical standards or basic R&D that private agents cannot profitably supply. They remedy deficiencies in markets, for instance, by providing information and technical assistance or common facilities to SMEs. They also plug specific gaps in markets, say by providing risk capital for technological activity where the private provision of venture capital is underdeveloped. They provide specialized facilities for industrial training, where economies of scale make it too expensive for firms to undertake particular training in-house. In some cases, institutions are responsible for spearheading innovation or coordinating R&D efforts among private enterprises.

One feature of the new technological setting in developed countries is the increasing interaction between firms and research, technology and training institutions. The outsourcing and specialization tendencies noted above also apply here. The changing nature of innovation and its growing science (as opposed to engineering) base make close linkages with science institutions (R&D laboratories and universities) imperative. The need for SMEs to keep up with rapid technological change makes it more important for them to interact with extension, R&D and service institutions. Rapidly evolving skill needs and the growing emphasis on continuous skill upgrading of employees makes it similarly important to link up with education and training institutions. And so on. Many institutions charge for their services, often at full market rates, as a result of pressures on government budgets.

This means four things. First, support institutions have to raise their skills, capabilities and facilities to meet new demands. Second, they have to be able to match their capabilities better to rapidly changing customer needs. Third, they have to win the trust and confidence of enterprises, particularly if they wish to charge for their services. Fourth, different institutions have to coordinate their respective services better to avoid duplication and meet overlapping demands more effectively. All developed countries have a large array of industry support institutions, which they are trying to reform and improve. This generally means instilling new values and management methods into the institutions, reorganizing them, merging them and sometimes privatizing them. The gradual nature of the reform—say, in the United Kingdom, where it has taken years to strengthen industry-university linkages—suggests that significant changes in values and attitudes are involved. Again, new forms of social capital are evidently needed to create effective institutional networks.

Most developing countries have adopted institutional forms from industrial countries. However, most industry-support institutions function far less effectively. As a forthcoming book by the present author and a colleague (Lall and Pietrobelli, 2002) shows for sub-Saharan Africa, many of these institutions are badly staffed and equipped, with inadequate equipment and few incentives to link to their clients. As a result, they perform their functions poorly, doing little to help industrial enterprises. The latter, in their turn, are unaware or distrustful of the institutions. Technical and economic deficiencies aside, there are also social-capital gaps that have to be overcome.

Within governments: The government has, as noted above, a critical role to play in building competitive industrial capabilities. As Malik argues (see Part 1, Chapter 1), the government has to set the right policies and have the capacity "to direct and manage these policies within a broader vision of societal transformation." Within the context of industrial development, the government also has to set a vision of the structure and orientation of industry. One vision may be to leave its evolution entirely to market forces, but this is certainly not the only available option. Other choices would be to specialize in resource-based or labour-intensive activities; to focus on technology-intensive activities within the context of multinational production systems; or to upgrade more autonomously, relying on domestic enterprises. These are not theoretical possibilities. As the dynamic economies of East Asia show, success can be achieved with all these different visions—but they need different sets of strategies and policies. Whichever vision is chosen, the government has to be firmly committed to industrial development; while this may sound banal and obvious, most developing country governments have not shown this commitment. One distinguishing feature of the "development state" in East Asia has been its clear, firm commitment to the overriding goal of efficient industrialization.

Once the vision is set, the government has to develop the capability to design appropriate policies and programmes to realize it. The vision must, in other words, be translated into achievable goals followed by concrete actions to achieve those goals, a complex organizational and learning process (Lall and Teubal, 1998). This involves collecting and analysing large amounts of information, within the economy and from other countries. It encompasses the process of deciding and setting priorities: Industrial priorities involve most other branches of government apart from the ministry directly concerned with industry. It also implies separating the executive and political parts of the government.

Once industrial priorities are set, factor markets and institutions have to be directed toward meeting the needs of these priorities. To the extent feasible, this also means changing the social-capital base to render new policies effective. The implementation of the policies may need new capabilities and attitudes within the bureaucracy; it also requires monitoring of progress and the ability to change policies as circumstances change. In fact, the ability to adapt policies and respond flexibly is probably more important than the ability to formulate complex plans and strategies.

Most governments lack the capabilities and social capital to make and implement industrial strategy. The political leadership and bureaucracy tend to be composed of different interests, making it difficult to arrive at a common vision or priorities. The formulation of policies cutting across traditional lines of authority may be hard, and the coordination and cooperation needed for continued implementation even harder. Monitoring, flexibility and the ability to learn from mistakes may be the hardest of all.

All this points to the need for capacities within the government to build coherence, coordination, independence and dedication. This can be seen as a specific and vital aspect of social capital.

Between government and industry: Effective industrial policy requires close coordination between the government and industry. The government must share its vision with the private sector, and win its understanding and support. It must collect accurate information on the needs, priorities and actions of the industrial sector to provide the right signals, incentives and support. Industry, for its part, must have clear information on government priorities and plans, and be assured of a voice in policy-making. Few governments in developing countries achieve this level of cohesion and stakeholder participation. It calls for considerable trust, sharing, honesty and dedication to a common purpose, all rather at odds with inherited structures of government and attitudes towards involving the private sector. The private sector similarly often lacks the internal cohesion to decide on national priorities and industrial priorities, and the trust and attitudes needed to coordinate with the government.

To conclude this section, we have used the concept of social capital broadly to illustrate the kinds of values, norms, attitudes and interactions that industrial transformation may require. The analysis is, of course, tentative and preliminary. It seeks to show that social relationships are relevant to industrialization, and that the compelling need to transform quickly the nature of industrial capabilities makes the consideration of these relationships more important and urgent. In brief, a strong base of social capital can offer the following benefits to industry: efficiency, specialization, innovation, flexibility, realization of clustering and scope benefits, stronger institutional support, lower risk and more effective policy direction and support.

Some Lessons from East Asia

The mature Tiger economies of East Asia, in particular Singapore, Korea and Taiwan, are rightly held up as best practices in industrial development policy. Starting with few

advantages, they have achieved world-class levels of industrialization in one generation. More impressive than their rates of growth, however, is the *quality* of their
industrial development. Their industrial sectors, while quite different from each other
in many ways, display enviable depth, innovation and flexibility. Despite differences in
strategy and vision, they are based on a strong human-capital and institutional base.
All the indications are that they have the capabilities to sustain high levels of income
and competitiveness in the future (Lall, 2001).

The above discussion would lead us to expect that these economies had, or
developed, the kinds of social capital needed to achieve this massive and rapid structural and technological transformation. It is difficult to test this proposition
empirically, since there is no meaningful way to measure social capital at the national
level. The extensive literature on East Asian industrial policy has focused on the economic tools employed, and the business systems and political economy that lay
behind the policy.[7] It has not, to my knowledge, addressed social capital explicitly,
though many of the writings touch on particular aspects. In general, the issue is
whether the social capital needed at various levels was present in the society or inherent to the culture (the Confucian ethic), or if it grew under force of circumstance or
because of government policies. If the former is true, the replicability of the East Asian
experience is correspondingly difficult; if the latter is the case, replication is more feasible, assuming the policy and economic conditions can be imitated.

The greatest gap in knowledge is probably at the microlevel. We know relatively
little of the social-capital base of enterprises, their management and organization,
labour attitudes and so on. The outcome in terms of performance clearly suggests that
they have been very efficient in accessing, mastering and using new technologies, and
over time in innovating products and processes.[8] The social mobility engendered by
massive shifts (e.g., the break-up of Korea after the Korean war, the move of mainland
Chinese to Taiwan as its rulers) allowed for an efflorescence of entrepreneurship. The
removal of strong land-owning classes and a good base of primary education led to a
relatively equitable pattern of development and a broader social commitment to
national development. All these factors may have contributed to a more disciplined,
willing and trainable labour force receptive to new technologies. At the same time,
labour legislation and practice were repressive, giving considerable power to the employ-
ers and allowing a very strong hierarchical set of relationships. We do not know enough
about how these relationships are changing as labour relations become more balanced
and the emphasis shifts to flexibility, use of ICTs and modern management techniques.

Korea and Taiwan deliberately fostered local inter-firm and inter-industry relations
from the early stages of industrial policy; in Singapore, the creation of local linkages
by multinational corporations came later. The emphasis on autonomous industrial
development in the first two Tigers led to a strong emphasis on local procurement of

---

[7] See, for a small sample: Amsden (1989), Ashton et al. (1999), Cheng et al. (1999), Evans (1999), Jones
and Sakong (1980), Lall (1996), Stiglitz (1996), Wade (1990), Westphal (2002), Whitley (1992) and the
World Bank (1993).
[8] Singapore is the exception here because the major source of management practices and technology
lay outside the economy, in the parents of the multinational corporations that dominated the industrial economy. However, foreign affiliates were able to deploy new technologies so efficiently presumably
because of the social capital embodied in the local labour force.

inputs and the diffusion of technology to local firms. The Korean reliance on giant conglomerates initially penalized the development of SME suppliers, offset later by a
deliberate effort to promote SMEs. Korean SMEs are today fairly strong in technological terms, and the *chaebol,* or business conglomerates, are committed to their
development. In Taiwan, SMEs were always in the vanguard of industrial growth and
exports, and they formed strong information networks to overcome the handicaps
imposed by small size. They also had strong networks with Chinese entrepreneurs and
engineers in the United States. Close links with overseas buyers and trading companies were another source of knowledge transfer. The evidence suggests that social
norms and attitudes were conducive to intense networking, with considerable collective learning taking place in both countries.

The government promoted the development of competitive industrial clusters in
all three economies. Each undertook a battery of measures to ensure that new technologies were made available to enterprises on terms that enabled the development
of local capabilities (Mathews and Cho, 1999, describe this for the semiconductor
industry). Singapore's recent industrial plans have been explicitly based on clusters,
identifying dynamic clusters for promotion and striving to fill gaps in the value chain
to strengthen and deepen their competitiveness. Korea and Taiwan developed their
industries, using protection, subsidization and other tools of policy (Amsden, 1989;
and Wade, 1990) along cluster lines to take advantage of economies of scope and
agglomeration. Both set up industrial and technology parks and cities. Both had
strong industry associations able to act in the competitive interests of their members;
set up supporting technology and training centres; and represent their members in
government bodies. The Taiwanese Government set up several innovation groups
(called R&D consortia) where advanced technologies were absorbed and developed
by groups comprising firms, technology institutions, trade associations and the
Government (Mathews, 2001).

This is all well known. What is difficult to decipher from the evidence is whether the
social capital necessary to form clusters, associations and the like was present *before* the
policies were launched or if it developed later in response. The likely answer is a bit of
both, but we need more evidence before we can pronounce this with any certainty.

Institutions supporting industry are strong in the Tigers. Each country has the full
complement of technology infrastructure institutions, extension services, linkage
promotion bodies, export marketing agencies, training centres and financing schemes
for innovation. For instance, Korea has a massive programme for promoting technological activity in the national interest by the chaebol and other firms.[9] Taiwan has one

---

9 The Designated R&D Programme has, since 1982, supported private firms undertaking research in
core strategic technology development projects in industrial areas approved by the Ministry of Science
and Technology. It funded up to 50 per cent of R&D costs for large firms and up to 80 per cent for SMEs.
Between 1982 and 1993, the programme funded 2,412 projects, which employed around 25,000
researchers at a total cost of around US $2 billion, of which the Government contributed 58 per cent.
This resulted in 1,384 patent applications, 675 commercialized products and $33 million in direct
exports related to know-how. Its indirect contribution in terms of training researchers and enhancing
enterprise research capabilities was much larger. The value of grants under the programme in 1994 was
$186 million, of which 42 per cent was directed at high-technology products like new speciality chem-
icals. The Industrial Technology Development Programme was started in 1987 to subsidize up to
two-thirds of the R&D costs of joint projects of national interest (National Research Projects) between

of the most comprehensive and effective programmes for SME technology support anywhere (Lall, 1996, chapter 3). Singapore has a superlative industrial training system. Each country has excellent ICT infrastructure. Each has created massive amounts of human capital, gearing education to the specific needs of industrial policy rather than simply overcoming generic failures in education markets (Ashton et al., 1999).

While there are certainly deficiencies, and the nature of social norms evolved over time as institutions became more effective, in general these countries succeeded in building strong support systems and linking them with enterprises. Again, we cannot say for sure if the social capital involved in institutional development in the Tigers was present before government initiatives were undertaken, and before industry grew and competed in international markets, or if it developed concomitantly.

Most academic attention has focused on government capabilities to formulate and implement risky and innovative selective interventions in these Tigers without being waylaid by sectional interests or massive rent-seeking. The political economy features of the development state in Korea and Taiwan are well studied: leadership committed to competitive industrial development, a broad education base, equitable income and land distribution, and the absence of strong rural groups. The special nature of the bureaucracy—with its strong skill base, competence and remuneration; relative insulation from politics; pragmatism; speed of reaction to change and harmony of interest with business—has been analysed extensively.[10] There was an early tendency to focus power in the executive branch of government. At the same time, policy vision, coherence, coordination and flexibility were achieved by a difficult process of experimenting, making mistakes, changing and learning. The specific institutional measures adopted were important: the Economic Development Board in Singapore, the Economic Development Bureau in Taiwan and the Economic Planning Board in Korea, for instance, acted as focal points to form policy.[11] There may have been strong social-capital elements underlying all these efforts, but clearly there was nothing inherent that sprang out ready-made to guide government policy.

Evans (1999) makes the strong point that the "myth of the super bureaucracy" in the Tigers can create undue pessimism in other developing countries concerning the replicability of their development strategies. He believes that there are practical lessons to be drawn from the Tigers for all economics. After describing the difficulties they

---

private firms and research institutes. Between 1987 and 1993, this programme sponsored 1,426 projects at the cost of $1.1 billion, of which the subsidy element from the Government was 41 per cent. In 1994, the programme gave grants of $180 million, with 31 per cent going to high-technology products. This marked a significant increase from $69 million in 1990. The Highly Advanced National Project (HAN) was launched in 1992 to support two activities: the development of specific high-technology products in which Korea could become competitive with advanced industrial countries in a decade or two (the Product Technology Development Project), and the development of "core" technologies considered essential for the economy and in which Korea wanted to achieve an independent innovative base (the Fundamental Technology Development Project). So far, 11 HAN projects have been selected, and during 1992-94 the Government provided $350 million in subsidies to them. In this brief period, the programme resulted in 1,634 patent applications and 298 registrations. See Chapter 3 of Lall (1996).

[10] One of the best analyses of Korea remains that of Jones and Sakong (1980) and of Taiwan that of Wade (1990). For an excellent comparative analysis see Evans (1999).

[11] However, Cheng et al. (1999) remark on the fluidity of the administrative structure in Taiwan that deals with industry; several different organizations are concerned with industrial promotion. In Korea, the military Government favoured much greater centralization.

faced in building their government apparatuses, he concludes that all governments have "something to build on" if they start modestly and focus their efforts on the most important tasks at hand (p. 80). They can clearly learn from the procedures and forms adopted in East Asia, where progress was also often hesitant. However, he does not underestimate the difficulties involved in countries with massive income inequalities, non-development–minded elites and the limitations imposed by the new rules of the game.

In terms of the present analysis, the evident conclusion is that certain elements of social capital *can* be fostered by policy and do not have to be present before strategies are launched. Moreover, of the important preconditions of East Asian success—equity, education, leadership commitment, bureaucratic independence and so on—some seem to be predominantly economic or political in nature. What is not clear is that they also contain social-capital requirements. Does the achievement of greater equity, the popular desire to invest in education, or the isolation of the bureaucracy from political forces reveal underlying social norms? Can the government coordinate well with business only where certain forms of personal interaction are well established? Or can we simply ignore the social aspects altogether on the assumption that they will fall in line once the economic and political conditions are in place? If not, which social norms and relationships are the really crucial ones, and what affects their development?

We do not yet know. And until we find out, we cannot really draw policy conclusions from East Asia (or on industrial development more generally). It is frustrating for a development economist to say this after working so long on industrial and technology policy, but there we are.

References

Amsden, A. 1989. *Asia's New Giant.* Oxford: Oxford University Press.

Ashton, D., F. Green, D. James, and J. Sung. 1999. *Education and Training for Development in East Asia.* London: Routledge.

Best, M. 1990. *The New Competition: Institutions of Industrial Restructuring.* Cambridge: Polity Press.

Cheng, T-J, S. Haggard, and D. Kang. 1999. "Institutions and Growth in Korea and Taiwan: the Bureaucracy." In *East Asian Development: New Perspectives,* edited by Y. Akyuz, 87-111. London: Cass.

Civic Practices Network. 2001. "Social Capital." (www.cpn.organization/sections/models/.)

Evans, P. 1999. "Transferable Lessons? Re-examining the Institutional Prerequisites for East Asian Economic Policies." In *East Asian Development: New Perspectives,* edited by Y. Akyuz, 66-86. London: Frank Cass.

Fukuyama, F. 2000. "Social Capital and Civil Society." An International Monetary Fund working paper, WP/00/74. Washington, DC: International Monetary Fund.

Humphrey, J., and H. Schmitz. 1998. "Trust and Inter-Firm Relations in Developing and Transition Economies." *Journal of Development Studies,* 34(4), 32-61.

International Labour Office (ILO). 1998. *World Employment Report 1998-99.* Geneva.

Jones, L. P., and I. Sakong. 1980. *Government, Business and Entrepreneurship in Economic Development: the Korean Case.* Cambridge: Harvard University Press.

Lall, S. 1996. *Learning from the Asian Tigers.* London: Macmillan.

———. 2001. *Competitiveness, Technology and Skills.* Cheltenham: Edward Elgar.

Lall, S., and C. Pietrobelli. 2002. *Failing to Compete: Technology Development and Technology Systems in Africa.* Cheltenham: Edward Elgar.

Lall, S., and M. Teubal. 1998. "Market Stimulating Technology Policies in Developing Countries: A Framework with Examples from East Asia." *World Development,* 26(8), 1369-1386.

Mansell, R., and U. Wehn. 1998. *Knowledge Societies: Information Technology for Sustainable Development.* Oxford: Oxford University Press, for the United Nations Commission on Science and Technology for Development.

Mathews, J. 2001. "The Origins and Dynamics of Taiwan's R&D Consortia." *Research Policy,* 30, 1-20.

Mathews, J., and D. S. Cho. 1999. *Tiger Technology: The Creation of a Semiconductor Industry in East Asia.* Cambridge: Cambridge University Press.

Nelson, R. R., ed. 1993. *National Innovation Systems: A Comparative Analysis.* Oxford: Oxford University Press.

Organisation for Economic Co-operation and Development (OECD). 2000. *A New Economy? The Changing Role of Innovation and Information Technology in Growth.* Paris.

Putnam, R. 1993. *Making Democracy Work: Civic Traditions in Modern Italy.* Princeton: Princeton University Press.

Stiglitz, J. E. 1996. "Some Lessons from the East Asian Miracle." *The World Bank Research Observer,* 11(2), 151-177.

———. 1998. "Toward a New Paradigm for Development: Strategies, Policies and Processes." Prebisch Lecture. Geneva: United Nations Conference on Trade and Development (UNCTAD). Reprinted in *The Rebel Within: Joseph Stiglitz and the World Bank,* edited by Ha-Joon Chang, 2001, 57-93. London: Anthem World Economics.

United Nations Industrial Development Organisation (UNIDO). 2002. *World Industrial Development Report 2002.* Vienna.

Wade, R. 1990. *Governing the Market: Economic Theory and the Role of Government in East Asian Industrialization.* Princeton: Princeton University Press.

Waglé, S. 2001. "Social Capital and Development: A Survey." A draft paper.

Westphal, L. E. 2002. "Technology Strategies for Economic Development in a Fast Changing Global Economy." *Economics of Innovation and New Technology* (forthcoming).

Whitley, R. 1992. *Business Systems in East Asia: Firms, Markets and Societies.* London: Sage.

Woolcock, M. 1998. "Social Capital and Economic Development: Toward a Theoretical Synthesis and Policy Framework." *Theory and Society,* 27, 151-208.

———. 2000. "The Place of Social Capital in Understanding Social and Economic Outcomes." *Canadian Journal of Policy Research,* 2(1), 11-17.

World Bank. 1993. *The East Asian Miracle.* Oxford: Oxford University Press.

World Bank. 2002. *World Development Report 2002: Building Institutions for Markets.* Oxford: Oxford University Press.

2 *ownership*

2.1 SHOULD WE MIND THE GAP?

CARLOS LOPES

Humanity now lives in a world of opulence that was unimaginable just one century ago. We have finally reached a stage where we can potentially live without hunger, control major diseases and harmonize our relationship with nature. Technical and scientific knowledge allow all major material problems to be solved. It is also a world that seems to generate wide consensus on economic solutions, political models and central priorities. Unfortunately, the appearances are deceiving. Other realities continue to mar the landscape, such as the remarkable endurance of oppression, constant violations of human rights, and unacceptable levels of deprivation and destitution.

Central to this contradiction is the accumulation model we have constructed for the reproduction of our societies, which relies on ever-increasing acquisition and growth. It is a model capable of producing enormous polarization and lost opportunities, particularly for those who are at the bottom of the pile. It is therefore not astonishing that now, more than ever before, the development equation is closely associated with the fight to reduce, and eventually eliminate, poverty. It is a moment to be sober and not prematurely triumphant. We stand in the crossroads, with the choice of reforming our systems and creating better responses for the challenges ahead.

Amartya Sen identifies expansion of freedom as the cornerstone of this transformation, "the primary end and the principal means of development." He says, "Development consists of the removal of various types of unfreedoms that leave people with little choice and little opportunity of exercising their reasoned agency"(Sen, 1999). It is the struggle to help remove these barriers that is central to human development. But to be effective in pursuing such a cause, it is necessary to question the systems, processes and instruments that have guided the development practice. No other area could benefit more from such a move than technical cooperation and capacity development.

The Pursuit of Happiness

In an increasingly globalized world, one common belief is that new possibilities, such as changing lifestyles and expanding horizons, will lead to happiness. The flip side of such opportunities may be the loss of social norms, value systems and rules, and changing expectations. The more humanity faces these trade-offs, the more we realize happiness is relative and an ever-shifting goal.

Social ties and networks mold many of our values and expectations. Many of our measurements of success only have meaning in comparison to others. For example, we all want to improve our lot, and consider that we have successfully done so when our children live in comparatively better conditions than we do. Similarly, being well off, for many, only has meaning when compared to the situation of others in the same social group—even after achieving enormous personal ambitions.

Social linkages also contribute to our sense of achievement. We know that a safe and happy life cannot be attained without various chains of solidarity, and it is seldom possible to achieve enormous progress without help. Recognition by others also may play a key role in the sense of self-realization and satisfaction. As humans, we are thus tightly interlinked with each other—even in the most individualistic societies—and many of our ambitions and successes are assessed in relation to others.

But there is one common thought that permeates most sensible analysis: Even when relative differences are taken into account, there is an absolute gap between the haves and have-nots, between rich and poor, between safe and unsafe societies.

At its inception, development aid was supposed to address this gap, particularly in skills and capital. The assumption was that for a period of time there would be a need for external input, and then it would become possible for countries to take care of themselves. Development aid was thus viewed in much the same way as raising children—poor countries would be provided with skills and support structures until they could start their independent lives.

This simple and candid analysis is in fact quite problematic. First, it appears to be based on the artificial idea that "development" is attainable by all, as if it were a linear process. In actual fact, the modern global system requires unequal access to resources in order for it to function. Under the current economic construct, development is not attainable by all—indeed, the lack of development by some is beneficial to others. Second, as we well know, the tendency to want to choose for our "children" what is best for them can easily be translated into a patronizing donor-recipient relationship. Third, nobody ever imagined sustainability was such a hard rock to sculpt.

Given the above, it is not surprising to find strong views against the benefits of development in general, and technical cooperation in particular. In his provocative pamphlet *Lords of Poverty*, Hancock argues for the end to the betrayal of public trust that the magnitude and generosity of the world's wealthy nations has generated through development aid. He considers that an "aristocracy of mercy" has devised a smoke screen that does not allow a culture of accountability to prevail (Hancock, 1989).

The fact that most of Hancock's facts are inaccurate, hearsay or personal anecdotes is irrelevant. His ideas are shared by many. In fact, his conclusions are remarkably similar to those of a great number of African scholars (Kankwenda, 2000)—who are supposed to crystallize the thinking of the most-affected recipients. Although for reasons almost opposite to Hancock's, they too believe in the mischievous effects of development aid: It creates dependency rather than sustainability; it has never generated real development; it has pervasive effects on capacity development; and it has contributed to the destruction of social capital.

A more sophisticated analysis of these issues underlines the fact that the economic models that serve as the basis for development aid interventions call for any possible surplus to be used as a payback dividend, rather than for it to be reinvested into development.

What was, therefore, the purpose of those who founded this approach?

It is helpful to recall the postwar context, which was dominated by growth theories of development (Rodenstein-Rodon, Harrod-Domar and others) leading up to the highly influential Rostow. The 1950s and 1960s were dominated by rather simplistic thinking that all development followed a similar pattern. The less developed were simply at a Rostow "stage" further back (Browne, 1999, 19-20).

From the genesis of modern development, the link between development and technical cooperation was established by President Truman's Point Four proposal (see Box 2.1.1). The fate of both was forever married to a specific understanding of the purpose of their existence: to fill a gap. In the words of President Truman, the purpose of Point Four was to use the advances of science and industrial progress to meet the growth requirements of poor nations, because their poverty was a handicap. In this way, the "human family would be able to enjoy a decent and satisfactory life" that would allow "freedom and personal happiness."

Five decades later, Hancock had this to say: "While it would be convenient to believe that the decision to launch large-scale aid programmes was the product of clear and uniform thinking on the part of the industrialized nations in the postwar era, the truth is otherwise. From the outset a number of quite different motivations were at

BOX 2.1.1: President Truman's Point Four programme

The first worldwide programme for technical assistance to developing countries came with US President Harry Truman's Point Four programme, which called for the American people to share their knowledge and technology with the developing countries.

President Truman spoke the common tongue of the American people and brought to office the values of the common man. In his experiences — ranging from small-town life and unsuccessful farming to the battlefields of World War I, from financial failure after the war to big-city politics and the revolutionary years of the New Deal in Washington — he had taken part in a great chronicle of American life. Although Truman did not attend college, he had an everlasting passion for knowledge, impressing his White House aides (educated in boarding schools and prestigious colleges) with his broad knowledge of history. His passion and high esteem for knowledge was expressed in a speech in September 1948, when he urged the US Congress to create the National Science Foundation, adding that "when more of the peoples of the world have learned the ways of thought of the scientist, we shall have better reason to expect lasting peace and a fuller life for all."

During his Presidency, Truman developed a larger role for the United States in world affairs than ever before. At the end of World War II, he had assumed command of the most powerful industrial nation on earth. It was a time of stunning advances in science and technology. With the premature death of Franklin Delano Roosevelt (only a few months after his fourth inauguration), Truman had become the "accidental" President. Later elected on his own right in 1948, Truman wanted his inaugural address to be a democratic manifesto directed at the peoples of the world, not just the American people. Prior to the inauguration, he had contributed to the unconditional surrender of Germany, the establishment of the United Nations, the launching of the Marshall Plan and the creation of the North Atlantic Treaty Organization (NATO). Not surprisingly, the first three points of his inaugural speech in January 1949 espoused the United Nations, the Marshal Plan and NATO. What caught everyone by surprise and grabbed attention, however, was his Point Four, which called for making American scientific advances and industrial progress available for the improvement of underdeveloped countries:

> "For the first time in history, humanity possesses the knowledge and the skill to relieve the suffering of these people. The United States is pre-eminent among nations in the development of industrial and scientific techniques. The material resources which we can afford to use for the assistance of other peoples are limited. But our imponderable resources in technical knowledge are constantly growing and are inexhaustible. I believe that we should make available to peace-loving peoples the benefits of our store of technical knowledge in order to help them realize their aspirations for a better life. And, in cooperation with other nations, we should foster capital investment in areas needing development."[1]

The idea behind Point Four had been initially suggested to the State Department by Benjamin H. Hardy, a public-affairs officer stationed in Brazil, representing the Office of the Coordinator of Inter-American Affairs. As a young reporter for the *Atlanta Journal*, he had seen how new technologies, introduced by Roosevelt's New Deal programme, had benefited poor areas in his native rural Georgia. He thought that American technology could do the same in places like Brazil. He proposed a global programme of technical cooperation with what were then known as the "underdeveloped" countries. His idea, however, was dismissed at the higher levels of the organization, only to be pulled from the discarded file when Truman complained that the first three proposals for new government policy were too timid to satisfy his desire for something more dramatic. President Truman warmly embraced the idea, and made assistance to poorer countries the fourth point of his democratic manifesto to the world, which can be seen as an extension, from the national level to the international arena, of his predecessor's New Deal.

After Truman's Point Four proposal, the Secretary-General of the United Nations immediately called together a working party of top officials from the specialized agencies to lay down a plan for the United Nations organizations to offer their contributions. The Expanded Programme of Technical Assistance (EPTA), the predecessor of UNDP, was formally established later that year by the Economic and Social Council (ECOSOC resolution 222 [IX] of 14 and 15 August 1949) and the General Assembly (resolution 30 [IV] of 16 November). UN resolution 200, which had been adopted on 4 December 1948, had focused on the underdeveloped countries' technological "backwardness" and had called for the organization of international teams of experts for the purpose of advising developing countries in connection with their economic development programmes.

---

[1] Inaugural Addresses of the Presidents of the United States, 1989.

work—and at work side by side. The result, today, is that the collective psychology of aid-giving is schizophrenic, shot through with contradictory urges and rationalizations, some of which are benign, some sinister and others just plain neurotic" (Hancock, 1989).

So much for the pursuit of happiness.

Clarifying Meanings

Part of the conceptual confusion about technical cooperation and capacity development is the result of the lack of clarity accompanying many debates on development. These debates routinely involve concepts that seem well known enough to be used in discussion without ever being defined. This common refusal—or even inability—firmly to pin down what many concepts mean has increased the general fuzziness of the debate, and has contributed to the confused nature of many development interventions. For example, although seized by many as central to the global political economy, "development economics" is still a marginalized discipline. Moreover, non-economic dimensions of development receive even less attention. This is partly due to the wrong historical link made between development and decolonization on one hand, and the focus on issues of particular interest to the developed countries—such as debt reimbursement, trade liberalization, environmental sustainability—on the other. These two preconceived ideas give the impression to many that development is about the countries that have not made it, when in fact it concerns us all.

Francois Partant (1982) proclaimed in the 1980s not the end of history,[2] but the end of development. His assumption was that the Western world was fast approaching a new understanding of its evolution. This particular view is an economic approach to evolution—it seeks to make optimal use of available resources without restraint or concern for the future.

Being naturally anthropocentric, this understanding places the human being at the top of a hierarchical distribution of roles. The environment, for example, is used for humanity's well being. Environmental regeneration thus becomes a hostage of economic productivity.

This linear approach presupposes that all societies aspire to make the best use of resources (which is economical); therefore, all societies aspire to be as capable as the most advanced ones. All societies should evolve to attain that same peak and move in one direction using a common historic route. This view also emphasizes that individuals are different, and it is normal to have inequalities and different capabilities. These differences are used to explain the different stages of development in which countries find themselves. If we backtrack a bit to the colonial period, we will find the same arguments presented in a slightly cruder version. Partant believed the contradictions of this view—including its unsustainability—had become so apparent by the 1980s that "development," as then conceived, was "dead."

---

[2] Referring to the well-known book by Francis Fukuyama.

As we know, metaphors don't always do the trick, and 20 years later we continue to debate the meanings that have created such diverse opinions.

In the 1990s, the *Human Development Reports* (HDRs) of the United Nations Development Programme (UNDP) represented a welcome shift when they put the emphasis on human capabilities and the expansion of choices as a better clarification of the development paradigm. From unquestionable end, development is now at the centre stage of harsh scrutiny. So is development aid. From the cold-war, crude rationale of "no questions asked," we are moving towards a focus on effectiveness and results. And central to the debate is the issue of how linear development is and how much room should be given to the actors of a particular society to exercise their choices in total freedom. From a technical origin, we have added a political dimension to development.[3]

Capacity Development and Ownership

In a recent book, William Easterly (2001) examines different economic models that did not lead to growth when their theories were actually applied in developing countries. Easterly also criticizes mainstream views on technological changes, education explosion and population control as the catalysts of growth. Despite some cases of success, structural adjustment, along with debt forgiveness, wasn't successful either, he argues. He finds that these failed panaceas for growth during the last five decades lacked sufficient understanding in actual application and practicality in the developing countries, and failed to offer the right incentives for the actors involved.

Easterly argues that these previous models and projects did not work because "the formulas did not take heed of the basic principle of economics: people respond to incentives." He explains that if incentives are right, growth occurs. In examining such incentives, he does not fully advocate for a free-market system, but emphasizes the importance of governmental intervention that does not discourage free-market elements and also creates various incentives for markets. He argues that especially in poor countries, interventions that provide knowledge, skills, education and technology are crucial for long-term growth, claiming that such elements of growth, otherwise unregulated, tend to concentrate where they already exist, thus making the rich get richer and the poor, poorer. Easterly also warns that government corruption "kills" growth by taking away incentives.

If there is little agreement on development economics, there is even less on capacity *development,* or capacity *for* development. It has been associated with individual capacity, organizational development, managerial capacity and institution building. The following pages focus on some key aspects that pertain to the relationship between ownership and capacity.

Development specialists nowadays resemble management consultants in that they tend to look at issues of capacity with the lens used by management theories. Economic vocabulary has been replaced by a pretense of management neutral

---

[3] This was already covered in the Hammarskjold Foundation Report *What Now?* (1975).

terminology, with direct references to increased efficiency, effectiveness, entrepreneurial creativity, client satisfaction and results-based management.

This change calls for a new view of capacity needs. But rather than overhauling their way of operating or redefining the contents of their programmes, most institutions dealing with capacity development have opted for a shortcut: better packaging for existing instruments in order to make them more suitable for a participatory approach. Obstacles in the way of change are rooted in personal and institutional inertia, as well as in issues of control, risk-aversion, extra workload, staff constraints, vested interests and power. Entrenched practices favour top-down, short-term development targets, while the incentive system disempowers and frustrates front-line field workers (Chambers, 2001).

Management consultants have proposed decentralized structures—which reflect global political and economic developments—with wider access to information. The assumption is that these new structures necessitate more vigorous beneficiary involvement in programme design and implementation. "A recognition that there is more to development than just economic productivity leads to a focus on processes as well as on products—on building institutional capacity and more effective dialogue between donors and recipients through the elaboration of methodologies such as participatory appraisal and evaluation" (Marsden, 1994).

Because there is a difficulty in finding a correlation between aid flows and economic growth, there is an increasing sense that greater focus on aid effectiveness is preferable to increased financial flows. This view not only provides justification for the sharp decline of aid flows, but also seeks to rationalize attempts to do more with less. In this context, there is a drive for setting targets as a tool for extracting value.

Targets per se are striped of meaning. The blind drive to meet them—ignorant to the thinking behind them and indiscriminate to the methods used to reach them—creates perverse incentives and distorted priorities that often lead to counteractive results. For example, in Britain, the target of reducing hospital waiting time led to the paradoxical shift in priorities towards considering minor disorders before major serious illnesses because the former can be dealt with more swiftly.[4]

There is a new emphasis on national ownership and indigenous processes as well. The proposals in UNDP's *Rethinking Technical Cooperation* (Berg and UNDP, 1993) introduced a systemic menu to deal with capacity from this perspective. But the conceptual challenge remains almost intact: What is meant by initiatives becoming national and promoting indigenous approaches?

The application of these concepts has been, in fact, extremely narrow in ambition. Donor concessions have been limited to the extent that national and indigenous approaches do not question the parameters that define mainstream views of what development is supposed to do and achieve. These elements are often defined by people other than the recipients of capacity-development initiatives.

---

4 "Missing the Point." *The Economist.* 28 April 2001.

It remains unclear how increased ownership—through national and indigenous approaches that are defined by new mainstream views—addresses the capacity issue, the new possible role of technical cooperation, and, more bluntly, the gap theory fundamentals. In other words, there is a need for unbundling the concept of ownership, from rhetoric to reality.

Empower without Power?

Empowerment is the central piece of any participatory manual. Empowerment literature goes back to Paulo Freire's alphabetization methods and the experience of rural appraisal systems. It is human-centred and strongly advocates for dialogue as a precondition for learning. From modest beginnings, this approach has since traveled quite far. It is now used as a mantra to demonstrate a cocktail of grassroots, community-based, civil society and social action initiatives. It has also been adopted by donor aid agencies at the highest level, such as the Organisation for Economic Co-operation and Development's Development Assistance Committee (OECD/DAC). Both the UN system and the World Bank have extensively used empowerment key words, if not the concepts themselves. It is therefore important to review, although admittedly too briefly, the implications of empowerment for capacity development.

There is a strong case for a close link between empowerment and ownership. Both concepts are rooted in the need for the recipients to be at the heart of the development process. The common sense interpretation for both, however, is hard to distinguish. At the centre of empowerment theories is the issue of values, equally present in the definitions of social capital and ownership. The purpose of empowerment is the expansion of choices and possibilities, the core of human development. Empowerment is about increasing capabilities. "Basic empowerment depends on the expansion of people's capabilities—expansion that involves an enlargement of choices and thus an increase in freedom" (UNDP, HDR 1990). The capability dimension is not only valuable in and of itself; it is also an important part of ownership. Participation is necessary for the development of capabilities. Participation, from the human development perspective, is both a means and an end (see Box 2.1.2).

As the word reveals, empowerment is about power. Perhaps because of this, its message has been limited to or associated with the grassroots, community and local governance level. To use empowerment at a national or macropolitical level would have been more controversial and potentially could have cut to the heart of highly sensitive power-related issues.

We can analyse empowerment from three angles: individual; local and community level; and state level.

Individual power and empowerment is the most familiar angle. It influences development practice quite substantially, given the fact that most of the transactions between individuals lack a clear accountability framework. Too much is left to interpretation. In the traditional donor-recipient approach, which produced the

BOX 2.1.2: "Capability" as defined in the Human Development Reports

When the HDRs first introduced the concept of capability in 1990, it was groundbreaking in that the concept provided a different lens by which to measure development. In the years since then, the HDRs have commented extensively on this issue:

"(A) society's standard of living should be judged not by the average level of income, but by people's capabilities to lead the lives they value. Nor should commodities be valued in their own right—they should instead be seen as ways of enhancing such capabilities as health, knowledge, self-respect and the ability to participate in community life" (UNDP, HDR 1996).

"In the capability concept the focus is on the functionings that a person can or cannot achieve, given the opportunities he or she has. Functionings refer to the various things a person can do or be, such as living long, being healthy, being well nourished, mixing well with others in the community and so on.... The capability approach concentrates on functioning information, supplemented by considering, where possible, the options a person had but did not choose to use. For example, a rich and healthy person who becomes ill nourished through fasting can be distinguished from a person who is forced into malnutrition through a lack of means or as a result of suffering from a parasite disease" (UNDP, HDR 1997).

"The main aim of human development is to develop and use all human capabilities. In order for that to be possible more focus needs to be given to institutional capability. Capabilities are not only qualities in themselves (which have the potential to be expanded and improved), but also tools to be used for the betterment of both the individual possessing those capabilities and the larger society. This cannot be achieved without the expansion of opportunities and choices offered by society's regulatory mechanisms, such as institutions that provide access to goods and services. The fuller use of human capabilities requires sustained economic growth and considerable investment in human beings. Skill formation, in addition to general education, promotes more productive use of human capabilities" (UNDP, HDR 1990). For instance, some low-income countries have demonstrated that it is possible to achieve high levels of human development if they skillfully use the available means to expand basic human capabilities.

"Basic empowerment depends on the expansion of people's capabilities—expansion that involves an enlargement of choices and thus an increase in freedom. But people can exercise few choices without freedom from hunger, want and deprivation. In principle, everyone is free to buy food in the market, for example, but this freedom means little if people are too poor to afford it" (UNDP, HDR 1996).

"Participation, from the human development perspective, is both a means and an end. Human development stresses the need to invest in human capabilities and then ensure that those capabilities are used for the benefit of all. Greater participation has an important part to play here: it helps maximize the use of human capabilities and is thus a *means* of increasing levels of social and economic development. But human development is also concerned with personal fulfillment. So, active participation, which allows people to realize their full potential and make their best contribution to society, is also an *end* in itself" (UNDP, HDR 1993). But capabilities development is not enough; capabilities need to be used. Development must enable all individuals to enlarge their human capabilities to the fullest.

"Fundamental to all these priorities are the equality of access to means of developing basic human capabilities, the equality of opportunity to participate in all aspects of economic, social and political decision-making, and the equality of reward"(UNDP, HDR 1995). "This equity is, however, in opportunity—not necessarily in final achievements. Each individual is entitled to a just opportunity to make the best use of his or her potential capabilities. So is each generation. How they actually use those opportunities, and the results they achieve, are matters of their own choice. But they must have such a choice—now and in the future" (UNDP, HDR 1994).

"Public policy must therefore be directed not only at building up people's capabilities, but also at matching these capabilities with opportunities—linking the supply of human capital with the demand for it.... When the supply of human capital and the demand for it are in balance—when capabilities match opportunities—a dynamic process of cumulative causation is set in motion that can raise growth and lower inequality" (UNDP, HDR 1996).

expert-counterpart model, a lot depended on the power relationship established by the pair. It is not difficult to imagine whose opinion prevailed. Today's donor-recipient relationship is no longer based predominantly at the project level, therefore individual power is exercised in a more sophisticated manner, through the influence on conceptual approaches, macroanalysis capacity and negotiation skills. However, another layer of power has appeared, with nationals replacing the international experts in the power pyramid. Often, these intermediate agents represent the external views rather than their own, are well entrenched in institutions funded from external resources, and act as gatekeepers to the development aid system.

Local and community level empowerment. Empowerment has powerful detractors too. Larry Summers (2001) challenges the recent emphasis on empowerment in development discourse. He disputes the claim that there are any valuable lessons to be learned in terms of local empowerment and ownership in the overwhelming development success of the East Asian countries. He further argues that there is a trade-off between empowerment and analytic rigour. He sees empowerment as an opposing element to economic methodology, which further compromises analytic rigour: "I am concerned that the move toward empowerment, rather than an economic approach, is standing in some ways for a reduced emphasis on the analytic element." To illustrate his claim, he gives education as an example. Once again presupposing inherent contradictions, he asks what is more important: intensive research of which reading curricula work best, or intensive consultation with villages about the design of curricula in their schools. Leaving aside the premise of universality, it is still unclear why the two cannot be complimentary to each other.

Summers further asks whether a client-centred approach means a closer partnership with the government or some broader relationship with the country. He argues that seeking to anoint representatives of civil society other than the democratically elected representatives of the people is inappropriate.

The reality of local empowerment is different from the economic views. Empowerment is a gain that is obtained by local struggles and increased self-confidence. It is not something that is given to people. Even with all the distortions of the current "empowerment and participation" practice, it is undeniable that it creates a two-way accountability at the local community level that enhances effectiveness, sustainability and impact. Empowerment is, after all, based on the human-capability approach and confirms the view of development as a social construct.

State empowerment shows that the more emphasis is given to upstream policy interventions, the more the debate on national and indigenous approaches will move the issue of empowerment up the ladder. The role of the state is central to this debate, as the state can still make or break the way its population participates in the development process.

The principle of a nation-state, promoted by the French Revolution, served as the basis for modernism and determined the direction of development theory until the 1980s. It is a theory full of pitfalls—not least the fact that most countries do not conform to the definition of real nation-states—but it provided a foundation for the concept of a protective, territorial and distributive state.

Since the end of the cold war, the role of the state has changed dramatically. Security and economic expansion have acquired a new meaning and have required a different state role, one more in tune with the need for strategic planning and market competitiveness. While most countries have counted on a strong state to build security, services and an integrated market, the internal role of the state has changed as well. It is no longer possible for the state to act as the unique development agent.

The state may no longer be the only interlocutor for development initiatives, but the lack of recognition of its role has created tension, confusion and a leadership crisis. Empowerment in this context is interpreted in different ways by different actors: Developing country state agents believe they have the right to decide on national options and priorities; empowered grassroots and civil society activities seize the opportunity to lay claim to a bigger share of the decision-making process; and external actors choose between the two extremes as they see fit—no longer recognizing anyone's central leadership role, and thus contributing to a leadership vacuum in weaker states.

Current technical cooperation guidelines reflect this disarray. Goran Hyden's (1995) four levels of governance are interesting to note here. He distinguishes a meta-level, which concerns the fundamental issues relating to the political system; a macrolevel, where national options and strategic policy priorities are defined; a meso-level, where policies are translated into operational programmes and public administration roles; and a microlevel, where projects are designed and implemented. This could serve as a basis to clarify roles and assign responsibilities.

References to Keynes are often heard as a justification for a clearer role for the state. The radical view of opposing markets to the state does not hold—it is a confused notion coming from the cold-war era. The reality is that public expenditure as a percentage of GDP is larger in developed countries than it was a few decades ago— and is even increasing in a number of them.

According to a recent World Bank report (World Bank, 2002), governments are not the sole actors in building and reforming institutions. Individuals, communities, multinational companies and other civil society actors are as vital in carrying out the change. These actors build institutions "often in partnership with each other," and influence the institutional changes in the process. Governments still are the main actors, as the providers of many market-supporting institutions (mainly via enforcing laws and protecting property rights). However, the report argues "the balance between markets and state power, and between business and social interests, is a delicate one in the course of institutional development."

The report's authors use a step-by-step approach to institution-building in order to promote market development. The first step, they maintain, is to understand three ways that markets support institutions, by: a) "channeling information," market conditions, goods and participants, b) "enforcing property rights and contracts," and c) increasing (or decreasing) competition in market transactions. They argue that rather than first focusing on the specific structures of institutions, policy-makers should use the proposed blueprint to identify what sort of a gap exists—what is missing and why it is missing—in their institutional settings. This mechanical view of how to "do it right" ignores social and political conditionalities in institution-building. It is impossible to offer a blueprint to deal with the latter. Each case is unique.

State regulation is perhaps the most important issue each country is currently facing. The role of the state in the assessment of trends and adjustments to competition seems today more important for developing countries than structural reforms. Short-term macropolicy has become so essential that the larger role of the state—such as providing social protection or social services, like education and health—is somehow hidden. This issue is particularly relevant in terms of what choices are given to developing countries. Are they being told to adopt the latest market fad without any guarantee that this will be right for them or good for their citizens? Is the universal design relevant for all? Are countries being obliged to follow a specific role for the state, depending on how dependent they are on external assistance? How does empowerment apply here?

One important, well-studied region, East Asia, provides interesting findings on the role of the state. In a volume reviewing the mistakes in past interpretations of the nature of the East Asian "miracle" (Stiglitz and Yusuf, 2001), a series of authors concur that the reasons behind the success are largely to be found in successful industrialization and absorption of international knowledge, whether in the form of new or disembodied knowledge. The key issues related to this success—a stable macroeconomic environment, high savings and interest rates, high-quality human capital, a merit-based bureaucracy, low-income inequality, export promotion—all point to a strong role for the state. The most contentious issue with regard to government intervention relates to its role in industrial policies, on two fronts: "the counterfactual and the aggregative quantitative significance of these interventions." While some authors insist that by "governing the market," the East Asian governments had slowed the growth of legal and regulatory institutions that would strengthen the market and remedy some market failure, others argue that changing conditions in the global economy are the reason for new demands on state regulation.

Concluding, Stiglitz admits that governments, as with any human institution, are fallible, and argues that in retrospect, perhaps the criticism that should have been leveled is that governments did not take strong enough actions, not that they intervened too much. Governments deregulated the financial sector when they should have been asking what was the appropriate set of regulations, and they did not do enough to ensure good corporate governance, which would have been necessary to create effective stock markets (Stiglitz and Yusuf, 2001).

Values

"Do we insist on the development of a set of universal values, or do we engage in a struggle to resist the monopoly over the explanations that such a set of values enshrines?"(Marsden, 1994).

According to Amartya Sen (1999), "The exercise of freedom is mediated by values, but the values in turn are influenced by public discussions and social interactions, which are themselves influenced by participatory freedoms."

Institutions that promote participatory freedoms are institutions that have a code of conduct inspired by progressive values. There is room for any agent to inspire such a value system. It is possible for even an external agent to play such a catalytic role. Capacity enablers, be they individuals, institutions, processes or resources, can all play a role in fostering public discussions and social interactions. These need not be confined to a self-reliant local or national group. Even admitting that the nature of development reproduces inequality and has not dealt at all with polarization, one can still find good justifications for using any entry point that expands participatory freedoms. In order for such a recipe to work, however, there are a number of fundamental elements that must be taken into account.

Instead of entering into a debate on economic choices, it is perhaps more relevant to focus on values. The state is a key agent in establishing a value system. Arguably there is no value system that does not refer to the state, even the ones opposing it. For instance, "One of the key ingredients of an effective rule of law is that law and government faithfully reflect actual social behaviour and serve as an effective means of societal control. Sharp deviation between the two (formal law and practice) will create a limbo resulting in lawlessness and empty formalism" (Dia, 1996). The same can be said for economic orientation. If a government does not take into account the interests of internal constituencies and acts in total disregard of society, it can revoke fake formal economic systems that have little to do with the informal exchanges. Chibber advocates a "good fit" between the state's institutional capabilities and its actions. In well-developed states, administrative capabilities are normally strong, and institutionalized checks and balances restrain arbitrary action, even as they provide government organizations with the flexibility to pursue their public mandates. By contrast, states with weaker institutions need to give special attention to signaling to firms and citizens that they will refrain from arbitrary actions (Dasgupta and Serageldin, 2000). Unfortunately, in both cases—rule of law and economic behaviour—it is often possible to find *empowerment promoters* justifying polarization and the weakening of the government's role.

To promote commitment and ownership, a value system has to foster motivation, loyalty and allegiance to modern organizations. Quite often the fault-line for lack of ownership in developing countries has been attributed to negative perceptions of clienteles, patronages, institutionalized corruption and extended kinship relations. These problems exist, but they have been only superficially analysed, making it easy to explain failure, even though some of the most spectacular economic growth examples can be traced back to this very recipe.

According to Qian, private ownership and control work well in an environment with good supporting institutions, which is not the perfect world most developing and transitional economies live in. Over the short term, most rule-of-law institutions are likely to be deficient (Stiglitz and Yusuf, 2001). The example of the Republic of Korea shows we should not have a black or white view of state regulation. There is a need to nuance some of the casual relationships established with patronage, kinship and state support of private sector development.

Values are culturally determined. If true partnership among development actors is to be achieved, much more discussion is needed on the harmonization of values. A number of Asian miracle countries built their enormous achievements on values that otherwise would have been considered corrupt; as did most of the developed countries before them, way back in history. What is peculiar to the debate is the way we evaluate success, risk and failure. To what extent does empowerment require relating to a specific set of values, such as external values, even if they are painted as universal? Or local values and their possible multiple interpretations?

Bourdieu's argument (Partant, 1982) that instruments of control are formally based on "good faith" relationships, while disguising an unequal basis for the same, is a strong reminder of how we can pretend without doing—to have the symbol without the substance. Most management literature in the United States and United Kingdom argues that processes and value systems determine organizational behaviour on a scale that was not previously recognized. Political discourse also equates managerial capacity to political competence—which always promotes value systems.

Management is inherently about power and control. Power relationships are actually never far from development practice and need candid attention. Otherwise, one can take refuge in the neutral terminology of management and pretend empowerment is just a technical tool to enhance effectiveness and, of course, ownership!

Constructive Impatience

Two premises have impacted the debate and practice of capacity development. The first was the premise of the expert-counterpart model that those working as experts had a specialized knowledge, whereas the counterparts had local-environment knowledge. The second premise was based on an assumption from the gap theory—that an expert (an external, developed-country national) has a depository of knowledge that needs to be passed on to the recipient, a developing country national who lacks such accumulated capacity. Another way of looking at it is that the recipient is an empty vessel waiting to be filled with the knowledge of the expert. Critiques of technical cooperation have addressed the limits of this model.

Current practice within capacity development claims to be moving away from this model, but in general there has been superficial change without fundamental transformation. Instead of looking into what produces sustainable capacity, donor aid agencies sometimes simply replace the foreign expert with a national of the recipient country and limit the role of possible external expertise. They also call for more indigenous approaches. Despite these surface changes, the fundamentals of the donor-recipient relationship have not yet changed, nor have they been sufficiently challenged. Three key areas need particular consideration: what is to be considered national and indigenous; the role of the development "industry"; and the time-span of development interventions in general and capacity development in particular.

What Is Meant by National and Indigenous?

Quite often, national and indigenous means the participation of recipients in the process of design, monitoring and implementation of projects. Projects are part of a larger policy framework that quite extensively defines their possible scope. Two different levels need to be examined here: the project level and the policy level.

On project design, it is not rare for donors to impose a particular format. This is normally based on a log frame that varies from donor to donor. The nature of a project is very much enclave-based, since it is rarely fully integrated in national budgetary processes. To complicate things further, sometimes the local formal institution hosting the project is itself conspicuous.[5]

Monitoring is based on an accountability framework that has been increasingly linked to donors' results-based management. Public pressure for donor aid agencies to account for money spent has imposed a very tight financial reporting and output focus. This can marginalize the role for the recipient in the management process even further, especially if the systems do not allow flexibility in executing arrangements.

Evaluation methods are still struggling with the integration of participatory techniques in sizable activities. The experience of small-scale projects has not yet translated into universal use of participatory techniques. Finally, the move towards sectorwide approaches and greater integration into national planning processes has been donor-driven, and so far not contributed to the reduction of transaction costs. In fact, it has reinforced the gap theory fundamentals by giving it a clearer meso-dimension. Thus, project design, monitoring and evaluation are designed to fit into a pre-existing framework created by donors—not local recipients. Cracknell (2000) stresses the importance of participatory monitoring and evaluation by local people. He further argues that a participatory approach in evaluation not only creates more effective aid programmes, but also empowers local and poor people. He claims that "reversals and reorientations" in evaluation are necessary to make development aid more effective. The same point of view is shared by a group of evaluators that looked

---

5 According to Dia (1996), "Formal institutions, not being rooted in local culture, generally fail to command society's loyalty or trigger local ownership, both of which are important catalysts for sustainability and enforceability. These formal institutions are at odds with societal behaviour, expectations and incentive systems and therefore face a crisis of legitimacy and enforcement .... By contrast, indigenous institutions anchored in local culture and values can count on the sound pillars of legitimacy, accountability and self-enforcement."

into European development cooperation from the angle of its impact on poverty reduction (Cox and Healy, 2000).

Cox and Healy subsequently more deeply analyse a sample of projects and programmes to search for "good and bad approaches" based on evidence. Their findings include:

- "Both developing country partners and development agencies have a responsibility to reject top-down approaches that exclude the poor. Agencies can also seek to influence other agencies to promote a more participatory approach."

- Promoting greater participation is seen by the poor as good in itself, even if a project fails according to conventional criteria, such as directly increasing livelihood security. "Less tangible benefits are often highly valued by poor groups, including those bolstering their sense of their rights, their capacity to analyse and articulate their own needs and possible solutions, and their confidence and ability to participate in local political processes."

- "Participation by local implementers tends to result in greater ownership and helps generate demand for new services. It is not a panacea, however, and can result in pressure to dilute efforts over an unsustainably large range of activities."

- "Meaningful participation needs to be implemented in advance of infrastructure components rather than simultaneously, thereby influencing the design, location, and appropriateness of such physical investments."

On the policy level, the contradictions are much more fundamental. When structural adjustment programmes were introduced, the conditionality instrument entered the sphere of macroeconomics. This move is in direct contradiction with the desire for more nationally-owned, indigenously-led processes. Promoting a better use of the latter approaches during a time when recipients perceive increased impositions at the macrolevel is, of course, problematic. This has become central to the debate and has provoked a number of responses—including the launching of the Comprehensive Development Framework and Poverty Reduction Strategies.

The Poverty Reduction Strategy Papers (PRSPs) process has opened an interesting approach that seeks to consolidate budgetary support, debt forgiveness, central planning and participatory methods in a single package. Donors, through the OECD/DAC, have had encouraging discussions about the nature of ownership when applied to this package. For instance, the relatively modest role played by Parliaments and elected constituencies, the fact that PRSPs are "approved" by the boards of the World Bank and the International Monetary Fund (IMF), and the absence of explicit macroeconomic links to the instrument are all challenges that will test the ownership of the approach. These issues are also related to the view that commitment and good governance need to be expressed necessarily in a central way, making it reasonable to catalogue countries in categories of "good" and "poor" performers, which might undermine the principles of ownership espoused by the PRSP approach.

The issue of how to deal with ownership has thus become central. In order to have a stronghold on people's commitment, dedication and identity, there is a need for processes that allow for clear national legitimacy.

The Role of the Development Industry Cannot Be Ignored

After five decades of development practice, development experts have created a number of fads and propositions without changing many of their core practices. The resilience of the industry and its capacity to adjust to changing times is well established. It has become quite influential in the shaping of international agendas, and has reached out to new partners such as philanthropic institutions and the corporate world. The development industry is a disparate collection of experts and other project personnel, such as consultants, development scholars, advocacy and communications experts, nongovernmental organizations (NGOs), and bureaucrats in donor agencies and international organizations. The industry is currently dominated by management consultants. They embody the new roles assigned to technical cooperation, the core of the development industry.

Technical cooperation approaches have centered on the creation of individual capacities and building institutions. There is probably wide agreement that the success rate in the first area has been extremely high. The problematic area of institution-building presents a different picture. It is established that the role of external agents in successful institution-building is often marginal. This view builds on the compared experiences of sub-Saharan Africa—with loads of capacity initiatives and little to show—and other regions, which have less infusion and more progressive records of institution-building. The current focus on defined tasks, measurable outcomes, learning mechanisms, and comprehensive and integrated planning has provided a new lease on life to the industry. The percentage of resources funding technical cooperation activities in developing countries has not been reduced in the last decade, despite the new approaches that have been introduced.

The development industry continues to have a thinking monopoly. By constantly creating new methodologies, jargon, initiatives and defined niches, it has overwhelmed the absorptive capacity of key recipients, making it impossible for them to really nationally own processes and introduce indigenous knowledge. The interest in indigenous *management* is an attempt to address these issues. It is far too early to assess a possible shift.

The Time-Span of Development Interventions

The project logic framework, now enhanced by results-based management, puts its emphasis on outcomes—although it uses input budgeting most of the time. The policy frameworks recently introduced in the development partnership discussion equally stress the importance of tangible targets. In fact, targets, and monitoring targets, are likely to be much more central than before. These tendencies go along with the spirit and logic of corporate management tools. They allow for a clear focus, established and measurable expectations, and identification of actions and priorities in accordance with realistic goals and objectives. Given the increasing influence of management con-sulting and the changing roles of the state, it is not surprising that these trends have become quite popular.

The problem that needs to be addressed is the impression that the time frames can still be based on the assumption of short-term results. Because of political, finan-cial and planning imperatives, there is a drive for showing results quickly. Changing political regimes at both ends—donors and recipients—legitimize such a drive. Immediate gratification and premium is central to financial markets. Television news underlines this reality through daily shows, and large companies prefer to buy rather than create capacity. The idea of security and stability is being replaced by the imper-ative of managing unpredictability and insecurity. The development industry follows this trend.[6] Yet contrary to trends and political or financial imperatives, fundamental change is a long, slow process.

The uneasiness regarding technical cooperation practices has not disappeared. Moreover, the growing contradictions surrounding it oblige a questioning of its fundamen-tal purpose in the current world configuration. There is growing tension among the key players. It is out of this tension that a new approach is expected to emerge. As a possible new approach unfolds, the interest on ownership issues allows for a constructive tension.

Capacity Malaise

The tensions surrounding technical cooperation have a lot to do with the perceived failure of a specific group of countries—the Least-Developed Countries (LDCs), of which a great majority are African. There is a certain degree of desperation among development specialists, because they see their own capacity being challenged by the very fact that they cannot uplift the performance of their main target group. The visi-bility of the failure obscures what can otherwise be presented as enormously successful achievements in other categories of countries. By circumscribing the debate to the capacity of the LDCs, the size of the challenge is not sufficiently recog-nized. The issue is one of poverty reduction most and foremost.

The latest World Bank estimates indicate that the average proportion of the pop-ulation in developing countries living below US $1 per day fell from 32 to 26 per cent between 1990 and 1998. The simple extrapolation of this trend to the year 2015 results in a headcount index of about 17 per cent—suggesting that the world is on track to reaching the global goal of poverty reduction between 1990 and 2015. Unfortunately, the story does not end here.

When East Asia is excluded, income-poverty in developing countries hardly declined—from 35 to 33 per cent respectively. Progress was less than half the rate

---

[6] Eduard Jaycox's introduction to Dia's book (1996) insists that the variety of high-impact, low-cost options for providing social services and infrastructure make the book's proposals for building sus-tainable institutional capacity realistic. He says that the book's "results and operational implications clearly show that, contrary to general belief, it is possible to achieve quick results in the field." Coming from someone who was then a World Bank Vice President known for strong criticism of technical coop-eration failures, this view indicates the magnitude of the challenge regarding time-span perceptions.

needed to reach the poverty goal. The number of income-poor in sub-Saharan Africa, South Asia, and Latin America and the Caribbean combined has actually increased by about 10 million each year since 1990.

Most of the human capital formation in LDCs has failed to produce desired results. Judging from the increase in the overall number of LDCs, the effects of globalization have further confirmed this reading. This is partly because of overconcentration on building human skills (rather than their retention and utilization), and on institution creation—"building" is in this context a misleading word—rather than institutional support and strengthening. But this is not enough to account for the lack of successful institutions. The huge number of high-achieving institutions in developing countries—although admittedly mostly in non-LDC countries—has produced evidence of what does and does not work. It might well be the case, therefore, that the specific circumstances of LDCs correspond simply to the price of unequal and non-linear development processes that produce winners and losers in an unequal world. This is a relevant discussion in light of the proposals from *Assessing Aid* (World Bank, 1998). The report makes the case for aid to be the midwife of good policies. For that to work, it acknowledges aid should be as much about knowledge as about money. And since the admission is that aid is subject to learning, we all have to insert in learning the reality that some of the worst development growth results came about through strong macropolicy conditionalities applied from the outside. And since the weaker states normally have to deal with the longest conditionality list, we need to account for "poor performance" in more sophisticated terms.

What provoked success in certain countries was a combination of factors, with ownership constituting just one such factor. In fact, ownership does not necessarily promote or hinder economic growth. But it is fundamental for human development (Marsh et al., 1999). It would help if we could admit that the circumstances under which an institution flourishes are far too complex to be reduced to a technical cooperation angle. In this regard, understanding the social fabric is key. Understanding the political dimensions is essential. Identifying the right type of knowledge requirements and tailoring the processes and solutions to respond to it are a must.

If the issues of capacity are to be seriously addressed, they cannot be dissociated from brain drain and what motivates it. Perhaps very radical solutions ought to be brought forward that take into account today's knowledge utilization and the emergence of one global skilled-labour market. These solutions would contribute to a more transparent debate. It is time we reinvestigated the notion that there is an international division of labour; if it exists, it is certainly governed by rules that are quite different from just two decades ago.

Key Issues to Master the Paradox

There are numerous possibilities for framing the ownership debate. From the vantage point of the arguments above, we can discuss key points to be made.

1. Human Skills Enhancement Is Always Good

Because we cannot just ignore human poverty—and for the good and valid reason that all human beings should be liberated from "unfreedoms"—one should consider any capacity investments as a value per se. These investments enhance the chances of individuals "making it," and expand their opportunities and choices, even though institutions might not benefit. Considering individual human skills enhancement as a value in itself relegates the discussion about cost-effectiveness and efficiency to a different level. In other words, the way investments in capacity development are made may not contribute necessarily to institution-building and may be too expensive for just personal gain, but it is still better than not offering the possibility to the developing countries at all. However, this begs the question of whether the current technical cooperation trends are the most suited for today's challenges. Most traditional forms of technical cooperation had their raison d'être (see Box 2.1.3), but faster change is now required.

2. There Is a Need to Balance External Input and Ownership

In order for capacity to go beyond the individual level, it is necessary to explore the paradox of enhancing access to external support while preserving ownership. Krishna in *Social Capital* (Dasgupta and Serageldin, 2000) emphasizes the problem of lack of ownership at the bottom layers and contrasts it with the success of assisted self-reliance groups. Ownership provides bonds of mutual trust and affection. There are three sine qua non for this to work: full control of the initial idea by the national agent; control of the resources assigned to capacity development, through their integration in national processes; and clear national agent decision-making power over the process. Perhaps the comments of Lee Kuan Yew regarding the role of the UN experts and his Cabinet's utilization of foreign technological assistance—i.e., a spirit of self-reliance instead of aid-dependency—could be a useful illustration of this point (see Box 2.1.3).

Hamdani summarizes his thoughts by stating, "Local capability development is both complimentary to and competitive with the use of imported technologies, and the right policy mix should aim at maintaining a balanced relationship by altering the modes of technology transfer, according to the level of indigenous capabilities and their potential for upgrading over time"(Dunning and Hamdani, 1997). Hamdani believes, "If all firms had access to the same technology, skills and markets, there would be no reason for foreign direct investment, and capital flows would take the form of portfolio investments or loans." No firm would take on the responsibility of foreign direct investment if it did not have an "ownership-specific advantage over its competitors." Firms create proprietary assets denied to them, either because of legal protection, or because they arise through investments in specific skills, knowledge and organizational capabilities. Furthermore, barriers to contestable markets and barriers caused by the increase in learning may also be produced. Learning and innovation produces skills that put firms at a competitive advantage.

Sanjaya Lall argues that the relationship between local capability-building and technology imports is both complementary and competitive. Overdependence on imports serves to slow down the learning capacity. Furthermore, a balance needs to be struck between foreign technological imports and the investment in human skills issued to advance technological improvements within countries, exclusive of outside aid (Dunning and Hamdani, 1997).

3. Capacity Development, Like Development Itself, Requires a Long-Term Time-Frame

There is a need to recognize that rejection of development aid is just another mechanism for producing inequality. The rule of thumb, therefore, should be how to best use aid for sustainability, while admitting it might entail some pervasive effects. The incentive system has to be appropriate to nurture homegrown transformation. Development aid practice will have to change the way in which it treats time. Sustainable development will take much longer to achieve than was previously recognized. Even with a long-term vision, development aid must have a clear end to its programmes and projects with clearly defined outcomes. This is particularly important when dealing with institution-building, because it frames the external support within the parameters of the national will.

4. Ownership Is Premised in Self-Esteem and Self-Confidence

Without self-confidence, it is not possible to identify ownership. But ownership in itself is not necessarily a positive factor in development. Examples of dictators claiming ownership to repress dissenting opinions is a sober reminder that ownership and self-confidence need to be related to specific values. But this being said, there is no development without ownership, self-confidence and self-determination. Self-esteem, like self-confidence, is a global evaluation reflecting a view of our accomplishments and capabilities, our values, our bodies, others' responses to us, and even, on occasion, our possessions. Self-esteem has been reported to be positively correlated to desire for control, hope, achievement, motivation and self-determination, and negatively with anxiety, aggression and loneliness.

5. Ownership Is Better Exercised within a Clear Accountability System

There is a need to clarify the contractual arrangements obliging the two parties within every development initiative—much like the private sector does. There should be an understanding, however, that there are predictable and substantial funds available, that the selection will be fair (i.e., with the participation of independent-minded mediators who do not belong to one of the parties), and that no predetermined conditionality is universally applied. Edwards (2000) argues that without the spirit of cooperation, "conditionally becomes a 'ritual dance around the Tower of Babel' incapable of generating any ownership over change and corrupting the relationships in which authentic partnership is based."

6. The Development Industry Is Undermining Harmonization

Capacity development need not be hostage to existing development industry pressure. Conceptualization of capacity development can be better defined, with tangible

BOX 2.1.3: Singapore's Lee Kuan Yew and traditional technical cooperation

Founded as a British trading colony in 1819, Singapore became an independent state in 1965 under the leadership of Lee Kuan Yew. He served as its first Prime Minister, and was regularly re-elected from 1959 until he stepped down in 1990. At the time of its independence, Singapore faced daunting economic and social problems. Unemployment was high and rising (in 1957 the unemployment rate was 5 per cent, rising to 9.2 per cent in 1966). There was an acute shortage of housing and inadequate health facilities, compounded by a high population growth rate of 4.4 per cent per annum between 1947 and 1957.

For the first two decades of its independence, Singapore enjoyed continuous high economic growth, largely outperforming the world economy. Its GDP growth rate never fell below 5 per cent and rose in some years as high as 15 per cent. At the same time, Singapore managed to maintain an inflation rate below world averages.

Singapore's GDP grew 15 times in one generation, from US $3 billion in 1965 to $46 billion in 1997 (in 1965 dollars). Annual per capita income grew from less than $1,000 at the time of independence to nearly $30,000 today, the eighth highest in the world in 1997 and 1998, and the ninth in 1999. The general literacy rates have increased by 20 per cent for males and 46 per cent for females. The literacy rate today is over 90 per cent, one of the highest rates in Asia. There is 56 per cent literacy in two or more languages.

Singapore's economic growth in the past 35 years occurred in the context of a unique combination of political, economic and social factors. A tiny island without natural resources, adequate water supply or a defense capability of its own, Singapore was gripped by uncertainty over its survival at the time of its independence. The three and a half years of Japanese occupation (1942-1945) were alive in the memory of Singapore's first-generation leaders, whose decision-making was largely predicated on the struggle for survival. The fear of being swallowed and the cold-war atmosphere influenced the domestic political climate.

The United States' anti-Communist strategies in Asia played a favorable role in the growth of Singapore and the rest of the East Asian economies, providing security guarantees, foreign and development aid, and open access to American markets. Having converted some of the British military facilities to commercial and industrial purposes and retrained laid-off workers for new jobs, Singapore later became a supply center for American forces and provided ship repairs during the increasing American involvement in Indochina, the beginning of a service that made Singapore the first port in the whole world.

Lee Kuan Yew, the founder of modern Singapore, is the ultimate example of a supporter of building national ownership. He believed that a trained, knowledgeable workforce and a strong, efficient government were imperative to the successful transition from a third to a first world country. Merit was high on the list of priorities in Singapore. Highly concerned about its talent pool, the Government even created incentives for men to marry equally educated women. Lee's realization that talent is a country's most precious asset, especially in resource-poor countries like Singapore, further led to numerous policies aimed at reducing brain drain and bringing foreign talent to Singapore.

According to Lee, the Confucian values of respect for order, harmony, diligence and hard work were crucial for the country's achievements. Lee contended that Confucian societies, unlike Western societies, believe that the individual exists in the context of the family, friends and wider society, and democracy not only cannot work there but also is unwelcome, for Asians see in it "a breakdown of civil society with guns, drugs, violent crime, vagrancy and vulgar public behavior." These highly controversial views influenced particular authoritarian types of institutions. But one can argue they did recognize civic engagement as fundamental.

Lee was determined to prevent foreign aid dependency and create instead a spirit of self-reliance:

> "Assistance should provide Singapore with jobs through industries and not make us dependent on perpetual injections of aid. I warned our workers, 'The world does not owe us a living. We cannot live by the begging bowl.'"

His strong views did not impede the use of the most traditional types of technical assistance. According to Lee:

> "We placed our hopes on a United Nations Technical Assistance Board team [the predecessor of the United Nations Development Programme] that arrived in October to survey a proposed industrial site at Jurong and advise on the types of industry suitable for it. We were fortunate in the choice of the leader, Dr. Albert Winsemius. A Dutch industrialist, he spent three months in Singapore and made the first of his many contributions that were to be crucial to Singapore's development. He was a practical, hardheaded businessman with a grasp of the economics of post-World War II Europe and America. He was to play a major role in our later economic planning."

Winsemius served as economic adviser to Singapore for 23 years until 1984. In order to overcome Singapore's disadvantages, Lee came up with an arbitrary strategy. The first step, of leapfrogging the region, was suggested to him by a UNDP expert who had visited Singapore in 1962 and then met again with Lee in Africa in 1964. He had described to the Singapore leader the Israeli experience with export-led growth. Similarly, Singapore could avoid its not so well-intentioned neighbors and link up with America, Europe and Japan, "and attract their manufacturers to produce in Singapore and export their products to the developed countries."

> "If Singapore could establish First World standards in public and personal security, health, education, telecommunications, transportation and services, it would become a base camp for entrepreneurs, engineers, managers and other professionals who had business to do in the region. This meant we had to train our people and equip them to provide First World standards of service. I believed this was possible, that we could re-educate and reorientate our people with the help of schools, trade unions, community centers and social organizations."

Lee concluded that "without foreign talent, we would not have done as well." As is clear by the attributions of the engineer of Singapore's miraculous growth, even the most traditional role of technical assistance, provided in the first years of the country's establishment, served an important role for the take-off of Singapore's economic growth. Today's reality is certainly quite different.

Source: Lee (2000a and 2000b).

ways of measuring ownership and other key dimensions. It can be rooted in each country's value system, respectful of the points made above. All the actors within development can attempt to harmonize their many views on institutional and social value systems as a way of building the trust required for a renewed effort for capacity development.

Policy conditionality is being challenged. But project conditionality has to go too. Gatekeepers between local communities or other actors and several layers of decision-makers complicate accountability and contribute to disillusion with technical cooperation. Focusing on capacity shifts the approach towards better support to institution-building and organizational development.

7. Technical Cooperation Costs Introduce Wrong Incentives

On costs, the issue of misallocations on the recipient side is often based upon a flawed reading of the costs of technical cooperation. Capacity development, or assuming ownership over technical cooperation, is not always the overriding motive on the recipient side. Recipient perceptions of technical cooperation as a "free good" makes for inefficient allocations and practices. Opportunity costs (such as matching budgetary allocations to technical cooperation inflows); costs of maintaining and servicing technical-cooperation-engineered projects, institutions, equipment, etc.; and, most importantly of all, the cultural costs of technical cooperation—hoisted on the recipient through the dominance of donor priorities, norms and procedures—are significantly underestimated. A better understanding of costs to the recipient side would enable a more demand-driven regime. The absence of a market price for technical cooperation distorts priorities and makes choices subject to a perverse incentive system that is not based on indigenous priorities.

8. The Political Dimension of Development Has to Take Central Stage

The political dimension of development is becoming more acceptable in the debate. A clear definition of the roles each actor should play is necessary, with empowerment and leadership issues addressed upfront and without cynical back-door motives. The catalytic role governments play in fostering ownership and creating the conditions for institution-building has to be recognized. After all, facilitation is the number-one task of a newly defined state. Instead of referring to enabling environments in an abstract way, development actors have also to promote socially defined and nationally owned targets within an enabling environment.

References

Bagla-Gokalp, Lusin. 1998. *Sociologie des organisations.* Paris: La Decouverte.

Berg, Elliot, and the United Nations Development Programme (UNDP). 1993. *Rethinking Technical Cooperation: Reforms for Capacity Building in Africa.* New York: United Nations Development Programme.

Browne, Stephen. 1999. *Beyond Aid: From Patronage to Partnership.* Aldershot: Ashgate.

Chambers, Robert. 1997. *Whose Reality Counts? Putting the First Last.* London: Intermediate Technology Publications.

———. 2001. *The New Dynamics of Aid: Power, Procedures and Relationships.* Brighton: Institute of Development Studies.

Cox, Aidan, and John Healey, eds. 2000. *European Development Cooperation and the Poor.* London: Overseas Development Institute.

Cracknell, Basil Edward. 2000. *Evaluating Development Aid: Issues, Problems and Solutions.* New Delhi: Sage Publications.

Dahl, Gudrun. 2001. *Responsibility and Partnership in Swedish Aid Discourse.* Uppsala: University Printers.

Dasgupta, Partha, and Ismail Serageldin, eds. 2000. *Social Capital. A Multifaceted Perspective.* Washington, DC: World Bank.

Dia, Mamadou. 1996. *Africa's Management in the 1990s and Beyond. Reconciling Indigenous and Transplanted Institutions.* Washington, DC: World Bank.

Dubar, Claude. 2000. *La crise des identités: l'interprétation d'une mutation.* Paris: Presses Universitaires de France.

Dunning, John H., and Khalil A. Hamdani, eds. 1997. *The New Globalism and Developing Countries.* Tokyo: United Nations University Press.

Dyke, Nancy Bearg. 2001. *Alleviating Global Poverty: Technology for Economic and Social Uplift.* Aspen: Aspen Institute.

Easterly, William. 2001. *The Elusive Growth: An Economist's Adventures in the Tropics.* Cambridge: Massachusetts Institute of Technology Press.

Edwards, Michael. 2000. *Future Positive: International Cooperation in the 21st Century.* London: Earthscan.

Fukuyama, Francis. 1992. *The End of History and the Last Man.* New York: Free Press.

Hancock, Graham. 1989. *Lords of Poverty.* New York: The Atlantic Monthly Press.

Hobsbawm, Eric. 1999. *The New Century.* London: Abacos.

Hyden, Goran. 1995. "Toward a New Model of Managing Development Assistance." In *Development Management in Africa: Toward Dynamism, Empowerment, and Entrepreneurship,* edited by Sadig Rasheed and David Fasholé Luke. Boulder: Westview Press.

Kankwenda, Mbaya. 2000. *Marabouts ou marchands du developpement en Afrique.* Paris: L' Harmattan.

Koen, Peter H., and Olatunde J. B. Ojo, eds. 1999. *Making Aid Work: Innovative Approaches for Africa at the Turn of the Century.* Lahan and Oxford: University Press of America.

Krause, Keith, and W. Andy Knight, eds. 1995. *State, Society and the UN System: Changing Perspectives on Multilateralism.* Tokyo: United Nations University Press.

Lee, Kuan Yew. 2000a. *The Singapore Story.* Abridged version. Singapore: Federal Publications.

———. 2000b. *From Third World to First: The Singapore Story 1965-2000.* Singapore: Singapore Press Holdings.

Lopes, Carlos. 1996. "La cooperation technique, concept marque par l'histoire." *Politique Africaine,* June, 69-82.

Mamdani, Mahmood. 1996. *Citizen and Subject: Contemporary Africa and the Legacy of Late Colonialism.* Princeton: Princeton University Press.

Marsden, David. 1994. "Indigineous Management and the Management of Indigenous Knowledge." In *Anthropology of Organizations,* edited by Susan Wright, 35-40. London and New York: Routledge.

Marsh, Ian, Jean Blondel and Takashi Inoguchi. 1999. *Democratic Governance and Economic Performance, East and Southeast Asia.* Tokyo and New York: United Nations University Press.

Mbembe, Achille. 1996. *De la Postcolonie: essai sur l'imagination politique dans l'Afrique contemporaine.* Paris: Editions Karthala.

McCullough, David. 1992. *Truman.* New York: Touchstone.

Partant, Francois. 1982. *La fin du development. Naissance d'une Alternative?* Paris: Francois Maspero.

Rikkila, Leena, and Katarina Sehm Patomaki. 2001. *Democracy and Globalization, Promoting a North-South Dialogue.* Helsinki: NIGD.

Rist, Gilbert. 1996. *Le Developpement. Histoire d'une croyance occidentale.* Paris and Po: Presses de Sciences.

Saasa, Oliver, and Jerker Carlsson. 1996. *The Aid Relationship in Zambia. A Conflict Scenario.* Lusaka: Institute for African Studies; Uppsala: Nordic Africa Institute.

Sakamoto, Yoshikazu, ed. 1994. *Global Transformation.* Challenges to the State System. Tokyo: United Nations University Press.

Sen, Amartya. 1999. *Development As Freedom.* New York: Oxford University Press.

Stiglitz, Joseph E., and Shahid Yusuf, eds. 2001. *Rethinking the East Asian Miracle.* Washington, DC: World Bank and Oxford University Press.

Summers, Larry. 2001. "Remarks at the (World Bank's) Country Directors' Retreat," 2 May.

United Nations Development Programme (UNDP). 1990-2000. *Human Development Reports.* New York: Oxford University Press.

Weder, Beatrice. 1999. *Model, Myth or Miracle: Reassessing the Role of Governments in the East Asian Experience.* Tokyo: United Nations University Press.

World Bank. 1998. *Assessing Aid: What Works, What Doesn't, and Why?* Washington, DC.

———. 2002. *World Development Report 2002: Building Institutions for Markets.* Oxford: Oxford University Press.

2.2 INCENTIVES, GOVERNANCE AND CAPACITY DEVELOPMENT IN AFRICA

THANDIKA MKANDAWIRE

Il n'y pas de développement "clés en main." Le seul développement viable et valable est le développement clés en tête

   (Ki-Zerbo, 1992).

When donors take the driver's seat, Africans move to the back seat. When donors try to do the same thing in Vietnam, Vietnamese get out of the car

   (anonymous).[1]

For nearly 20 years, African economies have lived through what are often referred to as the "lost decades." One major feature of the region's economies has been dependence on economic aid and, increasingly, on technical cooperation. The failure to get African economies growing in a sustainable manner in this period has sparked questions as to the appropriateness of aid policies pursued during the last two decades. More specifically, significant doubts have been raised as to the appropriateness of the technical cooperation provided to Africa and the extent to which such assistance has contributed to building capacity within African countries.

   To understand technical cooperation and capacity-building in Africa, we have to address a number of questions: What are the roots of the crisis? To whom is capacity directed and enhanced? Who possesses such capacity, for what purposes, and with what means? We also have to reflect on the role of the state in the process of development. No administrative structure can exist in a policy vacuum. Good administration in the context of a weakened state and in the absence of any specific goals is a contradiction in terms. The objective of technical cooperation and capacity-building is to contribute to a country's economic development and eventual self-reliance. Although there has always been a tendency to reduce development to economic growth, economic development has been understood as a transformative process encompassing a wide range of actors working on different fronts and needing some kind of coordination mechanism.

   One important aspect of the structural adjustment years was the displacement of both development and the quest for self-reliance from the central preoccupation of policy-making. Instead, the new central focus became stabilization, which obviated the

---

[1] In a similar vein, Jan Valdelin notes: "I fear that Eurocentrism in business and aid circles is greater when it come to Africa than Asia. Sometimes the discussion about the need for *management* in Africa almost assumes colonial proportions" (Valdelin, 1998, 208). Inside Africa, the acceptance of the back seat is attributed to a "colonial mentality" within African government circles. Either way, the evocation of colonialism does not speak well of the current practice of technical assistance.

need for development institutions that were necessarily closely linked and self-reinforcing. The crisis of the "development model" that had dominated policy-making in post-independence Africa created opportunities for a wholesale assault, not only on the technical aspects of the models, but on virtually everything associated with them, especially the capacity of the state at various levels—ideological, administrative, financial, etc. Key measures of stabilization—such as devaluations and lowering of tariffs— could be introduced by a limited number of people in the finance ministries and central banks. The implication of this has been the strengthening of the institutions associated with stabilization at the expense of the so-called "spending" ministries associated with development programmes. The weakening of the state and the subsequent erosion of existing capacities (and the loss of the capacity to expand these capacities) were all consequences of policies designed to limit the power of the state. It is within the context of this radical shift in policy objectives and instruments that we should understand the direction of technical cooperation and the growing dissatisfaction with it.

One often forgotten fact about the African civil service is its relative newness. Its rudiments only appeared in the final years of colonial rule. Two features of this service came to haunt post-colonial Africa. First, its "layered" colonial administrations were not meritocratic. Second, colonial administration was confined largely to law-and-order functions to facilitate the mercantile *mise en valeur tasks;* it was not designed to address complex issues related to development and redistribution. In 1960, Kenya, putatively one of the better-administered colonies, had 60,000 civil servants to serve a population of 10 million. Nigeria, with four times this many citizens, had 72,000 federal and regional civil servants (Goldsmith, 2001a). In the immediate aftermath of the colonial period, there were extremely low levels of overall education and serious shortages of skilled personnel. "Africanization" became a highly politicized process, to be achieved virtually at any cost. In the process, given the association of previous hierarchies with the colonizers, some skills may have been lost and unqualified people engaged. It became clear almost immediately after independence that the size, training and even outlook of the inherited bureaucracies were not appropriate for development and administration.

In the immediate post-independence era, states, public administrations and civil services were generally viewed as a positive, modernizing force. Political scientists, drawing on Weberian notions of governance, may have expressed reservations about the ability of the system to perform well given the particularistic and ascriptive recruitment relations that prevailed in "traditional" institutions. They believed, however, that a good start had been made towards achieving more universalistic and meritocratic procedures. Among development economists, the view was that the state could maximize social welfare, subject to a number of constraints. For much of the 1960s and 1970s, the main policy was indigenization and expansion of the civil service to assume new tasks that went with national sovereignty and an expanded development agenda. Considerable progress was made in this respect, thanks partly to a significant expansion in secondary and tertiary education, and the availability of study programmes linked to indigenization. And, despite cronyism and the fusion of private and public interests, most African bureaucracies performed reasonably well during the first decade of independence, when economies grew and social services expanded (Mkandawire, 2001; Sender, 1999).

However, one should not gloss over the fact that the expansion of the civil services faced considerable questioning. Early criticism came from leftist movements, who complained about the emergence of a "bureaucratic bourgeoisie" and "labour aristocracy" that had merely indigenized colonial privilege. They criticized the overextended state, which wasted economic surplus. They bemoaned the urban bias in government policies, which served a restricted constituency. They also complained about the growing evidence of ethnic or regional favouritism in recruitment processes. This strident criticism notwithstanding, it was assumed that state capacity was important for development, and that national initiatives—reformist or revolutionary—could lead to changes. This is in sharp contrast to the criticism from the right, which has dominated the thinking about African states since the beginning of the 1980s. This new criticism was driven by radically different premises and an anti-statist ideology.

Undermining State Capacity

The crisis of the public sector is linked to the fiscal crisis faced by African states and to the adjustment policies that have been pursued to address that crisis. In orthodox interpretation, the fiscal crisis is squarely the result of the profligacy of African states, which spent widely to maintain their patronage systems. Although this points to part of the truth, it is too cynical to relate to the fact that the imperatives of accumulation and legitimacy played an important role in the process. Governments had to push their budgets to the limit to handle the demands of supporting economic growth and development (through investment in physical and social infrastructure) and to manage the "social contracts" that were to provide a modicum of peace in the post-independence period. Adjustment tended to view public investment as crowding out the private sector, and its political economy reduced African politics to nothing more than simple rent-seeking. Consequently, one central tenet of adjustment has involved rolling back the state.

While it is true that any kind of response to the fiscal crisis of the state may have justified drastic reductions in state expenditure, both the cognitive framework through which the problem was conceived and the actual solutions proposed led not so much to the rolling back of the state, but to a drastic erosion of its capacity. The incapacitation of the state was premised on a number of beliefs and perceptions about the motives, capacities and commitment of African bureaucracies. In the culturalist view, African states, which in the 1960s and 1970s had been hailed as the instruments par excellence for modernization, were now seen as the incarnation of all the forces of retrograde tradition and underdevelopment. Contrary to earlier views that states represented the modern side of the modern/traditional dichotomy, they were now seen as hopelessly and incurably steeped in Africa's debilitating culture, in which "clientalism," "economies of affection" (Hyden, 1980) and "politics of the belly" (Bayart, 1993) guided all social action.

From an economics point of view, African institutions were infested by rent-seekers who had captured state policies to serve their narrow interests (Bates, 1981). This had rendered the state incapable of pursuing long-term development goals. In this view, bureaucrats were part of the coalition that had produced disaster. The only solution to such rent-seeking was the removal of the source of such rents—state interventionist policies.

A more technocratic view questioned the analytic capacity and the bureaucratic acumen of the African state. From this perspective, African states were seen to be in desperate need of technical cooperation and external guidance. In one version, it was generally considered prudent to work on the assumption that such a bureaucracy and its capacities could be ignored. Such a belief induced a tabula rasa view of African institutions. One consequence was the cultivation among donors of a culture of unbridled experimentation. New ideas, institutional arrangements or projects were introduced and abandoned according to the dictates of fashion, with no consideration of what all this might mean for existing institutions, since such institutions were considered nonexistent or moribund.

A fourth approach, which built on the three above, was what one might call the imperial approach. It was founded on the principal-agent, game-theoretical analytics, where the principal—who wants "good policies"—was the donor. The agents—who were deemed to be self-seeking and corrupt—were the recipient countries. The donor's problem was then to create incentives to induce the agents to act in the desired manner, and to establish institutions able to monitor the agenda and sanction any laxity or misdemeanours on the agent's part. The regime of conditionalities that has shaped donor-recipient relationships during the last two decades has been the inevitable consequence of this approach.

One combined effect of all these views was pervasive doubt about state capacity and a set of self-fulfilling predicaments. The doubt ruled out prospects for the self-regeneration of the state, or for its own internal reform into a more effective actor in the development process, and nourished the idea that "ownership" of policy should be taken away from the state. To avoid clientalism and rent-seeking, the state could be squeezed fiscally and even politically. This weakened state would then exhibit an incapacity to carry out its basic functions (partly because of demoralization, moonlighting by the civil servants, corruption, etc.), which could be used to argue that the state in Africa is not capable of handling development and needs to be stripped down further. And so we witness in Africa the reinforcement of policies that continue to erode the economic and political capacity of the state, even as considerable noise is made about good governance and capacity-building.

States can commit two types of errors: errors of omission, where the government fails to do what it ought to do; and errors of commission, where the state does too much and oversteps its bounds (Goldsmith, 2000). Much of the preoccupation with public sector reform in Africa has evolved around dealing with the latter. The standard view of the state has been that it is somehow overextended. Much of this thinking has become so much part of conventional wisdom that radical proposals on state reform are made without the slightest concern for the implications of such reforms on existing capacities, and without a detailed analysis of the institutional make up of the state. The reasoning has been largely deductive—a state that performed activities, which it should not have performed in the first place, must be bloated. There has been no consideration of the fact that a state overstepping its bounds in certain areas could be woefully inadequate in others. Since Africa performs poorly, it must be the case that there is something peculiar about the African state, hence the search for an African state sui generis. Yet comparative research clearly suggests that there is little difference between states in Africa and in other developing countries, including those that have performed exceedingly well.

Goldsmith (2001b) summarizes the latest evidence on the relative size of the African bureaucracy, all produced by either the World Bank or the International Monetary Fund (IMF). The first results are from the study by Shiavo-Campo, which measured the share of the number of civil servants for 100 people. The study shows that the average ratio for sub-Saharan Africa (1.5) is less than that of Asia (2.6) or of Latin America (3.0). Interestingly, Mauritius and Botswana—the best-performing countries in terms of growth, and with bureaucracies touted as efficient—have more than three times the African average: 5.5 and 5.8 respectively. An earlier study conducted in the early 1980s by the IMF, before the wave of retrenchment, used regression analysis to construct an index, which was the ratio of actual employment to the predicted level (multiplied by 100). The study shows that the average score for the 17 African countries included in the study was 92, or 8 percent less than predicted. Only Botswana and Mauritius are in the "overbureaucratized" group. A more recent study using the same approach on data for the 1970s, 1980s and 1990s arrives at a similar finding, and concludes that, adjusting for the level of development, urbanization and exposure to external risk, public sector employment in Africa is about average for developing countries.

A third measure is the ratio of government wages and salaries to other goods. The data show that Africa's ratio is below average, so that public personnel expenditures in Africa crowd out *less* spending compared to developing countries in general. For the 11 African countries for which data are available, downsizing has reduced the total number of central government workers by 9 per cent during the 1980s and early 1990s. As a consequence, spending on public wages and salaries also dropped from 7 per cent of GDP in 1986 to 5.8 per cent in 1996. Again a difference can be found in Botswana and Mauritius, where both total public employment and the share of the central wage bill in total public expenditures increased. In conclusion, the evidence of the African state as bloated or a "lame Leviathan" simply does not exist. A World Bank study (Schiavo-Campo, 1996) has the following observations:

> In many countries in sub-Saharan Africa, the civil service has sharply deteriorated in almost every way since the 1970s (Botswana is one of the few exceptions). Beginning in the 1980s, a succession of fiscal stabilization programmes has reduced government employment in Africa to the lowest level of any developing region. Thus, although additional downsizing may be necessary in some countries, most do not need to shrink the workforce but to overhaul the entire civil service system.[2]

---

[2] One should note here that the "overhauling of the entire system" has been a licence for reckless experimentation with African institutions.

The end result is that today Africa is the most undergoverned region in the world. The state has been reduced to the colonial *mise en valeur* proportions to maintain law and order and to ensure export of primary commodities:

> The state in Africa has come full circle to the small government of pre-colonial days; but with the additional hysteresis effect from past shocks of a seriously depleted current institutional capability, and deterioration in the current quality and scope of social services and infra-structure provision, coupled with a fiscal position highly vulnerable to changes in foreign aid (Aron, 1996).

According to the World Bank, African states had "sometimes tended to overshoot the mark" in their efforts to create the recommended minimalist administrations (World Bank, 1997b).

Notwithstanding this empirical evidence, the IMF stated that "there is still scope for further downsizing" (Liner and Modi, 1997). Retrenchment has continued, as a result of fiscal constraints.

Incentives

At the heart of the problem are issues related to incentives and governance. The state, as any employer, must motivate its employees by providing security, honour, stability, civility and fulfilment. In this both material and moral incentives are important.

Material Incentives

Standard explanations of the crisis of the African state—corruption, traditional African values that fuse the private and public spheres, patron-client relations, etc.—make sense only when discussed within the context of the effects of changes in the incentive structure for public service. The most obvious forms of incentives are the material ones, including job security. Capacity development requires provision of adequate remuneration to public sector employees. Modern bureaucracies are founded on the premise that individuals who work in them will serve the public good as opposed to catering to personal or sectional interests. This presupposes a basic income or living wages that will allow public servants to carry out their duties without succumbing to extraneous pressures.

During much of the period of adjustment, wages and salaries in the public sector have fallen sharply, with the consequence that many civil servants are compelled to use multiple coping strategies in order to defend incomes through struggles for resources in the informal sector. In a number of cases, these strategies intensify conflicts of interest and lead to downright corruption. Civil servants increasingly become less shielded from pressures of kinship, family or other private networks because of the collapse of public service provision and the need for civil servants to keep their livelihood options open. This resultant venalization of African bureaucracies may be most difficult to reverse.

One way of addressing problems of material incentives has been experimentation with new forms of management—the so-called new public administration (NPA). In recent years, donors have attempted to overhaul the incentive structure in certain arenas of the public sector, such as tax offices or projects run by donors, using higher salary scales and other benefits. These attempts may have produced positive results in capacity development within the specific areas in which they were implemented. But these success stories constitute islands within a larger public sector that is maladjusted and mired in crisis. Indeed, partial gains in a few activities may have hurt the larger system by compounding the confusion over incentives and by fragmenting the system. The gains thus appear as distortions of the public sector's incentive structure. They tend to fuel bureaucratic rivalry, prevent the growth of an esprit de corps, and frustrate efforts to maximize returns from technical cooperation in a nationally coherent manner.

One should add here that the adoption of NPA has been premised on the capacity of both the state and the private sector to deliver. Such things as subcontracting, privatization and competition require state capacity for evaluation, monitoring and regulation. There was also the assumption of the existence of "markets" where the services the state required were traded. In their absence, donors, themselves state bureaucracies with limited competence in the area, have sought to create such markets or institutions that would emulate markets. Where the so-called NPA methods have been prematurely introduced—often in the context of the state's poor regulatory and monitoring capacity—nonexistent or monopolistic markets created by donor identified providers, corruption, pillaging of assets and uncontrolled monopolies have emerged to subvert reforms.

The Problem of Moral Incentives

Deployment of capacities for nation-building has always demanded more than material incentives. Bureaucracies have been driven by a wide range of moral incentives, including "catching up," nation-building, military superiority, etc. In Africa, such moral incentives played an important role in the heydays of independence. The self-confidence, enthusiasm and commitment that were so evident in African bureaucracies in the 1960s and 1970s were contagious, as reflected in many African students, who anxiously rushed home after graduation to participate in the exhilarating projects of nation-building. Much of this esprit des corps began to erode in the 1980s, in some cases because those who had spearheaded the national project had been overthrown, or their self-aggrandizement had led to disillusion, or there was no clear sense of direction. The role of moral incentives is now generally obscured by the predominance of approaches that privilege greed and self-interest as the only driving force for human endeavour. In the new thinking, the distinctiveness of the public service, with its emphasis on esprit de corps and vocation, is rejected and replaced by the view that merit pay is to be the single most important driving instrument.

Governance and the Incentive Framework

In discussing incentives, we need to recognize the framework within which incentives are deployed. It is such a framework that explains the responsiveness of those to whom incentives are directed. The system must ensure fair rewards, and offer a sense that one is engaged in a meaningful exercise with legitimate institutions possessing means adequate to the task. The incentives must be transparent and consistent (or at least not self-defeating). In other words, an effective framework requires sound governance institutions that enjoy the confidence of most sections of society and those engaged by them, and that are designed to perform the assigned tasks.

Ownership and Identification of Needs

One important aspect of governance relates to ownership of policies. In current policy discourse, African governments are berated for not "owning" their policies by precisely the same institutions that insist on owning the policies themselves. One of the early concerns of African policy-makers was over the poor identification with the state on the part of citizens, the state being largely seen as a remnant of foreign rule. Nationalists were keen to be seen to own the policies. Every case of indigenization was proudly announced over national media. Although doubts remained about the national character of the state, some progress had been made in ridding it of its colonial baggage. However, whatever gains were made in making a dent in this image of the state was reversed by the end of the 1990s. Under the new forms of control and conditionality, neocolonialism, with its concerns for the sensitivities of the new nations, appeared in retrospect a milder affair. In quite a number of dramatic cases, posts that had been Africanized reverted to expatriate hands, to the chagrin of local experts and the humiliation of the nationalist project.

We noted how the prevalent view was that the pursuit of "good economics" was being subverted by "bad politics." This understanding was based on the assumption that the Washington Consensus was absolutely the right thing to do, and opposition to it was the result of the nefarious machinations of interest groups and politicians (Bates and Krueger, 1993). The certainty with which these views were pushed made it impossible to believe that there might actually be reservations. Since the civil service system and parastatals were considered as the most important sources of patronage, the public employees were simply part of the "bad politics" syndrome (Herbst, 1990). In a context where local technocrats were viewed as having no moral commitment to the task of economic development, there were two logical ways of proceeding. One was to attempt to circumvent or undermine institutions dominated by local elites; another was to create new structures to reach the poor directly. As Jan Valdelin observes:

> In extreme cases, donors went so far as to consciously plan projects as a *bypass,* simply to avoid the public sector in the recipient country. In a bypass, aid funds are controlled from start to finish by the donor, or at least by companies that are the direct agents of the donor. This model is in many ways the ultimate expression of a lack of trust in the recipient's ability, in combination with a lack of faith in the long-term possibility of improving capacity in the recipient's public sector (Valdelin, 1998).

The consequence was, as in the case of Ghana, "a parallel government controlled if not created by the lender agencies" (Hutchful, 1988, 12). One of the most striking consequences of such parallel governments is the parallel documentation that circulates among donors and national governments. Donors and nationals read different literature on the same problem, with literature produced by the former often marked as confidential. Not even versions of the budgets are the same.[3] In mild cases, this "bypass" has taken the form of support of nongovernmental organizations (NGOs), who presumably are national institutions. For some, the delegitimization of the state that this signalled was equated with the strengthening of civil society. For others, this implied a donor-recipient relationship within a principal-agent framework in which the donor, the principal, wanted development, while the recipient, the agent, simply wanted material gain.

Under such a framework, the stage was set for a conditionality-driven relationship. After years during which conditionalities were the norm, the donor community increasingly came to realize that imposed programmes were rarely, if ever, successful. The option of circumventing local elites in the development process was patently absurd. External imposition weakened the administrative capacity and undermined the moral authority of the state, which was now seen to have accepted external diktat. It also generated hostility from groups whose knowledge and skills were valuable to the success of any policy, and who had the capacity effectively to put the spanner in the wheels of donor-driven projects. The Organisation for Economic Co-operation and Development (OECD) donors increasingly began to see how ownership was low in Africa, and called for transferring it to Africans. However, the "ownership" reserved for Africa did not include generation of indigenous policy but adoption of pre-packaged policies.

This was achieved in two ways. First, key position papers that supposedly reflected government opinion, such as those for meetings of the Paris Club, were at times drafted by donors who then turned around and praised the recipients for their thoughtful propositions. Killick (1997) reports that "letters of intent," which are ostensibly from governments, were almost invariably drafted in Washington, with governments left trying to negotiate variations in a document presented to them. He adds: "It is difficult to imagine a procedure more subversive of ownership." The second approach was to identity certain key individuals who belonged to the same "epistemic communities" as the expatriate experts and empower them. In the absence of such individuals, courses were organized, lucrative travel grants were made, fellowships were provided. These "capacity-building" exercises had more the character of cloning than the production of people with critical analytical skills. Consultancy arrangements were made from which "nationals" could champion the externally driven policy agendas as their own. Nationals were seconded from international positions to national institutions and selected individuals had their salaries topped up. The overall effect has been that the so-called "dialogues" took on the character of the conversation between a ventriloquist and a puppet—a process unlikely to enhance the

---

3 And as Nicholas van de Walle observes: "The national budget that is officially passed in the legislature may come to matter less than what has been promised to the donors.... For instance, a recent report noted that the Tanzanian government presented different budget estimates in 1995 to the consultative group of creditors and to the national legislature. In one, it projected a surplus, in the other a deficit" (van de Walle 1996).

capacities of either of the participants. Berg cites this kind of dialogue as one of the "learning blockages":

> ...there is a lack of autonomous intermediaries in heavily-aided countries. Donors spend much of their dialogue in discussion with captured institutions and officials who are direct beneficiaries.
>
> What is most pertinent from the learning perspective is that genuinely critical dialogue, the best source of feedback, is rare, narrowing the information flow to donors about what is really happening" (Berg, 2000, 32).

Dialogue should not only be a polite way of imposing one's agenda, but an important component in the exchange and transfer of knowledge.

Proliferation of Tasks for Weakened States

Wrong diagnosis and the jaundiced view of the state have produced a number of paradoxes for neoliberal projects. Structurally adjusting an economy was a state activity that required much more capacity than was implied by simple retrenchment. Most of the measures proposed actually needed a strong state to see through the major structural changes implied by the policies. The strength refers not only to the repressive capacity to ride roughshod over putatively well-organized interest groups, but the more important political capacity to win adhesion to programmes among large sections of society, and to develop the analytical and technical capacity to implement the programmes.

The major changes in development thinking in the 1970s and 1980s related to the recognition of the importance of markets. Rather than viewing markets in a complimentary relationship with the state, the new approach tended to view the market as the dominant force, and when the role of the state was admitted at all, it was more in the mode of the night watchman to secure property rights. This position was arrived at not only through the anti-statist ideology, but also through a view of the market as working according to the specifications of models of perfect competition. Such markets, with their assumptions of perfect information, costly transactions, and infinite flexibility and foresight, need no bureaucracy. Ironically, it was precisely during this period that some of the more elaborate models of imperfect information, externalities and market failure in general were being developed. These new theories pointed to problems of transaction costs in real markets; to the need for public institutions to enforce competition; to possibilities of underinvestment by the private sector in socially valuable activities; and to problems of coordination, especially of investment decisions.

In addition, "new growth theories" rediscovered a whole range of determinants of economic growth that were central to development economics and that provided a rationale for government intervention, since they assert that the contribution to overall social production of some investments is higher than their contribution to the income of individual agents. Government policies, therefore, that foster such activities would be welfare-enhancing (Barros, 1993). On the basis of econometric exercises, the number of determinants of growth has increased pretty much at the discretion of individual econometricians and the availability of data sets.

Beyond these changes in economics theory, there were also pressures from the international community for African governments to implement all kinds of agendas adopted in international forums. NGOs played an important role in widening this agenda. Domestic pressures for more government activity grew as well, especially in light of the increased democratization of national politics.

Privatization

We have thus far focussed our attention on the public sector, largely because much technical cooperation is from public institutions to public institutions. However, given the prominent role of NGOs and the private sector, it is important to consider the technical capacity of these actors. The intention of privatization under structural adjustment was to create what Johnson (1987) characterized as a "soft authoritarian" state whose main task was to create an enabling environment for the private sector by augmenting market rationality and reducing risks and uncertainty, but not by engaging in market distorting interventions that characterized prior policies of developmental states. In all this, privatization programmes have rarely considered the capacity of the private sector to respond adequately, the assumption being that it was adequate and only needed unleashing from the tentacles of an interventionist state.

However, experience and the privatization debacle revealed that the capacity of the private sector to use available capital productively couldn't be taken for granted. Concrete measures are required to remove enduring institutional and behavioural impediments and to nurture the private sector into greater productivity. Furthermore, in economies in which the private sector is expected to play a major role, the capacities required are not only those of the private sector but also those of the public sector, in terms of managing the market economy. This also means building institutional linkages between the private sector and the state. Privatization is a state activity requiring state capacity to regulate the process, ensure competitive markets, safeguard standards, etc. Such economies have also discovered that the growth of the private sector, to which they had become fervently committed, was being hampered not by an overextended state, but by a weakened state. Some donors now admit that their own experience with aid largely geared to state-to state relationships has not prepared them for the task of promoting the private sector.

Globalization and State Capacity

Literature on globalization points to how the process is undermining the capacity of states and limits their room for manoeuvre. The weakening of the capacity to tax highly mobile capital and the need for the state to "signal" foreign investors have contributed to limiting the state's agenda. However, we should bear in mind that, in the absence of comprehensive global governance institutions, globalization must be "serviced" by public institutions at the national level (Sassen, 1998). Consequently, while eroding the capacities for addressing domestic issues, globalization has placed a high premium on national skills to service the global economy. National institutions must have the regulatory capacity to ensure that the rules of the game are upheld.

They must maintain infrastructure, provide a skilled and healthy labour force, etc. The costs of servicing the global economy at the national level can be enormous. It has been estimated that just drafting the laws to meet the intellectual property rights requirements in World Trade Organization regulations would cost Tanzania US $1-1.5 million (Finger and Schuler, 1999). In light of this, African countries are now under enormous pressure to acquire skills to meet the new norms of a globalized world. This extraversion of the bureaucracy so that it performs well on the international scene while performing poorly domestically takes us back to earlier criticism of the neocolonial or dependent state. It also brings us back to the question: capacity for whom and for what?

The eclectic and rather Procrustean explanation of economic growth, the multiplicity of "stakeholders," the demands of a globalized world and popular pressures have, paradoxically, increased the laundry list of what governments should do, even as the dominant ideology calls for a minimalist state. Virtually every donor can now find a variable in these equations that justifies their intervention. This proliferation of tasks forced the OECD to raise the pertinent question as to whether what was now going on was "capacity-building or spreading bewilderment" (OECD/DAC, 1995).

Credibility of Technical Cooperation and Mutual Respect

One new word in policy discourse is the "credibility" of policy, especially to the private sector. In the case of Africa, we are essentially talking about credibility to foreign capital. African states are now subject to ratings by an array of international institutions such as Transparency International, the World Economic Forum and the Bretton Woods Institutions. Public expenditure reviews are conducted with virtually no involvement from local people.[4] What is often overlooked in all this is that if technical cooperation is to be effective, it also has to be credible to the beneficiaries so they are motivated to embrace the new skills it requires.

And yet there is little discussion on how to ensure the credibility of technical cooperation, and there is little ongoing evaluation of such technical cooperation by recipients, presumably on the proverbial injunction of not looking a gift horse in the mouth. There is as yet no agency rating donors or foreign investors as worthy partners in the national development process, and given the asymmetry of power and needs, we are unlikely to see the emergence of such agencies. Misjudgements made during the last two decades have not done much to enhance such credibility. Donors have pressed for projects whose feasibility local experts doubted, and they have changed positions without explaining exactly what went wrong before. Positions and knowledge held by local experts for years have been announced as new discoveries by visiting experts. As an example, over the period of retrenchment many local observers of national administrations pointed out that (a) the rule-of-thumb and cookie-cutter trimming of bureaucracies did not take into account local conditions; and (b) the reduced capacities would not be up to the task even in its putatively reduced form. The cognitive dissonance that this produced among local experts could only be demoralizing.

---

[4] The marginalization of Africans from the reform process is illustrated by the fact that of the 113 public expenditure review exercises completed up to 1993, "only three included local members on the review team, not one in Africa where most were done and where the ownership problem was most acute" (Berg, 2000).

A fundamental problem of technical cooperation in Africa is that the supplier not only pays for it, but also claims it is being demanded. Technical cooperation is built into aid funding in a "take-it or leave-it manner." Only in a few cases is the technical cooperation provided and the price tag on it anywhere close to what African governments themselves would accept if they paid for it. The question is not simply that it would be out of reach of national budgets. Rather it is that very rarely are African technocrats convinced that the technical cooperation they are receiving is worth it. And in many cases, they are not even allowed to examine the curriculum vitae of the experts. They simply come with the aid package, and any attempts to disentangle them from the package would be futile and often foolhardy.

The identification of needs by donor funded consultancies and the possibilities of conflicts of interest that this raises have also created scepticism about the disinterestedness of donors in the process. Consulting teams whose well-being depends on the identification of gaps will tend to downplay or denigrate existing capacities, while exaggerating the crucial importance of their continued presence in "capacity-building." There is often little sensitivity to how local experts will take the detailed negative accounts of their expertise by visiting consultants. One should add here that the pro-lending ethos of the aid bureaucracies, which involves sustaining a high level of lending, is partly an end in itself. The consequence is that donors tend to overestimate local commitment and capacity.

The sense of frustration with the capacity-building process in one field—research—comes out from Kinyanji's *cris de coeur*:

> The notion common among certain donor agencies that Kenyans do not have the necessary skills to conduct research or that their institutions do not have the necessary capacity to train adequate numbers of such people are myths and, at best, falsehoods propagated by people whose true intentions are to make the never-ending training of Africans their lifetime career (Kinyanji, 1983, 302).

Given the role played by foreign elites in the management of African economies, it is remarkable that so little is said about the social relations between these elites and their local counterparts. And yet there can be no doubt that some modicum of mutual respect and commonness of purpose is essential to the attainment of what are putatively common objectives. In the case of Africa, the transfer of knowledge is taking place between two alienated elites—the locals and the foreigners. Resentment of foreign expatriates by local counterparts results from various perceptions: the erosion of national sovereignty; the hurt professional pride of people who feel they are being directed by, at best, professional equals; the envy of the high remuneration of foreigners; or concerns about having to spend so much time on a project whose value one is not convinced of. Expatriates, in turn, may be disdainful towards counterparts. This may be the result of a perception that they have come to rescue the country from predatory local elites; the reluctance of their counterparts to exert themselves adequately in the projects' work; or the perceived rampant corruption of a civil service engaged in "multiple survival strategies." Matters have been made worse by the erosion of the salaries of local elites through devaluations and inflations.[5] The sum total

---

[5] The contrast with the past is clearly brought out by Kenneth King when he writes: "What is intriguing about the huge movement of graduate teachers from North America and Europe to the newly independent

of all this is a social and psychological environment in which mutual exchange of ideas and learning are made extremely difficult. As far back as 1983, the World Bank, in commenting on "better management of expatriates," recognized much of this, noting, "The Bank's experience indicates that when the 'psychological distance' between expatriates and their local counterparts is minimized, the value of technical cooperation is much enhanced" (World Bank, 1983, 133).

There is also a dilemma expressed in donor circles about problems of a close relationship with local conditions and personnel. On the one hand, it is deemed necessary for donors to become acquainted with the real situation, partly to guard against the imposition of inappropriate and misguided headquarters-designed conditions or projects. On the other hand, there is a fear that field staff may "go native," becoming advocates of "their" countries, making selectivity and objectively-based decisions more difficult (Killick, 1998, 191).

Enclavization of Capacity

One disturbing feature of current efforts at capacity-building and use of local technical capacity is the privileging of those skills deemed appropriate to the donors' projects. We should bear in mind that the emphasis of structural adjustment has been on austerity, and not on growth and development. The implication of this has been the strengthening of institutions in the bureaucracy usually associated with the implementation of adjustment measures—such as finance ministries and central banks—and at the expense of the so-called "spending" ministries that implement development programmes. Governments are being forced to raise their technocratic capacities in the economic policy field in order to be able to implement market reforms, send credible signals to investors and enjoy debt relief from donors. Increasingly, in a large number of countries, a small pool of experts, often found in finance and trade ministries as well as in central banks, is vested with extensive powers in navigating economies and shaping public policies (Bangura, 1994). The presence of these technocrats is supposed to give private investors confidence in the country.

The temptation and practice have been to fence off reform projects so as to insulate them from an inefficient system. The "autonomy" given to these elements is only with respect to domestic actors, since "credibility" demands that they are subject to external "agents of restraint" (Collier and Gunning, 1993) and that, at the ideational level, they belong to the epistemic community conversant with the new global discourse. An extreme case of this was the "dream team" arrangement of Kenya, which clearly demonstrated that creating enclaves does not work, and civil service reform efforts should be directed at the overall system.

Adjustment programmes have often undermined local capacities and have tended to divert national capacities away from national projects towards donor-driven ones. While employment in the public sector is declining, employment in the burgeoning

---

states is that the process did not feel like what could later be called an aid project. These expatriates had regular contracts with ministries and universities, and some relatively small supplementation on their return.... This rather extraordinary episode which lasted for 10-15 years has been little analysed...it was...responsible for forming (or reinforcing) a very powerful commitment amongst the expatriate personnel to the countries (and continent) in which they temporarily worked" (King, 2000, 166-7).

consultancy industry has increased. This industry engages in "data mining," which often requires collaboration with civil servants who are paid for what should routinely be their job. One effect has been that national institutions—private and public—have been priced out of the markets for some of their most skilled citizens. Donors and NGOs can offer competitive remuneration for their projects, whereas governments are unable to pay their staff living wages; already scarce skilled employees migrate from the disadvantaged public sector to the arms of donor and NGO projects, and the remaining staff in the core service become overworked or engage in multiple survival strategies. We thus have the bizarre situation in which skilled Africans find the public sector unattractive or not fully rewarding, and are willing to develop the capacities of donor agencies and Western institutions, while foreign experts become firmly entrenched in the policy-making institutions of African states. Rather than focusing on enhancing the impact of local development efforts, the preponderance of aid interests ties up large amounts of scarce resources to enhance the effectiveness of aid, even when it is recognized that aid is not the catalyst, let alone the only development initiative taking place in the country. As a consequence, local administrators are left with little time for their own problems and initiatives.

All this is now common knowledge among donors and is publicly acknowledged. For example, the World Bank has admitted that external interventions:

> ...may actually have made matters worse on the capacity-building front because they have tended to "exacerbate Africa's capacity problems through approaches that have been supply driven and geared to satisfying internal institutional demands rather than the capacity-building needs of the countries."

> ...the donors' flawed approach in Africa is in part attributable to host governments' failure to develop a coherent vision of capacity-building, leaving the field open for donors to impose their own ideas.

> Despite their stated intentions to promote sustainable development and local capacity, donors have often behaved in a way that has either had no impact on local capacity or, worse, has eroded it. Donors have been too quick to seize the initiative for policy-making and project and programme preparation from local agencies. This has often been met by complacency on the country side; the result has been to reduce demand for local capacity development and an atrophying of existing capacity. A closely related point is that national authorities have rarely been strongly "committed to" or had "ownership of" capacity-building efforts. Most, instead, have been driven by external donors (World Bank, 1996).

Disembedding the State

We noted how much of the writing on African states bemoans the bureaucracies' lack of autonomy from interest groups and society at large. By delinking the state from its social roots while subjecting it to external "agents of restraint" through a battery of conditionalities and technical cooperation, the call for state autonomy has been tantamount to a call for isolation. Bretton Woods conditionalities have tended to distance the state from local vested interests. This alienation is supposed to provide the necessary autonomy to ensure decisions that enhance national interests. It is often claimed that it was such insulation that explained the East Asian "miracle states."

Analysis suggests that the view of the autonomy of the state in the Asian miracle countries is an oversimplification, and the argument for state technocracies pursuing development in complete isolation from societal pressures is a myth that is not empirically founded. In the seminal work on the developmental state, Johnson underlines the intimacy of its relationship with the private sector and the intensity of its involvement in the market as a crucial feature (Johnson, 1981). Subsequent writing on other developmental states has underscored this point, leading to the useful, albeit problematic, notion of "embedded autonomy." It describes the nature of state autonomy in these societies as circumscribed by the dependence of the state on the activities of the private sector for its development project (Evans, 1992). For democratic states, the issue is the embeddedness of the bureaucracy within a realm of democratic decision-making. The bureaucracy is an instrument of a democratic state. The "embeddedness" of the bureaucracy is then an aspect of democratic control of the bureaucracy. Note that this does not conflict with the need for efficient and meritocratic bureaucracy. Indeed, this requirement of embeddedness may be more important in a democracy.

Domestic Conditions

The effectiveness of technical cooperation ultimately depends on internal conditions. It is these that can adapt, tame, utilize, resist, deflect or subvert technical cooperation. The history of technological acquisition and "catching up" clearly suggests the importance of what Abramovitz refers to as social capability, understood to include educational levels, physical infrastructure, corporate governance, political stability, interpersonal trust, civil cooperations, etc. (Abramovitz, 1986 and 1995). Indeed, many negative effects of technical cooperation may reflect local weaknesses. A number of internal factors have contributed to undermining national capacity to absorb technical know-how. Here we can only discuss these in a very telegraphic matter.

The first of these factors is the neglect of education. No amount of incentives can serve as a substitute for competence. Indeed, placing incompetent people in high and well-remunerated positions can do enormous damage to the whole system of incentives. And so as we revisit the whole issue of incentives in Africa, we have to keep in mind the production of human capital. Each model of development implicitly or explicitly contains within it the structure of human resources requisite to its implementation. During the post-independence period, the rapid expansion of tertiary and secondary schools reflected nationalist ambitions for the industrialization of Africa and the desire to transcend the *mise en valeur* view of colonial development, which as we noted, did not need much skilled labour. The model of adjustment proposed for Africa did not need a highly skilled labour force, a point that was to be given scientific respectability by the studies on rates of return that persuaded many donors to withdraw support to tertiary education and forced governments to cut support for universities, with serious consequences for African economies. In the 1980s, some donors questioned the value of supporting university education. Not only did this lead to dwindling resources for existing institutions, as many donors stopped funding higher education, but it also fostered a brain drain, exacerbating the already dire situation African universities found themselves in. Michael Chege's observation is apt here:

> All considered, the diminution of human capability resulting from the degradation in health, education and skills amounts to the single most enduring handicap for the continent's long-term economic recovery. For in the light of current theories of economic growth, expounded most explicitly by Paul Romer and Robert Lucas, the strongest and most sustained prospects for national productivity growth are premised on positive rates of change in human capital combined with steady augmentation of physical assets (Chege, 1997, 322).

The second factor is lack of clarity about ends, and the lack of focus and determination to accomplish those ends upon which agreement has been reached. For technical capacities—national or foreign—can only be used effectively if the goals are clear and consistently pursued. Lack of vision by the political leadership and policy instability are not conducive to long-term thinking about skill acquisition and resource deployment.

A third issue has been the decline of a sense of self-reliance and its replacement by a mendicant posture in which help is sought even before exhausting readily available national capacities. An aspect of the decline in self-reliance is the collapse of national savings. Savings rates in Africa are in most cases lower today than they were in the 1960s and 1970s. In 1995, Africans south of the Sahara saved US $8 billion as compared to $10 billion in 1970 (in constant 1975 dollars). Had the rate of savings in 1995 been as high as it was in 1975, the amount would have been $11 billion. The shortfall is close to what these countries received in aid, and would have been much higher had the growth rates of the 1970s been attained under adjustment. A state that is dependent on foreign funding for its basic activities cannot expect undivided loyalty from a technocracy aware of this dependency. Related to this is the fiscal basis of the state. One factor that has driven bureaucracies in other societies to deliver services has been the extent to which they need to obtain taxes from the public. This reliance on incomes from the citizenry has in many ways contributed to some sense of accountability. In Africa, aid and mineral rents have probably diminished this imperative, with the consequence that bureaucracies have at times confined themselves to servicing mining enclaves or foreign sources of aid. As we noted above, this "enclavization" or "extraversion" of the bureaucracy has implications for the learning process and for the relationship between the technocracy and national constituencies.

The sense of autonomy and national purpose among technocrats depends to a large extent on the posture of the political leadership. To the extent that national leadership has yielded too much of national sovereignty to external forces, it is unrealistic to expect technocrats to be assertive about national objectives and priorities. Time and again, local experts are overruled by foreign experts who can always count on the support of the head of state or of a minister. At issue here is the question of accountability and sovereignty.

The fourth major constraint on the use of technical capacity are the authoritarian/personalized politics that have substituted arbitrary placement of personnel for merit. Not only does this practice block the usual channels of exchange, but it also stifles a culture of inquiry and free exchange of information. Despite democratization, many African countries have yet to resolve basic governance problems such as ensuring that elected representatives reflect the will of the people, protect civil and political rights, accept the principle of alternation of power and presidential term limits, and create effective channels through which civil servants and governments can be pressured to deliver good public services. Related to the above is the lack of accountability and the presence of corruption. Recent movements towards democratization hold the promise of addressing this problem, although the growing technocratization of policy-making is likely to limit the effectiveness of democracy in ensuring responsible and accountable administration.

The fifth problem is the unresolved "national question," which has often contributed to a multiplicity of points of view that have not all been reconciled to the exigencies of the modern state or the local version of it. Perhaps the most devastating example of this has been ethnicity, or the much bemoaned tribalism, which in some cases has scuttled all attempts at establishing national and meritocratic public administrations. The waste that ethnic discrimination causes in terms of deployment of national skills needs no elaboration. At the centre of the problem is the issue of equality or sense of inclusion in the formation of governments and staffing of the public sector. Standard explanations, such as those relating to neo-patrimonialism, only make sense when discussed in the context of the larger problem of African politicians' failure to construct appropriate governance institutions to manage diversity and promote inclusion in the public sector.

Finally, there is the problem of the absence of elite consensus on goals. One important conditioning factor for incentives is elite support for the governance of the public sector. Technical cooperation for capacity development will be ineffective when political authority is weak or hotly contested by highly polarized groups in society. Development will not take firm roots in Africa if its elites are uncomfortable with the rules of the game and express or hold fears about exclusion. They may be tempted to adopt the kinds of opportunistic strategies that have plunged many of these countries into multiple crises. Technical cooperation will not yield positive results in this kind of environment. One should also be aware here of the failure of African governments to link up organically with their own intelligentsia (Mkandawire, 2000).

With the growing importance of the private sector, the relationship between different elites—in this case between those in the public and private sectors—is premised on both shared national goals and self-interest. Government officials want to draw the private sector into their national projects, and they need information and revenue from the private sector. The private sector, in turn, needs to know government intentions and that it can expect a whole range of services from the public sector. In most cases, governments are hampered by the current policy regime by not being allowed to introduce policies that favour local business over foreign ones, while, at the same time, being required to enter dialogue with local business. With nothing to offer, it is unlikely that business will find the state bureaucracy a worthy partner.

Concluding Remarks

In recent years, there has been widespread recognition of what has gone wrong with technical cooperation to Africa and of the need to enhance the capacities of African countries. There is also recognition that instead of the lean and fit continent they sought through reining in the state, the reformers have produced emaciated states with demoralized civil services, and reduced political legitimacy and capacity. However, in most cases, the recognition of past errors does not seem fully to include the extent of the damage and the enormity of the task of redeploying existing capacity, rebuilding old capacity and creating new capacity. There is also no clear admission that some of the damage was attributable to the dominant economic vision of international financial institutions and their perception of the political economies of African countries. Unless such a vision is questioned, it is difficult to imagine how any new capacities can be created and how existing ones can be usefully deployed. A new understanding is needed that transcends the narrow scope of these institutions.

In reforming technical cooperation and capacity, the issue of incentives has become important. We have argued that the issue is not just of material incentives, but of moral incentives as well. We have also argued that in order for these incentives to have the intended effect, we have to take into account the overall incentive framework, consisting of goals, values, means, social arrangements, ownership and governance. Existing frameworks have tended to blunt the effectiveness of incentives; it is essential that fundamental changes are made to such frameworks as part of enabling African countries to "borrow" or build the technical competence required for development and social transformation.

A number of the problems of technical cooperation may be inherent to the relationships surrounding it. How else does one explain the fact that the problems persist after a slew of studies and recommendations, and after all the mea culpas from both donor and recipient countries? To reduce the negative aspects of aid, African countries will have to be more assertive of both needs and capacities. This, in turn, will mean greater mobilization of their own resources—human, financial and material—before rushing off to aid missions, so that aid is merely complimentary to their national efforts and not the driving force. Historically, countries have acquired technology through buying it, encouraging immigration of skilled labour, or by "stealing" it through violation of patent laws or industrial espionage. What Africans are apparently persuaded of—that they can develop through the free acquisition of technology—is unprecedented and, from all indications so far, a non-starter. To tame "technical cooperation," Africans will have to be selective, and that will involve paying for the services. There is a lot of talk among donors of an exit strategy from an aid relationship that has proved unsatisfactory. One hears little from the African side on their own exit strategies. Doesn't an African saying remind us all, "The hand that receives is always under the one that gives?" (cited in Landes, 1999).

References

Abramovitz, M. 1986. "Catching Up, Forging Ahead, and Falling Behind." *Journal of Economic History,* XLVI (1), 406.

———. 1995. "Elements of Social Capability." In *Social Capability and Long-Term Economic Growth,* edited by B. H. Koo and D. H. Perkins. London: Macmillan.

Aron, J. 1996. "The Institutional Foundations of Growth." In *Africa Now: People, Policies and Institutions,* edited by S. Ellis. London: James Currey.

Bangura, Y. 1994. "Intellectuals, Economic Reform and Social Change: Constraints and Opportunities in the Formations of a Nigerian Technocracy." Dakar: Council for the Development of Social Research in Africa.

Barros, A. 1993. "Some Implications of New Growth Theory for Economic Development." *Journal of International Development,* 5(5), 531-58.

Bates, R. 1981. *Markets and States in Tropical Africa.* Berkeley and Los Angeles: University of California.

Bates, R., and A. Krueger. 1993. *Political and Economic Interactions in Economic Policy Reform.* Oxford: Basil Blackwell.

Bayart, J. F. 1993. *The State in Africa: The Politics of the Belly.* London: Longman.

Berg, Elliot. 2000. "Why Aren't Aid Organisations Better Learners?" *In Learning in Development Co-operation,* edited by Jerker Carlsson and Lennart Wohlgemuth, 25-40. Stockholm: Expert Group on Development Issues.

Chege, M. 1997. "Paradigms of Doom and the Development Management Crisis in Kenya." *Journal of Development Studies,* 33(4), 552-67.

Collier, Paul, and Jan W. Gunning. 1993. "Linkages Between Trade Policy and Regional Integration." Nairobi: AERC.

Durevall, Dick. 2001. *Reform of the Malawian Public Sector Incentives, Governance and Accountability.* Helsinki: United Nations University.

Einhorn, Jessica. 2001. "The World Bank's Mission Creep." *Foreign Affairs,* 80 (September/October).

Evans, P. 1992. 'The State as Problem and Solution: Embedded Autonomy and Structural Change." In *The Politics of Structural Adjustment: International Constraints, Distributive Conflicts and the State,* edited by S. Haggard and R. Kaufman. Princeton: Princeton University Press.

Finger, J. M., and P. Schuler. 1999. *Implementation of Uruguay Round Commitments: The Development Challenge.* Washington, DC: World Bank.

Goldsmith, A. 2000. "Sizing up the African State." *Journal of Modern African Studies,* 38(1), 1-20.

———. 2001a. "Africa's Overgrown State Reconsidered."

————. 2001b. "Institutions and Economic Growth in Africa." In *Restarting and Sustaining Growth and Development in Africa,* edited by M. F. McPherson.

Herbst, J. 1990. "The Structural Adjustment of Politics in Africa." *World Development,* 18, 7.

Hutchful, Eboe. 1988. "From 'Revolution' to Monetarism: The Economics and Politics of the Adjustment Programme in Ghana." In *Structural Adjustment in Africa,* edited by Bonnie Campbell and John Loxley. London: Macmillan.

Hyden, G. 1980. *Beyond Ujamaa in Tanzania: Underdevelopment and an Uncaptured Peasantry.* Berkeley: University of California Press.

Johnson, C. 1981. "Introduction: The Taiwanese Model." In *Contemporary Republic of China: The Taiwanese Experience,* edited by J. H. Hsiung. New York: Praeger.

————. 1987. "Political Institutions and Economic Performance: The Government-Business Relationship in Japan, South Korea, and Taiwan." In *The Political Economy of the New Asian Industrialism,* edited by F. Deyo. Ithaca: Cornell University Press.

Killick, T. 1997. *Conditionality, Donors and the Political Economy of Policy Reform in Developing Countries.* London: Overseas Development Institute.

————. 1998. *Aid and the Political Economy of Policy Change.* London: Routledge.

King, K. 2000. "A Personal Reflection: Learning and Development Aid, 1960-2000." In *Learning in Development Co-operation,* edited by Jerker Carlsson and Lennart Wohlgemuth, 164-80. Stockholm: Expert Group on Development Issues.

Kinyanji, J. 1983. "Who Conducts Research in Kenya." In *Education Research Environments in the Developing World,* edited by S. Shaeffer and J. Kinyanji. Ottawa: International Development Research Cooperation.

Ki-Zerbo, J. 1992. "Le développement clés en téte." In *Le Natte des Autres: Pour un développement endogéene en Afrique,* edited by J. Ki-Zerbo. Dakar: Council for the Development of Social Research in Africa.

Landes, David S. 1999. *The Wealth and Poverty of Nations: Why Some Are So Rich and Some So Poor.* New York: W. W. Norton and Company.

Liner, I., and J. Modi. 1997. *A Decade of Civil Service Reform.* Washington, DC: International Monetary Fund.

Mkandawire, Thandika. 2000. "Non-Organic Intellectuals and 'Learning' in Policy-Making Africa." In *Learning in Development Co-operation,* edited by Jerker Carlsson and Lennart Wohlgemuth, 205-12. Stockholm: Expert Group on Development Issues.

————. 2001. "Thinking About Developmental States in Africa." *Cambridge Journal of Economics,* 25(3), 289-313.

Organisation for Economic Co-operation and Development (OECD). 1996. *Geographical Distribution of Financial Flows to Aid Recipients.* Paris.

Organisation for Economic Co-operation and Development/Development Assistance Committee (OECD/DAC). 1995. *Development Cooperation.* Paris.

Picciotto, Robert. 2001. "Banking on Reform." *Foreign Affairs,* 81 (January/February).

Sassen, S. 1998. *Embedding the Global in the National: Implications for the Role of the State.* Chicago: University of Chicago.

Schiavo-Campo, S. 1996. "Reforming the Civil Service." *Finance and Development,* 43(3), 10-13.

Sender, J. 1999. "Africa's Economic Performance: Limitations of the Current Consensus." *Journal of Economic Perspectives,* 13(3), 89-114.

Valdelin, Jan. 1998. "Aid Management." In Institutional Building and Leadership in Africa, edited by Lennart Wohlegemuth, Jerker Carlson and Henock Kifle. Uppsala: Nordiska Afrikainstitutet.

van de Walle, Nicholas. 1996. "Globalisation and African Democracy." Annual meeting of the African Studies Association. San Fransisco.

World Bank. 1983. *World Development Report.* New York: Oxford University Press.

———. 1996. *Partnerships for Capacity-Building in Africa.* Washington, DC.

———. 1997a. *Revitalizing Universities in Africa: Strategy and Guidelines.* Washington, DC.

———. 1997b. *World Development Report 1997: The State in a Changing World.* Washington, DC.

2.3 POWER, NETWORKS AND IDEOLOGY IN THE FIELD OF DEVELOPMENT

GUSTAVO LINS RIBEIRO

Another conceptual crisis is unfolding within the field of development and technical cooperation, prompting a most proficuous conjuncture to promote change within the related discursive formations. If we are to go beyond the recycling of theories and concepts, new formulations need to be based on a critique of the larger field of development activities.[1] After several decades of development, there is no room left for innocence. Inspired by Durkheim's (1968) well-known argument that religion is society worshipping itself, I understand development as economic expansion worshipping itself. That means we need to know the belief system underlying this devotion as well as the characteristics of the power field sustaining it.

Power, the central notion in this chapter, has many definitions. My own conception is based on a combination of three different sources. For Richard Adams (1967), power is the control that one party posseses over another party's environment. Of the several visions of Max Weber, I will retain that of power as the capacity to make people do things they do not want to do. Eric Wolf's (1999) notion of structural power underscores the capacity that historical relationships and forces—especially those that define access to social labour—have to create and organize settings that constrain people's possibilities for action, and to specify the direction and distribution of energy flows. Power, thus, is about (a) being the subject of one's own environment, and being able to control one's own destiny, i.e., the course of action or events that will keep one's life as it is or will modify it, or (b) preventing people from becoming such empowered actors. Since development is always about transformation (Berman, 1987), and typically occurs through encounters between insiders and outsiders located in different power positions, ownership of development initiatives is anchored in and influenced by situations where power inequalities abound. The difficulty of implementing change within the development community is intimately related to the fact that it is a power field.

Development As a Power Field

Bourdieu (1986) defines a field as a set of relations and interrelations based on specific values and practices that operate in given contexts. A field is heterogeneous by definition; it is made up of different actors, institutions, discourses and forces in tension. Within a field, everything makes sense in relational terms by means of oppositions and distinctions. Strategies of cooperation or conflict among actors determine whether a particular doctrine is hegemonic, regardless of its successes or failures (Perrot et al., 1992, 202-4). The development field is constituted by such actors as those representing various segments of local populations (local elites and leaders of social

---

[1] I share Rist's opinion that critique needs to be "understood in its Kantian sense of free and public examination rather than its ordinary sense of unfavourable judgement" (1997, 3).

movements, for instance); private entrepreneurs; officials and politicians at all levels of government; personnel of national, international and transnational corporations (different kinds of contractors and consultants, for example); and staff of international development organizations (officers of multilateral agencies and regional banks, for instance). Institutions are also important members of this field; they include various types of governmental organizations, non-governmental organizations (NGOs), churches, unions, multilateral agencies, industrial entities and financial corporations.

The structure and dynamics of every development field are marked by different power capabilities and interests that are articulated through historical processes of networking. Development encompasses different political visions and positions ranging from an interest in accumulation of economic and political power to an emphasis on redistribution and equity. In consequence, power struggles are common among actors, within and across institutions. Differentiated power nodes operate within the web of relationships and are concretely expressed by the disparities existing between, say, the capabilities and actions of the World Bank and those of a small NGO in India. Barros (1996), in her study of environmental global movements and policies, coined the notion of "nuclear agents," those with more power to influence a field's configuration and tendencies (in her case, the United Nations, the World Bank and mainstream NGOs). The development field's most powerful actors and institutions are those alluded to by the label "development industry." They strive for the reproduction of the field as a whole, since their own interests are closely connected to the field's existence. The least powerful actors and institutions are local groupings disenfranchised by development initiatives. Those initiatives that destroy the relationships between indigenous peoples, their territory and culture—such as forced resettlements to build dams—provide the most obvious scenario of the vulnerability of local populations vis-à-vis "development."

The nature of the power distribution within the development field will depend on the processes through which networks are formed and on the chararacteristics of the resulting institutional interventions in the development drama.

Networking and Consortiation: The Making of Institutions

Networks related to economic expansion and growth are not new. Since the industrial revolution, they have operated in the construction of large-scale infrastructure projects (LSPs), such as canals, railroads, dams and other major works, the quintessential examples of "development projects."[2] LSPs have structural characteristics that allow them to be treated as "extreme expressions" of the development field: the size of the capital, territories and quantities of people they control; their great political power; the magnitude of their environmental and social impacts; the technological innovations they often cause; and the complexity of the networks they entail (Ribeiro, 1987). They put together impressive quantities of financial and industrial capital as well as

---

[2] My choice of focusing on large-scale projects is a methodological one. I am following Kroeber's (1955) idea of studying "the most extreme expressions" of a range of phenomena to better understand them. First military engineers and then civil engineers played a major role in the structuration of this field beginning in the 18th century (Ribeiro, 1987).

state and technical elites and workers, fusing local, regional, national, international and transnational levels of integration.[3] As a form of production linked to the expansion of economic systems, LSPs have connected relatively isolated areas to wider and more integrated market systems. Non-linear flows of labour, capital and information among such projects have happened on a global scale (Ribeiro, 1994 and 1995). Large-scale projects have relied on powerful institutions—such as governmental and multilateral organizations, engineering schools, banks and industrial corporations—that have played important roles in the political economy of the last two centuries. Many of these institutions have become centres for the diffusion of ideas on new and ever larger projects; of technological innovations; and of the categories, models and ideologies of industrial progress and expansion.

Why should we mind these historical connections? Precisely because the field of development is the heir of many of the beliefs and practices that have been generated and transmitted within the field of large-scale projects. The circuits linking projects on national and global scales have made up a multilocated web through which information and people have circulated. Technical and managerial solutions have been exchanged and sometimes improved in projects presented as showcases for the implementation of new methods and technologies. Because of their huge environmental and social impacts, LSPs have vividly portrayed the unbalanced power relationships between local populations and developmentalist outsiders. These projects have also prompted an increase in the reaction capacity of local actors through social movements and NGOs. People have started to understand the inequalities inherent to this kind of economic expansion. Foreign capital, expatriate professionals and technicians have often taken the lion's share of the richness produced by such enterprises.

The connections among projects over time as well as the intergenerational continuity that exists within many of the professions involved in LSPs make us more aware of the need to trace similar connections and continuities in other core areas of the development field. Knowledge about LSPs also fosters a view of development as a force of expansion historically intrinsic to globalization, and reveals such expansion as planned interventions that rely on the establishment of networks of engineers, technicians, politicians, lobbyists, public servants, and financial and industrial capitalists. Personal relationships are of utmost importance to navigate through the complex webs of interests existing in and around projects; they are also the foundations on which many networks, across and within professional categories, are based and through which brokerage occurs. These networks frequently join local, regional, national, international and transnational interests. They are perfect to invigorate the wider, more complex field of development because they allow for the establishment of different, often ad hoc coalitions between various actors in the field. To the extent that

---

[3] Based on Steward (1972), I view levels of integration as a spectrum formed by local, regional, national, international and transnational levels, with different powers of structuration. For the sake of simplicity and clarity, I make the following equation: The local level corresponds to the location of our immediate phenomenological daily experiences, i.e., the set of loci where a person or group carries out regular daily activities, interacting with or being exposed to different social networks and institutions. The regional level corresponds to the political/cultural definition of a region within a nation, such as the South in the United States, or Galicia in Spain. The national, international and transnational levels refer to the existence of the nation-state, and to the different existing relationships within and without it.

this flexibility permits pragmatic and sometimes heterodox alliances that can prove to be effective in many circumstances, it is also responsible for a certain lack of accountability.

In spite of their vital role in maintaining the synergy of the development field, networks are too fluid to provide the regularity, stability, rational planning and foresight needed for development interventions. Networking pragmatism, thus, is an effective instrument, reflected in the strong ability of networks to move from local to national, international and transnational scenarios; but it also engenders a relative loss of homogeneity among the resulting collective subjects, who often exist as target-oriented coalitions that are dismantled once the task is accomplished. This is why networks may be characterized as pragmatic, fragmented, disseminated, circumstancial and even volatile actors. Their strength comes from these characteristics and from a heterogeneity that enables them to match the fluidity of a changing political and economic field with more effectiveness than traditional actors, who are often bound by the need for internal ideological, organizational and political coherence and cohesiveness (with its consequent weight and institutional investment of energy). Such an apparent unity serves as an external identity that qualifies traditional actors as representative of a segment, a corporation or of precisely delimited interests. But the weakness of networks also comes from networking pragmatism, which hinders networks from becoming actors who could have a longer and stronger presence if they were consolidated into a more homogeneous and coherent subject with a shared programmatic objective.

In consequence, networks are joined by other entities within the field of development. When networks reach a point where they have well-defined, lasting interests and goals, they tend to become institutions based not only in personal relationships but also in bureaucratic rationales. Institutions are the crystallizations of networks that have clear-cut projects in sight and within the foreseeable future. "Institution-building" involves a great amount of technical cooperation and monitoring, and is a form of domesticating the unpredictable environments where "development" occurs.

Development institutions are bureaucracies of different size and complexity. As Max Weber (1977) has pointed out, bureacracies are a form of domination, of exerting power. The larger the development initiatives, the larger the bureaucracies related to them and the stronger their capacity to exert power, especially over institutions and actors operating at lower levels of integration. With their hierarchies, rules and reproductive needs, bureaucracies are machines of indifference (Herzfeld, 1992):

> Accountability, Weber tells us, is what bureaucracy is all about; and accountability is what many bureaucrats invest enormous amounts of efforts in short-circuiting or avoiding. A cynic might define power...as the right to be unaccountable (ibid., 122).

This "right to be unaccountable" has motivated many reactions and much opposition to development bureaucracies worldwide. Counterhegemonic networks, made up of NGOs, social movements, unions, churches, etc., have played fundamental roles in protecting the interests of local populations against the great quantity of power amassed by development institutions. Many of the now frequent criticisms development institutions themselves express about the nature of their operations have to be understood in light of the pressures and struggles of such counterhegemonic networks. The fact that bureaucrats or technocrats of development agencies critize their own modes of operation is not necessarily a contradiction, as it may seem in the first place. It is inherent to the rationale of bureaucracies to produce their own criticism, as a way of disseminating and naturalizing the very bureaucratic structure they seem to criticize and, sometimes, oppose (Herzfeld, 1992). In fact, and this is especially true in the history of development, the capacity to produce excuses for failures, to recycle formulations and to create new panaceas is part of the "idioms of self-exoneration" (ibid., 46) in many institutions.[4]

Bureaucracies are also power fields. Criticism and opposition to mainstream policies are related to the power struggles that develop within and without institutions at certain junctures. The dispute within the World Bank over the Narmada River Basin Development Project in India is an example of the intricacies of such political struggles (Rich, 1994). Criticism, though, has limits. In spite of the efforts institutions make to censor their staff, sometimes staff make alliances with counterhegemonic networks at their own risk. The punishment for such heresies is often outright dismissal; the bureaucratic orthodoxy and theodicy needs to seem immaculate.

Max Weber (1977, 708) had already noticed the impossibility of a pure form of bureaucratic domination. Within the development field, personal relations are critical in such relevant moments as recruitment of new staff members and promotion of like-minded political allies. In fact, the prominence of "instrumental friendship," a major engine of networking, is so strong in large bureaucratic organizations that networks usually congeal into cliques within those settings (Wolf, 2001a, 174 and ff.). Especially in situations of power imbalance, cliques have "important instrumental functions in rendering an unpredictable situation more predictable and in providing for mutual support against surprise upsets from within or without" (ibid., 179). Wolf concludes that "an interesting perspective" about large organizations "may be gained by looking upon them as organizations of supply for the cliques, rather than the other way round" (ibid.).

Institutions also become engaged in several networks within the field of development. They make up networks in complex historical and political processes. I named these processes consortiation, to call attention to their resulting entity: the consortium (Ribeiro, 1994). Institutions are the building blocks of consortia that, in turn, become new institutions that may become the units of new and more complex consortia. Consortiation is fundamental to understanding the development field, since it is the galvanizing process that transforms networks of institutions into consortia destined to fulfill delimited roles as defined by a given "project."[5] Consortiation is a

---

[4] Building on Weber's concept of theodicy, a concept related to the various ways in which religious systems sought to interpret the apparent contradiction of evil persistence in a divinely ordered world, Herzfeld (1992, 7) proposes that "secular theodicy...provides people with social means of coping with disappointment. The fact that others do not always challenge even the most absurd attempts at explaining failure...(may be) the evidence of a very practical orientation, one that refuses to undermine the conventions of self-justification because virtually everyone...may need to draw on them in the course of a lifetime."
[5] The following arguments are based on my study of the construction of the Yacyretá dam (Ribeiro, 1994). Keeping the differences in mind, consortiation also happens in smaller projects and in those that are implemented in the name of "sustainable development" (Pareschi, 2001).

political process, commanded by power groups that operate at upper levels of integration. It is a chainlike movement that—through the organization of new task-oriented economic and administrative entities—actually links, within a project, international, national, and regional institutions and capitals. It is a way to reinforce capitalist relationships in a pyramidal fashion, where upper levels hegemonize lower levels. The consortium is the concrete social, economic and political entity that articulates different power groups. The political-economic process of consortiation directly affects the potential of projects for development. Consortiation implies that projects reinforce competition and the concentration of capital and power among capitalist firms; it facilitates the process of capital and power concentration by eliminating weaker competitors and co-opting a few selected ones.

Consortiation involves a two-way process. On one hand, it allows selected smaller units to participate as junior partners in tasks larger than what their financial, technological and managerial capacities would allow. On the other hand, it is a way of facilitating the access of larger corporations to new and often protected or highly disputed markets. Through different discourses on a project's potential for regional and national development, the weakest partners in the associative chain legitimate their claims for larger participation. Regional development is thus a common argument among companies that operate at the local or regional level in competition with national or international corporations. By the same token, national development is the argument national corporations use to defend their interests over international and transnational capital. Given the two-way characteristic of consortiation, the discourses on regional and national development may be an argument that the strongest partners, that is, those representing larger capital or power concentrations, use to legitimate the need for the project. The eloquence of the development argument is evident when the co-optation of smaller unities down the scale is needed.

Consortia are a means corporations have to optimize the use of different networks that must be activated for reaching different economic and political goals. For instance, a consortium operating at the conjunction of the international and national systems, and formed by national and transnational power groups, may lobby both national and international-multilateral institutions. Forming a consortium always implies a negotiation, a process based not only on economic and managerial criteria. The intervention of powerful actors—the controllers or owners of state, national and transnational capital—generates a field of power negotiations that is eminently politically structured. Choosing national partners, for instance, is a strategic decision that takes into account that strong political support within the national state may be more valuable than financial or technical support. In fact, the definition of each partner's share in a contract is due at least as much to political articulations, networkings and lobbying as to the technical assessment of a partner's technical, production and financial capacity. Consortiation is, thus, at the same time, a tool for economic expansion and a means of establishing a political field where brokers of different networks establish their conditions for participating in actual projects. From the ground up, development is the ideology/utopia that cements the diverse stakeholders, networks and institutions.

Development: An Ideology and Utopia of Expansion

Ideologies and utopias are essentially related to power. They express disputes over interpretations of the past (ideology) or of the future (utopia), and struggle to institute hegemony by establishing certain retrospective or prospective visions as the truth, as the natural world order (Manheim, n.d.; Ricoeur, 1986). Since World War II, development as a system of beliefs has always been involved with particular readings of the past and formulations about the future on a global scale (Ribeiro, 1992). In his analysis of development, Escobar (1995) considers it as equivalent to colonial discourse. From a different angle, Gilbert Rist (1997, 218) treats development as a system of beliefs organically related to the worldwide expansion of integrated market systems, and as the "mobilizing slogan of a social movement that created messianic organizations and practices."

The end of the Soviet Union (1989-91) prompted striking rearrangements within the world system and opened the way for the consolidation of different ideologies and utopias of global reach. In the 1990s, two related discourses became hegemonic: sustainable development and globalization. Both seem to be reaching their limits as mobilizing slogans for the 21st century, opening a new round of ideological/utopian struggles and new opportunities for change. For radical or minor reforms of development and cooperation, a critical knowledge of development's value systems and grammar is as crucial as laying bare its structuration as a power field. The exposure of the obsolescence of hegemonic discourses is always necessary in order to go beyond them. What is at stake is whether social actors will accept new discourses on their fates.

Development is one of the most inclusive discourses in common sense and within the specialized literature. Its importance for the organization of social, political and economic relations has led anthropologists to consider it as "one of the basic ideas in modern West European culture" (Dahl and Hjort, 1984, 166), and "something of a secular religion," unquestioned, since "to oppose it is a heresy almost always severely punished" (Maybury-Lewis, 1990, 1). The scope and multiple facets of development are what allow its many appropriations and frequently divergent readings. The plasticity of development is central for the assurance of its continued viability; it is "always in the process of transforming itself, of fulfilling promises" (DSA, n.d., 4-5). The variation of the appropriations of the idea of development, as well as the attempts to reform it, are expressed in the numerous adjectives that are part of its history: industrial, capitalist, socialist, inward, outward, community, unequal, dependent, sustainable, human. These variations and tensions reflect not only the historical experiences accumulated by different power groups in their struggles for hegemony within the development field, but also diverse moments of integration of the world capitalist system.

Since the 19th century, and more so after World War II, the increased pace of integration of the world system has required ideologies and utopias that could make sense of the unequal positions within the system, and that could provide an explanation through which people placed in lower levels would believe that there is a solution for their "backward" situation. It is not by accident that development terminology has usually involved the use of metaphors that refer to space or order in a hierarchical way: developed/underdeveloped, advanced/backward, first world/third world, etc. This hierarchy is instrumental to the belief that there is a point that may be reached by following some kind of recipe kept by those nation-states that lead the "race" for a better future. By using the term "development," instead of accumulation or expansion, undesirable connotations are avoided: such as the difference of power between the units of the system (within or among nation-states) in economic, political and military terms; and the fact that development is "a simple expression of a pact between internal and external groups interested in accelerating accumulation" (Furtado, 1978, 77).

Development operates as a system of classification by establishing taxonomies of peoples, societies and regions. Edward Said (1994) and Arturo Escobar (1995) have shown the relationship between creating a geography, a world order and power. It may be said with Herzfeld (1992, 110) that "creating and maintaining a system of classification has always...characterized the exercise of power in human societies." Classifications often produce stereotypes useful to subject people through simplifications that justify indifference to heterogeneity. Stereotypes can hardly hide their power functions under the surface of the idiom of development and cooperation, the lexicon of which is full of dualisms that refer, in static or dynamic ways, to transient states or relationships of subordination (developed/underdeveloped; developing countries; emergent markets; see Perrot et al., 1992, 189). Stereotypes may also become keywords—such as aid, help, donors/recipients, donors/beneficiaries—that clearly indicate, in not so subtle ways, the power imbalance between two sets of actors and legitimate the transformation of one set of them into objects of development initiatives.

Development's claim to inevitability is but another facet of its claim to universalism. The fact that development is part of a wider belief system marked by Western cultural matrices poses great limitations to its universalist claims, and is another reason why, in many non-Western contexts, local people are reluctant to become development subjects. It is hard to disagree that there is no universal method for achieving a "good life" (Rist, 1997, 241). Development's prehistory reflects such Western discursive matrices as the belief in progress (which can be traced back to ancient Greece: see Delvaille, 1969; Dodds, 1973) and others related to such important turning points as the Enlightenment—a crucial moment for the unfolding of the economic, political and social pacts of modernity and its associated ideologies and utopias (industrialism, secularism, rationalization and individualism, for instance). Leonard Binder (1986, 10-12) recognizes, in certain theories of development, an even narrower matrix: the image of the United States, "as some liberals would like us to be." More recently, in the late 1980s and early 1990s, sustainable development reverberated with notions of proper relationships between humankind and nature that were typical of Protestant, urban middle classes in countries such as Germany, England and the United States (Ribeiro, 1992).

In reality, development is another example of a globalizing discourse, similar to what Appadurai calls ideascapes—"elements of the Enlightenment worldview, which consists of a concatenation of ideas, terms and images, including 'freedom,' 'welfare,' 'rights,' 'sovereignty,' 'representation' and the master term 'democracy'" (1990, 9-10). In this connection, terms such as "ethnodevelopment," coined to refer to indigenous models of development or to alternative models that would respect local values and cultures, are oxymorons. They undoubtedly reflect legitimate aspirations, but are located on the fine and paradoxical line of accepting development as a universal category.[6]

I will briefly mention other anthropological issues that make development's pretension to universalism problematic. The first one is the existence of notions of time that are radically different (Lévi-Strauss, 1980). Development relies on a conception that envisages time as a linear sequence of stages endlessly advancing towards better moments. One implication of such a Western construct is that growth, transformation and accumulation become guiding principles of polities. But in many non-Western societies, time is understood as cycles of eternal recommencements, favoring the flourishing and consolidation of contemplation, adaptation and homeostasis as pillars of their cosmologies. Along the same line, we cannot underestimate the role of the control of time—particularly of the clock, the mother of mechanical complexity—in economic development in the past centuries (Landes, 1983). Synchronicity and predictability are the basis of capitalist and industrial labour relations. Another major divide is the transformation of nature into a commodity, a historical process related to the unfolding of capitalism and modernity (Jameson, 1984) that seems to be reaching its climax with capital exploring the code of life (biotechnology) and virtuality (cyberspace and other technological forms of virtuality are more and more crucial to economic activities). Many of the impasses between developers and indigenous peoples have been based on this cosmological difference. What for some are mere resources, for others may be sacred places and elements.

Cultural shocks form the wider scenario where the issues of language and rationality are located. Language in general, and written language in particular, is a major barrier for communication within the development field. To cooperate, people need to understand, and communicative competence is not a resource equally distributed within development networks. Furthermore, linguistic competence, as Bourdieu noted (1983 [1977], 161 and ff.) cannot be separated from power analysis. Who speaks, to whom, through what media, and in what constructed circumstances are vital elements of any communication process. The relation between written language and power is even more evident, as writing is central to the development of states and to bureaucracies, making it possible, among other things, to present rules as impersonal artefacts (Goody, 1986). Herzfeld (1992, 19-20) links the idea of a perfectly context-free, abstract language and the Western model of rationality to a desire for

---

[6] On ethnodevelopment, see Stavenhagen (1985) and Davis (1988), for instance. In the book *Autodesarrollo Indígena en las Américas* (1989), ethnodevelopment was substituted for "indigenous self-development," apparently because the indigenous participants of the symposium organized by the International Work Group for Indigenous Affairs "did not like the concept of 'ethnodevelopment' and preferred to conceive of development as a type of self-determination" (IWGIA, 1989, 10). Critical anthropological readings of Western ideologies/utopias pose dilemmas that may hurt one's own political predilections. Accountability, for instance, is clearly not a universal category. In his cross-cultural study of bureaucracies, Herzfeld (1992, 47) concluded that "accountability is a socially produced, culturally saturated amalgam of ideas about person, presence, and polity.... (I)ts meanings are culturally specific, and its operation is constrained by the ways in which its operators and clients interpret its actions. Its management of personal or collective identity cannot break free of social experience."

transcendence that is typical of "Judeo-Christian and Indo-European concepts of the superiority of mind over matter." The "ability to represent some forms of language" as context-free is where "the exercise of power lies" (ibid., 119).

Illiteracy is a major barrier within the development field, especially for those projects defending local participation. Planning is the heart of the rational development initiative, and it relies on the establishment of written rules and instructions that need to be followed if efficiency, bureaucratic accountability and goals are to be attained. Projects are the artefacts that summarize the need for control over time, people and resources. Accounting, legal definitions, plans, rational goals and the use of technologies are highly dependent on sharing the same cultural horizon and on certain levels of education. Project failure is almost certain if developers are unable to make people in the field understand what a project is, and how to implement or use it. This historical and sociological predicament is the raison d'être of technical cooperation and of capacity development. It is also a main cause of processes such as the export of the intelligence of projects to foreign centres and brain drain—two perverse effects that reinforce structural inequalities among nation-states. Since culture and education are structural determinants of the lifeways of societies, and do not change at the pace that development projects require, expatriates or outsiders from other regions of a same country are often sent to compensate for local deficiencies. Their commitment to local life is temporary. They are often members of networks that reproduce themselves in national, international and transnational levels of integration.

It is true that transformation is the core of development as ideology and utopia, and that many times transformation is longed for by local people of different cultural backgrounds. Indeed, it is in the nature of some innovations to captivate people, since the changes they bring about may make their lives more comfortable, safer and healthier. The reasons why some people accept change while others don't are complex. But at least three points need to be made about transformations, change and technological innovations: (a) the nature of the transformation and of the context where it will be introduced define whether change will be welcome or not; (b) transformations, change and technological innovations are cultural artefacts that always involve and affect power systems; and (c) they impact social, cultural and environmental systems in varying degrees (from sheer disaster to minor palatable changes). There is no doubt that some projects may enhance a community's access to modernity. But it is also true that "development" does not mean structural changes in power distribution, this being the source of much critique against it. Rist puts it straightforwardly: "Those in power have no interest in change (whatever they say to the contrary), and those who want change do not have the means to impose it" (1997, 243).

The Power Imbalance: Who Is the Subject of Development?

"Development dramas" are complex kinds of encounters that join local actors and institutions with outsiders. The fact that outsiders may pretend to plan a community's future is indicative of their differential power in the encounter. In such circumstances, a dichotomy is installed. On one hand, there are the goals and rationales of the planners; on the other hand, the destiny and culture of the communities. Before the existence of a development project, local people could hardly conceive that their fate was susceptible to being hijacked by an organized group of people. In reality, planning—i.e., determining ahead of time how a certain reality will be—implies the appropriation by outsiders of local populations' power over their own destiny. From being subjects of their own lives, people become objects of prescient technical elites.

Development creates two kinds of subjects, one active, the other passive. Passive-subjects are people transformed as objects of development mandates— forced resettlement represents the extreme case. Ownership will hardly occur, if at all. Local actors are frequently confronted with the odd options of either establishing patron-client relationships with developmentalist outsiders, or struggling to regain control over their lives and environments. In fact, such passive-subjects are prone to resist development, since they relate to its most authoritarian face. But development also creates active-subjects. The agents of development are local people who are likely to become allies of development initiatives because they can identify benefits and interests they have in common with outsiders. The existence of these two kinds of subjects shows that ownership of development initiatives depends heavily on two variables differently distributed within the development drama. One is access to power, to being able to control one's own environment and to avoid being the object of outsiders' will or of the imperatives of structural, faceless, expansionist forces. The other is access to knowledge and information that enables actors to understand what is happening and, more importantly, what will happen to them. Resistance or participation are the results of the ways these variables are combined. Self-confidence and ownership can thrive only where actors feel they have power over their environment.

There are two current modes of generating active/passive-subjects and of dealing with them. The top-down approach tends to create passive-subjects. This authoritarian mode is based on networks that co-opt local elites, establish no compensatory policies for those impacted by projects, and have no preoccupation with local models and cultures. The bottom-up approach intends to create active-subjects and is more ownership-friendly. This participatory mode turns out to be an attempt to compensate for the structural loss of power that characterizes the relations between local populations and outsiders when a project is initiated. Participation and partnership become buzzwords that cannot mask the fact that everyone in the development drama knows where ultimate decision-making power is located. It is true that this mode is more sensitive to local cultures and models, including indigenous models of management (on the latter, see Marsden, 1994).

Both approaches usually share an instrumental notion of culture. Culture becomes a "managerial technology of intervention in reality" (Barbosa, 2001, 135). Such a functional notion conceives culture as a set of interrelated, adjusted, coherent behaviours and meanings that can be identified and valued in terms of their positive or negative impact on the attainment of goals. This notion of culture fits well within the development field, because it adjusts perfectly to the terminology and rationale of planners. But it misrepresents at least two major considerations about culture: (a) contradiction and incoherence are part of human experience; and (b) culture is embedded in and traversed by historically defined relations of power (therefore, cultural change always relates to power change).

Indeed, whatever the approach, top-down or bottom-up, local power and political systems will always be impacted by development interventions. Given the characteristics of the networking and consortiation processes typical of the development field, local power systems are modules of wider power circuitries that are ruled by upper-level institutions. As we know, transnational, international, national and regional institutions and actors tend to have more power within the networking/consortiation processes because they start with and can move more resources. The authoritarian top-down approach tends to reinforce existing political elites that acted as brokers in the past. It tends, thus, to reinforce previously existing differences in class, gender, age, race and ethnicity. In contrast, the bottom-up participatory approach tends to introduce new leadership, thereby creating new tensions within the pre-existing power and political systems.

Both approaches produce "brokers" (Wolf 2001b, 138), who usually amass a great quantity of power. Such middle-people connect the intersections of different levels of integration and serve the interests of the groups they intermediate between. But "they must also maintain a grip on...(the) tensions (between the groups they serve), lest conflict get out of hand and better mediators take their place (ibid.)." In consequence, gatekeepers proliferate within the development field and consume much of its resources. These mediators create power networks of their own (made up of NGOs, consultants, officers of multilateral agencies, union and social movement leaders, etc.) within which much of the technical cooperation actually happens. Brokers are necessary in any development field, because mediation is intrinsic to networking and consortiation processes. But to enhance cooperation, gatekeepers, i.e., brokers specialized in accumulating personal power, need to have their power regulated. Many of the results of development projects are related to the nature of the brokerage system and the power effects and distortions it may generate.

Programmatic Challenges

In this chapter, I presented the main limitations and pressures affecting technical cooperation and development. There are no easy solutions for the conflicts of power created by the development field. Only by changing the characteristics of the power distribution within this field will technical cooperation and development really change. This implies that all actors and institutions within the networks have to "do" politics consciously and constantly to keep their interests alive. The socialization of knowledge of risks and opportunities involving change brought by development is important to improve the quality of the information that actors handle in these political arenas. In consequence, networks need to be democratic assemblages of institutions and actors with the real capacity to decide and intervene, especially if the outcome of such decision-making processes does not please the most powerful interests involved in a given project. To achieve these goals, public spheres to discuss and decide development issues need to be fostered, multiplied and made ever more inclusive. The diffusion of a democratic pedagogy should traverse the whole development field and its networks, from upper-level managers and state officials to grassroots leadership. The associative processes typical of the development field should be opened to participants in such ways as to equalize the power of actors operating at all levels of integration. These are major tasks for all interested in transparency, accountability and the strengthening of civil society. They will encounter much resistance among powerful actors interested in the status quo and among those for whom democracy is not a value.

To move forward in a globalized world, where multiculturalism is increasingly a transnational political issue, we must admit that development is not everyone's object of desire. Rather, much more open perspectives should be fostered, visions that are sensitive to different cultural and political contexts. Concomitantly with the redistribution of power within the development field, different principles and sensibilities need to be disseminated. Development cosmology and idioms have to be radically reformed. Development cannot insist on supposing that the West is universal. Technical cooperation cannot continue to use a language contaminated with metaphors of inequality and hierarchy. If local populations and institutions do not devise themselves as active-subjects of development, ownership will remain a problem, and technical cooperation will reinforce structural inequalities among nation-states.

Globalization processes, especially those related to the new technologies of communication, are promoting many changes in the relationships between local and global settings. The position of local subjects has evolved in ways that may shift the balance towards more participatory approaches within the development field. In spite of its unequal distribution, the Internet is enhancing the capacity for intervention among NGOs and social movements. This virtual public space is the techno-symbolic environment of the transnational virtual-imagined community, and a most useful tool to reinforce local voices and articulations of heterogeneous political actors in a transnational world (Ribeiro, 1998 and 2001).

On a more integrated planet, new challenges arise and call for cosmopolitan political and technical elites prone to accept the global development field as a heteroglossic community, where power imbalances need to be constantly negotiated in political and cultural terms. Conflict is the alternative to making heterogeneity a central value for promoting human conviviality, creativity and capacity of innovation.

References

Adams, Richard Newbold. 1967. *The Second Sowing: Power and Secondary Development in Latin America*. San Francisco: Chandler Publishing Company.

Appadurai, Arjun. 1990. "Disjuncture and Difference in the Global Cultural Economy." In *Global Culture,* edited by Mike Featherstone, 295-310. London: Sage Publications.

Barbosa, Lívia. 2001. *Igualdade e Meritocracia. A Ética do Desempenho nas Sociedades Modernas.* Rio de Janeiro: Fundação Getúlio Vargas Editora.

Barros, Flávia Lessa de. 1996. "Ambientalismo, Globalização e Novos Atores Sociais." *Sociedade e Estado,* XI(1), 121-37.

Berman, Marshall. 1987. *Tudo que é Sólido Desmancha no Ar.* São Paulo: Companhia das Letras.

Binder, Leonard. 1986. "The Natural History of Development Theory." *Comparative Studies in Society and History,* 28, 3-33.

Bourdieu, Pierre. 1983 (1977). "A Economia das Trocas Linguísticas." In *Pierre Bourdieu,* edited by Renato Ortiz. São Paulo: Editora Ática.

———. 1986. *Questions de sociologie.* Paris: Editions de Minuit.

Dahl, Gudrun, and Anders Hjort. 1984. "Development As Message and Meaning." *Ethnos,* 49, 165-85.

Davis, Shelton H. 1988. "Indigenous Peoples, Environmental Protection and Sustainable Development." A sustainable development occasional paper. International Union for Conservation of Nature and Natural Resources.

Delvaille, Jules. 1969. *Essai sur l'Histoire de l'Idée de Progrès jusqu'à la fin du XVIII siècle.* Geneva: Slatkine Reprints.

Department of Social Anthropology (DSA). n.d. Development as Ideology and Folk Model, a research programme of the Department of Social Anthropology at the University of Stockholm.

Dodds, E. R. 1973. *The Ancient Concept of Progress, and Other Essays on Greek Literature and Belief.* Oxford: Oxford University Press.

Durkheim, Emile. 1968. *Las Formas Elementales de la Vida Religiosa.* Buenos Aires: Editorial Schapire.

Escobar, Arturo. 1995. *Encountering Development: The Making and Unmaking of the Third World.* Princeton: Princeton University Press.

Furtado, Celso. 1978."Da Ideologia do Progresso à do Desenvolvimento." In *Criatividade e Dependência na Civilização Industrial.* Rio de Janeiro: Paz e Terra.

Goody, Jack. 1986. *The Logic of Writing and the Organization of Society.* Cambridge: Cambridge University Press.

Herzfeld, Michael. 1992. *The Social Production of Indifference: Exploring the Symbolic Roots of Western Bureaucracy.* Chicago: The University of Chicago Press.

International Work Group for Indigenous Affairs (IWGIA). 1989. *Autodesarrollo Indígena en las Américas.* Copenhagen.

Kroeber, Alfred. 1955. "On Human Nature." *Southwestern Journal of Anthropology,* 11, 195-204.

Jameson, Frederic. 1984. "Postmodernism, or the Cultural Logic of Late Capitalism." *New Left Review*, 146, 53-92.

Landes, David S. 1983. *Revolution in Time: Clocks and the Making of the Modern World*. Cambridge: Harvard University Press.

Lévi-Strauss, Claude. 1980. *Raça e História*. Lisboa: Editorial Presença.

Manheim, Karl. n.d. *Ideology and Utopia*. New York: Harvest Books.

Marsden, David. 1994. "Indigenous Management and the Management of Indigenous Knowledge." In *Anthropology of Organizations*, edited by Susan Wright, 41-55. London: Routledge.

Maybury-Lewis, David. 1990. "Development and Human Rights: The Responsibility of the Anthropologist." Paper presented at the International Seminar on Development and Human Rights, Brazilian Anthropological Association and University of Campinas. Campinas, April.

Pareschi, Carolina C. 2001. *PD/A e PP-G7: construindo modelos de ação e interação do desenvolvimento sustentável*. Unpublished manuscript.

Perrot, Marie-Dominique, Gilbert Rist and Fabrizio Sabelli. 1992. *La Mythologie Programmée: L'économie des croyances dans la société moderne*. Paris: Presses Universitaires de France.

Ribeiro, Gustavo Lins. 1987. "Cuanto Más Grande Mejor? Proyectos de Gran Escala: una Forma de Producción Vinculada a la Expansión de Sistemas Económicos." *Desarrollo Económico*, 105, 3-27.

———. 1992. "Environmentalism and Sustainable Development: Ideology and Utopia in the Late Twentieth Century." Environment, Development and Reproduction. Textos de Pesquisa 2. Rio de Janeiro: Instituto de Estudos da Religião (ISER).

———. 1994. *Transnational Capitalism and Hydropolitics in Argentina*. Gainesville: University of Florida Press.

———. 1995."Ethnic Segmentation of the Labour Market and the 'Work Site Animal': Fragmentation and Reconstruction of Identities within the World System." In *Uncovering Hidden Histories*, edited by Jane Schneider and Rayna Rapp, 336-50. Berkeley: University of California Press.

———. 1998. "Cybercultural Politics: Political Activism at a Distance in a Transnational World." In *Cultures of Politics/Politics of Culture: Revisioning Latin American Social Movements*, edited by Sonia Alvarez, Evelina Dagnino and Arturo Escobar, 325-52. Boulder: Westview Press.

———. 2001. *El Espacio Público Virtual*. Unpublished manuscript. Read at the Universidad Autónoma Metropolitana. Iztapalapa, Mexico; August.

Rich, Bruce. 1994. *Mortgaging the Earth: The World Bank, Environmental Impoverishment, and the Crisis of Development*. Boston: Beacon Press.

Ricoeur, Paul. 1986. *Lectures on Ideology and Utopia.* New York: Columbia University Press.

Rist, Gilbert. 1997. *The History of Development: From Western Origins to Global Faith.* London and New York: Zed Books.

Said, Edward. 1994. *Culture and Imperialism.* New York: Alfred A. Knopf.

Stavenhagen, Rodolfo. 1985. "Etnodesenvolvimento: uma dimensão ignorada no pensamento desenvolvimentista." *Anuário Antropológico,* 84, 11-44.

Steward, Julian H. 1972. *Theory of Culture Change: The Methodology of Multilinear Evolution.* Urbana and Chicago: University of Illinois Press.

Weber, Max. 1977. "Sociología de la Dominación." In *Economía y Sociedad, 695-1117,* Fondo de Cultura Económica (Mexico).

Wolf, Eric R. 1999. *Envisioning Power: Ideologies of Dominance and Crisis.* Berkeley: University of California Press.

———. 2001a. "Kinship, Friendship, and Patron-Client Relations in Complex Societies." In *Pathways of Power: Building an Anthropology of the Modern World,* 166-83. Berkeley: University of California Press.

———. 2001b. "Aspects of Group Relations in a Complex Society: Mexico." In *Pathways of Power: Building an Anthropology of the Modern World,* 124-38. Berkeley: University of California Press.

3 *knowledge*

"Scan globally, reinvent locally" (Joseph E. Stiglitz)

3.1 THE NETWORK AGE: CREATING NEW MODELS OF TECHNICAL COOPERATION

SAKIKO FUKUDA-PARR AND RUTH HILL[1]

Driven by economic globalization and technological transformations, the network age is rapidly replacing the industrial age. This historic shift is altering the rewards and penalties for acquiring and using knowledge and information in global markets and in national development efforts.

These changing realities are setting new challenges but also providing new tools for capacity-building in development, reshaping the agenda for the future of technical cooperation. This chapter reviews these implications and argues that while capacity-building is more critical than ever in this new environment, the conventional tools of technical cooperation are even more obsolete than before. The network age is also making possible the emergence of new modalities for knowledge-sharing, access to information and capacity-building, which in turn are helping to set new priorities for development cooperation that overcome many of the failures of conventional technical cooperation. A new model of development cooperation for capacity-building is emerging for the network age.

---

[1] This chapter reflects the authors' personal views and does not represent the policy of the United Nations Development Programme (UNDP). The authors welcome comments.

The Network Age: Increasing the Rewards for Knowledge and Capacity

Technological transformations of the last decade have combined with economic glob-alization to change the structures of production and many other human activities into networks. What is special about today's technological advances?

- First, knowledge and information are being codified, stored and made acces-sible at levels unimaginable in earlier decades. Recent breakthroughs in biotechnology are enabling the codification of information about the genetic makeup of all living matter. And the rapid advances in information communi-cation technology (ICT) have made possible storing, processing and communicating information at levels that were previously inconceivable. The exponential increase in web sites is making this information readily accessi-ble, and the spread of the Internet is linking people in communications networks (see Figures 3.1.1, 3.1.2 and 3.1.3). Today it matters less what a person knows than what information and knowledge she has access to and can utilize.

FIGURE 3.1.1   **FIGURE 3.1.2**   **FIGURE 3.1.3**

Biotech information   **More people have access...**   **...to more information...**
Millions of Internet users   Number of web sites

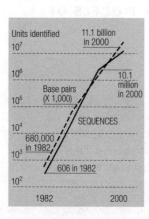
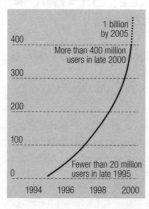
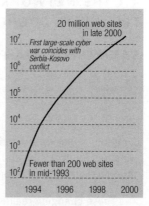

- Second, information and communications are pervasive inputs into almost everything that we do—from producing food and weapons to participating in politics—and so have pervasive impacts. Thus, ICT and biotechnology are transforming societies and economies, not just making incremental changes (Freeman, 1988; Castells, 1996 and 2000; Cox and Alm, 1999; Gilder, 2000; Webster, 1995).

- Third, the scientific progress of today is more rapid and more fundamental than before. For example, as stated by Moore's Law, computing power doubles every 18 months. Individuals, organizations, businesses and countries need to be constantly aware of and adapting to the rapidly changing technological environment. Such changes drive the global marketplace, and businesses that do not take advantage of technological advances can become marginalized.

- Fourth, technology-based activities are a burgeoning segment of the global economy—high-tech was the fastest growing sector of the global economy from 1985 to 1998, expanding by 13 per cent annually. A study of 68 countries accounting for 97 per cent of global industrial activity during this period shows high-tech production grew more than twice as fast as total production in all but one country.

- Fifth, advances in ICT are driving down the costs of information storage and communications to zero. Computing power not only doubles every 18 months but does so at a decreased cost. For example, the cost of sending a trillion bits of information from Los Angeles to Boston declined from US $150,000 in 1970 to 12 cents in 1999. And the amount of DRAM storage available for $1 increased by 30,000 times, from 0.0002 to 5.9 DRAM (see Figures 3.1.4 and 3.1.5).

FIGURE 3.1.5

The cost of computing–how much memory will a dollar buy?
Megabits of DRAM storage

FIGURE 3.1.4

...at a lower cost.
Transmission cost

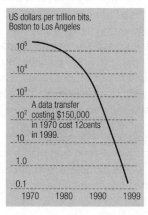

Economies are increasingly knowledge-based—dependent on the generation, distribution, and use of knowledge and technology (OECD, 1999). This is reflected by increased investment in intangibles, such as research and development (R&D), education and software. Between the mid-1980s and the mid-1990s, investment in intangible assets in the Organisation for Economic Co-operation and Development (OECD) countries increased by 3 per cent. Since the mid-1990s, the top 20 pharmaceutical companies have doubled their R&D spending (Arlington, 2000). Investment in these intangible assets is now as large as investment in fixed capital equipment (OECD, 2000). Knowledge-intensive business services, such as computers, R&D and training, are among the global economy's most rapidly growing sectors. Combined worldwide sales in the five most prominent knowledge-based service industries (communications, financial services, business services, education and health services) exceeded US $7.4 trillion in 1997, up from $5.8 trillion in 1990 and $3.4 trillion in 1980 (in 1997 constant dollars; OECD, 2000). World exports of goods and services as a percentage of GDP more than doubled from 1960 to 1999—from 13 to 27 per cent.

As knowledge becomes the basis for much economic activity, it also becomes the source of a firm's competitive edge. ICT has enabled the codification of much knowledge as well as easier and cheaper diffusion of that knowledge. As a result, firms tend to focus on their tacit knowledge, and externalize activities that do not involve core competencies. They participate in networks that provide them with valuable knowledge. Collaboration has become a fundamental component of many firms' strategies. The number of strategic alliances has grown in both number and scope, rising from just over 1,000 in 1989 to more than 7,000 ten years later; the number of deals made in 1999 alone increased by 40 per cent (OECD, 2000). Interestingly, the sectoral distribution of strategic alliances has drastically changed in recent years. In the early 1990s, manufacturing firms accounted for more than half of all alliances. Today, agreements in the services sector outpace those in all other sectors and represent almost three-quarters of all cooperative relationships. Most strategic alliances have an international dimension. Between 1990 and 1999, more than 67 per cent took place between firms from different countries.

Economies and societies are restructuring into networks that link actors across communities and countries. Networked structures of production and other activities are replacing hierarchically organized and geographically concentrated structures constrained by high costs of transport and communications. For example, global corporations are spreading production activities globally; outsourcing is a common feature of virtually all businesses and organizations; and global value chains of many actors—subsidiaries, consultants, contractors—make up competitive and dynamic structures (Sweeney, 2000). Globally, the outsourcing market is now worth more than US $100 billion.

These changes are the beginning of a trend that marks the historic shift from the industrial to the network age. Just as the industrial revolution replaced manual power with the steam engine, today's technology revolution is augmenting brain power.

A New Environment for Technical Cooperation

If development is about the transformation of production systems and society (see Part 1, Chapter 1), these historic shifts are reshaping the future. Change has only begun, and as writers like Sagasti and Castells point out, these historic shifts are redefining development challenges and priorities (Sagasti, 2001; Castells, 2000). For technical cooperation in particular, this new environment has several significant consequences in terms of the capacities needed and, more fundamentally, in the tools available to build capacities for development.

Changing Capacities

The network age alters the capacity-building challenges for developing countries. Capacity—meaning well-functioning institutions and policies, skilled people and a leadership with vision—matters more as the shift to the network age has increased the rewards and penalties for both individuals and organizations in terms of their knowledge and competence. Global value chains are creating niche opportunities for developing countries. India's success in exploiting the ICT and ICT-enabled outsourcing niche markets is a spectacular example (see Box 3.1.1). As this case shows, when local private initiatives exploit new market opportunities, the results can be astounding. The case of the pharmaceutical industry in Brazil also highlights how utilizing local and technical knowledge can be highly successful. The reverse also presents risks—the consequences of being out of the global value chains can mean being marginalized from the most dynamic aspects of the global economy, as well as the benefits of global progress. Where possible and necessary, local private sector activity should be encouraged and facilitated by the public sector.

BOX 3.1.1: Exploiting Niche Opportunities in Networked Production

India is exploiting the growing niche opportunities of the global ICT and ICT-enabled networks in such areas as credit card administration, insurance claims, business payrolls, and customer, financial and human resources management. Some 185 Fortune 500 companies are outsourcing their software requirements to Indian firms. There are 1,250 companies exporting software. As a result, ICT sector output rose to 330 billion rupees by 1999 (US $7.7 billion), 15 times the level in 1990. Exports grew from $150 million in 1990 to nearly $4 billion in 1999. One study estimates that this figure could reach $50 billion by 2008, leading ICT to account for 30 per cent of India's exports and 7.5 per cent of its GDP. (Human Development Report 2001; Chandrasekhar, 2001.)

The network age not only increases the rewards for capacity but also alters the types of capacity that are needed. Network structures require more:

- specialized skills—to find niches in global networks for research, production, services and other activities;

- adaptability and flexibility—to be able to follow the rapidly changing economic environment and global technological advances, and to adopt and adapt new ideas, methods and technologies that can best meet emerging needs and opportunities; and

- science- and technology-based knowledge, skills and training—studies consistently show basic education increases the rate of technological innovation and adoption among farmers and workers.

The new environment also requires different kinds of capacity to manage the process of development in a technology-driven global marketplace. Examples include:

- the capacity to negotiate rules of globalization;

- the capacity to negotiate intellectual property rules that safeguard social objectives, such as protection of indigenous knowledge systems, access to essential technology products and promotion of technology transfers; and

- the capacity to participate in global networks, especially those related to production and to knowledge creation and diffusion.

New Tools and Approaches to Sharing and Creating Knowledge Networks

The restructuring of activities along globally networked value chains is most visible in manufacturing production but is also taking place in other activities. Networks are now an important part of global research and technology development. Scientific research is increasingly collaborative across institutions and countries. Between 1981 and 1995-97, the share of scientific publications with a foreign co-author more than doubled in many OECD countries. In Brazil, cross-country collaboration increased by nearly 25 per cent, and in Kenya, it increased by 9 per cent. In 1995-97, scientists in the United States co-authored articles with scientists from 173 other countries, scientists in Brazil with collaborators from 114 countries, in Kenya with 81 and in Algeria with 59 (National Science Foundation, 2001). An increasingly collaborative approach to knowledge creation is also evident in rising instances of cross-border ownership of inventions. The share of patents invented in collaborations between OECD and foreign co-inventors almost doubled between the mid-1980s and the mid-1990s (OECD, 2000).

Networks of development practitioners across the globe are emerging, sharing relevant knowledge, information and know-how about best practices. These networks link development practitioners in different sectors and project areas, fostering collaboration between individuals and institutions and providing forums in which knowledge and information on best practices can be shared. UNDP's internal Subregional Resource Facility (SURF) systems, the World Bank's Global Development Network (GDN) and the networks among Southern African Development Community (SADC) countries are all examples of such linkages.

The establishment of knowledge communities around specific areas of practice through UNDP's SURF system has allowed the programme's 134 country offices truly to become a network on which UNDP's strength is based. Eighteen months after the creation of the SURF system in the latter half of 1999, membership had reached over 12,000 (see Box 3.1.2).

The World Bank's GDN encourages capacity-building, networking and knowledge creation across institutions—among research institutes, policy-makers and donors. The network focuses on critical research areas and builds on seven regional networks that span the developing world and draw on networks in the OECD. The GDN helps research and policy institutions by fostering vibrant global, regional and electronic networking activities designed to ensure the latest research, best practices and new ideas are shared across the development community. It is intended to strengthen the capacity of these institutions to contribute to national and global policy debates.

Among the SADC countries, knowledge-sharing initiatives enable practitioners in different areas—water management, food security, seed security, health care, etc.—to exchange experiences in building capacity. The South Africa Health Network, a national network of health professionals established in South Africa, is a particularly well-developed network that makes full use of information and communication technologies to connect people in the health profession, providing a forum in which they can share ideas and the latest health care knowledge. Through modules covering topics ranging from malaria to traditional medicines, the system aims to facilitate and enable interaction and an iterative information flow among researchers, health services professionals, industry players, health policy-makers and communities.

These are just three examples of the universal trend in the last few years of growth in the numbers of global knowledge-sharing networks at different levels—within and between institutions, and among development stakeholders at the regional and global levels. Almost all global development institutions have established some form of knowledge-sharing to ensure the best knowledge of the organization is available to all whenever it is needed. Some other examples include the organizational learning work of Bellanet, an international initiative working with the development community to increase collaboration; the Food and Agriculture Organization's FarmNet, which facilitates the exchange of knowledge and information among rural people; Healthnet's global network of networks of health professionals; and the OneWorld network, which connects nongovernmental organizations (NGOs) working for human rights and sustainable development around the globe.

Regionally, there has also been an explosion in the numbers of knowledge-sharing networks. A few examples are: in Latin America, the Technology Foresight Network of the United Nations Industrial Development Organisation (UNIDO) and the International Centre for Science and High Technology (ICS); in sub-Saharan Africa, the African Development Policy Network and the Southern African Development Culture and Communication Network; in East and South Asia, Electronic Networking for Rural Asia Pacific, which is supported by the International Development Research Centre (IDRC) and the International Fund for Agricultural Development (IFAD); and in South Asia, Bytes for All. Every month, Bellanet is contacted by five to ten civil society organizations in the South, who introduce their programmes and invite Bellanet to enter a dialogue regarding areas of possible collaboration.

BOX 3.1.2: Creating a Human Development Network

SURFs in UNDP

The role of UNDP and its country offices is to help governments do their jobs better. Providing the right information at the right time is crucially important. In 1998, the question arose as to how UNDP head-quarters could ensure it provided country offices with the information they needed. As an experiment, UNDP established a small network on sustainable livelihoods between New York and eight country offices around the world. When one of the eight offices questioned headquarters on an issue, that office and all other country offices (often facing the same issues) would receive a response. But as the questions began, the eight selected offices also started answering each others' questions, discovering an immense pool of knowledge among the network members. In the following January, UNDP scaled up the network to around 40 people, and in the second half of 1999, email groups were organized around six thematic focal points. These were common to many country offices and were subjects in which staff had developed considerable expertise—poverty, environment, government, microfinance, ICT for development and the National Human Development Reports (NHDRs). Full-time facilitators anchored in the corresponding units at headquarters were recruited to support the networks.

Since then, the SURF networks have generated knowledge-sharing within UNDP and facilitated the emergence of communities of practice through a format that is inexpensive and based on demand. Some SURF networks work better than others, however, and in all cases, it has been hard to foster the sense of community among network members that is needed to turn these networks into communities of practice. There have also been problems in bringing headquarters in and in changing the culture of UNDP to create incentives for knowledge-sharing. Now that the networks have been established, there is a need to ensure that the knowledge shared over the last few years is not lost. A comprehensive knowledge collection exercise should accompany this revolutionary step in connection.

The National Human Development Report SURF

The NHDR SURF network brings together over 330 people. It was established with the aim of support-ing members of UNDP's country offices involved in producing NHDRs. The network has been a huge success in meeting this objective over the last two years. Now it comprises UNDP staff, NHDR teams, and a number of experts and consultants, and is turning its focus to building capacity for furthering the objectives of human development nationally, regionally and globally.

Within UNDP, the NHDR SURF is considered the most successful of these networks. Like all effective networks it is:

Demand-driven: There was a real need for the network in the form of unmet demand for advice on pro-ducing human development reports. Most country offices had staff working on the production of national or regional reports. While they worked autonomously, they faced many of the same issues.

Purpose-driven: The NHDR SURF worked well quickly because it is output-oriented—discussion and best practices evolve around the issues related to producing the NHDRs.

Tightly focused in its purpose: The NHDR network concerns a specific topic—how to make the NHDRs better. Members know why they are on the network and what they expect to get out of it.

Based on high levels of trust: Trust is crucially important to the development of knowledge communi-ties and is built both through repeated good contributions and through direct and indirect personal knowledge. Since it is vital to bring network members together, NHDR participants met in Beirut in June 2001.

How It Works

During the course of preparing an NHDR, a country team needs external advice on a variety of issues, such as on the use of a Purchasing Power Parity (PPP) measure of income within the statistical work of the report, or on the outline of the report being proposed. As a part of the NHDR network, the team can post a question on PPP or ask for advice on the outline and receive immediate expert feedback from members around the world who have produced similar reports. They may receive a response in 24 hours and are guaranteed a response in five days—much quicker than the weeks it used to take.

The Impact

The NHDR network has had a huge impact in building capacity on national human development issues and measurements, and has allowed UNDP headquarters to have access to the expert knowledge that has been established. Network members working on NHDRs in Cameroon, Lao and Yemen are just some of those who have received advice on the outlines of their reports, and recommendations on data and people to work with as they complete their reports. Best practices in the production of regional human development reports have also been shared.

Capacity-building has not been limited to the production of reports, although at first this was the main role of the NHDR SURF community. In 2001, debates also took place on sustainable human development equilibrium models, the contribution of NHDRs to the monitoring of the 2015 development targets, the creation of training materials on human development, operationalizing human development for strategic planning and the role human development policies play in poverty eradication. The debate on building sustainable human development equilibrium models, for example, enabled members of the network to receive advice on building such a model, examples and articles detailing where such models had been constructed, and the data required. The community member in Vietnam who had originally posed the question was thus equipped with the tools needed to understand the feasibility of using such a model for formulating and evaluating policy there.

Another way in which capacity has been built is through the development of national networks. The production of an NHDR brings together many different actors, and these actors can be institutionalized in a network beyond the production of a report. Some national networks were established relatively early, such as in the Philippines in 1992. Other networks have started to develop through the capacity built by the SURF network—such as those in Armenia, Benin, Bolivia, Kyrgyzstan, Mozambique and Russia. The recently established network in Kyrgyzstan has developed an inward-looking national human development portal (in contrast to the national development gateway designed more for external audiences). The portal connects business people, government officials, donors, consultants, students and scholars. It is designed to engage the local population in discussions on concrete issues related to the country's development priorities throughout the year, not only during the preparation of the NHDR. They get feedback on the NHDR but also on issues such as Poverty Reduction Strategy Papers (PRSPs), the Comprehensive Development Framework (CDF), regional development plans and the government's national development strategy.

Recent and Future Developments

In its first two years, the focus of the NHDR network has been on the individual products—the reports themselves. As the network expands in membership, and becomes more mature, it is entering an exciting new phase in which the focus is shifting towards making contributions to the field of human development and its measurement. The network is becoming a lobbying force and instigator of change at the national, regional and global levels.

In some countries, country-specific NHDR networks have emerged, and in some areas regional and professional NHDR networks are starting to form as well. The global NHDR network will benefit from the development of these local networks, and thus it has encouraged their growth. Local NHDR networks further encourage national capacity-building and the adoption of the human development approach. It is also easier for non-UNDP actors to become more involved in local networks. UNDP now needs to learn to participate as a partner and not as an owner, as these networks must live in the country and be demand-driven. The human development approach is a composite bringing together many different elements, and national networks benefit similarly with respect to the membership of the network. Ideally, the network should involve experts in different fields, representatives of different social groups, and members of national and regional research institutions, political and economic commissions, universities, media and statistical agencies. These networks can bring a passion to issues of national human development. By facilitating knowledge-sharing, they can build the national capacity to succeed in meeting these challenges and help provide the tools needed to overcome them.

(Tadjbakhsh, 2001a and 2001b; Glovinsky, 2001.)

Such sharing and creation of information and know-how is replacing the transfer of know-how through the "expert-counterpart" model of technical cooperation and knowledge transfer. But such networks can be subject to the same weaknesses of being donor-driven (see Box 3.1.3).

ICT makes possible not only the creation of networks but also access to global information in a way that was never possible before. The remotest village has the possibility of tapping a global store of knowledge far beyond what one would have imagined a century ago, faster and more cheaply than anyone imagined only a few decades ago. A school in rural Tanzania can go from having few textbooks to having access to the world's best libraries through connecting to the Internet. In Chile and Mexico, FAO projects have applied computer technology to establish information networks for agricultural producers and farmers' associations. These networks have provided essential information on topics such as crops, markets, prices, weather, social services and credit facilities.

Networks among development practitioners and access to global knowledge systems can substitute for conventional technical cooperation, by which knowledge was thought to be embodied in an individual (expatriate) to be imparted to other individuals (nationals).

Towards a New Model of Development Cooperation in a New Paradigm

Increasingly, entrepreneurs in developing countries will find niches in the networks rising across the globe. In particular, organizations and businesses will participate in and benefit from networks of production and of knowledge creation, diffusion and use.

The appeal of networks as a new model of technical cooperation for capacity-building is that they bypass the root causes of the failures of the last decades of technical cooperation, which are by now well known (Berg and UNDP, 1993; Fukuda-Parr, 1996). These causes include, among others, the donor-driven nature of technical cooperation and a faulty notion of the expert-counterpart model in which knowledge is transferred from a Northern expert to a Southern counterpart.

Old models of technical cooperation have been entrenched in a paradigm of knowledge and society that gave little recognition to the dynamics of how knowledge is generated, adopted and used (Sagasti, 2001). The paradigm assumed that knowledge resided in the North and could be transplanted in the South. A more realistic paradigm of knowledge and capacity-building would be to recognize that:

- much of the knowledge on development resides in the South and not in the North (Denning, 2001);

- knowledge not only resides in individuals but also in institutional experiences and databases; and

- capacity development is fostered through learning by doing.

BOX 3.1.3: The Global Development Gateway: A Critique

The Global Development Gateway (DG), is one of the knowledge-sharing activities conceived by the World Bank. The DG aims to create a common platform for knowledge-sharing and dialogue through a global gateway and series of country gateways that are "easier to access and navigate than the often bewildering wealth of information on the Internet" (World Bank, 2001). As people share information, they may build communities of practice around particular development challenges.

This aspect of the World Bank's knowledge management strategy has been criticized heavily. While some critiques are based on real problems with the initiative, many of the complaints about the DG arise from frustrations with World Bank activities in the past. The main issues have been:

- **Supply - not demand-driven:** The overall budget to date for establishing the Development Gateway has been US $7.2 million. An additional $1.8 million has been allocated to finance the start-up phase of country gateways in 32 countries. Yet there is no guarantee that the information collected and uploaded is the information that people want. Honest consultation needs to establish whether there is real recipient need. Similar projects already exist, so there has to be an analysis of what is being done elsewhere and an outline of project need. The World Bank could play an important role in financially supporting existing initiatives.

- **Lack of participation in the development of the gateway:** The focus on supply rather than demand is also evidenced by the lack of real participation of the development community in the creation of the DG. There was a strong reaction against the formation of a portal such as this by the World Bank, but the concerns were not heeded. There are feelings that this is another example of the World Bank's top-down relationship with the community it hopes to serve.

- **Governance issues:** A balance of power needs to be struck between the World Bank and other partner organizations in running the Development Gateway Foundation, the independent organization that will manage the DG portal. Particular attention should be given to ensuring the full participation of people from the South in managing and controlling the DG.

- **Creating a monopoly of development information:** There is a fear that through the DG the World Bank will begin to monopolize development knowledge. The large sums of money behind the gateway relative to the sums of money available to other similar initiatives brings about unfair competition.

- **A hierarchy of development knowledge:** The aim of the portal is to provide access to premier information on development, which creates an uncomfortable authority situation. It establishes a hierarchy of knowledge—suggesting that if something is accessible through the DG it is a universal truth. Yet the World Bank is not a neutral provider of development information. Offering high-quality information requires an editorial policy, but this may result in a bias towards the information accessible through the gateway. Editorial activities are needed, but there should be a plurality of them—the DG offers only one. A huge amount of knowledge won't be accessible by the gateway, and the omissions will be unintentionally systematic. Knowledge that is outside the technocratic and scientific community—indigenous knowledge—will tend not to be included. "Just as it is difficult for the Polish or Malian filmmaker to win international film distribution, let alone a Hollywood Oscar, so it is difficult for the uninvited to contribute to the mainstream web sites, and of course impossible for the unconnected" (Panos Institute, 1998). Yet it is this unconnected knowledge that is often most important.

- **Fails to exploit the empowering nature of the Internet:** ICTs have driven the cost of storage, retrieval and communication down, enabling the smallest entity to develop web sites and information bases. Economies of scale are now applicable to the network, not to the individual producer—allowing a multiplicity of sites to develop and a multiplicity of voices to be heard. The DG suggests the Bank has failed to understand that the Internet encourages horizontal networking and multiple voices rather than centralized planning and coordination. Country development communities have complained about a top-down approach in the design and content of country development gateways. External consultants have often come in and established the gateways themselves. As two commentators note:

For the Internet to become an empowering tool for the billions of people living in poverty, what is needed is to stop seeing it as a broadcasting tool for those with a message, gospel or dogma wanting to reach "them" and to see it instead as a tool for communities to articulate their own message, reduce the costs of transactions they conduct themselves, communicate with whom they want to communicate.... The challenge is to find ways that allow for investors, industry and the international development community to play their role in bridging the "digital divide" by empowering communities (Roberto Bissio, 2000).

What we need in the new "knowledge society" is diversity; a multitude of knowledge brokers, a Babel of banks. Where ICTs can make a real difference is in providing access to these different and competitive databanks, which in turn enables all of us, through the media and civil society forums, to engage in well-informed, constructive and democratic debate (Panos Institute, 1998).

Knowledge does not exist without ownership by someone. As conceived now, the DG cannot exist as a neutral portal allowing a forum for development debate. The structure of the DG could alter to encourage this to a greater degree, but maybe what is best is for a plurality of development portals to exist.

Building a new model of development cooperation that recognizes these realities will give greater ownership to local communities in establishing programmes for change. A model is needed that strengthens the ability of the local private sector to act and increases the capacity for relevant development knowledge to be tapped into easily.

Such networks—in which businesses, public institutions and civil society institutions create partnerships, with each focusing on their niche specialization—present an alternative to traditional forms of technical cooperation. But while private businesses and civil society organizations might find profit and other incentives to participate in networks, public strategies and investments are needed to bring public institutions into networks. Institutional innovations and new forms of incentives need to be created. Public institutions in the North and the South are already doing this on a small scale. Initiatives fostering access to information, sharing of knowledge and best practices through networks, and partnerships among institutions that cross national borders can be a more empowering form of development cooperation that can strengthen capacities based on the utilization of expertise and knowledge in the South.

Knowledge networks and communities of practice enable knowledge-sharing and capacity-building. While information and communication technologies allow collection, storage and access to explicit knowledge that has been codified, much knowledge remains tacit, embodied in individuals and institutions. Such knowledge is "sticky" in that it is hard to pass it from one person to another. "We know more than we can say" (Stiglitz, 1999). Communities and networks enable this knowledge to be transferred. Also, access only to information without knowledge of the local situation is of little use. The context in which knowledge arises is often crucial to understanding and exploiting it. Through the connection of practitioners in a knowledge network or a community of practice, a forum is established in which knowledge can be shared, allowing global information and knowledge to be successfully adapted to the local context. Building capacity through knowledge-sharing thus does not only involve the storing of data and information, but also human interaction and understanding.

Within institutions, knowledge networks and communities of practice ensure full utilization of the wealth of knowledge built up by years of experience among the people of the organization. As organizations mobilize their knowledge base through such networks, it becomes possible for all individuals in the organization to utilize the best knowledge the organization has at any given point. These tools of knowledge-sharing are increasingly being used beyond organizational boundaries. They are applied to areas of practice across organizations, allowing best practices in the field to be shared and used. They are also starting to exist along regional and national lines, allowing people from different areas of practice but with the same goal—poverty reduction, for example—to communicate, share experiences and ideas, and develop a comprehensive approach to the problems at hand. The same principles ensure effective development of such networks and communities. Briefly:

1. The better defined a network is, and the more focused it is on a specific issue, the more useful the knowledge-sharing will be.

2. The higher the level of trust within the network or community, the greater the volume and honesty of knowledge flows. Trust between members of the network or community can be facilitated by sharing pictures of other network or community members, setting up face-to-face meetings, and keeping the network or community small, including by developing sub-networks when the original network becomes too big.

3. Networks and communities need to live, and as such need to be developed from the bottom up and allowed to follow their own agenda, sharing knowledge the individual members need. There does, however, also need to be a network or community facilitator ensuring that questions receive an answer and that debate remains active and alive. Striking the balance is key.

Much can be learned from the World Bank, which has developed a comprehensive approach to knowledge-sharing both within and across its organizational boundaries (see Box 3.1.4).

As knowledge networks and communities of practice increasingly develop across organizational boundaries, the old hierarchies of knowledge-sharing are broken down. As southern membership of these global networks increases, the greater the flow of knowledge from South to North will become, allowing so-called experts in the North to learn from the realities of experiences in the South. Encouraging active southern membership of communities of practice is vital to allowing this to happen. The South can benefit from membership in such communities, as local cultures are able to draw on their local and indigenous knowledge, which they can then reinterpret and develop in light of the most useful approaches from elsewhere. But the benefits in the way development institutions in the North do development will be much greater, as knowledge systems in international institutions become responsive to knowledge flows from the South.

BOX 3.1.4: Knowledge-Sharing at the World Bank

The World Bank has taken knowledge management seriously, deciding to adopt a comprehensive knowledge management strategy costing US $43.25 million per year that will transform the Bank into a "knowledge bank." The knowledge-sharing network within the Bank includes, among other activities initiated in the last few years, the Global Development Network to foster knowledge-sharing among research institutes, policy makers and donors, and the Development Gateway, which establishes a mega development portal.

This level of commitment to knowledge-sharing has paid off. In 1999, Larry Prusak, director of the IBM Institute of Knowledge Management, led an external panel of knowledge management experts to assess the relevance and impact of the Bank's knowledge-sharing programme. The knowledge management strategy was found "far-sighted in conception and sound in its fundamentals. It positions the Bank to play a key role in the world economy of the 21st century." In February 2000, the World Bank was acknowledged as one of the five top knowledge management organizations in the United States. In June 2000, an annual survey of experts of Fortune 500 companies also selected the Bank as one of the top ten Most Admired Knowledge Enterprises (MAKE) in the world.

As these knowledge-sharing activities of the Bank become more established, further institutional change is needed to ensure the realization of the goal of a knowledge bank:

- Partnership is key to the horizontal networks the Bank is seeking to develop, yet the experience of some NGOs who have partnered with the Bank has been that there needs to be more institutional change at the Bank in order to allow this to become a reality.

- The Bank's operating paradigms have not changed, despite the fundamental indications suggesting they should that have been generated by knowledge-sharing. The Bank still operates in a very centralized way that does not fit with the fact that it operates around the world in many different local contexts. Fostering ownership has thus not been possible. Structural change is needed to allow increased ownership.

In 1992, the Centre for Indigenous Knowledge for Agriculture and Rural Development (CIKARD) began an effort to collect and preserve indigenous knowledge pertaining to development. Indigenous knowledge networks in 131 countries are maintained on topics such as indigenous innovations and decision-making structures. Intended to facilitate sustainable local development, this information is available both to professionals, practitioners and lay individuals within the local community and experts around the globe. South-North knowledge flows need to be fostered, and knowledge systems in international institutions need to be responsive to these knowledge flows. Development cooperation based on such flows is empowering and effective.

As southern networks develop through the establishment of regional and national networks, the opportunity for the South to learn from the South also becomes greater. The South holds much relevant development knowledge for other southern countries. The real experts on development are those who live the reality on a day-to-day basis. In this age of accelerating change, it is even more important for different stakeholders in the South to share knowledge, which allows quick learning on best practices as contexts change rapidly. In Cameroon, for example, 44 organizations and individuals subscribe to WAZA (the Sustainable Development Networking Programme Cameroon mailing list), receiving several short articles each week on a variety of subjects related to sustainable development in Africa. WAZA provides networking opportunities to subscribers, who add their own news bulletins to the mix and break off into smaller email discussion groups based on specific topics. Dr. Martin Sama, a researcher in tropical medicine and medicinal plants, is a WAZA subscriber. "Just yesterday, I got information about the Ebola virus," says Dr. Sama. "That is important to me as a medical researcher." South-South knowledge flows need to be encouraged. As international institutions learn how to share their knowledge more effectively, they can help developing countries devise similar capacities.

It is crucial that local entrepreneurial activities are encouraged so as to allow this increased knowledge transfer to be utilized. Private sector initiatives need to be facilitated by the provision of necessary credit and legal institutions as well as investments in infrastructure. The capacity of a community to reinvent locally will depend crucially on the opportunities for entrepreneurial activities available to individuals and firms.

I do not want my house to be walled in on all sides and my windows to be stuffed. I want the cultures of all lands to be blown about my house as freely as possible. But I refuse to be blown off my feet (Gandhi, 1959, 159).

The strength of southern involvement in communities of practice and of the local private sector to act is necessary to ensure that local communities are not blown of their feet.

Conclusion

The network age offers a fundamental challenge to the reform of technical cooperation. Will technical cooperation be able to reform so that the transfer of knowledge and the building of capacity that it hopes to achieve take into consideration the advances in our understanding of knowledge transfer, namely the importance of connection rather then codification? If technical cooperation operates through a new mode, establishing knowledge networks and recognizing the fundamental truth that the South has much to learn from the South, then knowledge becomes a powerful force for action, and a two-way flow of knowledge can be established. When knowledge is shared in this manner, local ownership of development processes becomes possible. Facilitating local entrepreneurial activity is necessary to allow these knowledge flows to make their way into action. The ideal embodied in the phrase "scan globally, reinvent locally" becomes a reality.

References

Arlington, Steve. 2000. "Pharma 2005: An Industrial Revolution in R&D." *Pharmaceutical Executive,* 20(1), 74.

Berg, Elliot, and the United Nations Development Programme (UNDP). 1993. *Rethinking Technical Cooperation: Reforms for Capacity Building in Africa.* New York: United Nations Development Programme.

Bissio, Roberto. 2000. Letter to Dr. Mamphela Ramphele, World Bank, on the Global Development Gateway.

Castells, Manuel. 1996. *The Rise of the Network Society.* Oxford: Blackwell.

————. 2000. "Information Technology and Global Capitalism." In *On the Edge: Essays on a Runaway World,* edited by Will Hutton and Anthony Giddens, 52-74. London: Jonathan Cape.

Chandrasekhar, C.P. 2001. "ICT in a Developing Country: An India Case Study." Background paper for the *Human Development Report 2001.*

Cox, W. Michael, and Richard Alm. 1999. *The New Paradigm: Federal Reserve Bank of Dallas Annual Report 1999.* Dallas.

Denning, Steve. 2001. "Knowledge Sharing in the North and South." A presentation. Bonn, 3 April.

Freeman, Christopher. 1988. "Technological Change and Economic Theory: An Introduction." In *Technical Change and Economic Theory;* edited by G. Dosi, C. Freeman, R. R. Nelson, G. Silverberg and L. Soete; 1-8. London: Pinter.

Fukuda-Parr, Sakiko. 1996. "Beyond Rethinking Technical Cooperation." *Journal of Technical Cooperation,* 2(2), 145-57.

Gandhi, Mahatma. 1959. "English-Learning." In *Collected Works, vol. 20.* Delhi: Government of India.

Gilder, George. 2000. *Telecosm: How Infinite Bandwidth Will Revolutionize Our World.* New York: Free Press.

Glovinsky, Steve. 2001. Correspondence on the development of networks within UNDP. July.

Lall, Sanjaya. 2001. "Harnessing Technology for Human Development." Background paper for the *Human Development Report 2001.*

National Science Foundation (NSF). 2000. *Science and Engineering Indicators for 2000.* (www.nsf.gov/sbe/srs/seind2000/start.htm.)

Organisation for Economic Co-operation and Development (OECD). 1999. *OECD Science, Technology and Industry Scoreboard 1999: Benchmarking Knowledge-Based Economies.* Paris.

————. 2000. *Science, Technology and Industry Outlook 2000.* Paris.

Panos Institute. 1998. *Debate and Development: A Series of Panos Perspective Papers: Information, Knowledge and Development.* (www.oneworld.org/panos/knowlpap.htm.)

Sagasti, Francisco. 2001. "Knowledge Explosion and the Knowledge Divide." Background paper for the *Human Development Report 2001.*

Stiglitz, Joseph. 1999. "Scan Globally, Reinvent Locally: Knowledge Infrastructure and the Localization of Knowledge." Keynote address at the First Global Development Network Conference. Bonn.

Sweeney, Douglas. 2000. "The Networked World, New Technologies and the Future." *Journal of Human Development,* 1(2), 183-90.

Tadjbakhsh, Sharbanou. 2001a. "Some Thoughts on National Human Development Networks." New York: United Nations Development Programme.

———. 2001b. Correspondence on National Human Development Report networks. August.

United Nations Development Programme (UNDP). 2001. *Human Development Report 2001.* New York: Oxford University Press.

Webster, Frank. 1995. *Theories of Information Society.* London, New York: Rutledge.

World Bank. 2001. "Creating, Sharing, Applying Knowledge for All: Strategy for the Future." (www.worldbank.org/knowledgebank/research.html.)

3.2 INTEGRATING LOCAL AND GLOBAL KNOWLEDGE, TECHNOLOGY AND PRODUCTION SYSTEMS: CHALLENGES FOR TECHNICAL COOPERATION

JUANA KURAMOTO AND FRANCISCO SAGASTI

Introduction

Knowledge has acquired a crucial relevance at the dawn of the 21st century. The acceleration of scientific and technological advances and their explosive diffusion have changed the way economies and societies work. We do not rely anymore on cheap inputs to increase and improve production processes and economic growth. Nowadays, we rely on cheap information.

Two factors have contributed to the reduced price of information. On the one hand, the release of information transforms it into a public good, at least in principle. It is a non-rival good, because no matter how much we use a specific piece of information, it will not be reduced. It will still be available for another person to use it. Information is also a non-excludable good, because two agents can use the same piece of information at the same time. Even when the mechanisms to protect information are tight—for example, patents—information always leaks.

On the other hand, the advances in information and communication technologies (ICT) have permitted low-cost storage and widespread access to information in almost all areas of human activities. The Organisation for Economic Co-operation and Development (OECD) refers to ICT as "...a key technology to speeding up the innovation process and reducing cycle times...it has fostered greater networking in the economy, it makes possible faster diffusion of codified knowledge and ideas, and it has played an important role in making science more efficient and linking it more closely with business" (Dodgson et al., 2001; citing OECD, 2000).

Although cheap information creates huge opportunities for economic development, only a few countries are taking advantage of it. A minimum level of capacity is required in educational, research, government and productive institutions to transform information into useful knowledge, and also to discern which pieces of information are useful to solve a country's specific problems.

Knowledge, as opposed to information, is created in a specific context shaped by geographic, economic, social or political factors. Knowledge creation is not automatic; it requires a process of learning. When individuals learn, they usually build theories and conceptual frameworks that provide coherence to, and allow them to reflect on, their experiences. Theories are tested in the realm of action, and reflection on the results of these actions leads to additional knowledge and to improved theoretical understanding. Thus, knowledge creation requires systematic gathering of information and feedback in response to specific needs (Albu, 1997). It is also a cumulative and endogenous process, which continuously builds on previous pieces of absorbed and adapted information. This is why it is so difficult to transfer knowledge successfully from one location to another.

Knowledge contributes to economic development by giving people the capacities to solve the specific problems they face, satisfy their needs and further increase their capabilities. In particular, knowledge contributes to generating the technologies that are used in the production of goods and services that improve the quality of life. A country's capacity to devise effective solutions is supported by an institutional setting that promotes the creation, absorption, adoption and diffusion of knowledge, and which also matches such knowledge with the needs and preferences of the population. In developing countries, this problem-solving ability and the supporting institutional arrangements must take into account the solutions that have been devised in local settings and in response to rather specific problems. This implies paying attention to indigenous knowledge and technologies, which usually have been accumulating slowly over a long time and through trial and error.

The recognition that knowledge plays an important role in development has led, particularly during the last half century, to a variety of initiatives for development cooperation and to transfers of knowledge from developed to developing countries (Sagasti and Alcalde, 1999). To a large extent, many of these initiatives were inspired by the Marshall Plan, which provided financial and technical assistance to Europe after World War II. Between 1947 and 1951, the United States injected the 1997 equivalent of US $88 billion in balance-of-payments support and soft loans to most countries in Western Europe, and also provided technical assistance and access to US managerial and manufacturing know-how. Five decades later, the Marshall Plan's key features make it highly regarded as a model for international cooperation programmes. These include the cooperative and multilateral nature of the plan, which involved both donor and recipients in its design and implementation, and the incorporation of training programmes for European businesspeople, which transferred valuable technical and management know-how to the private sector. The limited and temporary nature of the plan has also been considered a desirable feature. In sum, the Marshall Plan has been deemed the most successful international cooperation programme in history (Jenkins, 1997; Rostow, 1997; Holt, 1997).[1]

However, as other contributions to this volume indicate, the international cooperation and technical assistance schemes devised and put in practice to help developing countries have had, for the most part, a rather limited impact. To a large extent, this is because they have relied on the transference of generic information, without addressing the organizational, economic, financial and political constraints that shape and condition the use of cooperation and assistance in the recipient countries. As a result, conventional technical assistance programmes have often eroded ownership, commitment

---

[1] The Marshall Plan's success owed much to the specific historical and geographical context in which it was carried out, because it involved the industrial reconstruction of countries that had decades or even centuries of manufacturing experience, a well-educated labour force and the institutions needed to support a modern economy.

and independent action at the national and local levels in developing countries (Morgan, 2001). In many cases, countries became dependent on such programmes to support significant parts of their production systems, and faced the loss of their own indigenous knowledge in their efforts to adopt the foreign versions. As a result, developing countries have not been able to create an endogenous knowledge base.

This chapter presents a conceptual framework to examine the ways knowledge and technology creation contribute to economic development. It then explores how indigenous and local knowledge can be integrated into production systems. The chapter concludes with some suggestions on the way technical cooperation could help in making better use of traditional knowledge and technologies.

Knowledge, Technology and Production: A Conceptual Framework

The concept of development has changed over time. According to the largely economic view of this concept that prevailed for a good part of the 20th century, development was practically synonymous with economic growth (Arndt, 1987; Bezanson and Sagasti, 2000). Developed countries were defined as those that achieved high per capita income, which allowed their populations to purchase a large amount of goods and services. Therefore, the implicit objective of development was to produce wealthy and even opulent societies. One of the conditions for achieving this was to improve productivity levels, which, in turn, implied structural transformations in the economy and the reassignment of production factors from low to higher productivity sectors.

Partly due to the cumulative character of productivity gains, which accrue disproportionately to those countries that have already achieved high levels, the outcome of the race for higher productivity during most of the second half of the 20th century was an increase in income disparities. Not only did rich countries become richer than poor ones, but high-income regions—and even wealthy individuals within regions—also became wealthier. As a reaction, during the 1980s, improvements in the level and distribution of income began to be seen as crucial to attaining development with equity, and poverty reduction programmes became one of the main tools to achieve this goal. More equitable income distribution was associated with successful development, particularly in European countries and Japan, while those countries that were considered far from successful in almost any measure—for example, many African and Latin American countries—had much greater levels of income inequality.

One of the perverse effects of poverty and deprivation is the undermining of people's self-esteem and capacities, which in turn leads to further poverty and deprivation. Partly as a result of the contributions of Mahbub ul Haq (1976), the International Labour Office (1976) and especially Amartya Sen (1981, 1984), there was a shift in the focus of development thinking during the 1980s that led to placing human beings at the centre. For example, according to Sen, the important question is what goods and services can do for people's lives, rather than how many goods and services people can produce during their lifetime. This was illustrated by comparing life expectancy with income levels: In 1985, China, with an annual per capita income of US

$310, had a life expectancy of 69 years, while in Mexico the figures were $2,080 and 67 years, and in Oman they were $6,700 and 54 years (Sen, 1989). From this perspective, the goal of development becomes the enrichment of human life and the expansion of capabilities, and this requires not only access to goods and services to satisfy basic needs, but also recognition in society and self-actualization, all of which provide the freedom to choose individual life options.[2]

It is possible to identify three approaches to development, each with its own strategy implications for the road that developing countries should follow. In the approach that focuses primarily on productivity gains, countries are supposed to replicate patterns of industrialization traversed by the more advanced economies, which implies a process of major economic transformation from traditional agriculture, crafts and self-subsistence activities to modern sectors, particularly industry. These modern sectors have to take the lead in the economy, because their higher productivity will increase people's income and allow them to buy more goods and services. This also requires the use of modern imported knowledge and technologies.

In the development-with-equity approach, the government plays a key role in redistribution of income, seeking to provide equal opportunities for improvement to all parts of the population (CEPAL, 1990) and to balance growth with social justice. Although it has often been argued by proponents of the productivity-gains approach that governments should first foster economic growth and then redistribute wealth, for otherwise they would be just redistributing poverty, it has been clear for a long time that redistribution and growth are not incompatible (Chenery et al., 1974). For example, the World Bank pointed out that to increase the income of the poor in Latin America to a level above the poverty threshold would only require 0.7 per cent of the regional GDP or an income tax of 2 per cent on the richest quintile (World Bank, 1990). In any case, whether growth is fostered before or after redistribution, the fact is that sustainable economic growth depends on productivity increases, which, in turn, require access to foreign knowledge and technology.

Sen's capabilities-and-freedoms approach views education as a key factor in the process of development, but an education that is specifically oriented towards enhancing the capacities of human beings to thrive in the context where their lives unfold. Productivity is also important, but primarily to the extent that it helps increase the production of goods and services required by specific populations to enhance their capabilities, for not everybody needs or wants mass consumption goods. In consequence, among other things, this approach leads to a revaluation of indigenous knowledge and technology, in so far that they satisfy the needs and conform to the preferences of specific segments of the population that are not fully integrated into the market for mass consumption goods.

All these approaches envisage different roles for knowledge and for the way in which it interacts with production systems. Sagasti (1979) provides a conceptual framework to examine the interactions of science, technology and production systems

---

[2] This approach was central to the development of the Human Development Index by Mahbub ul Haq and his collaborators, who issued the first *Human Development Report* in 1990. It is now published annually by the United Nations Development Programme (UNDP).

that are at the core of the different economic performances of countries (see Figure 3.2.1). While this framework was devised at a time when productivity gains were seen as the key to development, it has stood the test of time in part because it allows incorporation of a variety of issues that have been — and still are — relevant to the design of development policies and strategies, such as the role that indigenous knowledge plays in local production systems, and the various ways in which science, technology and production in the developing world interact with their counterparts in developed countries.

According to this conceptual framework, science seeks to generate knowledge to understand natural and social phenomena, and to provide explanations that give sense to human existence. Technology can be considered as a set of organized responses to confront the challenges posed by the physical and social environment. Production provides goods and services to satisfy the needs of a community and of the individuals that compose it. These three components, considered in a dynamic fashion as currents in constant change, are structured and linked to each other through a set of institutional arrangements, and are immersed within the broader social, cultural and political context of human societies.

Figure 3.2.1 indicates that a close interaction between science and technology in developed countries nurtured the evolution of productive activities. Without the capacity to generate scientific knowledge, to transform it into technologies that are then used in the production of new and better goods and services, these countries could not have achieved their high rates of economic growth. The close and continuous interaction between science, technology and production led to the creation of an endogenous scientific and technological base. This consists of the accumulation of scientific research and technological development capabilities that make it possible to generate new knowledge, and also to modify, adapt and recombine existing knowledge, which is then deployed to produce goods and services. In turn, through learning-by-doing and learning-by-using processes, the utilization of knowledge and technologies in the productive sector leads to incremental technical innovations and to the further accumulation of technological capabilities.

Although the interactions between science, technology and production are presented in a linear pattern, they usually do not take place in this way. There are substantive overlaps between these three spheres, to the extent that in some highly advanced economic sectors, scientific research, technological development and productive activities are tightly bound, mutually reinforcing and cannot be considered separately. The linear model of innovation, which states that scientific advances push technological innovations that result in new products or processes, is no longer valid — if it ever was. In developed countries, it is more common to find that firms finance basic research to obtain direct access to scientific advances and also to inform researchers about their requirements and needs. Conversely, research performed by universities and scientific institutions increasingly reaches industrial application through the establishment of spin-off companies.

**FIGURE 3.2.1: RELATIONS BETWEEN SCIENCE, TECHNOLOGY AND PRODUCTION
IN DEVELOPED AND DEVELOPING COUNTRIES**

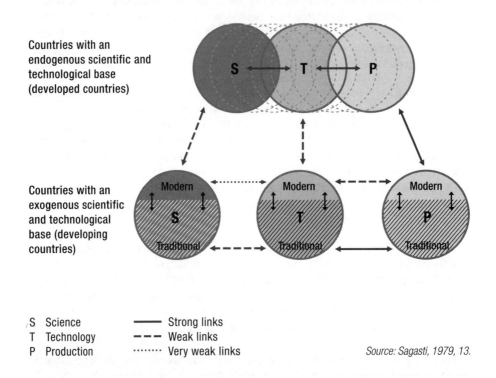

Countries with an
endogenous scientific and
technological base
(developed countries)

Countries with an
exogenous scientific
and technological
base (developing
countries)

S Science   —— Strong links
T Technology   --- Weak links
P Production   ········ Very weak links   *Source: Sagasti, 1979, 13.*

These modifications in the innovation process in developed countries have given
rise to new innovation models, such as the "innovation journey" approach of Van de
Ven et al. (1999), which views innovation as a non-linear dynamic system that incorporates managerial and organizational factors and external collaborative activity; the
"innovation systems" approach of Lundvall (1992) and Nelson (1993), which focus on
the interrelationships among the wide variety of agents engaged in technological
change and innovation processes in market economies; and the "triple helix"
approach proposed by Etzkowitz and Leydesdorff (2000), which highlights the role of
institutions, especially in a knowledge-based economy.[3]

One of the implications of the evolution of these conceptualizations of the innovation process in the advanced nations is that the distinction between the various
"capacities" associated with the generation and utilization of knowledge becomes
fuzzy. Since innovation can occur on the shop floor, production capacities also include
the modification of the technology as it is used. Furthermore, the extended notion of
technology, including "soft" components such as work organization and supervision,
adds more complexity to the delimitation of capacities.

---

[3] This approach can be considered as an update of "Sábato's triangle," which was widely used in the
1970s to examine the interactions between government, industry and scientific institutions (Sábato
and Botana, 1968; Sagasti, 1982).

In contrast, and for a variety of reasons, developing countries have not been successful in generating such an endogenous scientific and technological base. Their worldviews have differed widely from those of Western society, where science superseded religion and myth as a means to explain and understand natural phenomena. The widespread use of the scientific method—a set of procedures that link the manipulation of abstract concepts and symbols to observations and experiments—increased the stock of systematized and codified knowledge in Western societies. In other parts of the world, religion and myth continued to codify knowledge under the assumption that God's will and divine interventions, or even mysterious and mystical forces, structured the relationship between society and its physical environment (Jamieson, 1994). Furthermore, in some cases, the absence of writing and the low levels of literacy added to the constraints that limited the creation and diffusion of modern knowledge. Thus, science, as we understand it, was mostly absent in these regions.

In addition, the evolution of the stock of technologies available to respond to the challenges of the physical and social environment was largely a result of localized trial-and-error processes, and the transformations experienced by the production system were also the result of slow changes made to adapt to local conditions and demand (Herrera, 1975). To the extent that developing countries interacted with their Western counterparts during the last four centuries, they acquired—if at all—a very thin layer of imported modern scientific, technological and productive activities that usually remained isolated from each other. Therefore, with practically no interactions between modern science and both indigenous and modern technologies, and with very little relation between modern technological activities and the system of production, it became virtually impossible to create an endogenous scientific and technological base. Production systems were largely traditional and remained highly localized, relying mostly on traditional technologies (Sagasti, 1980). Paradoxically, the overlap of traditional knowledge, technology and production in developing countries mirrors the close interactions that emerged in their developed country modern counterparts as they built their endogenous science and technology bases.

The engagement of most developing countries in the dynamics of international markets, intensified by the globalization process of the last two decades, has created direct relationships that link each one of these national science, technology and production spheres in the developing world with their counterparts in the developed countries. Foreign direct investment has become an important mechanism to connect production systems in developed and developing countries; and goods and processes designed in the former have been imported or incorporated into local production activities in the latter, thus allowing for an expansion of the consumption options of high-income consumers in developing countries. The requirements of foreign subsidiaries and of more advanced local firms has led to technical knowledge flows from developed to developing countries, and helped to establish incipient technology markets, where solutions devised in rich countries have become available to satisfy domestic production needs, either for local consumption or export. The increase in information flows associated with the worldwide expansion of modern science has helped to replicate in developing countries—but in a rather stunted and diminished way—some of the scientific institutions that had evolved in the Western countries over long periods. As a consequence, developing country scientists have established rather strong links with the centres of scientific excellence in the North, but largely lost sight of the research needs of their own countries.

While modern science, technology and production systems in developing countries have forged strong links with their counterparts in the advanced countries, they have had little or no interaction among themselves at the domestic level. In contrast to what happened in the developed countries, this has led to the creation of an *exogenous* scientific and technological base, whose precarious and disjointed character limits its capacity to provide appropriate scientific and technological responses to the needs of production systems and the population. Even in those cases where some capacity has been accumulated in the scientific, technological and production systems, considering each on its own, the institutional settings and incentive systems have privileged links with their developed country counterparts that have hindered the convergence—and in some cases encouraged the divergence—of science, technology and production in the developing world.

For example, the national science and technology councils in Latin America, as well as the government agencies that promote scientific and technological research in specific productive sectors, have had little or no interaction with firms, financial agencies, educational centres and technology service providers (Vessuri, 1994). The main technological tasks performed by the region's productive agents have been limited to the adaptation of imported innovations without establishing tight and permanent links with local research and development entities. Thus, during the last several decades, the region has not been able to create innovation systems that work. Even in countries with a higher degree of institutional development in the area of science and technology—such as Mexico, Brazil and Argentina—the relationships among science, technology and production systems remains wishful thinking rather than a reality (Erber, 1999).

The task of building an endogenous scientific and technological base requires three sets of policies: (a) those that promote the growth and integration of domestic scientific, technological and productive activities, considering both their indigenous and modern components; (b) those that create linkages between a developing country's modern and indigenous knowledge, technology and productive activities, on the one hand, and the global science, technology and production systems, on the other; and (c) those that create favourable framework conditions for the efficient functioning of markets that are conducive to innovation, and for the selective upgrading and use of indigenous knowledge and technology.

The integration of knowledge, technology and production in developing countries requires, first, measures to establish, consolidate and guide the growth of institutions involved in the performance of scientific and technological programmes and projects, orienting them towards the needs of the productive sector. Second, it requires measures to promote the demand and application of locally generated knowledge by the production system, so as to avoid the divorce between science and technology capabilities and production and service activities. Third, there is a need for explicit measures oriented towards the identification of opportunities for selectively upgrading and utilizing indigenous technologies. Some of the policy instruments available for these purposes are institution-building, science and technology planning, financing of scientific and technological research, venture capital funds for innovation, the use of state purchasing power to generate demand for local knowledge, tax credits to promote innovation, technical norms and standards, measures to encourage the creation of clusters of innovative firms, information systems for indigenous technologies, sector specific policies to encourage the efficient use of indigenous technologies (for example, in agriculture, small-scale industry, crafts and housing), and incentives to promote the blending of modern with indigenous technologies.

In terms of making links to external sources of knowledge, other policies should aim at forging working relations between science, technology and production in the developing countries with their counterparts in developed countries. The idea is to take advantage and benefit from more advanced sources of knowledge, while at the same time strengthening local institutions. The effective use of imported knowledge requires a certain degree of autonomy and self-reliance on the part of domestic research organizations, technology agencies, and productive enterprises and agents, particularly with regard to decisions about the knowledge to be acquired and the way in which it is to be used. Some of the policy instruments available for these purposes include measures to increase imports of technology and knowledge-intensive goods, promote exports of progressively more complex goods and services, encourage direct foreign investment, make effective use of licensing and related means of technology transfer, and promote international scientific cooperation. Initiatives to take advantage of technical assistance should be included in this second group of policies, which is aimed at building endogenous science and technology capabilities. Although, as the articles in this volume argue, this requires major changes in the conception and practice of technical assistance.

The establishment of an appropriate framework to promote innovation and the efficient utilization of indigenous technologies requires a host of complementary or "implicit" policies, most of which are not exclusively or directly related to science and technology, but are made with other objectives in mind (Sagasti, 1976). Nevertheless, their influence can be decisive in terms of facilitating the creation and consolidation of an endogenous science and technology base, the establishment of effective links with external sources of knowledge, and the articulation of innovation systems. Table 3.2.1 indicates some of the measures that are involved in the creation of such an appropriate framework.

Integration of Indigenous Knowledge into Production Systems

According to the conceptual framework presented in the preceding section (see Figure 3.2.1), the design of strategies and policies to build an endogenous science and technology base in developing countries must take into account the coexistence of modern and indigenous knowledge, technology and production. In these countries, large segments

TABLE 3.2.1: EXAMPLES OF POLICIES THAT CREATE FAVOURABLE CONDITIONS FOR INNOVATION

Maintaining a stable macroeconomic environment that encourages long-term investments by productive agents
Competition policies to increase innovation-driving competitive pressures, but also to facilitate collaborative research
Regulatory reform policies to lessen administrative burdens and institutional rigidities
Financial, fiscal and administrative measures to facilitate the flow of capital to small and medium firms
Labour market policies to increase the mobility of personnel and strengthen tacit knowledge flows
Communications policies to maximize the dissemination of information and enable the growth of electronic networks
Regional development policies to improve complementarities between government initiatives at different levels
Protection of intellectual property, but with mechanisms and safeguards for preserving local and traditional knowledge, and for allowing the use of foreign knowledge in emergency situations
Development and maintenance of an efficient transport and communications infrastructure
Education and training policies to develop human capital, with an emphasis on science and technology
Creation of information centres where domestic firms can get information on foreign technology markets and providers, thus reducing information disadvantages in technology transfer negotiations

Source: Casabonne and Sagasti (2000).

of the population subsist with incomes that are below the poverty line; they cannot access the products and goods offered in modern markets. In fact, 80 per cent of the world's population depends on indigenous knowledge to meet their medicinal needs, and at least half relies on indigenous knowledge and crops for food supplies. Knowledge about these indigenous goods and services is embedded in the community and has usually been developed outside the formal education system. This does not mean that indigenous knowledge creation rests on an informal or disorganized innovation system; on the contrary, it stems from what may be called a "cooperative innovation system" that operates in the setting and at the pace of daily living, and is associated with the immediate agro-ecological context of indigenous populations (RAFI and UNDP, 1995).

Indigenous knowledge provides a basis for local level decision-making in matters of food security, human and animal health, education, natural resource management and various other community-based activities. Thus, it is closely related to different aspects of survival and subsistence, generating in that way a vast body of knowledge. For that reason, it is extremely valuable (MOST and CIRAN, 1999).

Given that indigenous knowledge is crucial for survival and often contributes to improving the quality of life of poor populations, there is a strong need to register, upgrade and disseminate such knowledge. Indigenous knowledge is rarely codified and systematized—or it is codified in highly idiosyncratic ways, which make it difficult to transmit (at least according to scientific and technical standards). It therefore depends on its depositaries or users for its diffusion, which usually takes place by imitation, exchanges of goods and the recounting of oral traditions. In many cases, indigenous knowledge has been lost because there are no reliable mechanisms to store it, and because the dominance and presumed superiority of Western ways have led to situations in which traditions were ignored, neglected and discarded. Box 3.2.1 refers to a study conducted in Peru regarding indigenous and modern worldviews.

The local specificity of traditional and indigenous knowledge has also become a constraint for its application on a wider basis. Indigenous technologies and products are found in specific regions and, even when they might be suitable for other places, technologies are applied and goods are produced in limited amounts. This happens, in part, because people that use this kind of knowledge follow the rationale of a pre-capitalist system in which artisanal work and custom-made production are the rule.

Nevertheless, as the Rural Advancement Foundation International (RAFI) has pointed out, the role of indigenous knowledge has made and continues to make important contributions to modern science, especially in the agriculture, pharmaceutical and biotechnology industries. These improvements have not been the result of passive accumulation, but have flourished from a cooperative innovation system, in which the community as a whole is involved and works with a holistic approach. The recognition and understanding of this cooperative innovation system makes it complementary to the modern or institutional innovation system. According to RAFI, the latter "tends to produce highly specific 'micro' improvements that then have broad application in such fields as molecular biology or microelectronics. The cooperative system, on the other hand, tends to produce 'macro' system innovations that can only be applied at the local level (for example, because they involve a complex mix of plants, insects and soil)" (RAFI and UNDP, 1995).

The growing needs of low-income populations, together with the limitations of domestic economies in providing the means to satisfy these people's needs, require innovative solutions to promote the wider dissemination of efficient indigenous methods of production and services. The key here lies in the word "efficient," which must be interpreted in the wider sense of contributing to creating capabilities and freedoms, and to improving equity, and not only in terms of narrow technical criteria that focus just on productivity increases.

For this purpose, it is first necessary to make an inventory of indigenous techniques and of the situations in which they have been successfully applied. Rajasekaran (1993) proposed a method for recording indigenous knowledge systems that involves the participation of key people such as local extension agents, local school headmasters, credit cooperative officials and workers, among others. These observers are usually immersed in the local settings where production and service activities take place, and can therefore observe, document and evaluate indigenous technologies and practices. They should also become thoroughly familiar with, and even embedded in, the local cultural and social environment in order to grasp people's

BOX 3.2.1: The worldview of the Andean peasant farmer

María Angelica Salas's study of systems of knowledge in the Peruvian Andes raises important issues regarding indigenous visions of the future. As part of this study, a number of peasant farmers were asked to make drawings that expressed their vision of a desirable future, depicting themselves, their social relations and their relationships with nature.

One drawing that showed the countryside looking very much like an urban or industrial landscape prompted a reaction from other peasant farmers who, somewhat disconcertedly, observed that the bare hills and the absence of crops could not be associated with a better future. Furthermore, they could not imagine a future without their homes, their relatives, the sun, the moon or animals. This expressed their reaction against the tendency to deny their Andean identity by replacing it with a vision of modernity in which the rural world is rendered in non-Andean terms. By contrast, the elements that appeared most frequently in the drawings were associated with the specific environment in which the peasants lived. The drawings contained symbols of Andean culture (the mountains, the crop parcel, the Andean community, the family) and other elements that expressed cultural interaction (roads, trucks, schools).

By examining the symbolic meaning of the more common elements depicted, Salas was able to identify the outlines of a vision of society that differs from the urban and industrial model. Peasant farmers have a relationship with nature in which sacred and economic elements are closely intertwined; furthermore, they feel that their ties with nature are built on reciprocity relationships. This same principle reinforces the strong family and community ties that shape the identity of Andean men and women. Also, the participatory and direct democracy mechanisms that organize community life make it possible to address the tensions that exist between individual and collective initiative in the solution of problems. These ties are protected from the threat of dispersion by people's respect for the history and knowledge embedded in their oral traditions, rituals, songs, dances and other forms of expression of Andean cultural diversity.

As part of her study Salas also organized a workshop between elder peasants knowledgeable in potato farming with scientists from the International Potato Research Center based in Lima. She was able to contrast their alternative worldviews with regard to the cultivation of potatoes, but found that the technical solutions devised by farmers and researchers did not differ too much in their fundamental aspects.

Source: Salas (1996).

beliefs, values and customs, which will allow observers to understand the decision-making processes in terms of the selection and use of indigenous technologies and practices. The accounts and recordings of indigenous knowledge and techniques provided by these observers should not contain just technical descriptions, but also include information about the wider social, cultural, political and ecosystems context in order to facilitate their diffusion and to make them more useful for policy-making and planning purposes (MOST and CIRAN, 1999).

Second, it is also necessary to evaluate, modify and further develop these technologies and practices, partly by injecting into them modern knowledge and technology components, through what has been referred to as "technology blending" (Bhalla, 1994). Local populations in developing countries face problems that require practical and effective solutions in their localities, a task to which indigenous knowledge can make a contribution. For this to happen, it is necessary to devise strategies, create institutions and adopt policies to foster a sustained interaction between the depositaries of indigenous knowledge, techniques and practices on the one hand, and scientific researchers and engineers on the other. In doing so, it is necessary to always keep in mind the local and specific character of these solutions, so that the new technology options that emerge from this process will be useful and acceptable to local populations.

These two steps amount to a selective screening and upgrading strategy to identify and improve indigenous technologies, but they must entail maintaining the essential characteristics that appeal to those who use and benefit from these technologies. The design and implementation of such a strategy requires committed, forward-looking and culturally sensitive political leadership, a rather unusual combination in most developing countries. Box 3.2.2 provides an illustration of what can be done in this regard.

Technical Cooperation and the Integration of Indigenous Knowledge into Production Systems

The development cooperation experiment in general, and technical assistance programmes in particular, were devised and put in practice at a time when the productivity-increase approach—embedded within the larger paradigm of modernization—dominated development thinking and practice. The institutional and programmatic arrangements that emerged during the 1950s and 1960s for this purpose conformed to this approach, placing emphasis on the unidirectional flow of knowledge from rich to poor countries. There was, to a large extent, disregard for whatever was available locally. Traditional ways, knowledge and beliefs were generally seen as a hindrance to modernization and economic growth.

As the contributions to this volume clearly show, it is time for a reappraisal of the ways in which international cooperation for development, and technical assistance in particular, are conceptualized and delivered.[4] Changes in the approaches to development and the poor performance of conventional technical assistance programmes have gradually led to a revaluation of indigenous knowledge, technology and production. From the perspective of this chapter, it is necessary to examine the role that technical assistance can play in the process of building an endogenous science and technology base, and in the integration of indigenous and modern knowledge, technology and production. The three sets of policies mentioned above at the end of the second section of this chapter—those related to the domestic integration of knowledge, technology and production; those that establish links with the global knowledge, technology and production systems; and those that create a favorable policy environment for the first two—provide an entry point to address these issues and will be addressed in turn.

Integration of knowledge, technology and production at the local level

The first set of policies are geared to the integration of domestic science, technology and production, considering both their traditional and modern components, and comprise several routes toward creating endogenous science and technology capacities that make full use of traditional knowledge. A first route involves the selective screening and upgrading strategy described in the preceding section, which focuses on the

---

4 For an attempt to suggest new directions for development cooperation, see the 1999 Hopper Lecture delivered by the second of the authors of this paper (Sagasti, 1999).

BOX 3.2.2: Support and preservation of indigenous knowledge and technology: The case of India

India provides a good example of how governments can support the preservation and promotion of indigenous technologies.

First, India has devised its Indigenous Knowledge Systems National Programme, which is led by a highly respected scientist. This programme has the aim of auditing, documenting and supporting research associated with indigenous knowledge. In addition, there are other, more specific programmes to promote and popularize these knowledge systems, and India has developed a large database on indigenous knowledge and biodiversity heritage.

Second, although India does not have formal laws to prevent anyone from appropriating knowledge from the indigenous community, it has made various efforts to protect indigenous knowledge. Through an amendment of its Patent Act of 1970, India does not grant patents to subject matter that, prior to the date of filing the patent application, was available to the public by means of use, written description or in any manner in any country, or which was used by local and indigenous communities. India is also screening patents to set precedents by challenging those that are based on prior knowledge and to which India can lay claim.

Third, India has wide institutional platforms to screen, preserve and promote research on indigenous knowledge. These platforms include the National Botanical Research Institute, the National Institute of Immunology, the Toxicology Research Institute, the Central Institute of Medicinal and Aromatic Plants, and the Council for Scientific and Industrial Research, among others.

Fourth, India has managed to provide a market for indigenous knowledge via the validation of alternative medicinal and health care systems, and the accreditation of hospitals and clinics that apply these alternative methods. Finally, although there is no formal mechanism for integrating indigenous knowledge and innovations at the school or university levels, different initiatives are aimed at training people and at promoting research.

Source: RAFI and UNDP (1995); DACST (2000).

identification of indigenous knowledge and technologies that could be improved before incorporating them into productive activities.

A second route consists of focusing on the complex interactions that take place within indigenous production systems, attempting to understand their logic and functioning before seeking to inject modern or upgraded indigenous technologies and knowledge components. For example, biological and social scientists have pointed out the complexity and sophistication of indigenous natural resource management systems, and indigenous communities have nurtured and used many species of plants that have therapeutic uses (Warren, 1992). The idea that there are indigenous innovation systems, which evolve and change in response to challenges and stimuli that are different from those of market-based innovation systems, has superseded the notion that indigenous production systems are passive and static. In this regard, Gupta (1990) has identified four factors that influence farmer experimentation in local settings: ecology, because innovations result from the interactions between crops, soil and climate; history, because the memory of major events such as crop failures conditions the willingness to assume risk; serendipity, which refers to improved practices that are discovered accidentally; and economics, which refers to the incentives, needs and efficiency considerations that induce farmers to innovate and adopt new practices.

Efforts to revalidate indigenous knowledge systems in farming using the "selective screening and upgrading" and the "indigenous innovation systems" routes (which overlap to a certain extent and may be considered complementary) make use of a participatory approach to knowledge generation, in which the research agenda is defined by identifying the problems faced by farmers, rather than by responding to the concerns of policy-makers or the interests of scientific researchers. This has facilitated the interaction of traditional and modern knowledge, technology and production practices, and has proven to be quite effective in tasks such as germ-plasm screening—particularly because farmers have extensive empirical knowledge about the ecological factors that affect variety selection (Haugerud and Collinson, 1991). The participatory approach keeps the indigenous knowledge system of farmers as a base, facilitates farmer participation from the beginning and their acceptance of research results, and enables scientific researchers to get direct feedback from the farmers (Rajasekaran, 1993).

A third route to the integration of modern and indigenous knowledge, technology and production focuses on the specific problems faced by local populations in developing countries in terms of satisfying their needs and living with dignity. This route brings the full arsenal of modern science and technology to help devise production systems appropriate to these objectives, and incorporates elements of indigenous knowledge and techniques as they appear relevant. An example of this approach is the work of the group Development Alternatives in India, which has focused for more than a decade on the creation of economically, socially and ecologically sustainable livelihoods by developing and marketing technologies and production systems that are appropriate to local conditions.

Development Alternatives and its commercial arm, the firm TARA, have established research, development and testing facilities for the design of technologies geared to the production of goods for local consumption and to the generation of employment at the local level. These technologies are designed keeping in mind economic, technical and ecological efficiency criteria, and also the need for them to be convenient and acceptable to their users. Development Alternatives and TARA have adapted a franchise distribution system, in which the technologies and business methods are generated in their central laboratories and offices; local partners are identified, recruited, trained and given technical support through licensing agreements; and the local partners then provide the limited amounts of investment capital (which is sometimes raised with the help of Development Alternatives and with government support) required to establish the local production and distribution facilities. The technologies and products that have been developed and marketed through this system include highly efficient wood and coal domestic cooking stoves, machinery to manufacture paper and cardboard, water pumps, multiple use presses, machinery to manufacture stabilized mud bricks, looms and knitting machines, appliances for processing and storing food, and integrated energy systems for rural villages (Koshla, 1996).

The role that conventional technical assistance can play to support the integration of modern and indigenous knowledge and technology into production systems through these routes is quite limited. Instead, what is required are programmes to spread best practices, which would involve exchanges of information and knowledge between developing countries,[5] and capacity development initiatives that create the local conditions for such integration.

Establishing linkages with the global knowledge, technology and production system

The second set of policies—those geared to the creation of linkages between developing countries and the global knowledge, technology and production systems—includes a variety of measures related to scientific cooperation, technology transfer and the expansion of production facilities from developed to developing countries. However, for the most part, these linkages do not relate to indigenous knowledge or traditional technologies. The main and most visible exception refers to the pharmaceutical, agricultural, biological products and biotechnology industries, which have shown significant interest in indigenous products and native plants that have valuable genetic and therapeutic properties. This has led to a multiplicity of initiatives from research institutions and businesses in developed countries to obtain access to local knowledge and products associated with the rich biodiversity of many developing countries.

Indigenous communities have made important contributions to agriculture, and to the pharmaceutical and biotechnology industries (see Box 3.2.3). For this reason, a growing global network of institutions, mostly universities and research centres in developed countries, is making efforts systematically to record and store indigenous knowledge. Warren (1992) reported at least ten centres around the world devoted to the collection of indigenous knowledge. In the early 1990s, the value of developing country germ plasm to the pharmaceutical industry was estimated to be at least US $32 billion per year, although developing countries received only a fraction of this amount for the biological materials and knowledge they contributed (RAFI and UNDP, 1995).

There are also cooperative ventures geared towards mobilizing local and global knowledge to make better use of biodiversity resources in developing countries. For example, there is a project aimed at harnessing indigenous South African knowledge about biodiversity (Center for International Development, 2001). The project involves a consortium composed of a team of South African biochemists, indigenous healers and plant experts, professionals from public research institutions and local universities, as well as foreign research partners. The mix of people, ideas, cultures and interests involved in the project is helping to pull together indigenous and modern knowledge systems. Their interactions have also led to questions related not just to technology and knowledge, but also to issues such as how to share benefits and risks between the various partners, how to deal with asymmetric power relations within the project, and how to build trust to facilitate the flow of ideas and information between the partners.

The interest in preserving the genetic resources associated with biodiversity has led to the establishment of facilities for the *ex situ* conservation of indigenous germ plasm, usually in well-established institutions in the developed countries. The most notable exceptions are the centres associated with the Consultative Group on International Agricultural Research (CGIAR), which has established several facilities in

---

[5] On this matter, see Rath and Lealess (2000).

BOX 3.2.3: Indigenous knowledge and therapeutic plants in Australia

The smoke bush (Conospermum) is a plant that is widespread in Western Australia; indigenous people used it for a variety of therapeutic purposes. During the 1960s, the US National Cancer Institute, under license from the West Australia Government, collected and screened the smoke bush for scientific purposes. In 1981, some specimens were sent to the United States to be tested for possible anticancer chemicals, but no cancer resistant properties were found. In the late 1980s, the smoke bush was tested again for potential substances that could cure AIDS. In the early 1990s, the West Australia Government granted a license to an Australian multinational pharmaceutical company to develop a substance named Conocurvone, which is able to destroy the HIV virus in low concentrations. Some estimates stated that the West Australia Government could receive royalties exceeding US $100 million by year 2002 if the substance is successfully commercialized, but there are no clear provisions for indigenous people who had first identified the plant for its therapeutic and healing properties.

Source: Davis (1998).

developing countries (Lima for potatoes, Manila for rice, Mexico for wheat and corn, among others). More recently, there has been a move to promote *in situ* conservation, primarily by encouraging indigenous communities to take an active role as stewards of the genetic resources in their own communities. This approach has the advantage of being more cost effective. For example, the cost of germ-plasm storage under gene bank conditions was estimated to be around US $128 million during 1993-2000, but this amount could have been cut in half through the active participation of indigenous communities in conserving biodiversity in their own local settings (RAFI and UNDP, 1995). In addition, *in situ* conservation provides intellectual recognition to the native communities and opens the opportunity to interact with modern innovation systems on a more equal basis.

The linkages between indigenous knowledge about biodiversity and the global science, technology and production systems raise the thorny issue of the distribution of short- and long-term benefits, which in turn are related to international agreements on intellectual property rights. These agreements are biased towards developed country governments and corporations, and do not recognize the right of indigenous communities to enjoy part of the economic benefits obtained by private firms when they are granted patents based on indigenous resources.

According to Posey and Dutfield (1996, 75):

> Traditional communities may have their own concepts of intellectual property and resource rights. However, industrializing countries are under pressure to adopt the European and North American concepts of intellectual property, which, by guaranteeing the right of legal individuals to profit from their innovations, are widely believed to promote development. Intellectual property rights have usually been inimical to the interests of indigenous communities, but there are ways in which these laws can serve the interests of these communities.

These two authors indicate that the process of acquiring and defending intellectual property rights poses a daunting challenge to most indigenous communities, for this requires good legal advice, financial resources and access to information, all of which are usually beyond the reach of these communities. They review the current international agreements regarding patents, petty patents, copyrights, trademarks, trade secrets and breeder's rights, and conclude that they are generally inappropriate and inadequate for defending the rights and resources of local communities. Among other reasons, these forms of protection are purely economic, while the interests of indigenous peoples are only partly economic, being linked as well to self-determination. According to Posey and Dutfield, "cultural incompatibilities exist in that traditional knowledge is generally shared and, even when it is not, the holders of restricted knowledge probably do not have the right to commercialize it for personal gain" (Posey and Dutfield, 1996, 92). Nevertheless, they suggest that under certain circumstances, intellectual property rights might be beneficial, but argue that it is more important to develop alternative methods of protection, compensation and self-determination, and therefore advocate a system of "traditional resource rights."[6]

There have been other suggestions to modify the existing system of intellectual property rights, which was initially designed in the era of the industrial revolution to protect factory machinery. From the beginning, it has focused on "novel" products rather than on the discovery of something that naturally occurs, and granted patent rights to individuals firms but not to communities. For example, to protect indigenous knowledge, it would be possible to devise some sort of "passport" containing all the available information about the origin of the genetic material, so as to clearly identify where it comes from at the time of recording it in gene banks or cell libraries, and when filing a patent application. If the patent claimers fail to disclose this information, they could lose the rights granted by any patents emanating from the material.

To overcome the limitations of the patent system, RAFI has suggested the adoption of special forms of intellectual property protection designed specifically for biodiversity. Among them are the inventors' certificates that would not necessary grant monopoly control or financial compensation, but would provide non-monetary awards and non-exclusive licensing arrangements. These certificates could, in addition, vary the period of protection, define conditions of the transfer of technology, and establish compulsory licensing arrangements. Another suggestion is to create the position of a world intellectual property rights ombudsperson, who would investigate complaints from indigenous communities, and from governments and organizations acting in consultation with indigenous communities (RAFI and UNDP, 1995).

Other alternative mechanisms to protect indigenous knowledge are related to benefit-sharing approaches through contracts and agreements signed by enterprises and indigenous communities. For example, the International Co-operative Biodiversity Groups (ICBGs) provide the framework for establishing contractual arrangements. This initiative rests on an integrated conservation and development programme, in which countries and communities that are stewards of genetic resources share the benefits of research results and of any future drug discoveries, thus providing incentives for further conservation efforts (Davis, 1998). A similar scheme was devised and put in practice by the National Biodiversity Institute (INBio) of Costa Rica, which pioneered an integrated approach to biodiversity mapping and prospecting (see Box 3.2.4).

---

[6] For an African perspective on how to deal with intellectual property rights see Mugabe, Barber et al. (1997). For a Latin American view, see Perkoff et al. (2001).

Most of the proposals mentioned above to make the intellectual property rights regime less hostile to indigenous knowledge are still evolving, but provide an idea of what could be done to recognize the importance of indigenous knowledge, and also to protect the rights of indigenous communities when linking their knowledge and technologies with modern production systems.

Technical assistance can play a role in assisting local communities in their intellectual property rights negotiations with private corporations and research institutes from developed countries. Several international agencies and nongovernmental organizations (NGOs) have established programmes along these lines, and have also promoted the exchange of information and the sharing of best practices among indigenous communities. In addition, some of these international institutions have also played an advocacy role in arguing for changes in the existing intellectual property rights regimes.

Creating a favorable policy framework

The third set of measures to create endogenous science and technology capabilities—those geared to the establishment of a policy environment conducive to innovation, and to the selective upgrading and use of indigenous knowledge and technology—covers a wide variety of topics, most of which are not directly related to knowledge and technology issues. Nevertheless, some of these—notably trade, financial, fiscal and credit policies—can hinder efforts to revalue indigenous knowledge, technology and production.

The main characteristics of a policy environment that is conducive to innovation in a modern market economy are well known. Table 3.2.1 listed some of the measures required to create an environment that stimulates firms and other productive agents to engage in innovative behaviour. For example, macroeconomic stability is essential to encouraging forward-looking attitudes by entrepreneurs and managers, and this, in turn, leads to investment in research and development whose results are often seen in the medium and long term. In addition, a well-functioning financial system, competition policies that spur efficiency, sensible regulatory policies that protect the public without placing an excessive burden on business, and a fair and effective tax system are among the requirements for an environment that promotes innovation. However, it is essential to avoid rigidities and ideological excesses in the application of these policies. Instead, it is necessary to adopt a pragmatic stance that takes fully into account local conditions. Some international financial institutions, such as the International Monetary Fund, have not excelled in this task through their dealings with developing countries.

The policy frameworks and conditions that promote the integration of indigenous and modern knowledge and technology into the production system are less well known and accepted. For example, designing and putting in practice the "selective screening and upgrading" and "technology blending" strategies described earlier in this chapter requires the preservation of reasonably efficient indigenous technologies and productive activities, where efficiency is understood in a broad sense, and not just in technical and economic terms, and the interactions with a local setting are fully taken into consideration. Unless this is the case, indigenous knowledge and technologies

BOX3.2.4: The National Biodiversity Institute of Costa Rica

Costa Rica's National Biodiversity Institute (INBio) was set up in 1989 as a public-interest, nonprofit civil association, and is an example of what can be done to acquire knowledge of, conserve and utilize biodiversity in a rational and sustainable manner. It is financed primarily through contracts for the sale of services, and from grants made by foundations and international organizations. Its main activities are:

Biodiversity inventory. INBio is in charge of the national biodiversity inventory, compiled on the basis of material and information gathered by a group of men and women living in communities close to the national parks. They are known as "para-taxonomists" and receive intensive practical training in the fundamentals of biology, ecology and taxonomy; specimen collection and preservation techniques; data management and information processing; and administration and management of technical equipment. The para-taxonomists gather specimens and process them in 23 stations set up all over the country, and the information is subsequently sent to INBio headquarters.

Search and promotion of sustainable uses of biodiversity. This takes place through "biodiversity prospecting," which consists of the systematic search for new sources of chemical compounds, genetic material, proteins, micro-organisms and other products of potential economic value to the pharmaceutical, cosmetic, agro-industrial and biotechnology industries. The process begins with the location, detailed description and collection of specimens; the compounds contained in these specimens are then identified in a preliminary manner; and those with economic potential are then handed over to firms and institutions associated with INBio. If any of these compounds reach the stage of commercial exploitation, the firm or institution pays a royalty to INBio, which has developed research agreements for bio-prospecting with academic centres such as the University of Costa Rica, Strathclyde University and Cornell University, and with private companies like Bristol Myers Squibb, Merck and Co., Givaudan Roure and Diversa. These generate over US $1 million per year to support INBio's activities, as well as other conservation initiatives.

Generation and dissemination of knowledge and information. INBio publishes information about biodiversity; has developed several multimedia products; maintains and continuously updates a large web site with more than 10,000 pages of free information; conducts workshops and training programmes on biodiversity; develops educational materials for schools; and also provides consultancy and advisory services. In 2000, the group inaugurated INBiopark, a large educational facility with three to four types of ecosystems and installations specially designed to house permanent and temporary exhibits on biodiversity in Costa Rica and the rest of the world.

Source: Agenda: PERU (2001, Box 5.4).

are likely to erode and disappear. However, this requires a policy framework that allows for, and even encourages, the coexistence of modern and indigenous technologies with different productivity levels. At the very least, such policies—which may include government subsidies, free extension services, access to credit, and temporary protection for local farming, crafts and small-scale industries—should be in effect during a transition period to allow the selective technology screening and upgrading and technology blending strategies to work. However, this runs against the dominant version of common sense in macroeconomic policy, which propounds a level playing field of uniform policies for all economic activities and firms, regardless of their size or ownership (a better description might be a level playing minefield stacked against traditional and indigenous production!).

Moreover, many policy reforms advocated by international financial institutions and academic experts from developed nations (and adopted by many developing countries during the heyday of structural adjustment programmes) work against the possibility of preserving and integrating indigenous and modern knowledge and technology in the production system. For example, an accelerated process of trade liberalization and tariff reductions, implemented without temporary measures to assist local producers, may wipe them out with a flood of cheap imports; the privatization of public financial institutions and financial liberalization measures may reduce the availability of credit to peasant farmers and small traditional firms; and fiscal reform measures can lead to the elimination of price support schemes for farmers, limit access to affordable agricultural inputs and do away with free public extension services. While care should be taken to avoid maintaining temporary support measures beyond their usefulness (as was the case with the high tariffs associated with import substitution in Latin America), without a policy framework geared to what Sachs (1980, 1987) has called the active "management of technological pluralism"—which would facilitate the coexistence of technologies with different productivity levels—it will be very difficult to incorporate modern and indigenous knowledge and technology in the production systems of developing countries.

Technical assistance can play a useful role in helping to establish appropriate policy frameworks, primarily by distilling and transmitting best practices gleaned from the experiences of developing countries, while taking care to reinterpret them anew in each different case. The concern about ignoring the diversity of specific situations, and of basing policy prescriptions on the prevailing conventional wisdom, was clearly articulated by Jacques Lesourne more than a decade ago in his concluding remarks at a symposium to celebrate the twenty-fifth anniversary of the OECD Development Centre:

> We...have to be wary of the latest fads in the development field. They are frequently transformed into simplistic and extremist ideologies which often cruelly mark the life of nations. The current welcome emphasis on markets is no reason for disregarding their shortcomings, and highlighting the weakness of the State as a producer must not lead us to overlook the contributions government policies have made to development in certain countries. Conversely, the failure of many attempts to foist doctrinaire socialism irrespective of realities on societies with their own long-standing structures must be acknowledged. There is not just one possible development model, although this does not mean that all models can work (Lesourne, 1989, 298).

This warning applies with particular force to the variation of technical assistance that goes under the name of "policy advice" from international financial institutions and academic advisers from developed countries. In the former case, this advice is usually buttressed with conditions for developing country access to the resources at the disposal of these institutions, and therefore carries significant weight. As the policy frameworks to facilitate the integration of modern and indigenous knowledge and technology in production systems do not register on the screens of international financial institutions, it will take much research, exchange of experiences and persuasion to transform technical assistance, and policy advice in particular, into positive forces for the revaluing of indigenous knowledge, technology and production.

Concluding Remarks

Taking into account the knowledge explosion that has taken place during the last five decades, the creation of an endogenous science and technology base must figure prominently in the design of development strategies and policies as we move into the 21st century. Most developing countries rely to a significant extent on traditional knowledge, technology and production activities, which have evolved over a long time through trial and error, in response to local conditions, and which cater to the needs of the poorer segments of their populations. In consequence, development strategies must open spaces and create opportunities for the integration of modern and indigenous knowledge and technology into production systems. Such integration should lead to improvements in the efficiency of traditional practices, but at the same time maintain the characteristics that render them useful and attractive to the poor and to indigenous people.

This requires efforts to understand the logic and functioning of indigenous production systems, and also to identify, select and upgrade traditional knowledge and technologies. Although several possible routes are available to do this, much more research and analysis are needed before a well-established body of knowledge emerges on how to integrate local (traditional, indigenous) and global (modern) knowledge, technology and production. These should be complemented with efforts to learn from the experience of other developing countries that have explored ways of preserving and revitalizing indigenous knowledge and technology.

The current set of technical assistance concepts, practices and institutions emerged, in large measure, at a time when the prevalent approaches to development were based on productivity increases and economic growth, and were embedded in the broader paradigm of modernization. These approaches were based on the transmission of supposedly superior knowledge from developed to developing countries, and paid little attention to traditional and indigenous knowledge and technology. The latter are now being revalued, as approaches to development have evolved over time and now focus on human capabilities and freedoms, as well as on equity considerations.

As the contributions to this volume highlight, the criticisms of development cooperation and of technical assistance leveled during the last two decades are forcing a reappraisal. At present, there appears to be little room for applying conventional technical assistance schemes to promote the integration of traditional and modern knowledge and technology into the production systems of developing countries. Perhaps such reappraisals, many of which are focusing on local capacity-building and capacity development, may lead to new conceptions and practices in international cooperation. As yet, there are very few institutions that have ventured forth to face this complex and potentially rewarding challenge. The most notable and successful of these has been the International Development Research Centre (IDRC) of Canada, which for over three decades has supported the development of local science and technology capabilities in developing countries, and which has sponsored many projects that revitalized traditional technologies.[7] Building an endogenous science and

---

[7] See the IDRC web site at www.idrc.ca.

technology base and revaluing traditional knowledge and technology will require many more institutions like IDRC.

References

Agenda: PERU. 2001. *Development Strategies for the 21st Century: The Case of Peru.* Lima: Peru Report.

Albu, Michael. 1997. "Technological Learning and Innovation in Industrial Clusters in the South." *Electronic Working Papers Series, 7* (September). Brighton: Science Policy Research Unit, University of Sussex.

Arndt, H. W. 1987. *Economic Development: The History of an Idea.* Chicago: University of Chicago Press.

Bezanson, Keith, and Francisco Sagasti. 2000. "Development." A contribution to the Encarta CD-ROM Encyclopedia.

Bhalla, Ajit. 1994. "Technology, Choice and Development." In *The Uncertain Quest: Science, Technology and Development,* edited by Jean Jacques, Francisco Sagasti and Celine Sachs-Jeantet. Tokyo: United Nations University Press.

Casabonne, Ursula, and Francisco Sagasti. 2000. *Policies for Building Science and Technology Capabilities in Developing Countries.* A working paper.

Center for International Development. 2001. *Global Governance of Technology: Meeting the Needs of Developing Countries.* A synthesis report. Cambridge: Harvard University.

CEPAL. 1990. *Transformación Productiva con Equidad.* Santiago.

Chenery, Hollis, M. S. Ahluwalia and C. G. Bell et al. 1974. *Redistribution with Growth.* Oxford: Oxford University Press.

The Department of Arts, Culture, Science and Technology of the Government of South Africa (DACST). 2000. "Indigenous Knowledge Systems: Study Tour to India." (www.dacst.gov.za/science_technology/iks/index.htm.)

Davis, Michael. 1998. *Biological Diversity and Indigenous Knowledge.* Research Paper No. 17. Parliament of Australia.

Dodgson, Mark, David Gann and Amon Salter. 2001. "The Intensification of Innovation." *Electronic Working Papers Series, 65* (April). Brighton: Science Policy Research Unit, University of Sussex.

Erber, Fabio. 1999. "Ajuste estructural y política científica y tecnológica." In *Proceedings of the Regional Workshop on Technological Innovation for Economic Development,* Second Meeting of the Science and Technology Inter-American Commission. Acapulco, October 30.

Etzkowitz, Henry and Loett Leydesdorff. 2000. "The Dynamics of Innovation: From National Systems and 'Mode 2' to the Triple Helix of University-Industry-Government Relations." *Research Policy,* 29, 109-23.

Ezaza, W. P. 1989. "The Main Environmental Issues and Options for the Sustainable Development of Agriculture Associated with the Use of Mineral Fertilizer and Agro-Chemicals." *Journal of Eastern African Research and Development,* 19, 73-82.

Gupta, A. 1990. "Documenting Farmers' Innovations or How Do People Survive Through Innovations in Risky Regions." Ahmedabad: Indian Institute of Management.

Haq, Mahbub ul. 1976. *The Poverty Curtain: Choices for the Third World.* New York: Columbia University Press.

Haugerud, A., and M. Collinson. 1991. "Plants, Genes and People: Improving the Relevance of Plant Breeding." *IIED Gatekeeper Series,* 30. London: International Institute of Environment and Development.

Herrera, Amílcar. 1975. *Modern and Traditional Technologies: An Approach to the Generation of Technologies Appropriate for Rural Areas.* Brighton: Science Policy Research Unit, University of Sussex.

Holt, P. 1997. "Like Welfare, Foreign Aid Shouldn't Go on Endlessly." *The Christian Science Monitor,* 7 June.

International Labour Office (ILO). 1976. *Employment, Growth and Basic Needs: A One World Problem.* Geneva.

International Development Research Centre (IDRC) of Canada. 2002. Institutional web site. (www.idrc.ca.)

Jamieson, Andrew. 1994. "Western Science in Perspective and the Search for Alternatives." In *The Uncertain Quest: Science, Technology and Development,* edited by J. J. Salomon, F. Sagasti and Celine Sachs-Jeantet. Tokyo: United Nations University Press.

Jenkins, R. 1997. "Special Relationships." *Foreign Affairs,* 76(3) [special section on the Marshall Plan].

Karanja, Nancy, J. Freire, M. Gueye and E. DaSilva. 2000. "MIRCEN Networking: Capacity-Building and BNF Transfer in Africa and Latin America." *AgBiotechNet,* 2 (March).

Koshla, Ashok. 1996. *Sustainable Livelihoods: The Central Issue of Human Security and Sustainable Development.* New Delhi: Development Alternatives.

Lesourne, Jacques. 1989. "Development at a Major Turning Point in Time." In *One World or Several?,* edited by Louis Emmerij. Paris: Organisation for Economic Co-operation and Development.

Lundvall, B. A. 1992. *National Systems of Innovation.* London: Pinter Publishers.

Morgan, Peter. 2001. A draft background paper on technical assistance. (www.undp-forum.capacity.org/forum/docs/20011029130509.doc.)

Management of Social Transformations Programme (MOST) and Centre for International Research and Advisory Networks (CIRAN). 1999. Best practices on indigenous knowledge. (www.unesco.org/most/bpikreg.htm.)

Mugabe, John, Charles Victor Barber, Gudrun Henne, Lyle Glowka and Antonio la Viña. 1997. *Access to Genetic Resources: Strategies for Sharing Benefits.* Nairobi: African Center for Technology Studies Press.

Nelson, Richard, ed. 1993. *National Innovation Systems: A Comparative Analysis.* New York: Routledge.

Organisation for Economic Co-operation and Development (OECD). 2000. *A New Economy? The Changing Role of Innovation and Information Technology in Growth.* Paris.

Perkoff, Bass, and Susan and Manuel Ruiz Muller. 2001. *Protegiendo la biodiversidad.* Montevideo: Priguazú Ediciones, Centro International de Investigaciones para el Desarrollo de Canadá.

Posey, Darrell A., and Grahan Dutfield. 1996. *Beyond Intellectual Property: Towards Traditional Resource Rights for Indigenous Peoples and Local Communities.* Ottawa: International Development Research Centre (IDRC).

Rural Advancement Foundation International (RAFI) and the United Nations Development Programme (UNDP). 1995. "Conserving Indigenous Knowledge: Integrating Two Systems of Innovation." Civil Society Organizations and Participation Programme. (www.undp.org/csopp/CSO/NewFiles/dociknowledge.html.)

Rajasekaran, B. 1993. "A Framework for Incorporating Indigenous Knowledge Systems into Agricultural Research, Extension, and NGOs for Sustainable Development." *Studies in Technology and Social Change* (Iowa State University), 21.

Rath, Amitav, and Sherry Lealess. 2000. "The Forum on South-South Cooperation in Science and Technology: An Overview Document." Report of a UNDP-sponsored conference in Seoul, 14-17 February. Ottawa: Policy Research International Inc.

Rostow, Eugene. 1997. "Lessons of the Plan." *Foreign Affairs,* 76(3) [special section on the Marshall Plan].

Sábato, Jorge, and Natalio Botana. 1968, "La ciencia y la tecnología en el desarrollo futuro de América Latina." *Revista de la Integración,* 3 November.

Sachs, Ignacy. 1980. *Strategies de l'écodeveloppement.* Paris: Economie et Humanisme et Editions Ouvriéres.

———. 1987. *Development and Planning.* Cambridge: Cambridge University Press.

Sagasti, Francisco. 1976. *Science and Technology for Development: Final Report of the STPI Project.* Ottawa: International Development Research Centre.

———. 1979. "Towards Endogenous Science and Technology for Another Development." *Development Dialogue,* 1, 13-23.

———. 1980. "The Two Civilizations and the Process of Development." *Prospects,* 10(2).

———. 1982. *La política científica en América Latina: un estudio del enfoque de sistemas.* Serie Jornadas. México DF: El Colegio de México.

———.1999. *The Future of Development Cooperation: Radical Break or Gradual Evolution?* Seventh annual W. D. Hopper Lecture at the University of Guelph.

Sagasti, Francisco, and Gonzalo Alcalde. 1999. *Development Cooperation in a Fractured Global Order: An Arduous Transition.* Ottawa: International Development Research Centre of Canada.

Salas, María Angelica. 1996. *Papas y cultura: acerca de la interacción de sistemas de conocimiento en los Andes del Perú.* Nijmegen: Derde Wereld Centrum.

Salomon, Jean Jacques, Francisco Sagasti and Celine Sachs-Jeantet, eds. 1994. *The Uncertain Quest: Science, Technology and Development.* Tokyo: United Nations University Press.

Sen, Amartya. 1981. *Poverty and Famines: An Essay on Entitlements and Deprivation.* Oxford: Oxford University Press.

———. 1984. *Resources, Values and Development.* Oxford: Basil Blackwell.

———. 1989. "Development as Capability Expansion." *Journal of Development Planning,* 19, 41-58.

Van de Ven, A. H., D. Polley, R. Garud and S. Venkataraman. 1999. *The Innovation Journey.* Oxford: Oxford University Press.

Vessuri, Hebe. 1994. "The Institutionalization Process." In *The Uncertain Quest: Science, Technology and Development,* edited by J. J. Salomon, F. Sagasti and C. Sachs-Jeantet. Tokyo: United Nations University Press.

Warren, Michael. 1992. "Indigenous Knowledge, Biodiversity Conservation and Development." Keynote address at the International Conference on Conservation of Biodiversity in Africa: Local Initiatives and Institutional Roles. Nairobi, 30 August-3 September.

World Bank. 1990. *Poverty: World Development Report 1990.* Washington, D.C.

3.3 TECHNICAL COOPERATION AND KNOWLEDGE NETWORKS

STEPHEN DENNING

TC looks like a Toyota Land Cruiser with a big agency sticker on the doors to announce who funded the vehicle;...TC looks like a big sign on a compound. Inside a place to park the cars, a generator to give light, and drive the air conditioners and refrigerators...And a room with computers and copying machines;...TC looks like people coming to the village to ask questions...Sometimes very polite and correct...Usually very intrusive and arrogant...When they go it takes us a long time to get back to normal....[1]

In June 1995, a health worker in Kasama, Zambia, logged on to the web site of the Centers for Disease Control in Atlanta, Georgia, and got the answer to a question on how to treat malaria

> *(Denning, 2000)*

Introduction

Technical cooperation is large in size, at US $14.3 billion a year, but small in impact. It produces notoriously disappointing progress towards its ostensible objective of sharing knowledge and building capacity, but has also proved itself largely immune to reform. This chapter examines the role of technical cooperation from the perspective of the knowledge revolution now underway in the developed countries, with particular attention to the contribution that knowledge-sharing networks might play in development assistance.

The chapter suggests that there are lessons from the global experience of sharing knowledge that help explain the disappointing cost-benefit performance of technical cooperation and indicate promising potential avenues for its reform. It identifies 12 lessons related to the nature of knowledge: (1) the centrality of sharing knowledge, (2) the need for voluntary knowledge-sharing, (3) the importance of local knowledge, (4) the importance of know-who, (5) the need for time to learn, (6) the need for autonomy, (7) the importance of tacit knowledge, (8) the challenge of unlearning, (9) the tacit knowledge of groups, (10) the impossibility of transferring knowledge, (11) the non-linear evolution of knowledge, and (12) the difficulty of sharing knowledge. It also

---

[1] Email from a United Nations Development Programme (UNDP) dialogue on technical cooperation, a synthesis of visits to rural communities in Africa over a period of several decades. It is part of a forthcoming book by Kirimi Kaberia, President and CEO of ATCnet, and Peter Burgess (www.atcnet.org; profitinafrica@aol.com).

reviews six lessons from knowledge-sharing programmes: (1) the limits of formal train-ing, (2) the limits of organizational engineering, (3) the limits of knowledge collections, (4) the need for indirect, organic approaches, (5) the promise of knowl-edge networks, and (6) the potential of open-source development.

Against this background, this chapter concludes that knowledge-sharing net-works are necessary—but not sufficient—to make a major improvement in the performance of technical cooperation.

The Global Knowledge Environment of the 1990s

Over the last ten years, the world has learned a great deal about what's involved in the sharing of knowledge between individuals and organizations and countries. The mod-est experimentation and evolution of technical cooperation in the development field itself is overshadowed by the scale of innovation in organizations more generally:

- The 1990s opened with the "learning organization" becoming a principal preoccupation in business and business schools.

- Technology, including the emergence of the World Wide Web, the spread of cheaper and more powerful computers, and the widespread access to cost-free email, has facilitated a burst of huge new communications possibilities around the globe.

- The overall pace of technological innovation has accelerated markedly, and concentrated geographical zones of new productive activity have emerged both in the North (e.g., Silicon Valley in the United States) and in the South (e.g., Bangalore in India).

- Knowledge management (a.k.a. knowledge-sharing) has become a ubiqui-tous managerial preoccupation in public and private sector organizations throughout the world. Some development organizations have come to be perceived as leaders in the field.

- The role of groups, networks and knowledge-sharing communities as a key factor in the sharing of knowledge and innovation has become very widely recognized. Even economists discovered the phenomenon and found a way to talk about it with the label of "social capital."

- Knowledge is increasingly perceived as the principal driver of economic growth and development in both the North and the South. This was reflected in the unan-imous UN Economic and Social Council (ECOSOC) resolutions of July 2000.

- The gap between the "haves" and "have-nots" is now perceived to exist not just in financial and physical resources but also in information and knowl-edge, with the gap usually seen to be widening and with serious consequences for the prospects of development.

- Some argue that the resultant changes are remaking the world economy to an extent unprecedented since the invention of the printing press, some 500 years ago, and will have huge and unpredictable consequences for every aspect of economic and social activity over the coming years.

The Question for Technical Cooperation

Given the scale of the changes under way, it is natural to ask: What is the relevance of these developments for the sharing of knowledge in development? In particular, what change should take place in technical cooperation?

- One prosaic answer is: "hardly any." In this view, flows of financial resources accompanied by conditionality and traditional technical cooperation are a necessary adjunct of international development assistance and should essentially continue as they are now, with some streamlining and refocusing at the margin, along with continued efforts to instill more of a sense of ownership in those being assisted.[2]

- A more expansive answer—at the opposite end of the spectrum—is to say that the emergence of networks makes technical cooperation essentially redundant. In this view, technical cooperation is based on an antiquated and mistaken understanding of the nature of knowledge—that it is located in the North and needs to be transferred by foreign experts to individuals in the South.

- There are other viewpoints in-between. Some argue, for instance, that knowledge networks can supplement, but should not replace, technical cooperation from the North, which remains an essential part of the development assistance toolkit.

- Still others argue that technical cooperation should change dramatically, but that, given the current political constraints, it is unrealistic to expect donor agencies to allow such change, and therefore the South should learn to make the best of a bad thing while continuing to urge reform on the recalcitrant North.

These divergent viewpoints suggest the need to review what technical cooperation might learn from broader developments in sharing knowledge. This could help determine whether technical cooperation has a future, and if so, what it should be.

Traditional Technical Cooperation and Its Results

The Nature of Technical Cooperation

Definitions of technical cooperation vary somewhat. A typical donor-driven formulation is:

> Technical cooperation encompasses the whole range of assistance activities designed to

---

[2] This viewpoint is implicit, and to a certain extent explicit, in the official papers now showing on the International Monetary Fund (IMF) web site in the discussion of the reform of IMF conditionality. See IMF (2001).

improve the level of skills, knowledge, technical know-how and productive aptitudes of the population in a developing country (OECD/DAC, 1991).

A recipient-driven description of technical cooperation might be closer both in tone and content to the quote that opens this chapter. Both formulations reflect different perspectives on the same reality. The underlying assumption of the donor approach to technical cooperation is a lack of knowledge on the part of the recipient, for which the remedy is a variety of methods, including the financing of experts for short or long periods, workshops, conferences, twinning, study tours, training, and, more recently, e-learning and web dialogues.

Technical cooperation is, to many observers, surprisingly large. Total technical cooperation grants amounted to more than US $14 billion in 1999, comprising about a fourth of total official development assistance. Donors generally perceive technical cooperation as "a key instrument for improving policies and project design, enhancing skills and strengthening implementation capacity, and for institutional development in general" (World Bank, 1996). The intensity of the discussion around technical cooperation stems from anxiety about the results that come from approaching the challenge in the traditional manner. Formal reviews suggest that perhaps only a third of technical cooperation projects are successful (ibid.). Anecdotal observation confirms that failure is consistent and widespread. The disappointment with the results of technical cooperation has led to concerns on both the donor and recipient sides.

Twelve Lessons from the Global Experience in Sharing Knowledge

The discouraging picture of technical cooperation as currently practiced prompts a look at the institutional scene beyond development. In the last ten years, there has been a revolution in the way organizations around the world are approaching learning and sharing knowledge. Although the lessons from the massive amount of activity under way are still being digested, and much remains to be learned, some themes have emerged that help explain the disappointing cost-benefit performance of technical cooperation and also indicate promising potential avenues for its reform.

1. The Centrality of Sharing Knowledge

In the new knowledge economy, knowledge-sharing is increasingly seen as the sine qua non for survival. The corporate world has realized that traditional hierarchical organizations cannot cope with fast-changing client demands unless they are able to share knowledge among employees, partners and clients. Innovations and the creation of new e-business lines depend on communal rather than individual knowledge. The community's knowledge is always larger than the individual's. Finding out what is known by someone else and adding one's own knowledge to that is faster and more efficient than an individual inventing a solution from scratch. This requires that organizations develop a knowledge-sharing culture and processes. In business, knowledge-sharing is now perceived not merely as an alternative strategic option but as a key to organizational survival.

Implications for technical cooperation: The centrality of knowledge has already spread to the development world, as reflected in the unanimous ECOSOC resolutions of July 2000. Information and knowledge are now perceived as principal drivers of economic growth and development in both the North and the South. If taken seriously, this would turn technical cooperation, which has been an adjunct of and support to financial assistance, into the central preoccupation of development. The enhanced priority of knowledge makes the poor results of technical cooperation even more disquieting. To date, only a few agencies have made sharing knowledge a strategic objective.

Even more important, organizations in the developing countries need to start seeing themselves, and being seen by donors, as knowledge organizations.

> The same logic that drives the international community to manage its knowledge applies with equal force to developing countries. They must establish their own knowledge bases, authenticate them from their own experience, interpret what is meaningful from their own perspectives, and create a future that meets their needs. As international institutions learn how to share knowledge more effectively, they can and should help developing countries to understand what is at stake in managing knowledge to nurture similar capacities. This will be a large-scale and long-term undertaking (World Bank, 1999, 143).

2. Knowledge Sharing Is Voluntary

It has long been recognized in teaching that you can't *make* someone learn. Schools and universities have always known that the learner has to want to learn before any significant learning takes place, and motivating students has always been a preoccupation. As organizations have tried to get their staffs to share their knowledge, they have found that the same principle applies to the knower as to the learner. Organizations have also discovered that *knowledge can't be conscripted.*[3] Knowledge can only be volunteered by the knower if the knower so chooses. The knower cannot be forced to reveal what he or she knows. Organizations have found that they could ask people to say what they know and they could force people to fill in forms, but this didn't mean that people actually revealed their knowledge. It was found that people only reveal what they know to people they trust will use it well.

Implications for technical cooperation: Technical cooperation reflects the same experience as the corporate world in that knowledge does not flow quickly and smoothly from one person to another, as if with the flick of a switch. Lack of demand for knowledge is a pervasive problem in technical cooperation projects, although this is in part the result of the interventions of gatekeepers who effectively prevent local demand for knowledge from expressing itself.

> **EXAMPLE #1: THE MINING REVENUES PROJECT:** A very poor country is currently implementing a technical assistance project to develop institutional capacity to deploy large revenues coming from a mine. The agency funding the project is headed by a former high-level official who is well connected but lacks drive. The agency sends regular supervision missions of experienced staff. When a supervision mission is present, the agency takes action to implement measures and sign decrees insisted on by the mission. When the mission leaves, the agency tends to lapse back into inaction until the next mission. Construction of the mine is on schedule. The capacity-building project is only six months behind schedule and

---

[3] I am grateful to Dave Snowden, the Director of IBM's Institute for Knowledge Management, who formulates the idea in this way.

implementation is rated as satisfactory. Although it is not obvious that any indigenous capacity to manage the expected mineral revenues is likely to be significantly enhanced by the project, all parties are reconciled to the arrangement. The mining company is happy that construction of the mine is proceeding on schedule. The country is happy that large revenues are imminent. The officials of the recipient country are happy that they have been able to satisfy the donors that a planning process is being put in place without any great disruption of business as usual in the country. The donor management is happy that the project is rated satisfactory. The agency staff are happy that they are well paid and that they continue to work on a large and interesting project. All players in the game are thus reconciled to what is happening. It is principally the non-players who might be unhappy with the situation—those who are concerned about the risk of the imminent mineral revenues not reaching the population of this desperately poor and undemocratic country whose president is a tribal chief supported by the military.

EXAMPLE #2: THE PRIVATIZATION PROGRAMME: A middle-income country is currently implementing a technical assistance project to enhance its capacity to carry out privatization. The implementation team comprises five staff resident in the country's capital for a period of around three years. Little privatization is actually occurring—or likely to occur—because the country assigns low political priority to privatizing its public enterprises. The project, however, has priority for the donor, who assigns top importance to using the private sector to promote economic development. The project is supervised by donor staff stationed in the country. The project is rated by the donor as "needing improvement," but no drastic action is strenuously insisted on or realistically expected. The project is therefore in a state of low-level equilibrium that none of the parties is inclined to disturb. The recipient country is content to satisfy the donor with this project that does not disrupt the political status quo. The donor is happy that a substantial portion of its assistance is devoted to one of its high priority objectives. The foreign experts resident in the country spend their time designing processes and reviewing privatization proposals. They are content to have well-paid assignments in an exotic country with moderately interesting work and with reasonable prospects of obtaining attractive assignments after this one. All players in the game are thus reconciled to what is happening. It is the opportunity cost of what else might be done with the money that causes concern.

EXAMPLE #3: GHANA TECHNICAL ASSISTANCE PROJECT: In Ghana, a free-standing technical assistance project—the Structural Adjustment Institutional Support Project approved in 1987—gave managers considerable flexibility to adapt to the country's changing conditions. This flexibility proved to be a weakness. Neither the Ghanaian task manager nor the World Bank supervision teams could withstand the pressure they faced to divert funds from high-priority uses such as training to low-priority uses such as vehicles and trips abroad for people only peripherally involved in furthering project goals. In any event, a project that was intended to spend less than 30 percent of its funds on equipment spent over 70 percent on such purchases (World Bank, 1996).

3. The Importance of Local Knowledge

Paradoxically, it is the very capability to ship advice around the world that has drawn attention to the importance of the context in which the advice arises. What appears to be a reliable finding in one context can turn out to be totally misleading and counterproductive in another. If one scans for knowledge globally, one also needs, before using it, to pay very close attention to the local context of the origin of the knowledge. The contrast between information and knowledge is striking. Although everyone who visits the World Wide Web is familiar with the sensation of swimming, or even drowning, in an ocean of data and information, there is increasing difficulty in finding reliable knowledge in areas where one really needs to know something. This is in part related to the dramatic pace of change that makes earlier knowledge obsolete. One well-known expert argues that most of what we think we now know is just plain wrong (Brown).

Implications for technical cooperation: Development assistance and technical cooperation tend systematically to undervalue local knowledge. There is to a certain extent an awareness that development assistance should attempt to be compatible with the local context, but efforts to fully understand this context are time-consuming. Moreover, deep understanding of the local context may reveal major incompatibilities with the set of assumptions that are governing the design of donor programmes, as in the examples described in No. 2 above.[4] Deep local knowledge can be seen as revealing "lack of ownership" or "resistance" to the assistance objectives being pursued by donors. The donor staff often know what is going on, but are not encouraged to record this knowledge as official facts because it would reveal the disconcerting gap between donor rhetoric and political reality.

4. The Importance of Know-Who

Given the difficulty in acquiring truly reliable knowledge in an increasingly turbulent world, there is a growing awareness that know-who is crucial. If one knows who knows something, and one knows that person, then one has the possibility of meeting or discussing, finding out the meaning, getting more context, eliciting additional information and discovering other avenues that might be explored, as well as getting some hint of what deep smarts might reveal. This possibility of hooking into a network of personal connections of knowledgeable people offers such an immense potential value that one person's network of contacts can become at least as important as what one knows oneself. Moreover, one person's network can be made available to others—or withheld. One's effective knowledge is related not only to what one knows oneself, but also to the number and quality of other experts that one knows and stays in contact with.

Implications for technical cooperation: The provision of individual experts may not add much value unless there are sustainable links to broader networks of expertise. More systematic efforts to nurture and link networks of expertise, particularly between practitioners in the South, are called for.

5. Taking the Time to Learn

The essence of usable knowledge is that people can internalize and integrate it into their conceptual frameworks and their way of doing work. People know something when they have found a way to integrate it into their thinking and behaviour. That often happens in the process of discussion. In fact, a great deal of learning happens outside the workplace. Inside the workplace, people get information. Outside the workplace, people start to construct their own understanding of what it means. Most of what people think they know has been learned by talking things through with other people or working together in shared problem-solving. People are constructing knowledge all the time, in conversation. They are personalizing it through telling stories, and in so doing, they are constructing it for themselves. The real expertise of experienced practitioners—sometimes called deep smarts—takes time to acquire, perhaps a

---

4 See also section No. 11 below: The Non-Linear Evolution of Knowledge.

decade or more to develop for slow or difficult skills. Coaching and apprenticeship are appropriate modes. Where time frames are short, all that can be transferred is simple explicit knowledge, such as "administrivia." The deeper tacit skills take much more time and more social context.

Implications for technical cooperation: The effort to shift the focus of technical cooperation towards short-term assignments of experts is understandable, but is likely to limit the acquisition of knowledge from such activities to fairly shallow and low-value knowledge.

6. Having the Autonomy and the Background to Learn from Knowledge

A Harvard University study has shown that in a large organization, teams that have access to wider knowledge do not produce higher quality products as a result of that knowledge *unless* the teams also have the *time* to digest the knowledge and the *autonomy* to make decisions on the basis of it, and the *combination of local and cosmopolitan knowledge* to make good use of it (Haas). Teams that have *no* access to knowledge in fact do *better* than teams that have access to knowledge but lack the time or autonomy to digest it or make decisions about it. This indicates that knowledge per se is not a plus without the means to apply it.

Implications for technical cooperation: Recipients' lack of time and authority to make decisions are plausible causes of the low productivity of some technical cooperation, since the overall environment of technical cooperation is frequently one in which recipient agencies are underbudgeted and overstretched. Staff are frequently underpaid and may be doing several jobs at the same time. Where development projects are appraised in advance, detailed implementation conditions may be contained in legal agreements that are not easy to change. In such settings, emerging lessons from implementation may not be easy to incorporate into a revised project design, particularly lessons that challenge the underlying assumptions of the original design. For technical cooperation to build genuine capacity, systematic efforts are needed to ensure that, where knowledge is being provided, recipient agencies have the time and autonomy to digest and implement what is being learned.

7. Capacity-Building and the Tacit Aspect of Knowledge[5]

Many large and important organizations have been surprised to find that every interesting piece of knowledge has two dimensions. It has the explicit dimension that can easily be talked about. But that explicit dimension also penetrates down into a dimension that can't be talked about very well, because it is embodied in people, in their practices, in their ways of thinking, in their ways of acting. People are largely unconscious of this tacit component of knowledge. It's not a question of converting the tacit (the know-how type of knowledge) to the explicit in order to pass it on. Thus, learning has to do not only with *learning about* something—e.g., by reading books—but also with how we *learn to act*. How does one acquire the capacity to act as a central banker or a doctor or a health worker or an engineer? How does one enculturate someone into

---

[5] This section and following sections on tacit understanding owe much to discussion with John Seely Brown (see Brown). Credit for ideas on disseminating the importance of tacit knowledge goes to Nonaka and Takeuchi (1995).

a profession? There is a massive amount of tacit practices and sensibilities and lenses that we use to see and make sense of the world and act effectively when we take on one of these roles. Firms have discovered that knowledge is not a commodity that can be captured and bottled and shipped about in boxes, but something that is peculiarly personal to the knower. They have found that knowledge cannot be fully explicated, no matter how long and hard the organization tries.

Implications for technical cooperation: Tacit understanding is central to the capacity-building objectives of technical cooperation, but has been little discussed. Strictly speaking, tacit understanding cannot be "transferred" at all in any simple sense: It must be "acquired afresh" or "rediscovered" by each new person. It is evident that the parachuting of foreign experts into developing countries for short periods to give advice or build capacity is unlikely to lead to the transfer of high-value understanding. The acquisition of tacit know-how is more likely to take place in apprenticeships, study tours, twinning arrangements, secondments, and settings where people can informally exchange views with knowledgeable practitioners on their experiences and issues of common concern. South-South exchanges have particular promise.

8. The Challenge of Unlearning and Societal Transformation

Organizations have also learned that the challenge of sharing knowledge is in many situations not so much one of learning something new, but rather one of getting people to unlearn what they think they already know. When it comes to unlearning, the problem is that people have to shed largely unconscious practices and sensibilities and lenses. But how can they shed something they barely know that they have? People have an interpretive frame, constituted by their own mental lenses. They might suspect that their current mental lenses aren't the lenses that they need for today's world, and they need something new to make sense of the world. Yet they can't even detect the presence of the existing lenses because they are already using them to see the world.

Implications for technical cooperation: The challenge of unlearning is huge in technical cooperation. The challenge of transformation in developing countries involves substantial unlearning of unproductive practices; current practitioners are generally oblivious to their lack of utility. Traditional rational approaches to learning are essentially ineffective when it comes to unlearning. The use of narrative to catalyse transformational thinking in change-resistant environments has shown promising results (Denning, 2000).

9. Transformation and Tacit Knowledge of the Group

What makes sharing knowledge even more difficult is that the tacit components don't live just *within* the individual. They also reside *between* people, in networks and groupings that are connected together in some way so as to create the organization. Shared stories reflect part of the explicit knowledge of networks. But for those stories to lead to action, they must have "tentacles" down into the implicit and the tacit understanding that is distributed across a number of people. In an organization that is working well, people are engaged with others in an interactive and systematic way, sharing tasks in a joint practice that has usually been created over time. The people learn to read each other in an intimate, textured, nuanced way. The ability to read others usually starts to shape the way people talk and leads them to evolve their own vocabularies and their own specialized ways of going about things. These are the tacit practices that lie in the group mind, as opposed to lying just in one individual mind. Understanding how to share knowledge thus involves understanding the social fabric of the organization. Organizations have discovered that they have to focus not only on how *individuals* encode tacit knowledge in their bodies but also on how the *organization itself* also encodes tacit knowledge. As people try to change organizational structures and processes and behaviours, they are actually becoming entangled with the tacit knowledge as well as the explicit knowledge of the organization. The trouble with the tacit knowledge of the organization is that, just as with the individual's tacit knowledge, it is very difficult to get hold of it, reflect on it and work with it.

Implications for technical cooperation: The social fabric and its related tacit practices are aspects of the organization of which the designers of organizational change, whether in business process re-engineering or traditional technical cooperation, are generally unaware. One can re-engineer a firm or provide technical assistance around processes that have been explicitly identified as good or even best practices, without understanding how those are situated in and linked with particular tacit practices and cultures in groups and networks of the ongoing organization. Many of the problems experienced both in business process re-engineering and technical cooperation stem from trying to make changes in organizations in ways that either do not connect with the existing practices of the organization or that sever essential connections between the explicit process knowledge and the tacit understandings that enabled those processes to work. If transfer of individual tacit understanding is difficult to envisage, the transfer of group tacit understanding is even more so: Clearly moving a single individual, however expert, from one organization to another will not by itself achieve this. Transformation of an organization requires that actions proceed from, and be in alignment with, a deep understanding of its social fabric.

10. The Impossibility of "Transferring" Knowledge

There has been a great deal of talk in the last ten years about what is involved in "transferring knowledge." Yet given the strange nature of tacit knowledge, which resides within a knower without the knower being fully aware of its existence, it is now apparent that it is not strictly speaking possible to transfer knowledge at all, except the simplest kinds of explicit knowledge. For each new knower to acquire knowledge, the individual must discover or rediscover the knowledge on his or her own and make it his or her own. It is only when understanding is embodied in the knowers—in their practices and behaviour, and in their ways of thinking and acting—that they can be accurately said to know something at all. For people to know something, they have to make it their own. When the context in which people make knowledge their own is very similar, then the similarity of the knowledge being used in different places may give rise to an impression that the same knowledge has merely been created in one place and rediscovered in another and thus in effect "transferred." But where the context is any way different, then it becomes obvious that the knowledge has not merely been redis-covered or transferred, but rather adapted and reinvented in the different context.

Implications for technical cooperation: The objection to the terminology of "transferring knowledge" is not a mere verbal quibble. Most of the unproductive prac-tices associated with the US $14 billion–per–year enterprise of technical cooperation rest on the incorrect assumption that knowledge can be and needs to be transferred from North to South and then made to "stick" to those to whom it has been so trans-ferred, when it is clear from the tacit nature of significant knowledge that it cannot be transferred at all. Further, the importance of local context means that even if such knowledge could be transferred, it would be inappropriate without considerable adap-tation and innovation in the new context. The presumption in technical cooperation needs to be one of adaptation and innovation, and not that of mere rediscovery or transfer.

11. The Non-Linear Evolution of Knowledge

The difficulties of sharing knowledge and unlearning mean that the advancement of knowledge in a domain or organization does not proceed in a simple linear fashion. Over the last 40 years, Thomas Kuhn's work has helped reveal that even scientists work within a given set of assumptions or models, which Kuhn (ambiguously) called "paradigms" (Kuhn, 1996). While the assumptions or models remain in place, scien-tists do normal science by solving problems within the paradigm and clarifying issues about the overall framework, fleshing it out in more detail. In this work, when anom-alies arise that can't be reconciled within the framework, initially they are set aside. People may go on for years believing one thing despite mounting evidence to the con-trary. The anomalies continue to build and theories emerge that challenge the prevailing paradigm. These theories are at first rejected, but eventually someone comes up with a theory that suddenly seems worth the trouble of throwing out the old paradigm, and then a major shift in thinking occurs. As the new paradigm emerges, people change their minds and wonder why they ever believed otherwise. Kuhn's work drew attention to the continued pervasiveness of these phenomena.

> When a new idea repudiates a past paradigm, the scientific community simultaneously renounces, as a fit subject for professional scrutiny, most of the books and articles in which that paradigm had been embodied.... Practitioners come to see it as progress. No alterna-tive is available to him while he remains in the field (Kuhn, 1996, 167).

Well documented in science, these tendencies are even more significant in the sharing of knowledge within and between organizations.

Implications for technical cooperation: Development assistance is conceived within a set of assumptions not unlike the paradigms that Kuhn identified in the evo-lution of science. Over time, the paradigms change, sometimes abruptly, and sometimes for reasons more related to politics in donor countries than anything relat-ed to evidence or the development process itself. One day population control programmes may be "in," and the next day they may be "out." One day debt relief for a country may be "unthinkable," and the next day it is "essential." One day "private sector development" is the centrepiece, while the next day it may be "poverty reduction."

Donor staff may do their best to maximize recipient ownership of development projects and technical cooperation programmes, but in reality, as in science, there is only
a limited possibility of pursuing a project or programme of technical cooperation that
does not comply with the prevailing donor paradigm. As Kuhn chillingly said about the
necessity of accepting scientific paradigms, "No alternative is available to him while
he remains in the field."

12. The Difficulty of Sharing Knowledge

Over the last five years, many organizations in the private and public sector in developed countries have leapt with enthusiasm into the idea of sharing knowledge, only to
find that implementation was much more difficult than they had envisaged. While
information and data could be shipped around the world instantly, knowledge was
more difficult and tricky.[6] Knowledge itself had many tantalizing and unexpected
characteristics that made its sharing problematic, particularly when direct command-and-
control approaches to management were adopted. One estimate is that only about
half of ongoing knowledge management programmes in the Global 1,000 firms are
being executed successfully.[7] Similar issues emerge when efforts are made to share
knowledge across organizational borders: In corporate mergers and acquisitions,
where two companies with different cultures try to join forces and share knowledge,
the track record is even more dismal than in knowledge management programmes,
with success rates said to be on the order of 20 per cent (Sirower, 1998).

Implications for technical cooperation: As in the corporate sphere, the sharing of
knowledge in technical cooperation is a risky undertaking. What is the extent of the
risk? What in quantitative terms would be realistic to expect? Efforts to establish reasonable quantified expectations of risk in development assistance generally, and in
technical cooperation in particular, have not met with success. Thus, while there is a
great deal of criticism of the donors about the failure rate of technical assistance, particularly in the poorest countries, there are no generally agreed parameters of likely
success. Even though past experience indicates that as few as one-third of technical
cooperation projects actually succeed, the prevailing assumption is that all *future
projects* should in principle succeed. It is the practice to write the risk sections of project appraisals as if to imply that all known risks associated with the project are being
in some way "dealt with." Technical cooperation is one of the principal ways in which
donors deal with risk. Efforts to persuade donors to allow staff to quantify the actual
risk of the project failing have not succeeded, apparently because an explicit and
quantified discussion of real risk associated with proceeding is in conflict with the prevailing donor paradigm, which reflects the theological expectation of universal success.

---

[6] Cf . the statement that begins the World Bank's *World Development Report 1998-1999:* "Knowledge
is like light." In practice, knowledge transfer usually travels at the speed of a donkey, not that of light.
[7] Source: Larry Prusak at the IBM Institute for Knowledge Management.

Six Lessons from the Global Experience of Knowledge-Sharing Programmes

As a result of what has been learned about the nature of knowledge, the actual practice of organizations in learning and sharing knowledge has evolved in quite striking ways, most of which have implications for technical cooperation programmes.

1. The Limits of Formal Training Courses

Formal training courses were an early casualty of the knowledge revolution. It isn't simply that "talk and chalk" programmes are expensive to organize and maintain. More important has been the realization that little learning is taking place in formal training programmes. No matter how the trainers adjust the course, it is, for each individual participant, always too much or too little, too soon or too late. If it is right for one person, it is wrong for someone else. Even where participants enjoy the course, the retention of what is supposedly learned is low. The major benefit from such courses, if any, is often the ability to make connections and establish networks with other practitioners or managers, in line with the insight that most learning occurs in informal settings. The better training institutes and corporate universities have tended to shift towards real-world problem solving for intact teams, so that training becomes an extension of the workplace—simply another place where the work of the organization gets done.[8] Lesser institutes have simply changed their name from training to learning, hoping that no one will notice that little learning is actually taking place.

Implications for technical cooperation: Formal training programmes in technical cooperation should be carefully scrutinized to see whether the potential benefits are warranted by the cost, and whether other cheaper and more effective ways to achieve the intended result are not available. Formal training is likely to make only a limited contribution to capacity-building.

2. The Limits of Organizational Engineering

In the early 1990s, there was a major effort to re-engineer organizations to make them more efficient and effective. Knowledge was treated as an object and the organization regarded as a machine. The appeal of this way of thinking was the sense (or illusion) of control. But the more the organization is treated as a machine, the more living parts of it—the people, the knowledge, the more innovative aspects of it—rebel and refuse to be so treated. Where the machine model is imposed as the solution to every issue, the organization becomes entirely ossified and eventually dies.

Implications for technical cooperation: Like business process re-engineering, the development project is a concept that assumes that it is possible to engineer organizational solutions to social problems. The project's resources and conditionalities may influence the internal behaviour of the recipient in the direction of supporting the project, but may also engender negative feelings, resentment and push-back that can ultimately cause the whole undertaking to fail (see Part 1, Chapter 2). Donors and

---

[8] Where top managers undertook the teaching, such as Jack Welch, the charismatic Chief Executive Officer of General Electric, then the training became in effect on-the-job learning.

recipients need to give more attention to ecological, organic and indirect approaches to development.

3. The Limits of Knowledge Collections

Nonaka's book *The Knowledge Creating Company* (Nonaka and Takeuchi, 1995) encouraged many firms to launch programmes to make knowledge explicit and build computer-based "corporate memories." The challenge was perceived as getting the knowledge out of people's heads and into the corporate memory so that knowledge could become a corporate asset and presumably so that employees could if necessary be made redundant. In this way, the company would no longer be held hostage to its employees and their tacit knowledge. The result of these efforts was that huge knowledge collections were assembled, but they were rarely used by the intended beneficiaries because they didn't fit people's needs. The existence of "best practice systems" perhaps reassured top managements, but the systems were usually ignored by people doing the work because they didn't take into account the social fabric of the organization. Organizations that focus completely on collecting knowledge with little or no effort to foster people connections end up with repositories of dead documents.

Implications for technical cooperation: From the experience of the private sector, major efforts to build large knowledge collections do not appear to be warranted per se unless there is an explicit and strong demand from identified users for the particular resources involved.

4. Need for Indirect or Organic Approaches to Sharing Knowledge

Connecting people who need to know with those who do know has proved to be much more successful in sharing knowledge. Connecting people is important because knowledge is embodied in people, and in the relationships within and between organizations. Information becomes knowledge as it is interpreted and made concrete in the light of the individual's understandings of the particular context. However, organizations that focus entirely on connecting, with little or no attempt at collecting, can be very inefficient. Such organizations will fail to achieve the leverage of knowledge-sharing and may waste time in reinventing wheels. A balance is needed between connecting and collecting. An emphasis on connecting people to share knowledge reflects an *ecological approach to knowledge*. It is impossible to extract knowledge from anything. Instead, one gardens. The gardener seeds, feeds and weeds the garden. Knowledge grows. It emerges out of a fertile field, tended by people interacting with people, groups, and networks and communities. The organization is seen as a living system, which is largely self-organizing.

Implications for technical cooperation: Most donor agencies are currently proceeding in an engineering mindset and would do well to adopt more of an ecological approach to technical cooperation. Connecting people together to share knowledge is one way to move in this direction.

5. The Promise of Knowledge Networks

With the growing recognition that most learning is informal, and that connecting people can help share knowledge, knowledge-sharing has begun to focus on human groupings under various labels—networks, communities of practice, thematic groups, learning networks. Whatever the label, the thrust is to nurture human groupings that have sufficient levels of trust that knowledge-sharing can take place naturally. Thus, networks have emerged as a principal organizing concept in sharing knowledge. Networks are messy but necessary. The approach reflects the organic nature of knowledge. Human passion is an essential element of these groupings; without it, the network loses energy and dies. The physical interaction of participants is usually found to be essential in launching such communities, but once they are launched, technology can extend the reach of a network around the globe. Yet it is also recognized that networks *alone* are ineffective for significant innovation, since networks may be purely social. To be productive, the life of the network has to revolve around knowledge. Increasingly, organizations at the cutting edge of knowledge management realize that *most high-value knowledge is in the heads of their clients,* as well as in those of their own staff.

The perceived value of client knowledge is driving firms to nurture community-like relationships with clients, partners and even competitors in ways that were unthinkable just a few years ago. The efficiency of knowledge-sharing networks, as compared with other methods of sharing knowledge, comes from the fact that when they function well, they provide knowledge "just in time" and "just enough." In formal training or the financing of experts, large expenditures occur whether or not anyone actually wants or needs the knowledge that the arrangement aims at transferring. By contrast, a network comes into operation when an actual member of the network identifies a real-life problem, and the members of the network only contribute if they perceive themselves to have useful expertise in the particular problem. Formal training or technical expertise thus grind forward regardless of their utility, while informal networks self-organize and self-adjust to meet the needs of members.

Implications for technical cooperation: Knowledge-sharing networks represent an obvious avenue for donors to improve the efficiency and enhance the value of technical cooperation. Networks exist within the staff of donor organizations or among practitioners in the developing countries, or combinations of the two. Organizations such as the United Nations Development Programme (UNDP) have been active promoters of knowledge-sharing networks to facilitate the sharing of experiences across internal and external boundaries. Even more interesting is the emergence of South-South communities, also being promoted on a pilot basis. At the same time, *knowledge-sharing networks are not a panacea.* Networks are efficient because they are closely related to an actual demand for knowledge. Where the demand is lacking, the network is inoperative. A knowledge-sharing network would obviously be ineffective to deal with the problems encountered in the three examples described in No. 2 in the previous section. Since there is no effective demand for knowledge in these cases, no knowledge is likely to be shared, even with the presence of a network. The gain, however, comes in terms of efficiency: Many millions of dollars are saved.

6. Demonstration of Network Power: Open-Source Development

In a world where key knowledge lies with clients, the boundaries of an organization start to look increasingly arbitrary and anomalous, and highly decentralized modes of operation are emerging. The most spectacular example of open-source development is Linux, where a large number of individual computer programmers scattered around the world succeeded over a decade in developing a computer operating system on which around 30 per cent of the world's servers now run, in effective competition with Microsoft. Linux was developed without any central organization at all. One reason for its success was the presence of a respected coordinator at the centre, who decided what was to be accepted in the system and what was not. But even more important was the willingness of multiple individuals to collaborate and use their collective cleverness. As the Renaissance writer Alberti said about the architecture of the ancient Greeks when they were confronted with the riches and power of Egypt:

> It was their part to surpass through ingenuity those whose wealth they could not rival (Alberti, 1991).

To the programmers of Linux, Microsoft was the 1990s equivalent of Egypt. They couldn't compete on wealth or power, so instead they used ingenuity. The ingenuity of Linux programming was a labor of love. The commitment to continuous improvement exploited the strength of the network to keep innovating. The existence of the Web now makes this kind of collaboration very widely accessible. Initially, Linux was seen as a phenomenon peculiar to computer hackers. It is now being perceived by some as a model for the way the new economy might undertake a wide range of activities.

Implications for technical cooperation: Open-source development appears to be an immensely promising approach when there are a number of people with expertise and passion around a subject, and when there is a credible coordinator to enable the group to come to closure on issues. Given its huge potential, those interested in this form of development should be actively exploring it.

Some Obvious Implications for Technical Cooperation

It has been evident for some years that technical cooperation could be massively enhanced by building on the lessons of the global experience of knowledge-sharing in organizations, particularly the fostering of informal knowledge-sharing networks.

a. **Fostering South-South knowledge flows:** Developing countries often learn best from each other, since the real experts on development are often those who live the reality of the problems on a day-to-day basis. Programmes that link practitioners in developing countries through real or virtual conferences across national boundaries can greatly accelerate these high-value knowledge flows.

b. **Fostering North-North knowledge flows:** For collaboration and openness to become the modus operandi of development assistance organizations, stronger partnerships among the major players are needed. The World Development Indicators offer a promising model, as do the partnerships emerging in various sectors such as the environment. The international community thus needs to function as an efficient connector and facilitator to promote the creation and dissemination of knowledge to enhance global welfare.

c. **Fostering South-North knowledge flows:** Development assistance needs increasingly to be seen as not simply a process of financing physical facilities, such as schools and cars, but also as a process that is invigorated by people's abundant ideas and inspirations. In this way, a culture can draw on its local know-how, including indigenous knowledge, which is then reinterpreted and developed in light of the most useful approaches from elsewhere. Knowledge systems in the international institutions need to be open and responsive to inflows from whatever source (World Bank, 1998).

While some development agencies have continued to press ahead with knowledge-sharing through networks as a central strategic objective, support of knowledge-sharing and knowledge-sharing networks for the developing countries is still being pursued on a limited and pilot basis. If donors were really concerned about getting recipient countries better access to knowledge, one would have expected them to embrace knowledge-sharing networks with enthusiasm, as an obviously more cost-effective approach than the expenditure involved in sending foreign experts to countries either for short- or long-term assignments. The fact that this hasn't happened on a significant scale tends to confirm that there are in fact other motivations driving donor support of technical cooperation. As Channing Arndt points out:

> Technical cooperation also meets more subtle, but very real, donor needs. Technical cooperation personnel serve as "ears" within local administrations. They provide donors with some reassurance that project money is not being misappropriated. They serve as a contact point that can be approached without the confusion of cultural barriers. They assure that project reporting and disclosure requirements are met…. Proposals to reform TC that fail to account for these deep-seated needs on the part of donors are unlikely to succeed (Arndt, 2000).

Hence, even if knowledge-sharing networks are much more efficient and effective ways of getting organizations access to relevant knowledge in a timely fashion than the sending of foreign personnel to the country, the knowledge-sharing networks will never serve as the "ears" of the donors and cannot meet these real but surreptitious donor needs. Recommendations to replace foreign personnel with knowledge-sharing networks are therefore likely to fall on deaf ears.

References

Alberti, Leon Battista. 1991. *On the Art of Building*. Translated by Neil Leach and Robert Tavernor. Cambridge: Massachusetts Institute of Technology.

Arndt, Channing. 2000. "Technical Cooperation." In *Foreign Aid and Development: Lessons Learnt and Directions for the Future,* edited by Finn Tarp and P. Hertholm. London and New York: Routledge Press.

Brown, John Seely. (www.creatingthe21stcentury.org/JSB3-learning-to-unlearn.html.)

Denning, Stephen. 2000. *The Springboard: How Storytelling Ignites Action in Knowledge-Era Organizations.* Boston: Butterworth Heinemann.

Haas, Martine R. *Acting On What Others Know: Distributed Knowledge And Team Performance.* An unpublished study.

International Monetary Fund (IMF). 2001. IMF Public Information Notice No. 01/92, 4 September. (www.imf.org/external/np/sec/pn/2001/pn0192.htm.)

Kuhn, Thomas. 1996. *The Structure of Scientific Revolutions.* Third edition. Chicago: University of Chicago Press.

Nonaka, Ikujiro, and Hirotaka Takeuchi. 1995. *The Knowledge-Creating Company: How Japanese Companies Create the Dynamics of Innovation.* New York: Oxford University Press.

Organisation for Economic Co-operation and Development/Development Assistance Committee (OECD/DAC). 1991. *Principles for New Orientations in Technical Cooperation.* Paris.

Sirower, Mark. 1998. *The Synergy Trap: How Companies Lose the Acquisition Game.* New York: The Free Press.

World Bank. 1996. *Technical Assistance: Lessons and Practices #7.* World Bank Operations Evaluation Department, 1 May. Washington, DC.

———. 1998. "What is Knowledge Management?" Background paper for *World Development Report 1998-1999: Knowledge for Development.* Washington, DC.

———. 1999. *World Development Report 1998-1999: Knowledge for Development.* Washington DC.

3.4 DEVELOPMENTS IN PRIVATE SECTOR KNOWLEDGE-BASED ENTREPRENEURSHIP IN THE SOUTH

SUNIL CHACKO

Introduction

In recent years, financial investment has started to flow into human capital, owners of intellectual property, and producers of knowledge- and research-based goods and services in the global South. The role of the private sector in developing technological excellence is not marginal by any means. This is a distinct departure from the past, when the main investment in the South, committed by partners of both the South and the North, went to sectors that depleted natural resources and left environmental hazards for people who already carried the heaviest burden of diseases and other social inequities. Today, such factors as technological advances, availability of efficient network media, ethnic diasporas and others have contributed to a positive path. Some countries have yet to capitalize on these benefits. Nevertheless, knowledge- and research-based development has been quietly but steadily transforming the future of the South.

The research enterprise, while often locally specific, is inherently global in today's communication and digital technology era. Whether it is in India, Brazil or in sub-Saharan Africa, technology is one unifying principle drawing on the strength of emerging knowledge-based private sector development in the South. Poverty reduction is linked to job opportunities and technological excellence, overwhelmingly generated in the private sector, particularly in new value-added areas where intellectual production of knowledge raises technological standards and capacity.

Central to this development are new paths that offer greater opportunities and faster progress to better living standards. Even as the United Nations Development Programme (UNDP) has been spearheading the new agenda for capacity-building of the South in the midst of communication technology advances, the network age enables these momentous opportunities to be shaped. Considerable experience in global cooperation in both public and private sectors has already been built over the past decades, and it is this experience and knowledge that creates confidence that new modes of technical cooperation are not just feasible, but essential for international development cooperation in the modern era of the knowledge-based economy. In the following chapter, individual entities are mentioned solely as example to illustrate growing trends.

The Role of the Private Sector in Developing Technological Excellence in the South

The Rise of Knowledge-Based Research and Development

There is little question today about the role of the private sector in catalysing techno-logical advancement and bringing its benefits within people's reach. Many times, the basic sciences are incubated and fostered during the most risky early stages by pub-lic resources at public sector institutions. For instance, the Internet and the Human Genome Project are recent cases in point. Basic research on both projects was initiat-ed with Government-led efforts in the United States. The private sector then went on to demonstrate its capacity to expand the technological advances through the "3Ds": discovery, development and distribution of goods and services to the marketplace, where people's demands interact with commercial opportunities. This basic role of the private sector manifests in the global South as well.

The pharmaceutical industry in the South used to be almost all concentrated on low-risk, low-cost, low-profit-margin generic drug production. Today, with technology and efficient instruments increasingly available in the world, the scenario of concen-trating industrial capacity in low-risk, low-cost and low-return areas has been changing in many countries. An illustrative case is the recent rise of the pharmaceuti-cal and biotechnology sectors in India, which have placed a heavy emphasis on research and development (R&D). Worldwide, high-revenue-generating companies spend enormous resources on R&D. Technology-oriented companies spend even more than what they earn, yet still are constantly funded because investors see the value of technology and the benefits of long-term research activities (see Table 3.4.1). Indian companies are rapidly moving in that direction. Compared to their spending on R&D of less than 1 per cent of revenue a decade ago, the current level of 4 to 6 per cent of rev-enue is a remarkable shift in priorities towards more knowledge-based investment.

India's pharmaceutical industry and public R&D institutions, for instance, togeth-er with the Government's new vision and the global reality of the Trade-Related Aspects of Intellectual Property Rights (TRIPS) in 2005, are reallocating internal resources on R&D for novel product discovery, and diversifying their operations in order to move up the global value chain.

Further, the Government of India now allows, in effect, a tax credit by exempting 125 per cent of R&D spending when companies conduct R&D through subsidiary research foundations, and 150 per cent for biotechnology research and clinical trials. The new environment has given a tremendous boost to the morale of scientists in R&D-oriented pharmaceutical and biotechnology companies, as well as in public sec-tor laboratories that are increasingly building partnerships with the private sector, a development actively encouraged by the Government.[1]

Already, some Indian pharmaceutical and biotechnology R&D companies have identified global opportunities that can build on traditional skills required for generic

[1] As one means to create a resource base for research that would strengthen neglected areas, the Pharmaceutical Research and Development Fund was established by the Government of India with about US $33 million.

TABLE 3.4.1: MOST RECENT ANNUAL R+D SPENDING AS A PERCENTAGE OF REVENUE

COMPANY	R+D IN US $ MILLIONS	REVENUE IN US $ MILLIONS	R&D AS A PERCENTAGE OF REVENUE
Genomics and Research-Oriented Companies in the North			
Celera Genomics	167.8	42.7	393%
Human Genome Sciences	225.5	22.1	1020%
Millennium Pharmaceuticals	268.7	196.3	137%
Vertex Pharmaceuticals	84.9	78.1	109%
Integrated Pharmaceutical and Biotechnology Companies in the North			
Boehringer Ingelheim	871	5,569	16%
GlaxoSmithKline	3,677	26,486	14%
Merck and Co.	2,344	40,363	6%
Pfizer	4,435	29,574	15%
Serono	263	1,240	21%
Indian Pharmaceutical Companies			
Cipla	9.1	241	4%
Dr. Reddy's Laboratories	9.2	223	4%
Ranbaxy	11.3	401	2%
Lupin	8	202	4%

Source: Annual Reports 2000.

drug production, particularly in chemistry, process/reverse engineering and manufacturing (Chacko, 2002). Under the process patent system, combined with other factors, home-grown innovations for the discovery of novel therapeutics did not flourish much in the past. However, current development in the private sector indicates that those skills needed for generic drug production have become the technology foundation for the next level of innovation.

Twenty Indian companies have secured international accreditation from the US Food and Drug Administration (FDA), the UK Medicines Control Agency (MCA) and other regulatory agencies in the North for specific medicines, enabling them to export.[2] Research on drug delivery systems, improved versions of existing drugs with fewer side effects, and derivatives of existing medicines have been identified by the Indian Government and the private sector as high-value areas to pursue and develop during this transition period, without much exposure to attrition or cost risks.

A company in Hyderabad, Dr. Reddy's Laboratories, has a considerable number of patents of which three anti-diabetes molecules are licensed to the global pharmaceutical giants Novo Nordisk of Denmark and Novartis of Switzerland. Dr. Reddy's expects to garner US $60-70 million in revenues if progress through the development pipeline continues. On the biotechnology front, recombinant technology has already been in use for some time in India. Multiple domestic companies now compete for market

---

[2] The UK Government's Trade Partners Programme.

share of the hepatitis B vaccine (along with Korean and Cuban companies, and large multinationals). In the past, recombinant technology was seen as too sophisticated for developing countries to master, and was the exclusive expertise of global technology leaders such as Chiron, Merck and SmithKline Beecham (now GlaxoSmithKline). Another Hyderabad-based company, Shantha Biotech, is a new entrepreneurial biotechnology company, and produced India's first hepatitis B vaccine with much lower costs, addressing the local public health needs by utilizing recombinant DNA protein production technology. Other therapeutic products resulting from biotechnology are in the company's pipeline.

This trend is not only confined to large and growing economies of the South and the North with an acknowledged technological and scientific base. Individual institutions in Africa are also moving towards upgrading their research output for new social and economic value creation. For instance, in Bamako, the US Government's National Institutes of Health (NIH), in collaboration with the University of Mali, has established a malaria research facility for the development of vaccines. In Cinzana, the agricultural research station maintained by the Syngenta (formerly Ciba-Geigy) Foundation and Mali's Institut d'Economie Rurale works on millet and sorghum improvement. Further, the Netherlands' African Studies Centre in Leiden promotes and undertakes social science and humanities research in Africa in cooperation with ten Dutch universities and African colleagues. These and numerous other cases throughout the South illustrate that research-based value generation has been undertaken even amid the intractable problems posed by low GDP per capita.

Value-Added Research and Production of Intellectual Property

The cost associated with pursuit of high-value, knowledge-intensive research is certainly high. Return on investment has to be above the cost of capital, so the issue of fostering the innovation and its research by safeguarding the legal entitlement for further development becomes critical. The clear title for ownership and intellectual property rights (IPRs) is the integral component for the knowledge- and research-based 3Ds noted above. The Indian health science research community, for instance, has been scoring quite good success in this new endeavour, along with researchers in a couple of other countries in the South.

A number of patents for proprietary new drug delivery systems, as well as improved versions and derivatives of existing medicines, have been filed in the United States, India and other countries. Many of them have already been granted patent protection. Indian patent holders in the private sector have successfully negotiated alliances with forthcoming global pharmaceutical giants to co-develop them further. For instance, Ranbaxy of India has licensed its new drug delivery system to Bayer of Germany. The system enables a once-daily dosage of Bayer's now world-famous anti-infective ciprofloxacin; it is now progressing through clinical trials in the United States.

Medicine utilizing traditional knowledge, abundant in the South, is also expanding the potential for value-added research and production of intellectual property to boost technological excellence in the South. After a battery of tests to identify active ingredients and numerous clinical trials to prove efficacy under controlled conditions, a traditional Chinese cure used by a traditional healer was approved by the FDA in September 2000. It is used to treat patients with leukemia whose disease has recurred or who fail to respond to standard chemotherapy. Arsenic trioxide is the active ingredient, and the concoction is today distributed under the brand name Trisenox™ by the US company Cell Therapeutics for use in the most prominent American cancer hospitals, such as Memorial Sloan-Kettering in New York and the Dana-Farber Cancer Institute in Boston (Waxman et al., 2001) The work of this US company and Chinese partners is adding value to the traditional knowledge of Chinese medicine by taking the drug through clinical trials, carrying out the data management and regulatory filings, and securing approvals from regulatory authorities, thereby making it available in the industrialized countries as well the place of its origin.

There are numerous similar cases of discovery of great drugs that originated from biological substances native to the South. However, many doubt whether these commercial successes are bringing the proper share of benefits to indigenous peoples and to the South, where the substances have been tested and used over centuries. Hernando de Soto (2000) calls for the underprivileged to have a formal stake in the economic system by means of acquiring clear legal title to their assets. This, needless to say, helps to lift up the entrepreneurial aspirations among millions of people in the world who live in poverty.

Another great path-breaker who has veered from the conventional thinking of the past in the South is Dr. R. A. Mashelkar.[3] He also forcefully advocates the importance of the knowledge-based ownership of goods and services in the world intellectual property system, for social, cultural, and, particularly, economic development. Dr. Mashelkar spearheaded the Pharmaceutical Research and Development Committee Report (December 1999) in India, which became a blueprint for a new focus on more research-based goods and services in order to move up the global value chain. The report stresses the value of R&D-based pharmaceutical, vaccine and biotechnology capacity development for industry and public sector R&D institutions. In addition, Dr. Mashelkar has a unique programme to foster and protect traditional knowledge and encourage innovation for its further development in India by linking age-old tradition with the modern medical science system. Medicinal property derived from nature is being catalogued—in particular, some 15,000 herbs, about 800 of which are commonly used as ingredients in the 5,000 year old practice of ayurveda and other traditional medical systems. For instance, clinical trials of active principles in Curcuma longa (turmeric, family Zingiberaceae) or curcumin; Boswellia serrata (family Burseraceae); and Capsicum annum have revealed value in treating arthritis (Majeed et al., 1997).

---

[3] Dr. Mashelkar is the Director General of the Council of Scientific and Industrial Research, and the Secretary of the Department of Scientific and Industrial Research of India.

Notable Factors in the Private Sector for Facilitating Technological Excellence

Where Computing and Biological Systems Coalesce

As UNDP's *Human Development Report 2001* points out, the Internet certainly has broken down the communication and geographical barrier for the global South, although challenges still remain. The Internet is helping to energize spirits across the world, forging links to the new technologies and new sources of funding. In the context of health science, digital and network technologies' contributions to such areas as the emerging fields of genomics, bioinformatics and proteomics, as well as clinical trials in both the North and South, have manifested a paradigm shift for the research community.

Figure 3.4.1 illustrates how the World Wide Web underlies each step in the 3Ds. The web has promoted access to online databases on genomic information. Further, online clinical trials software is particularly useful in standardized data collection, reporting and analysis. And this enrichment of clinical research is a critically important component for value-added research, particularly for the South.

Bioinformatics is a promising field, where computing capacity is required to process and manage the immense deluge of biological data generated by digitalgenomics. It involves the use of computers and associated software to gather, organize, store, analyse and integrate biological and genetic information, which can then be applied to new genomics-based rational and even personalized drug discovery and development. The increasing need for bioinformatics capability is directly related to the explosion of genomic information from the Human Genome Project, and from new technology related to combinatorial chemistry, rational drug design, high-throughput screening, microarrays and other advances in the biosciences. Further, both in-house and outside databases need to be integrated to maintain cutting-edge status. In all of this, the collection, warehousing, integration, annotation and analysis of biological information using code, software applications and databases are central. Gene sequences, protein expression, protein structure, protein-protein interactions, assay results and other information on drug development are stored and then need to be retrieved, analysed and cross-checked. Bioinformatics enables the pulling together of all the data for the study of biology as a functioning system. The changed world of new-medicines discovery treats bioinformatics as integral to almost every piece of medical and pharmaceutical research.

The same design skills for databases that store information in large corporations—for instance, on 100,000 employees, including their payroll, health care, other social needs, work-related accomplishments for bonuses, etc.—have to be utilized for medical benefits and potent medicine discoveries. Bioinformatics meets such demand, and it is becoming a crucial tool for building databases for genes, their sequence, functions, the proteins they code for, and the systemic and streaming interactions between them. Well beyond the monitoring capacity of notebooks and pencils and word-processing software, these essential research steps require giant, sophisticated,

FIGURE 3.4.1: NETWORKED 3Ds–DRUG DISCOVERY, DEVELOPMENT AND DISTRIBUTION

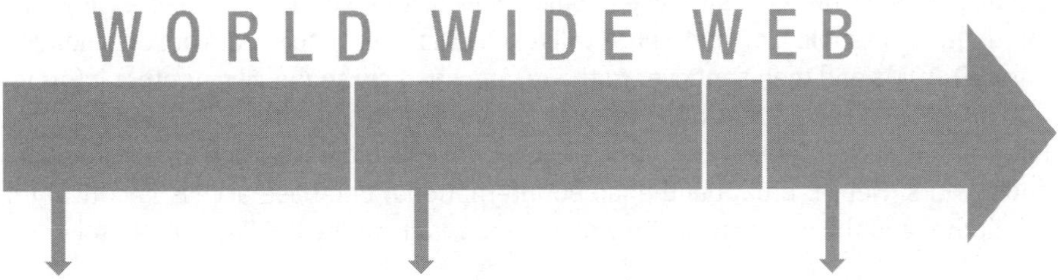

WORLD WIDE WEB

DISCOVERY
Finding the right targets
Expanding from 500 to 5,000:
receptors, enzymes, hormones

• Genomics and bioinformatics
• Proteomics
• Genomic chips
• Combinatorial chemistry
• High-throughput screening
• Toxicology
• Lead identification
• Lead optimization (medicinal
  chemistry)
• The "right" molecule is taken
  forward

INVESTIGATIONAL NEW DRUG
APPLICATION

DEVELOPMENT
Clinical trials
Phase I–Phase III

• Web-based clinical trials
• Essential to prove safety and
  efficacy in humans
• Ticket to entry for those whose
  work was unknown before
• $6 billion outsourced industry

NEW DRUG APPLICATION

DISTRIBUTION
Manufacturing and outreach

• Quality
• Reliability
• Wide reach

Source: Sunil Chacko

scalable databases. Indeed, the largest database programmes, such as Oracle and Microsoft SQL, had to be customized for biological research information—so large are the billions of data points that are being generated. Statistical tests are employed to determine the significance of patterns matching against nucleotide and amino acid sequences.

This also demands a great number of programmers, database designers, developers and administrators, for which a core competence of the South can be effectively deployed. This painstaking, labour-intensive, somewhat cumbersome work is manna for many dedicated programmers from the South. They thrived on the laborious precision needed for fixing the COBOL code during the Y2K days, and are gearing up for this much larger challenge. The ratio of scientists to bioinformatics software professionals is so highly skewed, sometimes 700 to 5, and that presents outsourcing opportunities for the software industry.

Indeed, because of the fast pace of scientific developments and the need to con-stantly access that information, web-enabled research applications are the most logical, and perhaps the only way, to go forward. Millions of new sequences of micro-organisms are stored in databases somewhere in the world. Unless accessing this information is enabled, obsolescence will result. By the time such data are downloaded onto CD-ROMs and then sent over to the researcher, new sequences or other informa-tion may have been added to the original database, thereby already making days-old information out of date. This is also the case for diverse knowledge disciplines and endeavours. Hence, broadband-enabled international database access is critical for the South, and the only way actively to enhance value in the intellectual capital era.

Several companies offer this technological excellence and make use of genomic information through partnerships with academia and public institutions of the North as well as the South. Incyte Genomics, based in California, has academic collaboration programmes and special pricing for access to its databases for public and nonprofit entities. Having access to cutting-edge bioinformatics knowledge databases is in the interest of many scientists in the global North and South. At the same time, it is in the company's interest as well to discover wider application of the data and further vali-date its knowledge-based services. Hence, Incyte found synergy where its interests as a private sector company and those of the larger research community came together (Chacko, 1999). Affymetrix, another California-based company, builds genomic chips for research; it too offers reduced prices for public and nonprofit entities.

In addition to customized solutions from numerous other companies, the public sector also provides data from the Human Genome Project and other ongoing research on public sites, including those of NIH and the Wellcome Trust. Researchers have a choice, and that is why it is essential, in achieving targeted access, to both study terms and special arrangements on a case-by-case basis, and negotiate specifically for the needs of research programmes in developing country institutions. This has been accomplished by some research entities in Africa, Latin America and Asia, which have already been making use of these knowledge-based products and services. In the net-worked environment, the availability and quality of information has become drastically different for researchers in the South today, and will be even more so in the future.

Application of Computing Power in Downstream Research

Information technology is not only revolutionizing upstream research. Clinical research also comprises an important R&D component in the overall drug discovery and development process, and requires 30-40 per cent (or sometimes higher) of the commonly estimated average expenditure per drug: $500-800 million. Today, comput-er technology makes it possible to organize patients and their data-monitoring system in clinical trials, managed with specialized software linked to the Internet. The digi-tized system prevents the high variability in non-standardized methods at the investigational site. Further, specialized training and available software for statistics and database management—such as Oracle Clinical Suite™, Clinsoft's (now a part of Phase Forward) Clintrial™ or Quad One's CliniOn™ for online clinical trials—have been developed. They are designed to reduce the error rate, thereby helping to manage data quality, validation of trials and even to detect new effects.

Quad One Technologies is a company based in Hyderabad that created a proprietary, customizable, web-based software programme, CliniOn™, for online multicentric Phase I-IV clinical research. Dr. Reddy's Laboratories has begun to use this web solution, which incorporates the flexibility and stability of Java applications with the far-reaching strengths of the Internet. The dynamics of the software combined with the web application allows data capture to be stored locally or on the Internet, and enables effective monitoring and more rapid analysis. It even caters to the typical settings of the South: The client server configuration is designed to work both in offline and online situations because many locations in India do not have continuous Internet access due to frequent lapses in electricity and for other reasons. These computer-aided approaches to the apparent problems facing many developing countries are more likely to improve the acknowledged shortcomings of clinical research capacity in the South.

A study also shows that medical practitioners in Japan attest to the importance of Internet resources. Doctors surf the Internet to examine clinical data for a new drug or comparative studies on similar drugs. They often find that the Internet provides better, or sometimes overwhelmingly better, information for clinical research and practice than the information provided by a medical representative of a company that produces the new drug.[4] Having roughly a 20 per cent share of the world drug market, Japan has a well-developed clinical research capacity. Each year, the national regulatory agency approves about 30 to 40 new drugs on average, with more than half of them having originated in domestic R&D entities. Coupled with the clinical trial requirement for the remaining new drug applications from abroad, the level of clinical research becomes significant.

While there is consensus that the North has extensive capacity, its quest is nonetheless relentless for new technology to maintain its competitive edge. Can the South, with its acknowledged capacity challenge, therefore afford to be complacent? In order to raise research output, it is very important to invest in new equipment and tools. We all personally witnessed the dramatic increase of productivity at each stage of progress on our own desktops, from the word processor to the personal computer, from sharing the computer at the office and the school lab to owning one's own at home, from Pentium I to Pentium 4. The cost savings have also grown enormously. The US-based data service company, Giga Information Group, has provided a startling comparison, noting for instance, the enormous savings of web-based self-help, which costs about one twentieth of what a conventional call center requires. In terms of health science research, microarrays, combinatorial chemistry and powerful sequencing machines are all revolutionizing output and saving vast amounts of time and cost in the North, particularly in the United States.

These technologies and forms of equipment are also embraced and recognized as a key for research capacity-building by scientists and researchers in the South. In Brazil, the nonprofit Ludwig Institute for Cancer Research has teamed up with local

---

4 Hidetoshi Naito, Shakai Joho Services, 1998.

government institutions[5] to utilize high-throughput sequencing to discover genes associated with stomach and breast cancers in São Paulo, where cancers comprise a leading cause of death. This follows on the successful work by the same team on sequencing Xyllela fastidiosa, the first plant pathogen to be sequenced and the cause of severe damage to citrus trees, which are central to the local economy. It was also the first bacterial genome to be sequenced outside the United States, United Kingdom or Japan. Further, the International Livestock Research Center, based in Kenya and Ethiopia, is an illustrative case from the African region in capitalizing on new digitalgenomics technology. It collaborates with The Institute for Genomic Research (TIGR), based in the United States, on sequencing Theileria parva, the causative organism of (African) east coast fever, a deadly cattle disease.[6]

Diaspora Connection for Financing and Transfer of Technical Know-How

Another major factor to facilitate the private sector playing a crucial role for research- and knowledge-based development is the ethnic diaspora connection, which transfers technical know-how and financing, mostly in the private sector. Remittances to developing countries from workers residing abroad total some US $60 billion (Martin, 2001), surpassing all foreign aid, which now amounts to about $53 billion (Brown, 2001).

The Israeli diaspora in America, for instance, has been an active catalyst in developing high-value industry and the country's capacity through various means. In the research field, cooperation between the United States and Israel is supported by the Binational Science Foundation, which has an endowment of US $100 million; the US-Israel Binational Industrial Research and Development Foundation (BIRD Foundation); and the US-Israel Science and Technology Foundation, which disburses grants jointly financed by the US and Israeli Governments. All these entities have as their goal the building of research and commercialization partnerships with private corporations in order to make the fruits of research available to the public.

Further, in the Israeli pharmaceutical sector, there are many milestone achievements tapping into the great talent of the diaspora. An Israeli pharmaceutical company, Teva, has been exporting generic medicines to the United States for 20 years. Founded in Jerusalem in 1901, the company gained momentum with the arrival of European scientists, chemists and technicians in the 1930s. Over time, its financial strength enabled it to create joint ventures in the United States in the 1980s, and acquisitions in the United States and Europe in the 1990s. Today, with revenues of US $1.75 billion, mainly from manufacturing and selling high-quality generics medicines, Teva is among the top 50 pharmaceutical companies in the world, with a marketing or manufacturing presence on all continents. It has been investing significantly in R&D and took a novel molecule, glatiramer acetate (Copaxone), through clinical trials and on to use in patients with relapsing-remitting multiple sclerosis, a debilitating autoimmune neurological disease that affects over a million people worldwide. Glatiramer was discovered at the Weizmann Institute of Science at Rehovot, a major public

---

[5] Over 200 Brazilian scientists are linked via networked infrastructure financed by the São Paulo State Research Foundation (FAPESP).
[6] Financing for the project includes the donation by Dr. Craig Venter, TIGR's Chairperson, of the $200,000 he received from the King Faisal Science Award.

research institution.[7] The institute is well known for its extensive links with US and European premier R&D institutions, and is well-supported financially and technologically by the diaspora. Teva was able to take glatiramer through clinical trials and license it for use in 22 countries, including the United States, Brazil, Switzerland and Poland, indicating that the company is well poised to make use of public-private partnerships for the benefit of patients needing new treatments.

The Chinese diaspora also has been well known for contributing to the impressive technological development in Asia Pacific countries. Members of the Society of Chinese Bioscientists in America, for instance, have been active in enhancing the health science research capacity, and are attracting great interest from both the public and private sectors of Asia Pacific countries. They cooperate actively in terms of developing technological excellence as well as in setting up systems for professional operation of the peer review system for research, which has been actively debated and modeled on the US system through the diaspora connection, and which helps the positive progress of research capacity. There are numerous systems in Asia Pacific countries that are modeled on the NIH and its crucial role as a public sector institution undertaking risky and costly but high-value basic research that can be eventually applied to fulfil social needs and encourage wealth creation by the private sector.

Numbering some 50 million people, the Chinese diaspora throughout the world generates an estimated annual US $700 billion in economic activity. Its liquid wealth may run as high as $2.5 trillion (Burstein et al., 1998). Chinese investors, in addition to manufacturing garments, toys and other consumer goods, have generally favoured investments in information technology, especially computer components and hardware, but they are gradually warming to other high-technology sectors, such as biotechnology, as well.

African-Americans have been particularly passionate and active in promoting the development of African countries in recent years. The African Growth and Opportunity Act (AGOA) was sponsored in part by members of the Congressional Black Caucus and enacted by the US Congress in 2000. The act addresses how African countries and the United States, through public sector incentives, can tap the power of the markets to improve the lives of citizens. It also allows African countries and companies to export goods duty-free to the US $1.2 trillion import market of the United States. US Congressional Black Caucus members have actively encouraged US financial institutions, such as the Export-Import Bank, to collaborate with African countries in providing loans, guarantees and insurance to upgrade health care access, technology and productivity. So far, in a short period of time, essential business networks have been built under the aegis of the act, and it is a major cornerstone achievement by concerned members of the African-American community for development in the African region.

Similarly, African-Americans, including the Congressional Black Caucus and church groups, have intensely lobbied and supported an increasing role for major donors in AIDS programmes and research. The Joint United Nations Programme on HIV/AIDS (UNAIDS) estimates that about 1,600 children become HIV positive every

---

[7] Glatiramer, believed to function as a decoy, was discovered by Drs. Michael Sela, Ruth Arnon and Dvora Teitelbaum after 27 years of work on synthetic molecules capable of provoking an immune response.

day. Research done in Uganda by a team of African and US researchers showed that giving a single oral dose of nevirapine (a non-nucleoside reverse transcriptase inhibitor) to an infected mother at the onset of labour, and a single oral dose to the newborn within 72 hours of birth, significantly reduces mother-to-child transmission. This research has led to programmatic efforts in Cameroon, Congo, Kenya, Malawi, Rwanda, Senegal, Tanzania, Thailand, Uganda, Zambia, Zimbabwe and other countries, along with a donation programme from the drug's manufacturer, Boehringer Ingelheim of Germany.[8] This sort of research elicits value-added, knowledge-based practice in tackling major public health threats.

Indian computer engineers and software programmers are also a networked world resource for development. The Indian diaspora, numbering somewhere around 20 million worldwide, is believed to generate economic activity totalling about US $400 billion annually.[9] Well-known personalities include Vinod Khosla, a founder of Sun Microsystems and now a venture capitalist; Purnendu Chatterjee, an investment fund manager for George Soros's Quantum Fund, who is now financing scholarships at a public research institution in New Delhi through collaboration with his India-based R&D pharmaceutical and biotechnology company; Vijay Vashee, a long-term, high-ranking manager of Microsoft; and Sabeer Bhatia, a founder of hotmail.com, the web-based e-mail system that was sold to Microsoft for nearly US $400 million in 1998. They have been busy fostering nonprofit and for-profit activities that constitute a powerful force in developing technological excellence in India, and facilitating the transfer of knowledge, capital and human connections—the spirit capital of entrepreneurs—that encourages the aspirations of many.

Further, on the heels of the impending Y2K computer glitch challenges, diaspora information technology entrepreneurs such as Satish Sanan of IMR Global (now merged into Canada's CGI Group), Bharat Desai of Syntel and others created a firm collaborative link between India's programmers and global Fortune 1000 firms. Correcting the year number of 00 to the 2000 stored in mainframe computers and associated software built between the 1960s and 1980s required COBOL software programming knowledge. Otherwise, mainframe computers and software would recognize the number 00 as the year 1900, thereby making major errors in computerized calculations and systems related to insurance, bonds and other financial services for which the period of time is central. COBOL, a programme that had long been semi-abandoned in favor of the newer, more powerful software programming codes, such as C, C++ and Java, was still being used by programmers in South Asia.

Information technology entrepreneurs working overseas knew this fact first-hand, and they established subsidiaries of their US companies in India to enable thousands of programmers to contribute to this task. Once chief information officers were able to see how effectively they could work offshore using 64-kilobits-per-second satellite-based connections (even before the Internet became the mainstay of communications), this led to further programming work as well as prospects in the post-Y2K era. Now, T1, T3 and other broadband, high-speed links form the pathway through which these

---

[8] Programme implementation is supported by the Elizabeth Glaser Pediatric AIDS Foundation and the Bill and Melinda Gates Foundation.
[9] IndiaWatch Foundation.

collaborations work today. These entrepreneurs have brought together capital, knowledge of global information technology supply and demand resources, and the trust that generated employment in developing countries in order to create opportunities for trained knowledge workers.

This development sparked a social transformation as well. In the minds of the population, software training became synonymous with higher future income, leading to changes in the target educational courses for young people and corresponding shifts in the dreams of their parents. Unlike most other professional courses, basic software programming can be taught in many new institutions, with certification examinations being conducted by major corporations. Proving one's worth takes place through the objective means of mastering written software code that can be examined and analysed. In many ways, this revolution in thinking about work and value was inspired by the story of Microsoft Chairperson Bill Gates, who is the world's wealthiest programmer, despite having no postgraduate degree in programming.

These ethnic diaspora groups, together with numerous other diaspora communities, are disbursed all over the world. Today, the World Wide Web connects these communities not on the basis of geographical boundaries but on their common interests. This channel is a great resource for technical cooperation and, by networked on-line means, this rich resource can be effectively utilized in reaching the focused goals of raising living standard and enhancing country capacity-building.

Multinational Corporations and Companies

Transnational companies play a notable role in private sector technological development in the South. Outsourcing, subcontracting, original equipment manufacturer (OEM) contract manufacturing, licensing both from the North and from the South, and regulatory compliance are precious channels for the private sector in the South to earn hard currency, gain technological excellence and access large-scale markets. Although there are some negative experiences in the South in which multinational corporations suppressed local industry or caused more harm than good, it is also true on the other hand that the presence of foreign companies and cooperation with overseas companies have contributed much to raising technological and industrial standards.

Swedish-Anglo pharmaceutical giant AstraZeneca's research foundation, Astra Research Foundation, is one example. It has undertaken infectious disease research in Bangalore, utilizing the latest discovery technology. Its anti-tuberculosis (TB) drug discovery programmes include novel targets based on the knowledge of the already sequenced TB genome, with 4,000 genes and 4.4 million base pairs. This digital information is linked to studies by microarrays and genomic chips—a new digitalgenomic research technology developed in the past few years in Silicon Valley in the United States. AstraZeneca has invested substantially in genomics and maintains a global network of R&D facilities, including genomics and anti-infective research centers in Boston and in Cheshire in the United Kingdom. The proposed collaboration with local scientists and academic institutions in India is expected to provide India's researchers with good exposure to the latest scientific knowledge and the use of digitalgenomics equipment.

Pfizer provides another example. Recognizing the research quality of a local Indian biotechnology company, Pfizer is offering the valuable transfer of know-how on quality control as a part of their strategic alliance for product distribution in the Indian market. This strategic alliance has provided a much more cost-effective solution to the identified research challenge.

There is also a handful of scientists in India who have worked at the local R&D facilities of global pharmaceutical giants, including Hoechst (now Aventis) and Ciba-Geigy (now Novartis). Both have long maintained R&D activities in India, even during the time when India's patent protection environment and market conditions were not conducive to fostering novel research.[10] These Indian scientists have now joined India's blue-chip pharmaceutical companies. Together with highly qualified public sector scientists, they have been laying the ground for new knowledge- and research-based development of health science in the country, and contributing to the successful discovery of new chemical entities for novel therapeutics.

South-North Industry Collaborations

Availability of Global Resources for the South

In the network age, money, human capital, specialized services, technology, tools and equipment can be sourced wherever they are most efficiently available. Collaborations between the South and the North to facilitate development are increasing as more resources and expertise are globalized. For drug discovery R&D, the challenge in biological screening and pharmacological testing are increasingly tackled by the availability of combinatorial chemistry and microarray technologies. Traditionally, toxicology and safety testing in India have been almost impossible, and today, many top companies still go abroad to North America and Europe to contract these studies to specialized service providers. The clinical research capacity in India has been another area that has lacked quality control and therefore suffers from a negative reputation. For this, too, there has been no choice but to rely on software aid and foreign contract research organizations abroad.

A form of strategic alliance and joint research with research organizations and companies in the North provides another route to achieve research and technological excellence. The joint research between the Indian pharmaceutical company Zydus Cadila and the Danish company Pantheco is a quintessential case in this regard. The Indian side can benefit from the know-how in areas in which critical expertise is lacking. Zydus Cadila aims to gain in preclinical and clinical development expertise, especially in Europe, and through getting patented drugs developed internationally. Pantheco, in return, will gain access to the core competence of the Indian researchers. The Indian company will undertake chemistry, preliminary screening and initial characterization of compounds with antibacterial activity. In this sort of alliance, the cost and profit sharing are integral parts of the deal.

---

[10] Dr. Noel deSouza, Director of R&D, Wockhardt Pharmaceuticals, India.

Knowledge Transfer from the South to the North

Expertise and technology transfer from the South to the North are indeed occurring globally across a broad spectrum of industries and markets. Pharmaceutical product manufacturing, particularly generic drugs, is one area where the South has accumulated know-how, and transfer of knowledge from the South to the North can be seen at the level of the individual enterprise. Technology and capital are highly mobile in various directions in the private sector.

In the field of the generic drug industry, in which Indian companies have also accumulated solid know-how, Sun Pharmaceuticals of India provided a small US-based generic drug company, Caraco Pharmaceutical Laboratories, with a much-needed cash infusion and expertise to secure FDA regulatory approval. Sun Pharmaceuticals has considerable experience in working with the FDA to obtain certifications for bulk actives and production facilities in India. Its Ahmednagar plant for active pharmaceutical ingredients is FDA approved, and its Ankleshwar plant, dedicated to producing cephalexin, is FDA certified for 7-aminodecephalosporanic acid.[11] Prior to Sun Pharmaceutical's equity participation, Caraco was struggling with serious management problems and unable to raise further cash. In August 1997, Sun Pharmaceuticals officially reorganized the company under new management. As a result, Caraco successfully secured FDA approval for production of two drugs in the US market, clonazepam and flurbiprofen, and has seven additional abbreviated new drug applications (ANDAs) pending at this time.

The FDA's approval process for generic drugs is not by any means simple. It can take between three to four years to satisfy the requirements before the approval is granted on an ANDA. The documentation required and the associated inspections cover sourcing of raw materials; formulation; scale-up batch; testing the identity, strength, quality and purity of raw materials; stability; and, most importantly, bioequivalence. In obtaining certifications from regulatory agencies in countries of the North, validation of the manufacturing process through in-process and postmanufacturing testing in consecutive production batches is a long and cumbersome procedure. At the same time, certification is a well-recognized means to enhance the value of products. The Good Manufacturing Practice certification is not only important for patients, but also constitutes knowledge-based value creation for producers.

A similar example comes from the industrial development process Japanese auto makers experienced during the 1970s. Prior to establishing the brand recognition achieved today, many Japanese auto companies started investing heavily in US manufacturers in the 1970s, and transferred production-related technology and manufacturing practices that led to the establishment of extensive production and distribution channels.

For technology capacity development and for market access, many private sector companies in the South are very committed and forthcoming. They invest in a joint venture, plants, distribution rights or the buyout of businesses to create a base in the

---

[11] In addition, Sun Pharmaceutical's Panoli active pharmaceutical ingredient (API) plant currently holds a European Certificate of Suitability (CoS) for pentoxifylline, indicated in intermittent claudication and peripheral arterial disease. Sun subsidiary MJ Pharma's plant holds UK MCA and South African Medicines Control Council approval.

North and gain technological excellence. Following the success of many private sector companies from middle-income countries, particularly from East Asia, India's pharmaceutical companies have been actively investing. Ranbaxy Laboratories has had a manufacturing base in the United States since 1995, having acquired a small generic drug manufacturer, and upgraded the technology and management expertise there. Ranbaxy also formed several strategic alliances with other companies in the United States, and today it is the eleventh largest generic drug company there. Antibiotics sold under prescription, analgesics and anti-inflammatories such as ibuprofen, antacids, and the nasal decongestant pseudoephedrine are some of the many over-the-counter products manufactured for the US market. Dr. Reddy's Laboratories is another upcoming and formidable international player from the South. The company has invested in subsidiaries in the United States, France and the Netherlands for generic drug production and distribution, including the anti-ulcer drug ranitidine, as well as for therapeutics discovery R&D. Having multiple revenue-generating products, both generic and novel discovery products, Dr Reddy's Laboratories successfully raised substantial funding from the international equity market by making its debut on the New York Stock Exchange in April 2001. These are a handful of examples of the larger trend in the private sector in the South.

Harnessing the Incentives and Resources of the Private Sector for Technical Cooperation

Capital Accumulation for Acquiring Crucial Technology

Flexibility in financing and mobilizing capital in the private sector are necessary resources and incentives for developing technological excellence. Private placements, public offerings on the financial markets, mergers and acquisitions and joint ventures are all means for entrepreneurs to raise necessary resources for high-value, knowledge-based operations. There are now such financial flows into the South, though still limited, and there are notable cases where this private investment led to great bio-science success. Foreign direct investment (FDI) of US $1 million is credited with sparking the creation of the first locally manufactured hepatitis B vaccine in India.[12] Domestic and other foreign investment followed. The growth of FDI flows into India has been substantial, from an average of $500 million in the years 1985-1995 to the current $2.3 billion. Nevertheless, there are wide disparities in the per-capita FDI between countries. China, excluding Hong Kong, attracted $41 billion. The bulk of the world's $1.3 trillion in total FDI pours into the United States, at $281 billion, and the European Union countries, at $617 billion (UNCTAD, 2001).

Capital formation is another incentive, allowing acquisition of crucial technology that is vital in raising research capacity. The early 1990s saw major economic reforms enacted in India that had a direct impact on software services and exports. Infosys is a major information-technology software company based in India, and its Chairperson, Narayana Murthy, described the reforms as having changed the Indian business context from one of state-centred control orientation to that of free, open market

---

[12] Chairperson Varaprasad Reddy. Shantha Biotech, Hyderabad, India.

orientation, at least for high-tech companies (Murthy, 2001). Job creation, export opportunities, wealth creation and capital formation translate well into economic development. Indian software exports have reached about US $8 billion per year, and have experienced a growth rate of about 30 per cent per year despite the recessionary world environment. Indeed, companies are moving up the value chain from upgrading legacy systems and maintenance to packaged software integration, network infrastructure integration and outsourced software R&D. Further, business process outsourcing is growing at 70 per cent per year.[13] All this growth is having a tremendous impact on investment in the next level of technology, as companies recognize the value of enhancing computerized operations. Efficiency gains that create job opportunities that benefit the poorest are a feature of these changes.

Forming Alliances with the Life Science Sector in the North

Two questions are very relevant for technical cooperation in the network age:

- How can multilateral institutions and governments collaborate with the private sector in the South to encourage its development; and

- What tools can multilateral institutions and governments use to accelerate the development of the private sector in the South.

Fostering knowledge- and research-based development between multilateral institutions, governments and the private sector in the South demands well-defined alliances, and an understanding of finance, scientific and technological aspects, and organizational and management issues. In the private sector, these assessments form the foundation for creating alliances in the pharmaceutical, biotechnology and genomic sectors, where strategic alliances are actively pursued to enhance core competence and value creation for a mutually shared mission.

For drug development, a collaborative deal is an intermediary step for fostering progress, as alliances of numerous pharmaceutical and biotechnology companies are leading to great success (of course failure, too) in the North. Understanding the technology specifics and market value, and gaining insight into recent partnership deals between the South and North enables us effectively to define the terms for potential new alliances between multilateral institutions, governments and the private sector.

A few analytical methodologies for private sector entities are very important tools. The methods have to be modified for the specifics of the public sector, and to make them applicable to multilateral institutions, governments and the private sector in the South. The following are a few of the tools that can be used to quantify the intangible assets—value—in the best possible way:

- Comparable analysis

- Discounted earnings analysis

- Milestone analysis

---

[13] National Association of Software and Service Companies, India.

These methodologies are also frequently used for R&D-intensive companies, since they often do not show a profit, but that does not mean that there is no value in the company. The size of the loss-making can reflect the extent of R&D investment. In Table 3.4.2, examples are drawn from some of the most successful genomic companies in the United States. The technology is the core component of their value, which makes valuation and quantification of health science sectors—pharmaceutical, biotechnology and genomics—quite unique and unlike other industry analysis.

Comparable analysis is used to estimate financial worth by examining similar companies or institutions. It can help in situations where the local stock market is illiquid, the company is privately held, or it is a nonprofit entity. Discounted earnings analysis makes use of earnings projections that are then discounted back using discount rates appropriate for the risk taken. Milestone analysis is much more straightforward, in that it estimates or measures those milestone achievements in R&D and payments that have been made or are anticipated from often larger companies for licensing technology, or outsourcing products or raw materials. Within strategic alliances, rational decisions on ownership, strategy, financing needs, projects to be pursued or discarded, etc. require careful assessment of what each partner is bringing to the joint endeavour, and the internal and external progress of the entity they create.

Specialized Analysis

Technical cooperation has been and will be a very vital input for countries' capacity development. Today, the private sector is increasingly involved and committed to newer forms of cooperation. Harnessing incentives and resources of the private sector for technical cooperation requires market intelligence, rigorous analysis of both the benefits as well as shortcomings of the private sector, and identification of the real needs for technical cooperation organized and sponsored by multilateral organizations. This need for private sector intelligence and related services seems to be growing for various important projects led by multilateral organizations. Comprehensive studies are useful in presenting opportunities to investors, donors and the managers of organizations. For instance:

- developing the methodology to quantify the demand for particular services and products that are important for the South;

- identifying and characterizing the very new or neglected market segments that are vital for the underprivileged;

- comparative financial analysis for prioritizing the agenda for management;

- information technology applications for setting new directions in health, social and development policies; and

- cost studies and output monitoring that pinpoint hidden costs due to cumbersome procedures.

TABLE 3.4.2: LOSS-MAKING COMPANIES CAN HAVE LARGE VALUATION BECAUSE OF THEIR PATH-BREAKING TECHNOLOGIES OR SERVICES

NAME OF COMPANY	REVENUE IN LATEST THREE MONTHS REPORTED	LOSS IN LATEST THREE MONTHS REPORTED	VALUATION
Affymetrix	$55.4 million	$4.8 million	$2.3 billion
Celera Genomics	$27.0 million	$15.6 million	$1.8 billion
Human Genome Sciences	$1.6 million	$24.9 million	$4.6 billion
Incyte Genomics	$57.3 million	$17.8 million	$1.3 billion
Millennium Pharmaceuticals	$82.0 million	$25.0 million	$5.6 billion
Myriad Genetics	$13.2 million	$1.2 million	$1.3 billion

Source: Company filings with the Securities and Exchange Commission. Valuation as of 28 December 2001.

The great common denominator in creating the field of mutual interest and cooperation for R&D partnerships is often missed or neglected. Catering to scientists in the South, the intermediary entities have to analyse the technology and identify the joint research area, particularly for new sciences. It is also true that there is a huge gap in information about the health science sector, R&D capacity and market data analysis in the South among mainstream players in the North.

Further, the relevant issue is that partners do not necessarily have to be giant corporations. Today, technology-intensive companies, often lean and nimble, and academic research institutions comprise the real engine of innovation in the case of the pharmaceutical and biotechnology sectors. In the United States alone, there are about 1,300 biotechnology companies, of which 300 are listed on stock markets; the rest are privately held. The industry is fast growing, with revenues rising from US $8 billion in 1993 to $22.3 billion in 2000, and it spent $10.7 billion on R&D in 2000.[14] Moreover, in Europe there are about 1,600 biotechnology companies. In China, India, Brazil, Taiwan, Singapore, Thailand and South Africa, all members of the World Trade Organization, the academic and business segments focused on new drugs, vaccines and generic medicines are also growing.

Therefore, strategic alliances are often created to build synergy. Large corporations identify various technologies and their owner entities to form alliances. Accordingly, financial and industry analysts on Wall Street attach a value so that investors commit more resources. For smaller companies or institutions, strategic alliances with large corporations are one form of incentive and an engine of growth – their R&D is continuously financed or rewarded via equity participation and other arrangements. Total sales within the global pharmaceutical market were US $317 billion in the year 2000 and growing—thereby generating considerable amounts of resources to fuel research alliances.[15]

---

[14] Biotechnology Industry Organization.
[15] IMS Health.

As for harnessing the incentives and resources of the private sector for technical cooperation, specialized analysis becomes the first necessary tool to generate neutral assessments to define the goal. Private companies function under a host of constraints, and high-social but low-financial-return projects are often left out in decision-making on prioritization, particularly in big corporations. For instance, the antimalarials discovery and development unit at pharmaceutical giant Hoffman La-Roche was eliminated some years ago because of the declining prospect of a financial rate of return on investment. Recognizing the importance and social value of continued research, a study was conducted to establish synergy among different actors—multilateral organizations, donor foundations, governments, corporations and academic institutions (Chacko, 1999). Subsequently, the vacuum left in antimalaria product discovery research was partly filled by the World Health Organization (WHO) joining hands with the Rockefeller Foundation and the Bill and Melinda Gates Foundation in creating a public-private partnership, the Geneva-based Medicines for Malaria Venture (MMV). Under MMV, research has been carried out in multiple locations at academic institutions that partner with pharmaceutical giants. The industry offers screening for drug discovery, in addition to development and distribution expertise that requires substantial economies of scale in reaching patients today.

The Role of Multilateral Institutions and Governments in Technical Cooperation and Private Sector Development

Demand-Side Initiatives

Solid identification of demand for technical cooperation in the South has to be carried out with concrete means. Today in the network age, the Internet helps scientists and entrepreneurs in the South greatly in identifying what is available to help build research capacity, and in comparing their needs to market and social realities. A chief executive officer of a health science company in the South, for instance, surfs the Internet and learns a great deal about the availability of various technologies. She reads online scientific papers that refer to these technologies, which are used in experiments featured in the papers. She identifies specific needs, and hopefully multilateral organizations and governments can identify larger trends from these needs that are prevalent in the South. Identifying the availability of technologies and determining realistic needs in that context has become widely practiced thanks to the Internet. The key is to crystallize the real and realistic demands of researchers and entrepreneurs in the South.

Various Approaches to Collaborations

For the long term, the challenge for the public sector may be how to maintain a proper stake in terms of investing public resources and the outcome of the investments. For instance, there are many important drugs—including the cancer drugs tamoxifen and paclitaxel; the AIDS drugs zidovudine, lamivudine, nevirapine and stavudine; the antihypertensive captopril; and the antidepressant fluoxetine—that were discovered and/or developed with significant public sector financial and technical support in the

United States.[16] These drugs certainly broke the treatment barrier for patients, and now the challenge will be how this benefit can be brought to uninsured patients or those who are barely able to pay increasing insurance premiums. Leveraging the public sector's stake for the larger public good has been an argument for some time now.

Government entities sometimes distribute money through various vehicles to private research companies, such as government agencies for small business development or venture capital funding in economically depressed regions. With the constraints on governments, however, it is unrealistic, and indeed rare, for them to be able to influence the public stake even though it is for the benefit of the underprivileged. An example was the government contract for screening medical compounds that a US Government research agency gave to an American developmental-stage R&D company. There were encouraging hits against a particular disease that has high social value, especially for the South, but it was practically impossible to generate interest in further development. It is highly doubtful if companies in the private sector who reviewed this result will ever take it further for product discovery of the drug, since the disease is known as a neglected one, and perceived to have marginal commercial value with high risk.

One avenue to address this challenge is by forming collaborations. Chiron Corporation (a middle-sized biotechnology company with strong R&D activities in the United States), PathoGenesis (now a part of Chiron), and the Global Alliance for Tuberculosis Drug Development (a New York-based nonprofit partnership entity for medicine discovery) are cooperating on tuberculosis R&D with financing from the Rockefeller Foundation and the Bill and Melinda Gates Foundation. Similarly, major networking company Cisco Systems has partnered with UNDP in its Least-Developed Countries initiative in support of 27 African and other countries for enhancing Internet connectivity. Another notable collaboration is the UNDP/World Bank/WHO special programme for research and training in tropical diseases, including for therapeutic and diagnostics development. There is also the American International Group/World Bank International Finance Corporation Fund for investment in Africa. These examples may present models for multilateral institutions, governments and private sector entities working for a very specific purpose in international development. Moreover, the South-oriented electronic network-based venture is something of a unique initiative, in the context of collaboration platforms.

Peer-to-Peer Computing in the Social or Business Enterprise

In the network age, the third-party intermediary for private sector and multilateral organizations and governments to cooperate and share knowledge can well be an electronic knowledge repository for information exchange in addressing an identified mission, for instance, public health issues of the South. The health challenge of infectious diseases in the South is vastly neglected in global drug discovery. Reflecting this reality, new strategies have to be formulated. An electronic interface could be a platform for information exchange and knowledge transmission to benefit patients, scientists, entrepreneurs and industry all over the world, along with partners from international and bilateral agencies, and committed donor foundations. Figure 3.4.2 represents a

---

[16] Three sources include Oxfam, the Consumer Project on Technology and the Joint Economic Committee of the US Congress.

system involving specialized databases, facilities for online communications and analytical tools. Via such means, researchers in the South could participate more fully and have an increased stake in product development against communicable and chronic diseases that affect large populations.

Unlike the well-known client-server computer networks, where information sharing occurs through central server hubs, peer-to-peer (P2P) is information sharing at the edges of networks. In many ways, e-mail is one form of P2P that has become the primary means of communications in international development. In addition, file transfer protocol (ftp), hyper-text transfer protocol (http), instant messaging and usenet news groups are other widely used means of P2P. On the technological side, an advantage of P2P is that it does not take up big bandwidth on servers; P2P networking, along with the necessary caching stations and routers, enables efficient bandwidth usage. As computing and the storage power of "client" computers follow a variation of Moore's Law, it is becoming possible for "central server" programmes to function on "client" machines in this networked era. Simultaneously, the spread of broadband is enabling videoconferencing through the web, another emerging P2P application central to cost-reduction in capacity development.

With communication and information technology, the means of global cooperation has become ever more democratized, with a much lower cost-burden and with high efficiency. Clients and providers both have a choice on where to present their needs and where to source their solutions, and this opportunity is increasing as more connectivity becomes available every day. Sub-Saharan African countries are certainly embracing this change. Internet-based initiatives and entrepreneurship, such as MaliNet, have started sprouting from the region to reach global resources.

Conclusion

Nations have boundaries and, at the same time, technology has no finite limit. In the quest for advanced optical broadband networking capabilities and universal outreach, it is not just the North and middle-income developing countries with a relative technological base in high-tech computing or biological systems who will benefit from the network era. Today, hard-working entrepreneurs and scientists in, say, Mali, Niger or Ghana have improved access to technology on the individual and institutional level, and this is utilized to enhance their goods, services and talents in global knowledge endeavours. Through the information communication medium that directly connects them to more than 3 billion web documents, a range of options exists, from virtual distance education to data management to equipment purchase in business-to-business marketplaces. In addition, software and the Internet make it possible for researchers located in sub-Saharan Africa to manage and supply weekly real-time data in a unified format with partners in the Netherlands and North America. This is the essence of value creation that upgrades the output of the intellectual production work of the South in the knowledge-based global economy. We have all witnessed how technology can level the playing field in many cases, particularly for the world's majority that is

FIGURE 3.4.2: AN ELECTRONIC KNOWLEDGE REPOSITORY AND INTERFACE
FOR INFORMATION EXCHANGE
HIGH-LEVEL DEFINITION DIAGRAM   © *Sunil Chacko*

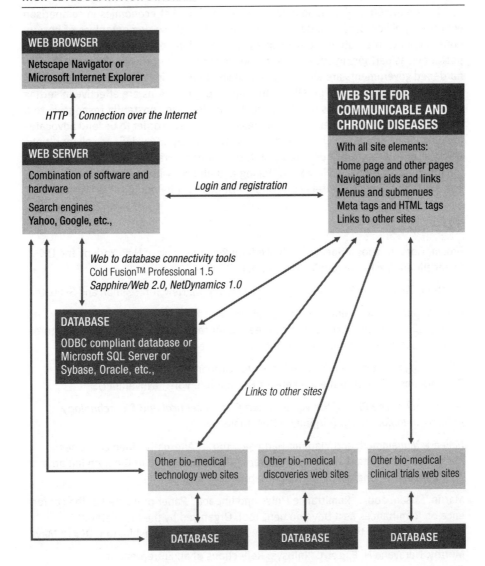

outside "the major league." Those groups and individuals willing to grasp a stake in the rising tide presented by the network era will empower the development process.

Nine hundred million people live in developed market economies in comparison with over 5 billion people in developing countries. In these demographics of horrendous inequity, international development organizations are uniquely and distinctly positioned as partners in addressing the needs of the underprivileged, for which overburdened governments are struggling to find solutions. Using their far-reaching global operations and associated prestige, multilateral organizations are effective in setting the agenda for pressing issues. They must, therefore, be constantly responsive to a changing world that is driven by technological advances, in order to be loud advocates for knowledge- and research-based development in adequately defined collaborations with the private sector. Undoubtedly, in the networked era of technical cooperation, the ingenuity in Bamako, New York, Beijing and all over will generate tangible development from the world's intellectual and knowledge capital far into the future.

References

Brown, Gordon. 2001. "Speech to the Federal Reserve Bank of New York by the UK Chancellor of the Exchequer." 16 November.

Burstein, Daniel, and Arne De Keijer. 1998. *Big Dragon*. New York: Simon and Schuster.

Chacko, Sunil. 1999. "Global Antimalarials Market: Market Quantification and Analysis." Presentation at a planning meeting for the Medicines for Malaria Venture at the Rockefeller Foundation. New York, September.

———. 1999. "Harnessing New Sciences for Orphan Diseases through Partnerships." Report to the Rockefeller Foundation, Vol. II (November).

———. 2002. *The Rise of the Value-Added Pharmaceutical and Biotechnology Industry in India*. Vienna (Virginia): eBIN Books.

Majeed, Muhammed, and Vladimir Badmaev. 1997. "Alternative Medicine Goes Mainstream for Better Health Care Delivery." Paper presented at the 49th Indian Pharmaceutical Congress. Thiruvananthapuram, December.

Martin, Susan. 2001. "Remittance Flows and Impact." Paper presented at the conference on Remittances as a Development Tool. Organized by the Multilateral Investment Fund of the Inter-American Development Bank. Washington, DC, 17 May.

Murthy, Narayana N. R. 2001. "Infosys: Reflections of an Entrepreneur." Commencement speech at the Wharton School of Business. Philadelphia, 20 May.

Soto, Hernando de. 2000. *The Mystery of Capital*. New York: Basic Books.

United Nations Conference on Trade and Development (UNCTAD). *World Investment Report 2001*. New York and Geneva.

Waxman, Samuel, and Kenneth C. Anderson. 2001. "History of the Development of Arsenic Derivatives in Cancer Therapy." *The Oncologist*, 6(2) [April], 3-10.

3.5 KNOWLEDGE OF TECHNOLOGY AND THE TECHNOLOGY OF KNOWLEDGE: NEW STRATEGIES FOR DEVELOPMENT[1]

JOSEPH E. STIGLITZ

It has now become commonplace that what separates developed from less-developed countries is not just disparities in resources, but gaps in knowledge and organization—in other words, how those resources are used to produce outputs.[2] By the same token, as attention has shifted from a narrow focus on GDP to a broader set of objectives—to broader measures of living standards and to equitable, sustainable, democratic development[3]—there has been a parallel emphasis on knowledge and technology. Simple and, in some cases, even cost-saving changes that influence behavioural patterns—from the installation of chimneys in primitive huts, to the location of latrines, to the use of saline solutions for rehydration, to impregnated bed nets—can make an enormous difference in health, productivity and overall well being.

Several factors have contributed to the impetus for the new focus on technology and knowledge, an emphasis that was reflected in the World Bank's *World Development Report 1998-1999* (World Bank, 1999), which focused on knowledge. First, there has been a change in the very concept of development. Today, development is thought of as a transformation of societies (Stiglitz, 1998b), and an essential part of the transformation is a change in mindsets, a movement from traditional to more modern ways of thinking that emphasize change, science and technology.

Second, the countries of East Asia, which have pursued the most successful development strategies, have emphasized technology, and their success is widely attributed to their ability to close the "knowledge gap."[4]

Third, changes in technology—the remarkable reductions in the costs of transportation and communication—that have led to globalization and the new economy[5] have emphasized the key role of knowledge and technology in the economy;[6] provided

---

[1] I wish to acknowledge the helpful assistance of Niny Khor, Marco Sorge and Nadia Roumani. This chapter can be viewed as a version of the remarks delivered at the founding of the Global Development Network in Bonn in December 1999 (Stiglitz, 2000). It also builds on ideas contained in the World Bank's *World Development Report 1998-1999: Knowledge for Development*, written under my direction as Chief Economist of the World Bank.
[2] For an earlier articulation of this view, see Stiglitz (1998a).
[3] See Stiglitz (1998b).
[4] See Amsden (1989), Wade (1989, 1990), World Bank (1993) and Stiglitz (1996). These perspectives are not inconsistent with those studies that claim that total factor productivity growth has not been particularly impressive (as flawed or unconvincing as this evidence might be). The studies only claim that the countries of East Asia "purchased" their knowledge through investments in human and physical capital.
[5] For discussions of the new economy see Shapiro and Varian (1999).
[6] This change in perspective, of course, antedates currently fashionable discussions of the new economy. The literature on endogenous growth (Romer, 1994; Grossman and Helpman 1994) perhaps paid insufficient attention to earlier literature on macroeconomic endogenous growth (see, e.g., Uzawa, 1969; Shell, 1969; Nordhaus, 1969; and Atkinson and Stiglitz, 1969, and the articles cited there) as well as the parallel literature on innovation (see, e.g., David, 1985; Rosenberg, 1974; Mansfield, 1977; and Stiglitz 1987).

unprecedented access to technology and knowledge more generally; and led to forms of industrial organization that have facilitated the transfer of technology across borders, particularly from the developed to the less-developed countries. Indeed, some view the new economy as a revolution in the way that ideas and knowledge are produced, just as the industrial revolution represented a revolution in the way that goods are produced. If the gap between the developed and less-developed countries was not to grow larger, the developing countries *had* to partake of this revolution, or at least had to take advantage of the parallel revolution in the manner in which ideas could be, and were being, transmitted. And just as the industrial revolution resulted in a change in "industrial organization," in the way in which society organized production, so have similar changes been occurring recently. The rationale for large, transnational firms lies not in economies of scale or scope of the conventional sort, relating to production (or the returns to maintaining global monopoly power), but in the broader dissemination and utilization of new knowledge.[7] Indeed, more than 25 per cent of all private research inside the United States today is by transnational firms, who recover a substantial fraction of their investments in research and development through sales abroad.[8]

The changes in the global economy have served to emphasize the importance of knowledge, and have enabled *some* of the developing countries to gain unprecedented access to knowledge and technology. The most obvious example is the Internet, which puts at the disposal of anyone who has access to it an amount of knowledge almost unimaginable a decade ago. A student or a manager in a capital city in Africa has access to a formal knowledge base far greater than virtually anyone in the most developed country a decade ago. However, the importance of transnational firms referred to in the previous paragraph as transmitters of knowledge should not be underemphasized.

While this chapter focuses on technological knowledge, it should be clear that there are many other aspects of knowledge, and some of what we have to say will apply to these other forms as well. I have already made reference to several examples of what might be called *social knowledge,* knowledge that affects how people live their lives. Besides the examples cited earlier, such knowledge includes knowledge about reproduction—over the long run, there are probably few things that are of greater importance than issues related to population. There is also *institutional knowledge,* knowledge about the creation and preservation of the institutions that mediate so much of life in every society, including the democratic institutions, which are central in the conduct of collective actions. The same forces that have facilitated the transfer of technical knowledge, and globalization of trade and capital flows, have brought about a globalization in this arena as well. There is a globalization not only of beliefs (e.g., in the virtues of democracy and the adverse effects of corruption), but also of some of the supporting institutions, such as a globalized civil society.

---

[7] Which indeed can be viewed as giving rise to economies of scale.
[8] World Bank (1998).

Does the New Economy Put the Developing Countries at an Increasing Disadvantage?

There has been an enormous concern about the dangers of a growing digital divide, a worry that changes in technology lie behind the increasing inequality that has appeared throughout the world.[9] Changes in technology can have the effect of changing the relative scarcity value of different skills; the new technologies put a premium on computer literacy on the one hand, and higher-order thinking skills on the other. If these changes work to the disadvantage of low-skilled individuals within a country,[10] they also work to the disadvantage of countries where there are a preponderance of low-skilled individuals. The new economy has helped markets work better—that is, more competitively. It has eliminated rents in many arenas, especially in the production of "commodities," although not in the production of ideas. But developing countries have a comparative advantage in the former; the developed countries in the latter. If that was the entire picture, however, then the changes associated with the new economy would work to the disadvantage of the developing countries.

There is another side that may offset, at least partially, these changes, and that is the increase in global competition, the barriers that imperfect information creates to market access. It is no longer the case that a few companies can control the flow of goods from the developing to the developed countries, thereby earning monopoly rents. While the imperfections of competition are two-sided, I suspect that the developing countries on the whole have more to gain, although some developing countries, particularly those that had closer historical connections with certain developed countries, may have more to lose. Today, there is often fierce competition among international companies from developed countries, for instance, in bidding for a telecommunications license in a developing country, thereby eroding the rents that these companies might otherwise receive. To be sure, companies and their governments often work hard to reduce such competition, and historically determined asymmetries of information often are quite effective in maintaining a modicum of market power.[11]

But the new technologies have not only facilitated the transfer of knowledge, they have facilitated the transfer of knowledge about knowledge production, thereby increasing incomes for those countries able to take full advantage of the new technologies; in particular, those countries with the human capital to do so. (Later, I shall discuss other relevant attributes of the economy.) Human capital is the essential requisite, and a few countries, such as India and China, have that resource. But many of the poorest developing countries do not. Thus, in the coming decades, while the disparity in income between, say, India and China and the more developed countries may well shrink markedly, there is a real risk that the disparity between the poorest countries, e.g., those in sub-Saharan Africa, may actually grow.

This is in spite of the fact that the new technologies might be able to make a greater difference for those countries. For instance, one of the problems that these countries face is their isolation; with the new technologies, in principle, they can

---

[9] See, e.g., Krueger (1993).

[10] In Hick's old classification scheme of innovations, they are labour saving. See Hicks (1935).

[11] Competitive bidding with asymmetric information does not, in general, erode rents. See, e.g., Wilson (1997).

become far more integrated into the global economy. That integration would have been more difficult under old, wire-based technologies, partly because of problems encountered with copper wires being repeatedly stolen. Moreover, the geographical isolation of farmers from markets has meant that farmers have been easily preyed upon by middlemen, among whom competition has been limited for a variety of reasons. There is some evidence that the new technologies have, at least in some circumstances, increased enormously the income of farmers, allowing them not only to benefit from reduced profits to middlemen, but also to arbitrage differences in prices across markets because they have a choice of markets into which to sell. Knowledge of market prices may also enable them to redirect planting in ways that enhance income.

In short, while improvements in technology increase incomes in general, they also lead to redistributions. The poor countries, on the whole, may or may not suffer as a result, although certainly some countries will without offsetting actions. The challenge then is to enhance the *potential* for partaking of the upside possibilities while minimizing the downside risks. Much of the remainder of this chapter is devoted to identifying policies and strategies that might achieve these ends.

Transmission and Adaptation

While the new technologies can thus bring enormous benefits to developing countries, those benefits do not come automatically. There was an old literature that emphasized "appropriate technology" (Sen, 1962; R. S. Eckaus, 1960). It stressed that because of large differences in factor prices, technologies that were developed for the more advanced countries might not be appropriate for the less-developed countries. While saving labor was a key concern in the former, generating jobs was a key concern in the latter. The problem that Atkinson and Stiglitz (1969) and others emphasized was that with most of the innovations occurring in the North, with *localized* technological progress, the North developed labor-saving technologies that *dominated*. Regardless of the factor prices, these technologies were superior to the "old" technologies. Suppose technology A uses more labour than B, and therefore would be the appropriate technology for a developing country. But then research on the capital intensive technology—which effectively leaves technology A unchanged—lowers both its capital and labor costs; the new technology B' then dominates technology A. Regardless of the large differences in factor prices, however, it pays the developing country to use technology A. At that juncture, it is irrelevant, or almost so, that technology A would have been improved or that a new technology A' might have been developed had the innovation process been controlled in the South.

If the less-developed country develops its own research capacity (or if multinationals engaging in research start focusing on how they can reduce their production costs in the developing countries where so much of their production occurs), then a new set of choices unfolds. There are at least two research strategies that might, at this juncture, be pursued. One entails adaptation, taking the technology B' and modifying it, say to B". An alternative strategy could be to look back at the old technology

A, and see if there could be modifications that at lower costs might result in a more cost-effective technology (e.g., the technology A' referred to earlier).

The textbook analysis just presented oversimplifies in two key ways. First, there are economies of scope and scale in innovation. The multinational, producing in many countries, may be looking for a versatile technology appropriate for a multiplicity of circumstances; if a significant part of his production occurs in the more developed countries, this will bias him towards an improvement in technology B (B'). This is especially the case given the nature of the learning/research process: Its engineers will be more familiar with technology B and its variants, and thus they have to invest less to think about how it might be improved.

On the other hand, diminishing returns may well have set in with the improvements in technology B; the absence of research on technology A may mean that large changes in costs can be attained with relatively little investment.

Compounding these advantages is the second broad point: What matters is not just factor prices, but a whole set of *characteristics* of the production process. For instance, a technology may be more or less sensitive to variability in the quality of the inputs (including labour) or to fluctuations in electricity voltage or to the climactic conditions. Those who live inside the developing country are more likely to be sensitive to these concerns. Indeed, once these dimensions of the production process are taken into account, it may no longer even be the case that technology B really dominates technology A. In any case, the process of adaptation requires altering technology B so that it can work, or work more effectively, under the conditions of the country.

Adaptation, in short, can be thought of partly as *localization:* using local knowledge to transform generally available technologies based on the circumstances of the particular country. But the process of localization has to, by and large, occur locally, and for a simple reason: Much of the relevant knowledge associated with localization is tacit, not codified. As a result, it can only be transmitted through direct contact. To be sure, the process of globalization has facilitated the extent to which contact occurs; but *deep* knowledge typically occurs only through repeated and extended interactions, a total immersion, and thus, by and large, the process of localization will occur more effectively within a country, or within a country with similar attributes. That is why it is imperative for developing countries to expand their technological capabilities for adaptation and development of new technologies.

It is now widely recognized that much, if not most, of the improvements in productivity are a result of small incremental changes—not the monumental changes like the invention of the airplane or the Internet. The knowledge about how production processes might be improved is often widely dispersed: Those involved in the production have tacit knowledge that is hard to codify and often hard to transmit. They know where problems are arising, even if they may not know precisely how to remedy the problems.

Earlier, I spoke of development as a transformation of society, a change in mindset, and, in particular, a mindset that focuses on change. This is true not only at the

level of the individual, but at the level of the firm: Firms need to be organized to facilitate the utilization of localized knowledge in order to make adaptation work.
Hierarchical-production organizations might have worked for steel mills, for production processes in which individuals are likely not to make many contributions to the
improvement in productivity. The technology itself locks in behaviour. But this is not
the case in the vast majority of productive activities today—as can be seen in the enormous differences in productivity in firms producing similar products, even in factories
of similar design.[12] The structure of an organization (or of a society) can thus facilitate
the adoption and adaptation of new technology.

What Can Governments Do?

There is a strong presumption for a role of government in the transmission and adaptation of technology. Knowledge is a public good; not only is it often difficult for firms
to appropriate fully the returns from their investments in technology, but such appropriation will typically result in underutilization of knowledge. That is, relying on the
private sector will result in underprovision and/or underutilization of knowledge. That
having been said, however, the role of government remains more ambiguous: While
there may be marked market failures, it may not be obvious that government is capable
of effectively remedying those failures.

There are some forms of public action that have received broader support than others.

Education

Government support of education, and especially technology/science education, is
one form of government action that receives widespread, though not universal, support.
In effect, such support increases the supply and reduces the price of this key input.

There is a view that government in developing countries should focus its attention
on primary education. There should be full cost-recovery for tertiary education. This
view is now increasingly discredited, even in those places where it was put forward
most strongly, such as at the World Bank.[13] If there are large spillovers associated with
innovation and adaptation, then it makes sense to subsidize the production. And it
may be more effective to subsidize the input than the output, because it may in fact
be difficult to assess what is and is not innovative activity. While a broad-based subsidy may also not be well targeted—many may not go into activities that generate
externalities—the income and other taxes that are typically collected from high-
income individuals itself introduces a discrepancy, which justifies government
subsidies, between private and social returns to education.[14]

---

[12] See, in particular, the remarkable set of studies by McKenzie (1990). See also Pack (1986).
[13] See World Bank (1999).
[14] The inability of individuals to borrow to finance their education may be viewed as a "market failure,"
but this market failure provides more of a rationale for a government loan programme than for a government subsidy.

Technology Policy

In many East Asian countries, government has taken an active role not only in promoting education, but in promoting technology directly by subsidizing high-tech industries. These "industrial policies" have been widely criticized, with the argument being that government does not do a good job at picking winners. There are two responses to this charge. First, the objective of government is not to pick winners, but to identify areas where there are large externalities and where private incentives are accordingly lacking. Second, some governments have in fact done a credible job at picking winners—winners who at the same time have generated enormous externalities. There is a long history of this in the United States, from the support of the first telegraph line between Baltimore and Washington in 1842, which opened the telecommunications industry, to the development of the Internet, which today is changing the way the economy is organized; and from agricultural research and extension services, which transformed agriculture in the 19th century, to the laser and transistor, which have transformed the 20th. Under former President Bill Clinton, US technology policy developed procedures and policies aimed at enhancing the likelihood of success, e.g., by requiring equity participation, by having broad-based programmes and by more extensive use of peer review.[15]

Intellectual Property

Intellectual property regimes affect the incentive to innovate/adapt because they enhance the ability of those engaged in the activity to appropriate the returns of their investment. But the effects on developing countries of stronger intellectual property regimes are more ambiguous than this assertion would suggest. Intellectual property is not just an output; it is also an input. Stronger intellectual property protection may increase the price of intellectual property as an input. Since, in general, developing countries are more users of knowledge than producers, one suspects that the net effect of stronger intellectual property regimes may be adverse.

It may be possible, however, to craft intellectual property regimes that are better, from the perspective of developing countries, than others, e.g., by strengthening protection in some ways in return for relaxing it in others.

Beyond Technology Policy: Macropolicy

Much of the process of adaptation and adoption occurs in specific firms, and the broader economic environment can play a major role in creating an environment that is either conducive or adverse to the interests of such firms. For instance, new, small- and medium-sized firms have played a particularly important role in technology development. Such firms need access to capital; they cannot rely on their own funds. What is thus required is both financial institutions that provide such funds and a macroeconomic policy that keeps interest rates low. Extreme stabilization policies, resulting in

---

[15] The unfortunate aspect of these reforms was that they eliminated much of the rent associated with technology subsidies, thereby undermining political support for them.

high interest rates, induce banks to lend to the government rather than to the private sector. They dry up both the demand for and supply of funds.

Beyond Technology Policy: Liberalization

Several aspects of liberalization policies affect firms that are engaged in technology adaptation. Some countries have acceded to demands to open up their markets to foreign banks in ways that have led such banks to become dominant. In some cases, this has dried up the supply of funds to local firms—including the firms that might potentially be engaged in technology adaptation. The foreign banks have done a better job in providing funds to established multinational firms engaged in importing goods into the country than in supplying funds to new firms within the country. (Such problems might be mitigated if governments imposed what might be thought of as generalized CRA—community reinvestment act—requirements, which would mandate that all banks, whether domestic or foreign, lend a certain fraction of their loan portfolio to small- and medium-sized domestic firms.)

Capital market liberalization is systematically related to an increase in the risk faced by a country, and such risk has particularly adverse impacts on new, small- and medium-sized firms.

Foreign Direct Investment

In some countries, such as Singapore and Malaysia, foreign direct investment (FDI) has not only been a key vehicle for growth, but also for the transfer and adaptation of technology. There are numerous policies that affect the attractiveness of foreign investment—and not necessarily those that have typically been stressed, e.g., by international financial institutions. For instance, while these institutions claim that capital market liberalization is essential if a country is to attract capital, the country that has been most successful in attracting FDI is China, which has yet to liberalize its capital account.

Not all FDI, however, brings technology with it, or at least technology that has significant spillovers to the rest of the economy. In many countries, FDI is concentrated in mineral resources, where there are few spillovers, partially because the technology in that sector has little bearing on relevant technology elsewhere in the economy, and partially because the mines or oil wells are remote from major population centres.

Having FDI is thus not enough. Some types of FDI are likely to have more spillovers than others. But countries may need to adopt policies that actively promote the transfer of technology. Malaysia undertook policies that did exactly that, with considerable success, and without the untoward effects that critics of these initiatives had predicted.

References

Amsden, Alice. 1989. *Asia's Next Giant: South Korea and Late Industrialization.* New York: Oxford University Press.

Atkinson, A., and J. Stiglitz 1969. "A New View of Technological Change." *Economic Journal,* 79, September, 573-78.

Chang, Ha-Joon, ed. 2001. J*oseph Stiglitz and the World Bank: The Rebel Within.* London: Anthem.

David, Paul. 1985. "Clio and the Economics of Qwerty." *American Economic Review,* 75(2) [May], 332-37.

Eckaus, R. S. 1960. "The Factor Proportions Problem in Underdeveloped Areas." *American Economic Review Supplement,* l (May), 642-48.

Grossman, Gene, and Elhanan Helpman. 1994. "Endogenous Innovation in the Theory of Growth." *Journal of Economic Perspectives,* 8(1), 23-44.

Hicks, John. 1935. *Theory of Wages.* London: Macmillan & Co.

Krueger, Alan. 1993. "How Computers Have Changed the Wage Structure: Evidence from Microdata, 1984-1989." *Quarterly Journal of Economics,* 108(1), 33-60.

Mansfield, Edwin, et al. 1977. "Social and Private Rates of Return from Industrial Innovations." *Quarterly Journal of Economics,* 91(2), 221-40.

McKenzie, Lionel. 1990. "Ideal Output and the Interdependence of Firms." In *Industrial Organization,* edited by Oliver Williamson, 34-52. Cheltenham: Edward Elgar.

Nordhaus, William. 1969. "An Economic Theory Of Technological Change." *American Economic Review,* 59(2), 18-28.

Pack, Howard, et al. 1986. "Industrial Strategy and Technological Change: Theory Versus Reality." *Journal of Development Economics,* 22(1), 87-128.

Romer, Paul. 1994. "The Origins of Endogenous Growth." *Journal of Economic Perspectives,* 8(1) [Winter], 3-22.

Rosenberg, Nathan. 1974. "Science, Invention and Economic Growth." *Economic Journal,* 84(333), 90-108.

Sen, A. K. 1962. *The Choice of Techniques.* Oxford: Basil Blackwell.

Shapiro, Carl, and Hal Varian. 1999. *Information Rules: A Strategic Guide to the Network Economy.* Boston: Harvard University Press.

Shell, Karl, et al. 1969. "Capital Gains, Income, and Saving." *Review of Economic Studies,* 36(105) [January], 15-26.

Stiglitz, Joseph E. 1987. "Learning to Learn: Localized Learning and Technological Progress." In *Economic Policy and Technological Performance,* edited by Dasgupta and Stoneman, 125-153. Cambridge: Cambridge University Press. 125-153.

———. 1988. "Economic Organization, Information, and Development." In *Handbook of Development Economics,* edited by H. Chenery and T. N. Srinivasan, Vol. I, 93-160. Amsterdam: North-Holland.

———. 1996. "Some Lessons from the East Asian Miracle." *World Bank Research Observer,* 11(2) [August], 151–77.

———. 1998a. *More Instruments and Broader Goals: Moving toward the Post-Washington Consensus.* World Institute for Development Economics Research Annual Lectures 2. (Reprinted in: Chang, 2001, 17-56).

———. 1998b. "Towards a New Paradigm for Development: Strategies, Policies, and Processes." Prebisch Lecture. Geneva: United Nations Conference on Trade and Development. (Reprinted in: Chang, 2001, 57-93.)

———. 1999. "Lessons from East Asia." *Journal of Policy Modeling,* 21(3), 311-30.

———. 2000. Scan Globally, Reinvent Locally: Knowledge Infrastructure and the Localization of Knowledge. In *Banking on Knowledge: the Genesis of the Global Development Network,* edited by Diane Stone, 24-43. London: Routledge. (Reprinted in: Chang 2001, 194-219.)

Uzawa, Hirofumi. 1969. "Time Preference and the Penrose Effect in a Two-Class Model of Economic Growth." *Journal of Political Economy,* 77(4) [Part II, July/August 1969], 628-52.

Wade, Robert. 1989. "What Can Economies Learn from the East Asian Success"? *Annals of the American Academy of Political Science,* 505, 68-79.

———. 1990. *Governing the Market: Economic Theory and the Role of Government in East Asian Industrialization.* Princeton: Princeton University Press.

Wilson, Robert. 1997. "Competitive Bidding with Disparate Information." In *The Economics of Information,* edited by D. K. Levine and S. A.Lippman, 45-7. Cheltenham: Edward Elgar.

World Bank. 1993. *East Asian Miracle: Public Policy and Economic Growth.* Washington, DC: World Bank and Oxford University Press.

———. 1998. *Global Economic Prospects.* Washington, DC.

———. 1999. World Development Report 1998-1999: Knowledge for Development. Washington, DC.

ABOUT THE AUTHORS

Sunil Chacko is Executive Director of the Science and Conscience Foundation in Geneva. He conducts science, technology, finance and equity analysis on the medical, digitalgenomics, pharmaceutical and biotechnology sectors. He has received an M.D. from Kerala University in India, a masters in public health from Harvard University and an M.B.A. from Columbia University, along with training in information technology and database/software programming. He has worked as a physician; as adviser to the Rockefeller Foundation on harnessing new sciences for technology development and partnerships; as a project director at the International Commission on Health Research for Development on applying debt-swap methodology for financing social development; and for the World Bank Group, Harvard University and the United Nations Children's Fund (UNICEF). He served as Chief Executive Officer of New Info Solutions, an Internet and medical technologies consulting company. His most recent publication is *The Rise of the Value-Added Pharmaceutical and Biotechnology Industry in India.*

Stephen Denning was the Program Director, Knowledge Management at the World Bank from 1996 to 2000. He now consults with organizations in the United States, Europe and Australia on knowledge management and organizational storytelling. He is the author of the book entitled *The Springboard: How Storytelling Ignites Action in Knowledge-Era Organizations,* which describes how storytelling can serve as a powerful tool for organizational change and knowledge management. In November 2000, Mr. Denning was selected as one of the world's Ten Most Admired Knowledge Leaders (Teleos), along with Jack Welch (General Electric) and John Chambers (Cisco Systems). He studied law and psychology at Sydney University and did a postgraduate degree in law at Oxford University before joining the World Bank, where he worked for several decades and held various management positions. For more information on some of the issues discussed in this book, see www.stevedenning.com.

David Ellerman is an adviser and speechwriter to the Chief Economist of the World Bank, previously Joseph Stiglitz and currently Nicholas Stern. His undergraduate education was in humanities at the Massachusetts Institute of Technology; he also has two masters degrees, in philosophy and in economics, and a Ph.D. in mathematics from Boston University. He has taught mathematics, economics, computer science, operations research and accounting at various universities, and founded a small consulting company in Eastern Europe before joining the World Bank ten years ago. His most recent book was *Intellectual Trespassing As a Way of Life: Essays in Philosophy, Economics, and Mathematics.* His essay in this volume is based on a recently completed book manuscript entitled *Helping People Help Themselves: Towards a Theory of Autonomy-Respecting Assistance.*

Sakiko Fukuda-Parr is currently the Director of the Human Development Report Office at the United Nations Development Programme. She was the lead author of the *Human Development Report (HDR) 2001: Making New Technologies Work for Human Development.* She was also lead author with Mahbub ul Haq of HDR 1995, on gender;

and with Sir Richard Jolly of HDR 1996, on growth, poverty, consumption and globalization, and HDR 1997, on human rights. She led the UNDP team on the 1993 publication—by the UNDP Regional Bureau for Africa and Elliot Berg—of *Rethinking Technical Cooperation: Reforms for Capacity-Building in Africa.* She is a graduate of Cambridge University, the Fletcher School of Law and Diplomacy, and the University of Sussex.

Ruth Hill is a research student at the Centre for the Study of African Economies, Department of Economics, Oxford University. From 2000 to 2001, she served as a consultant at the Human Development Report Office at the United Nations Development Programme. She worked on *HDR 2001: Making New Technologies Work for Human Development.*

Juana Kuramoto is an economist and Associate Researcher at the Group of Analysis for Development (GRADE). She is a Ph.D. candidate in technology and innovation policy at the University of Maastricht, and holds a masters of science in public policy from Carnegie Mellon University. Ms. Kuramoto has research experience in topics related to technological change and development, with a focus on issues such as the linkages generated between mining and the rest of industry, the technological change in the mining industry, and the contribution of mining to local and regional development. Recent publications include: *Las Aglomeraciones Productivas Alrededor de la Minería: El caso de la Minera Yanacocha S.A and Evolución y Desafíos de la Política Científica y Tecnológica en América Latina* (with Francisco Sagasti).

Sanjaya Lall is Professor of Development Economics at the International Development Centre and a Fellow of Green College at Oxford University. He was educated at Oxford and has been a staff member of the World Bank. He has acted as adviser and consultant to many international organizations and national governments on industrial development, technology policies and foreign direct investment. He has published extensively on these issues, with some 30 books and over 200 journal articles. His last book, *Competitiveness, Technology and Skills,* was published in 2001. His next one, *Failing to Compete: Technology Development and Technology Systems in Africa,* will appear in summer 2002.

Carlos Lopes has a masters in development economics from the University of Geneva and a Ph.D. in history from the Univeristy of Paris1-Pantheon-Sorbonne. After serving in the civil service of his native Guinea Bissau, he taught or conducted research in several universities, including in Lisbon, São Paulo, Mexico, Uppsala and Zurich, before joining the United Nations Development Programme in 1988 as a development economist. He is currently the Acting Director of UNDP's Bureau for Development Policy. Lopes has authored or edited 20 books on subjects related to development.

Khalid Malik is Director of the Evaluation Office at the United Nations Development Programme, following his assignment as UN Representative in Uzbekistan. Educated as an economist at the universities of Oxford, Cambridge, Essex and Punjab, he has held a variety of key managerial, technical and policy positions at UNDP. He is presently the Chair of the UN Interagency Group on Evaluation. Since 1998, he has been instrumental in the introduction of results-based management at UNDP, which is emerging as a critical factor in the reform of the organization. Jointly with the World Bank and key bilateral organizations, he has helped shape the emerging evaluation agenda and contributed to the global debate on the development effectiveness of aid agencies. He has edited books and authored articles on a range of topics, including poverty and inequality, science and technology, culture, evaluation and results-based management.

Thandika Mkandawire is the Director of the United Nations Research Institute for Social Development (UNRISD) in Geneva. He studied economics at Ohio State University and the University of Stockholm. From 1986 until 1996, he was the Executive Secretary of the Council for the Development of Social Research in Africa (CODESRIA). Recent publications include: "Thinking about Development States in Africa," in the *Cambridge Journal of Economics, and Our Continent, Our Future: African Perspectives on Structural Adjustment* (coauthored with Charles Soludo).

Devendra Raj Panday, who has a Ph.D. in public and international affairs from the University of Pittsburgh, is a former Finance Secretary and Finance Minister in the Government of Nepal. Currently, he is associated with several civil society institutions in Nepal and abroad, focusing on issues related to democracy, transparency, human rights, development aid and people-centred development. His recent publications include two books: *Nepal's Failed Development: Reflections on the Mission and the Maladies;* and *Corruption, Governance and International Cooperation: Essays and Impressions on Nepal and South Asia.*

Gustavo Lins Ribeiro is a Professor in the Department of Anthropology at the University of Brasilia. He holds a Ph.D. in anthropology from the City University of New York, and has published on large-scale construction projects, development as an ideational system, international migration, globalization and transnationalism. He has also served on the board of civil society organizations in Brazil and abroad. Dr. Ribeiro's book *Hydropolitics and Transnational Capitalism in Argentina* was published in Brazil, Argentina and the United States. Recent publications include "Cybercultural Politics: Political Activism at a Distance in a Transnational World," in *Cultures of Politics/Politics of Cultures,* and "Planeta Banco. Diversidad étnica en el Banco Mundial," in *Estudios Latinoamericanos sobre Cultura y Transformaciones Sociales.*

Francisco Sagasti is Director of the AGENDA: Peru programme of activities at FORO Nacional/Internacional. In addition to various academic, private sector and government advisory positions in Peru and other countries, he has been Chief of Strategic Planning and senior adviser at the World Bank; Visiting Professor at the Wharton School of Finance, University of Pennsylvania; and chairperson of the UN Advisory Committee on Science and Technology for Development. He holds a Ph.D. from the University of Pennsylvania and engineering degrees from the National Engineering University in Lima. He is the author of 20 books and monographs, including *The Uncertain Quest: Science, Technology and Development* (with Celine Sachs and Jean-Jacques Salomon); Democracy and Good Government (with Pepi Patrón, Nicolás Lynch and Max Hernández); *Development Strategies for the 21st Century: The Case of Peru; and Financing and Providing Global Public Goods: Expectations and Prospects* (with Keith Bezanson).

Joseph E. Stiglitz holds joint professorships at Columbia University's Economics Department, School of International and Public Affairs, and Business School. From 1997 to 2000, he was the World Bank's Senior Vice President for Development Economics and Chief Economist. Dr. Stiglitz served as Chairperson of the US Council of Economic Advisors and as a member of President Bill Clinton's cabinet from 1995 to 1997. Previously a professor of economics at Stanford, Princeton, Yale and Oxford universities, Dr. Stiglitz helped create a new branch of economics—the economics of information—which has received widespread application throughout the field. He also helped revive interest in the economics of technical change and other factors that contribute to long-term increases in productivity and living standards. Dr. Stiglitz was awarded the Nobel Prize in Economics in 2001.

Swarnim Waglé is a consultant at the World Bank. Trained as an economist at the London School of Economics and Harvard University, his academic interests span issues of growth, international trade, poverty and social relations. He is currently enlarging his Harvard monograph, "Claims and Resources: Civic Engagement at the Macro Level," for publication. A national of Nepal, he has also worked at the BBC in London and the United Nations Development Programme in Kathmandu.